Relationship Is the Transformative Space

Relationship Is the Transformative Space

Living in the Not Yet

DARRYL WOOLDRIDGE

WIPF & STOCK · Eugene, Oregon

RELATIONSHIP IS THE TRANSFORMATIVE SPACE
Living in the Not Yet

Copyright © 2016 Darryl Wooldridge. All rights reserved. Except for brief quotations in critical publications or reviews, no part of this book may be reproduced in any manner without prior written permission from the publisher. Write: Permissions, Wipf and Stock Publishers, 199 W. 8th Ave., Suite 3, Eugene, OR 97401.

Wipf & Stock
An Imprint of Wipf and Stock Publishers
199 W. 8th Ave., Suite 3
Eugene, OR 97401

www.wipfandstock.com

PAPERBACK ISBN 13: 978-1-4982-8041-9
HARDCOVER ISBN 13: 978-1-4982-8043-3

Manufactured in the U.S.A.   02/03/2016

Unless otherwise indicated, all Scripture quotations are from The Holy Bible, English Standard Version® (ESV®), copyright © 2001 by Crossway, a publishing ministry of Good News Publishers. Used by permission. All rights reserved.

Contents

Acknowledgments | vii

1 Introduction | 1
2 God's Heart | 12
3 Transforming-Salvation | 61
4 Devices in the Unveiling | 120
5 Enculturation and Presuppositions | 169
6 Reflecting God's Glory | 201
7 Summary and Conclusions | 246

Bibliography | 271

Acknowledgments

THERE HAVE BEEN A number of people to whom I am greatly indebted that have lovingly enabled the research and writing necessary to produce this book. First, is my family that inspires me and drives me to excellence: My wife, Ruth, whose deep love, support, dialogue, and patience have made room for the necessary focus of such a challenge as this. Loving thanks to my children, grandchildren, and siblings, who bring me sustaining joy, and inspiration. A special note of gratitude to my doctoral advisors, professors Dr. Lioy and Dr. Vorster, and Jessica Bratt (2005), who graciously allowed me to cite her paper, "Wolfhart Pannenberg: Imago Dei as Gift and Destiny."

There are many instructors in my life, both in formal and informal settings, some of whom I have only met in books and journals and debated with in those pages, and from whom I have learned a great deal. Some have been the most unassuming members of society. Others have been the famous, lauded, and acclaimed that have taught and advised me from university, lectern, pulpit, history, and face-to-face consult and encouragement. The incidents of my life, both trials and mercies, have taught me deeply and enriched me beyond measure. Whatever small light I may have been able to shine in this work is of God's exceeding mercy and grace that have nurtured me and made me capable. Finally, I offer deep gratitude to the excellent team of Wipf and Stock Publishers.

1

Introduction

THERE HAVE BEEN NUMEROUS and varied records of the human pursuit for God as first shown by the discovery of the scrawls of a half-animal-half-human in a cave of Dordogne, France, from the Paleolithic Age, dated about 30,000 years ago.[1] However, at the extreme, Harrod has argued that the first event may go back over 2,000,000 years.[2] And at the opposite extreme, Christian fundamentalism has argued against any evolutionary account of creation and of the first humans for a young earth (10,000–20,000 years) created with a built-in age of 4.5 billion years.[3] Although Genesis does not portray history in the sense of modern methodologies, the scientific evidence, rightly interpreted, does not conflict with biblical accounts and presents God-directed and precise biological evolution coming out of a less-than-idyllic swirl as the most viable explanation.[4] However, whether more recently or back into a nascent evolutionary forming, the human pursuit for God has reached across time, place, and all cultures and milieus.[5] The story of this search for God has been a particularly intense, violent, and lusty quest that, at times, is told and experienced in often-conflicting perspectives.

Mystics and contemplatives variously claim that the Judeo-Christian God in particular is experienced in both presence and absence and sought in positive (cataphatic) expression and the negative (apophatic) expression.[6]

1. Leroi-Gourhan and Michelson, "Religion of the Caves," 6–17.
2. Harrod, "Two Million Years Ago," 4–7.
3. Grudem, *Systematic Theology*, 295–97, 304–6.
4. Lioy, *Evolutionary Creation*, 25–26, 44, 85.
5. Cady, "Loosening the Category," 23–25.
6. McGinn, *Foundations of Mysticism*, xviii.

These differences of pursuit are not solely academic distinctions. Their paradigms portend existential outcomes. The nature of the Christian relationship with God directs or even determines any transformative affect of that relationship upon the life of the seeker, the initiate, and the seasoned disciple as we pursue or stammer toward spiritual transformation.

The new academic discipline "spirituality" probably began in France during the first half of the twentieth century and referred to a kind of liberation. Both ascetics and mystical theology seem to imply excessive inflexible and elitist concepts of divine activity. This prior concept is overwrought with distinctions between human nature and God's grace. Spirituality attempts to address a multifaceted range of human experience.[7]

More particularly, I propose spirituality or the lived experience of spirituality as one's conscious participation in life synthesis through an experiential integration of self-transcendence toward ultimate value.[8] But more accessibly, spiritual transformation mainly points to a basic change in the place or character of the sacred as life's significance.[9] Integration of our lives into the sacred is a change in spiritual quality, vivacity, function, character, or condition from one experiential level to another that may have collateral affects on soul, body, and creation. Such transformation shall alter our relationship with others as well as God. Also note that "transformation" is used and explored throughout this book except where the word "formation" is required for explanatory reasons. Although the terms "ascetical" and "mystical" are also used, my preference for the forms of "spiritual"—a term more focused on the human experience, especially as it relates to God—is also found throughout.

Admittedly, one may call the spiritual, transformation process sanctification, right and moral living, the Spirit-filled life, progressive *theōsis*, divinization, deification, divine filiation, or some other appellation to spiritual transformation. The problem we examine here is not the naming of the process or its state but rather the proposed process and state and who is included in what I shall mostly refer to herein as "proleptic, spiritual transformation" (PrōST). That is, by proleptic, I am indicating a spiritual transformation usually thought reserved for the *eschaton* as anachronistically enjoyed, to a great measure, in the present.

In addition to the examples that we can find in Scripture (e.g., Gen 2:7–9; Song; Mark 9:2–8; Gal 2:20; 2 Cor 3:16–18; 12:2–4; 1 Thess 5:12–26; 2 Pet 1:4; 1 John 3:2), there are extrabiblical spiritual writings and authors,

---

7. Endean, "Spirituality and Theology," 74.
8. Schneiders, "Christian Spirituality," 1.
9. Pargament, *Spiritually Integrated Psychotherapy*, 21.

too numerous to list here. These sources can be found starting in the first century CE onward (e.g., *First Epistle of Clement*, Clement; *The Shepherd of Hermas*, Anon; *The Cloud of Unknowing*, Anon; *The Practice of the Presence of God*, Brother Lawrence; *The Imitation of Christ*, Thomas à Kempis) through to present times (e.g., *Streams of Living Water*, Foster; *The Divine Conspiracy*, Willard; *The Wound of Knowledge*, Williams; *Subversive Spirituality*, Peterson; *The Return of the Prodigal Son*, Nouwen).

These writings exemplify, discuss, debate, and instruct on what we can experience of the spiritual and of God. Like *Celebration of Discipline*, by Foster, these writings often present various methods and disciplines intended to facilitate a way to these spiritual experiences and encounters with God. The extent of experienced spiritual transformation ranges from initiation to deification or divinization (Gk. *theōsis*). Here, we generally mean, by such terms (deification, divinization, and *theōsis*), a real knowledge of God and actual participation in God's divine life.[10] Rarely is deification or divinization spoken of in the fully developed, superlative meaning as a possibility for the present space-time continuum before eternity is entered.

The scholastic position, represented here by Thomas Aquinas,[11] speaks about "partaking of the Divine Nature, which exceeds every other nature . . . by a participated likeness." Although, my position posits a scholastic similarity (at least as held by Thomas) to Orthodoxy,[12] the route and methods may differ. We will set aside the controversies of Orthodox practices of Hesychasm, and its variants while holding to the desired possibility of direct experiential fellowship with God by which measures we can enjoy deification, as Paul says from glory to glory (2 Cor 3:18).

From a Reformed position, Carl Mosser[13] finds deification in both Luther and Calvin (particularly 2 Peter). Canlis[14] looks to Calvin and Irenaeus and argues that Irenaeus's anachronistic sense of deification is helpful in removing any competitive relationship between humans and the Creator. Although admittedly "*deconstructive* concepts" intended to destroy gnostic "radical incompatibility [laid] between heaven and earth" this deification makes us more like God in fellowship (Gk. *koinōnia*) or Triune, perichoretic relationship with God in one another (Gk. *perichōrēsis*), adoption presented as proof of such a deification.[15] Let's be clear, deification, here, is not in any

10. Meyendorff, "Liturgy and Spirituality," 350
11. Aquinas, *Summa Theologia*, 1140.
12. Plested, *Orthodox Readings of Aquinas*, 11, 27–28, 225.
13. Mosser, "Greatest Possible Blessing," 38–40.
14. Canlis, *Calvin's Ladder*, 188.
15. Ibid., 190, 237.

way meant as receiving God's essence (incommunicable), but rather only God's communicable attributes.[16]

While agreeing with Canlis[17] that deification is a matter of fellowship and relationship (Gk. *koinōnia*) with God, to be direct and clear, in this, I hold most closely to an Orthodox position that the image breathed (Gen 1:26; 2:7) into humans was the beginning, inviolate deposit of those communicable divine energies or nature of God ultimately resulting in deification.[18] Thus, the transformation spoken of here is a coming into a fuller expression of that which is communicable, by removing the dross caused in the fall and protracted willful acts on display throughout human history, that opens one to fellowship or *koinōnia*. It is God's communicable nature "[extending] to the whole human makeup, not excepting the 'cloak of skin'. . . penetrated by deifying grace . . . what God is by nature."[19] Grace is within the realm of deification in perfect conformity with God. Thereby, as we discuss below, transformation is removing that which may obscure, the *imago Dei* (God's image) from being most fully expressed in humans, without limit to one particular human facet but "the whole of human existence."[20] It contains an ontological (existence or reality) eventuality of full, unhindered, and expressed *imago Dei* as deification in relationship and expression not incommunicable divine essence.

Among the main Christian bodies, the Orthodox Church (followed by elements of the Catholic Church) has been the most forthcoming in offering a theology and model of full-orbed spiritual transformation toward deification or divinization. The Orthodox Church, in fact, has been unequivocally explicit to call such a potential spiritual transformation deification or divinization. The beginning of this process, according to the Orthodox Church, is available today, and yet they do not hold out the expectation for deification or divinization for the main population of Christians before eternity. It seems, to me, that Orthodox theologians are united in their belief that human culminating deification is not obtained until the *eschaton* with the so-called "third birth," but that a very clear and firm beginning should distinguish all Christians presently.[21] The church fathers and mothers, both early and later, have variously spoken of these experiences of God. Both the Orthodox Church and Catholic Church have owned these persons

16. Kärkkäinen, *One with God*, 30–31.
17. Canlis, *Calvin's Ladder*, 236.
18. Lossky, *Image*, 98, 110; Mantzaridis, *Deification of Man*, 15.
19. Lossky, *Image*, 139.
20. Mantzaridis, *Deification of Man*, 16.
21. Clendenin, "Partakers of Divinity," 377.

and mystical approaches in differing manners and degrees.[22] However, no distinction is made by me of the various Orthodox and Catholic churches except where it is pertinent to the discussion.

Whoever might claim ownership, the early church fathers (e.g., Irenaeus of Lyons, Clement of Alexandria, and Origen of Alexandria) spoke of deification.[23] This language better harmonizes with Orthodox theology. As Steeves[24] points out, in the final analysis, within the Byzantine period, Orthodoxy's considerable mysticism, intuition, and amalgamation was firmly fixed. This was in sharp contrast to the West's philosophical, scholastic, and forensic design.[25] History also records a number of smaller bodies of Christians that have reached for this "glory" (2 Cor 3:16–18). Among them are Friends of God, Brethren of the Common Life, Quietists, Quakers, Pietists, and Morovians.[26]

Where *theōsis*, deification, and divinization are not explicitly addressed by these early disciples and mystics, "union" with God is proposed by such as Bernard of Clairvaux, Meister Eckhart, Teresa of Avila, and John of the Cross.[27] Hero mystics of the Orthodox Church, such as St. Anthony the Great, St. Maximus the Confessor, St. Macrina (St. Gregory of Nyssa's sister), St. Symeon the New Theologian, and Gregory of Palamas all left the church with examples of the spiritual life. However, their ranks are suspiciously lacking in the writings of women,[28] while the Catholic tradition has a number of women who left mystical writings for posterity. Examples of female Catholic writing mystics are Hildegard of Bingen, Julian of Norwich, Teresa of Avila, and Therese of Liseux. The Orthodox Church and, to a less-defined degree, the Catholic Church are the two largest bodies that have continued with these beliefs, in varying modes.

In more recent times, but in no particular order, some representative mystics or contemplatives that have shaped much of the present spiritual, transformational thought and expectations are the writings of Madame Guyon, William Law, John Wesley, Evelyn Underhill, Andrew Murray, Ruth Paxon, Watchman Nee, Simone Weil, Dallas Willard, Jacob Böhme, Richard Foster, Cynthia Bourgeault, Thomas Keating, Thomas Merton, Bede

---

22. Campbell, "Asceticism"; McGinn, *Essential Writings of Christian Mysticism*, 149–57; Zizioulas, "Early Christian Community," 38–40, 116–19.

23. McGinn, *Essential Writings of Christian Mysticism*, 397.

24. Steeves, "Othodox Tradition," 806–8.

25. Ibid., 809.

26. Cairns, *Christianity through the Centuries*, 249–50, 378–82.

27. McGinn, *Essential Writings of Christian Mysticism*, 427–29.

28. Ashbrook-Harvey, email to Wooldridge about women mystics in the Middle Ages.

Griffiths from the Benedictines, and Mother Gavriellia Papaiannis from the Orthodox. Clearly, these representatives stand on the shoulders of the Scriptures, the early church fathers and mothers, and those mystics and seekers who have come before.[29] A few of these pioneers have already been cited above and others are cited within these pages.

Discussions about the extent of spiritual transformation range from the anemic to full-orbed experience. The church fathers and mothers have variously spoken of these experiences of God. Admittedly, the accusation of heterodoxy, aberrance, and even heresy sometimes trouble the words of these early innovators.[30]

Although there is a rich and long history of mystics, seekers, and "common people" simply desirous of the divine, there is no unified, broadly accepted understanding of spirituality. What spiritual conditions or attributes of God are communicably and fully available to humans has not been clearly and thoroughly presented and made available in Christian literature. More specifically, there does not seem to be much, if anything, addressing "proleptic spirituality transformation" (PrōST). That is, what of the "not-yet," if any, of these communicable conditions and attributes are available "now" for humanity to enjoy of God's restorative and progressive work of spiritual transformation.

Humans were originally created in the "image and likeness" of God (Gen 1:26–27), which creation in God's image joined with the natural world and expressed in both the immaterial and material worlds, that both ontologically and functionally makes them different than the animals of creation.[31] God's "image" (Heb. *tselem*) "does not consist in man's body which was formed from earthly matter, but in his spiritual, intellectual, moral likeness to God from whom [humanity's] animating breath came."[32] Additionally, Hamilton goes on to say that "likeness" (Heb. *děmuwth*) may amplify "image" and establish humans as fully representational of God.[33] Scripture references "image and likeness," "image" alone, and "likeness" alone. Despite the distinctions that might be found in these terms and the comparisons that can be made, I, while briefly discussing some considerations, do not defend any distinctions, comparisons, differences, or arguments about these words in any part or combination. Such consideration would be a

---

29. Chan, *Spiritual Theology*, 82–83, 103–9, 190; Foster and Griffin, *Spiritual Classics*, xi–xiv; Willard, *Divine Conspiracy*, 271–73.

30. McGinn, *Essential Writings of Christian Mysticism*, 481, 490, 511–12.

31. Lioy, *Evolutionary Creation*, 86, 89.

32. Harris et al., *Theological Wordbook*, s.v. "děmuwth."

33. Ibid., s.v. "tselem."

distraction from our purposes and unnecessary to our goals. Neither do I enter the debate of whether "is" or "in" the image is the correct rendering except to say that the human being both *is* the *imago Dei* and *in* the *imago Dei* however found among these pages.

Although there seem to be some "representational" elements in image, for example, functional dominion over the earth as consequence of being God's vice regents, these elements fail to address either the substantive or the relational theories of image. That is, as addressed below, what, if any, is the structural, essential, spiritual sameness, or possession of humans as God's image (substantive)? Moreover, what is the relationship of humans to God and creation in order to reflect God's image to God and creation in those relationships (relational)?[34]

The prior, present, and future condition of humanity is a labyrinth difficult to navigate and derive any coherent systematic. Yet the Scriptures seem to reveal God's desire for some large measure of relationship with and image bearing from God's creatures. A primary question continues to surface regarding the extent of that relationship and image and the effects of that relationship and image upon the heart of God and the condition of humanity and creation. Again, what of the "not-yet," if any, of God's communicable conditions and attributes are available "now" for humanity to enjoy of God's restorative and progressive work of spiritual transformation? Among the many secondary questions that can be asked regarding proleptic spiritual transformation (PrōST), the following shall be considered:

- ❖ What does God's heart, in relationship, imply toward an image-bearing human spiritually, and what, if any, are the implications on this from the Edenic fall?

- ❖ In what measure is God actively interested in the recovery of God's image in humanity as the remedy to the spiritual effects of the fall and in PrōST?

- ❖ What are the means by which God reveals or unveils God's heart, truth, and intents toward creation and humanity in particular in the plan of spiritual recovery/PrōST?

- ❖ What are the transformative and soteriological implications of PrōST?

- ❖ What are the possibilities, if any, to develop a unified theory regarding PrōST from the conclusions of this study?

Our primary aim is to investigate whether individuals must wait for the afterlife to have purification and spiritual transformation fully or largely

---

34. Herzfeld, "Imago Dei," 363.

"worked out"—that is, the possible opportunity to greatly "work out [one's transformation] with fear and trembling [now]" (Phil 2:12–13). This book investigates whether God's economy (Gk. *oikonomia*) or administration includes provisions for a present enjoyment of the *imago Dei* in transformation as inclusive of the life of Christ, and whether (to what degree) this transformation, as the *imago Dei*, is to be reflected and represented by humans in time and in relation to God and creation.

Our central theoretical argument is that humans were originally created in the "image and likeness" of God (Gen 1:26–27); however, the enjoyment and expression, *not* the essence, of this *imago Dei* has been greatly blemished, marred, and damaged by a God-defying willfulness of humanity (Gen 2:16; 3). Despite this rebellion, God desires a full restoration of the enjoyment and expression of his image. God has not forgotten this intent that humans would express God in this life as the Divine image (Rom 8:29; 1 Cor 15:49; 2 Cor 3:18; Eph 1:11; Col 2:13; 3:10; 2 Tim 1:9; 1 Pet 5:10). Moreover, I argue that *imago Dei* now carries something more—the God-man. God's image in Jesus the Christ now carries the existential realities of his incarnate life toward which PrōST (Proleptic Spiritual Transformation) drives in the now (Rom 8:29; 2 Cor 4:4; Col 1:5). We will reexamine the conventional partitioning of the "now" and "not-yet" for a potential new balance and paradigm in expressed PrōST toward *imago Dei*.

I shall limit our arguments to Christian traditions and expressions of faith,[35] and yet transversely include "pluralistic and interdisciplinary" fields as necessary to the subject.[36] However, a full-orbed and exhaustive inclusion of multiple scientific disciplines is outside the scope and intent of these pages. Yet, an enlarged approach is employed as informing disciplines weigh in on the concerns of this book. Thereby, we shall investigate a wide contextual perspective and draw from a broad area of Christian, spiritual traditions inclusive of Western and Eastern traditions but mainly from three: Orthodox, Catholic, and Protestant. Additionally, as warranted, subcategories of the main traditions shall be thoroughly researched and consulted along with sciences such as paleoanthropology, philosophy, and cognitive disciplines.

While biblical assessment on the subject of this book is at the leading edge, extrabiblical literature was broadly read and surveyed to measure and inform that assessment as well as the aims, goals, and objectives of our investigations. We view the Bible, within this approach, from an underlying progressive or trajectory hermeneutic.[37] We shall review both testaments

---

35. Schneiders, "Christian Spirituality," 1.
36. Van Huyssteen, *Alone in the World?*, 112, 159–60, 242.
37. Webb, *Slaves, Women & Homosexuals*, 30–34.

progressively unfolding God's full revelation and intent of a transformed universe in which such allowances as divorce and slavery are done away for fidelity and freedom (Gen 1:26–27; Prov 14: 31; Matt 7:12; 10:2–9; Acts 17:26; Gal 3:28; Phil 8:1–21);[38] where an eye for an eye gives way to turning the other cheek (Matt 5:39); where only loving one's clan gives way to also loving one's enemies and the world at large (Matt 5:4; 1 John 4:16).

The hermeneutic utilized in this study does not abandon the existential realities or position of the active interpreter.[39] This research employs an eclectic hermeneutic and thereby leverages various approaches into an eclectic postfoundationalism. For ease this broad and open approach is referred to as an eclectic hermeneutic, in which multiple interpretive techniques and principles are employed as appropriate. This often invites disparate elements of exegesis such as allusions, authorial style and leanings, genre, and earlier scriptural assumptions as well as history, grammar, and the sciences.

Primary sources are consulted wherever possible. Especially biblical texts, historically significant periods, modern sources, and sciences are transversely[40] consulted to best discern voices pertinent to the discussion. As in utilizing different modes of transportation as conditions demand, this study moves within this eclectic hermeneutic that is inclusive of postmodern interpretations.

Moreover, a "postfoundational approach" holds place seeking defensible rational to "intersect transversally with theological arguments . . . [as to] what it might mean to talk about human uniqueness today."[41] More precisely, using the thought of Badiou,[42] in which he places the "law of the future anterior . . . [from which] a post-evental truth is being deployed," a statement is veridical. That is, it is possible to determine the truth of the present, although a passing, post-evental truth. This postfoundationalism allows for communal and historical conditioning while holding that one can work and reach beyond such preconditioning of culture, prior and "received" knowledge, and human insularity.

Although I presume there is objective reality to be known and understood (foundationalism), a postfoundational-postmodern "theological condition" is applied as the materials indicate the need for deconstructing or "unpeeling" the layers obscuring seeing. This assists us in looking past the

38. Lioy, *Evolutionary Creation*, 55.
39. Palmer, "Postmodern Hermeneutics," 60.
40. Van Huyssteen, *Alone in the World?*, 12, 164, 242.
41. Ibid., 164.
42. Badiou, *Being and Event*, 401.

obvious, delivered truth to the underlying plurality, discontinuity, and complexity of the "un-deconstructible."[43] This approach mines and deconstructs meaning utilizing and transversing interdisciplinary constructs. Although I am not arguing for or defending deconstruction, here it assists and supports the eclectic hermeneutics of this study as an interpretive approach as the need presents.

The approach is not a mixture or even a combinant. It is the tension between memory, faithfulness, preservation to what has been given and yet variegated, something original, and a departure from the prior.[44] In this "deconstruction is treated as an hermeneutic of the *kingdom* of God" as an approach to interpretation that assists in seeing the prophetic spirit of the unpredictable and sometimes dissonant outsider—Jesus—who took a stand with the marginalized, disenfranchised, and downtrodden.[45]

Moreover, deconstruction occasionally supports this study by affirming but without being self-certain and positive. Here I do not use it as a position in opposition to Christianity or for that matter any other established or proofed belief or practice. Deconstruction is a disquieting tool by which we can examine a stance or belief, about how not to hold too strongly any given stance or belief. It presses against seeing or holding a stance or belief as decided with too much complacency and certainty, and rather encourages permitting oneself to be held.[46]

I have intended that postfoundationalism enfold deconstructive principles and the eclectic hermeneutic described above to provide space in which an understanding of proleptic spiritual transformation (PrōST) is best understood and presented.

- ❖ Utilizing an eclectic hermeneutic, research and gain an understanding of what God's heart, in relationship, implies toward human spirituality, and what, if any, are the implications on this from the Edenic fall.

- ❖ Utilizing an eclectic hermeneutic, research and gain an understanding of God's interest in recovery of his image in humanity and PrōST as the remedy to the spiritual effects of the fall.

- ❖ Utilizing an eclectic hermeneutic, research and gain an understanding of the means by which God reveals or unveils God's heart, truth, and intents toward creation and humanity in particular in the plan of spiritual recovery and PrōST.

---

43. Vanhoozer, "Theology and the Condition of Postmodernity," 4–5, 11, 13, 17.
44. Caputo, *Deconstruction in a Nutshell*, 6.
45. Caputo, *What Would Jesus Deconstruct?*, 26.
46. Ibid., 55–56.

❖ Utilizing an eclectic hermeneutic, research and gain an understanding of the transformative and soteriological implications of PrōST.

❖ Utilizing an eclectic hermeneutic, research and gain an understanding for the conclusions of this study and whether they imply a unified theory regarding PrōST.

2

God's Heart

PREFATORY

To ensure clarity and coherency of the intent of this work and the present chapter in particular, I offer the following. The prior chapter was introductory in scope and briefly laid out the book's background and problem, the aims and objectives in pursuing the intended area of discussion, the study's theoretical argument, and the means and methods of pursuit. The current chapter sets forth foundational considerations on which the following chapters build. In this chapter I speak to the ineffaceable drive within humans to find God. It is a reciprocated drive—a response to God who first sought and continues to seek humans—a correlate and concomitant seeking in response to God. Although surely not the final word, in this chapter we discuss God as Spirit and spiritual, by whom human beings have been created as *imago Dei* (God's image), showing God's heart as toward his creation and humans most especially.

A World in Relationship

I will also discuss here the incredible reality that humans are destined to join the perichoretic relationship that God has enjoyed from eternity past. Particularly, in his ascension and glory, Jesus sent the Spirit of adoption into creation so that human creation might enter this same perichoretic relationship with God.¹

In support, and although narrowly presented, a full development and defense of possible worlds and the etiology of evil is beyond the scope and my intent for this chapter or these pages in the main. I discuss certain conjectures ostensibly founded as key to the intent and subject of this study in affecting proleptic spiritual transformation (PrōST). For one, although human striving fails, and the finality of death is assured, God has created a world that cannot be defeated from God's purposes and intents.² The creation into which humans have been placed is good and in truth the best possible world in God's sovereign, omniscient, and omni-benevolent desire.³ It is intended and suited for "relationship with God."

Leibniz⁴ clarifies that God is at full liberty and free to use his will and power without hindrance or compulsion by outside forces or wills. God is free in always being self-led toward what is good and right. God is without restriction or displeasure in prosecuting his will. In this all humans were created as God purposed in display of his wisdom and benevolence to best realize this wisdom and will. This "need" of God, in free will, is without imperfection as is the "wrath" of God. However, I do not hold to a "Leibniz Lapse" that God could have created any possible world he might have wished.⁵ If humans are to have free will, a necessity of my argument, then they may, unlike God, by their free-actions, introduce evil, pain, and suffering.

The Anthropomorphic God

We will examine *imago Dei* further as it particularly relates to a foundational understanding to the main subject of this work, that is, the *imago Dei* now carries something more—the God-man. God's image in Jesus the Christ (*imago Christi*) now carries the existential realities of his incarnate life toward which PrōST (Proleptic Spiritual Transformation) drives in the now (Rom 8:29; 2 Cor 4:4; Col 1:5). We reexamine the conventional partitioning of the "now" and "not-yet" for a potential new balance and paradigm in expressed PrōST toward *imago Dei*.

---

1. Canlis, *Calvin's Ladder*, 204.
2. Lioy, *Evolutionary Creation*, 124.
3. Leibniz, *Theodicy*, 123.
4. Ibid.
5. Plantinga, *God, Freedom, and Evil*, 44.

In order to accomplish the goal of transformation, God has put down human rebellion through the incarnation of Christ who exampled God's heart (anthropomorphically speaking) regarding the intended life meant for humans. It is important, that we remember that wherever, in this book, human form, characteristics, attributes, behaviors, and functions are given as God's form, characteristics, attributes, behaviors, and functions it is used as an anthropomorphic (physitheism or anthropotheism) literary devise to describe God's condescension or accommodation in extending grace and mercy in relationship with humans. Beegle[6] provides candid help in that the incarnational mediation of Jesus the Christ necessitates a measure of cautionary Christian anthropomorphism; for it is in this that the finite human can know something more of the infinite, incomprehensible God whose thoughts and ways are not the thoughts of his creatures. In particular, many Yahwist (or J, one of the sources of the Pentateuch [Torah]) passages are boldly anthropomorphic in expression.[7]

The Mystery of God's Heart

It seems presumptuous to speak as though one might know something about God's heart. After all, God is transcendent, eternal, immortal, immutable, and invisible—the magnificent creator of the universe and the maker of heaven and earth and all their content, seen and unseen, experienced and never to be experienced. However, what is to be experienced of God is to be found in Christ as facilitated by the participation of the Spirit, who brings Christ and his benefits and through whom disciples find communion with God.[8] God, who is in unapproachable glory, is "outside," "above," "below," "before," and "after" space-time and yet contains space-time (Gen 1:31; Eccl 8:17; 1 John 4:12; 1 Tim 1:17; 6:16). God contains all; all is in God (Job 12:10; Dan 5:23b; Acts 17:28). God is the uncreated-creator and uncaused-cause of reality and all of its content. God sustains the entire "universe by the word of his power" (Col 1:17; Heb 1:3). As Anselm famously said, God is that being "than which nothing greater can be conceived."[9] Yet incomprehensibly and gloriously this God, who is transcendent, is revealed in Christ Jesus (John 1:18; 6:46; 8:19; 14:7–10) in whom humans participate

---

6. Beegle, "Anthropomorphism," 54.
7. Rad, *Genesis*, 26.
8. Canlis, *Calvin's Ladder*, 154–55.
9. Fairweather, *Scholastic Miscellany*, 75.

in communion in trinitarian immortality "in the Word, by the Spirit" only in "relational context."[10]

Although much is claimed regarding the revelations of God's heart in creation—experiential tales by individuals and communities—God and God's heart is at the deepest level a mystery. John Calvin[11] spoke to this mystery with poignant counsel in that the "most perfect way" to seek God is not to attempt to satiate one's curiosity by attempting to probe and investigate God's essence but rather to adore and meditate God as can be seen in his great works. It is by these works that God is close and known to his children, and by which he communes with his creatures.[12] Experience of God is variously further discussed below and throughout these pages along with other modes of God's expression.

Not only can God's heart be seen in his works, but as further considered below, the Judeo-Christian Scriptures display the heart of God and help derive God's desires (Ps 19:1; 50:6; 144:6; Rom 1:19–20). The anthropological personifications used in Scripture to describe God, although only partial and incomplete, are adequate to the task of revelation for human understanding (2 Tim 3:15–17). More pointedly, in the hands of the Yahwist, they are the "boldest anthropomorphisms" and necessary to God's, self-revelation.[13] God's heart is laid open in the histories, narratives, poetry, psalms, parables, allegories, and directives of Hebrew and Christian canon and deuterocanonical writings.

As testified by these writings, God determined to make known to humans the "mystery of his will" which serves God's purpose (Eph 1:7–10; 3:3). This mystery (Gk. *mustérion*) indicates that God's will, in plan, was hidden. God's self-revelation opens his heart to human knowledge and experience. Moreover, God's self-revelation now makes possible that we might join and serve God's heart-desire in fulfilling God's will and plan.[14]

The theory and theology of an unknowable God, a God that is exclusively transcendent, ineffable and "transcategorial, meaning beyond the range of our human systems of concepts or mental categories,"[15] is briefly discussed in chapter 4 below. Nevertheless, there is a vast list that can be numbered regarding the revelation of God's heart in Scripture and following that God is to some measure and at some level knowable. The evidential testi-

---

10. Canlis, *Calvin's Ladder*, 77.
11. Calvin, *Institutes*, 1.V.9.
12. Ibid.
13. Rad, *Genesis*, 25–26.
14. Chan, *Spiritual Theology*, 140, 223–24; Willard, *Divine Conspiracy*, 97–99.
15. Hick, "Who or What Is God?"

mony to God's heart as found in Scripture is indeed, a priori, multitudinous. Nonetheless, my intent and the subject are specific to spiritual transformation and the possibility of proleptic, spiritual reality. God's heart specifically regarding this subject graciously presents as seminal, knowable, vital, and central. It is the focus of this discussion.

Accomodatio

God accommodates himself to humans, the human situation, and human understanding often using anthropological language and analogy in order to reach humans within our own milieu and needs. Although elements of *accomodatio* (accommodation) can be found in the writings of Tertullian, Origen, and Clement of Alexandria, John Calvin is most recently better known (over a twenty-five-year rise [1952–1977]) for a fuller development of *accomodatio*, even conjectured as the heart of his theology.[16] This theological leaning is especially seen in Calvin's scriptural exegeses of related passages in such books as Genesis, Psalms, Ezekiel, Daniel, and John.[17] So that God might be known by human beings, the thought of *accomodatio* presents the idea of God's condescension to human ways and means (Gen 1:5).[18]

Some examples of God's heart include the following: God's heart is overflowing with love for his creation and creatures (John 3:16; Rom 5:8; 8:32; Eph 2:4; 1 John 4:9–10). God is desirous of beauty (Ps 8:1; 19:1; Eccl 3:11a; Acts 14:17; 17:24; Rom 1:18–19) and of righteousness and justice (Gen 6:6–7; Ps 23:3; 89:14; 97:2). God's heart is for the disadvantaged, downtrodden, orphan, widow, poor, sick, possessed, dispossessed, all nations, children, women, men, animals, the planet, the universe, and all disadvantaged issues, situations and involved people (Matt 5:1–11; 11:5; Mark 1:40–41; 10:14; Luke 4:18; Gal 3:8). God is for his kingdom (Dan 6:26; Matt 13:44–46; John 2:17). God is for the salvation of everyone (John 3:16; 1 John 4:9; Rom 4:25; 5:8; 1 Cor 15:22; 1 Tim 2:6; 4:10; Titus 2:11). Willard[19] writes large and helpful words about God's heart as referenced above and that he is against idolatry, covetousness, irresponsibility, and a host of immoral and unrighteous actions and thoughts (Deut 4–5; 2 Kgs 15:5; Matt 23:27–29; 2 Pet 2:9).

---

16. Wright, "Calvin's Accommodating God," 18.
17. Balserak, *Divinity Compromised*, 8–9.
18. Calvin, *Commentaries on the First Book of Moses*.
19. Willard, *Divine Conspiracy*, 129–34.

Relationship

From the beginning of the scriptural record, God displayed a heart and intent to share his essence with humanity as he created humans in his image and breathed into them his very life (Gen 2:7; John 5:21). Moreover, and to the point of this study, God's heart still yearns for a full, rich, and transformative relationship with us all (Ps 34:8; Song 8:1; John 14:23; 17:21–23; Rom 12:2; 2 Cor 3:18; 6:16).[20]

God seeks an intimate and vital relationship with humans and is "injured" by the loss of this relationship (Luke 13:34; 19:41; John 11:33; 13:21). God desires to be in conversational relationship with us as friends, freely living in God's will and glory (Exod 29:43–46; 33:11; Ps 23; Isa 41:8; John 15:14; Heb 13:5–6).[21] Toward this desire, after the Edenic fall, God's heart immediately reached out to restore fallen humanity to relationship within the Triune, perichoretic community, one another, and creation (Gen 3:8–11; Lev 26:12; Deut 23:14; 2 Cor 6:16).

As we discuss in the pages that follow, God's heart yearns to restore and deepen the rich and intimate conditions that he and other persons enjoyed as told in the story of Eden, as reflected in the parable of the Prodigal (Gen 2; 3:6a; Luke 15:11–32), and as elevated in the life of Jesus Christ: "You have heard it said, . . . But I say to you . . ." (Matt 5:44 et al.). God desires fellowship and intimacy with humans enjoying and living out his image to the full beginning now.[22]

God's will or economy (Gk. *oikonomia*) at the basic level is simply God's heart and desire and how he arranges or pursues the fulfillment of that heart and desire. God's economy, in creating such a world that is most conducive to his goals and means, is seen in the evolving and progressing world in which humans inhabit. God's heart and desire are toward a world that is the best possible—one that allows for the highest good (L. *summum bonum*) of God's creation with human free will seeking God.[23]

There is much in human present experience that would militate against such a conjecture as that presented above such as mental and physical defect, prejudice, hegemony, discrimination, hate, murder, poverty, homelessness, "natural" disaster, war, illness, malfeasance, and death. Although considered further below, under the section "Theodicy and Other Trials," a thorough

---

20. Grenz, *Social God*, 268; Van Huyssteen, *Alone in the World?*, 118–23.

21. Willard, *Hearing God*, 10.

22. Aquinas, *Summa Theologia*, 885–86; Hagner, *Matthew 1–13*, 134–36; Van Huyssteen, *Alone in the World?*, 155–57.

23. Augustine, *City of God and Christian Doctrine*; Brunner, *Man in Revolt*, 147; Leibniz, *Theodicy*, 123; Plantinga, *God, Freedom, and Evil*, 54–55.

examination of a coherent theodicy is beyond the scope of the present work. Nonetheless, I hold that this world as conceived by God is, in truth, the best catalyst for spiritual transformation. It is designed, and has continued to develop, as the best soil and means to transformationally develop the heart of God in each individual human in expression of God's image and in proleptic spiritual expression as is shown below.[24]

Best Possible World

It is not that God "needs" evil to accomplish his intents with humans. Human free will is needful to the full development of mature and transformed humans. A world in which humans are markedly free and thereby perform more good than evil is of greater value than a world consisting in no free persons whatsoever.[25] Unfortunately such free will not only presents the opportunity for personal evil, but also in fact, necessitated its actual introduction.[26] Even if such free will (Augustine's *improbra voluntas*, L.) potentiates and precipitates evil and suffering, a world in which such freedom is given, even if evil is consequential, is better for the development and transformation of humans. While I disagree with any ideation that God instituted evil (pain and suffering), whether often attributed to John Hick, the more narrowly held claim that challenges and temptations are inherently more valuable for developing virtues, in my view, still holds more value than would any imagined ready-virtue apportioned to individuals.

Plantinga,[27] for one, gives trouble to the Irenaean or modern interpretation of his theodicy as provided in Hick when he allows that a theist may not be able to provide the rational and surely not a provable case as to why God allows evil, and yet it is not a contradiction in allowing that God does allow evil.[28] It is beyond the purpose of this study to argue all of the causals and allowances driving evil proposed to be of God's means. However, I side with John Hick, who would say, "soul-making" (a Keatsian coinage often used by Hick), is God's purpose in these difficulties in what I refer to as the process of spiritual transformation. There is no contradiction in God's attributes of omni-benevolence and omnipotence in any of this.[29]

---

24. Aquinas, *Summa Theologia*, 47.
25. Plantinga, *God, Freedom, and Evil*, 30.
26. Ibid., 30–31.
27. Ibid., 11.
28. Ibid.
29. Ibid.

In truth, ready-made virtues displayed in spiritual transformation would be of no value having not been worked by trial and difficulty. Although Irenaeus' and Hick's free will theodicy is severely questioned, and although such a theodicy is not required for the thesis of this book, the reality of this world in which trial, pain, sin, and evil, are clearly present make Hick's "soul-making" or "person-making" fruitful. I deal with this postulate under the rubric of proleptic spiritual transformation (PrōST). Although I do not develop a full theodicy, understanding the issues of free will and best possible worlds is more fully dealt with in chapter 4. A world of both choice and God's sovereignty are presented throughout Scripture and consideration of the seeming tension between evil and an omnipotent loving God, again, is briefly discussed in chapter 4.[30]

DRIVE FOR THE DIVINE

Most particular, and to the point of this study as discussed above, is that God desires vital and intimate relationship with transformed human beings in reflection of his Son. Although often obscured and buried deeply within the soul, this ultimate destination is known and resonates in the human heart. Catherine of Siena speaks to this love of God at a devotional level in the *Dialogue* where she says of God, "Because you have fallen in love with what you have made!"[31] This desire of God, I propose, is the essential reason that human beings desire God in concordant, harmonious response, which response, is, at its core, a reflection of God's desire (1 John 4:10, 19). It is a response, reflection, and echo of the very image of God, responding, reflecting, and echoing back to God and to the whole creation (Eccl 3:11). Within this transmission or transaction is the necessary and naturally spontaneous worship generated by such an encounter with the living God.

In consideration of this drive and encounter, Calvin[32] speaks about the religious seed (L. *semen religionis*). God has deposited in all humans an understanding of "his divine majesty" to prevent them, by this divine conviction, from hiding in ignorance. Specifically, Calvin says, "God has sown a seed of religion in all men"[33] to sense divinity (*divinitatis sensum*). He goes on to present the case that although this seed resulting in a divine sense has been sown in humans it does not ripen and certainly does not bear fruit in

---

30. Collins, *God of Miracles*, 156–57; Pannenberg, *Systematic Theology*, 2:165–66; Plantinga, *God, Freedom, and Evil*, 30.

31. Catherine of Siena, *Dialogue*, 325.

32. Calvin, *Institutes*, I.III.1.

33. Ibid., I.IV.1.

season. Humans struggle under vanity and an obduracy measuring God by themselves and thereby missing how God has offered himself. We most often only see as driven by our own machinations. So human worship and service toward God is misplaced upon our own imagined goals driven by hearts not focused on and yielded to God.

In support of reformed epistemology, and Calvin in particular, Plantinga[34] considers such ontological posits of God, and I believe, by inference, God's attributes (real desires among them), to be properly basic and justifiable even lacking any possible foundational argument within a normative contention pressing against such a belief.[35] God created wise persons (L. *Homo sapiens*), humans, in such a manner that we are inclined or disposed to see God's working in the universe whether simple or grand.[36] Plantinga's argument is supportive of the religious seed (L. *semen religionis*) no matter how distorted, misplaced, vain, or obdurate humans may be in obscuring the resultant *divinitatis sensum*.

Setting aside Plantinga for the moment and pressing against the restrictions of classic foundationalism, empiricism, and scientific reason, Milbank's rigorous, epistemic analysis of *poiésis* (Gk.),[37] a doing, making, or performance is itself outside of accepted scientific postulation, unyieldingly suggests that in the "poetic moment" is a realization of the Beautiful. Here, in this aesthetic experience, is the place of the Christocentric revelation. It is "a narrative projecting forwards the divine horizon," experiencing this sacred narrative as Christ is supposed to have lived it.[38] Persevering in this work, and contrary to Milbank's resistance to a divine seed, one is drawn to this teleological eventuality. It seems appropriate to suggest that human understanding, based in *mythos* and *mimesis*[39] of Christ, becomes the "*mythos*," that we encounter driven by the *semen religionis* and are drawn to and desirous of the Divine in this *divinitatis sensum* exampled in Christ and implanted in all humans.[40] In speaking of *mythos* nothing is suggested or agreed that the present considerations, especially as they apply to Genesis 1, are to be understood symbolically but rather as "concentrated doctrinal content" and of topical interest for Israel then and all humans now.[41]

---

34. Plantinga, "Is Belief in God," 46.
35. Ibid., 42.
36. Ibid., 46.
37. Milbank, *Word Made Strange*, 123.
38. Ibid., 29.
39. Ibid., 127.
40. Calvin, *Institutes*, I.III.1.
41. Rad, *Genesis*, 47–48.

Archaeologists have long believed that abundant vegetation and increasing wild game led to farming and domestication of animals which led to permanent settlements in turn leading to organized religion.[42] Recent archaeological findings have replaced this time-honored, erroneous belief credited to V. Gordon Childe.[43] Beginning with geometric surveys, archaeologist Klaus Schmidt began unearthing the temple Göbekli Tepe in southern Turkey in 2003, which has been dated to 7,000 years before the Great Pyramid of Giza, some 11,600 years ago.[44] Study of Göbekli Tepe has led to the firm belief that organized religion gave rise to farming. That is, religion, worship, and the spiritual preceded farming. The wonderment at changes in the natural world led to religion which, in turn, led to the domestication of plants and animals, agriculture, and permanent settlement for the benefit of communal living and worship.[45] This discovery is significant in its suggestion that the intrinsic and overwhelming drive for the divine (*divinitatis sensum*) within humans is evidently responsible for community and progress in society as a display of *imago Dei* in the world. It is a response to divine general revelation and the God infused impetus within humans as God driven to seek the divine. Here relationship is born or at least shared in purpose among humans desirous of relationship with the divine and transcendent.

The spiritual condition of human beings is often difficult to determine especially in the knowledge that much of the creation story has been made "obsolete" by modern standards.[46] Nevertheless, Scripture seems to tell a story about God's desire for intimate relationship with and image bearing from his creatures. This desire does not imply any measure of anthropopathy and may be rendered will or wish (Gk. *theló*).[47] A full discussion regarding the attributes of God is not within the scope of this study; however, anthropomorphisms are used in consonance with Scripture. Metaxas[48] cites Dietrich Bonheoffer where he wrote a circular to the local church in Finkenwalde, Germany in 1939 and said, "Where God tears great gaps we should not try to fill them with human words." Although speaking of the terrible loss of the war, the point applied here is not to avoid the issue, but that although God is not a man (Job 9:32; Rom 9:20) he often speaks of himself

42. Mann, "Every Now and Then," 49.
43. Ibid.
44. Ibid., 39–40.
45. Ibid., 41–48.
46. Rad, *Genesis*, 48.
47. Strong, *Exhaustive Concordance*, 2309.
48. Metaxas, *Bonheoffer*, 349.

in human terms. What is more, not only does God speak of his "desire," but without the satisfaction of his desire for the divine in resonance with God's desire for humans. Without this resonance humans cannot find fulfillment or satisfaction, and therefore, remain frustrated from God as their "source."[49] God's desire or will that humans be holy, in fellowship with him, follow his commandments, and a host of other intents and directions for humans, speaks to God's desire and will for humans in harmonious communion (Gen 3:9; Lev 26:12; 1 John 4:19; 1 Pet 1:16). Moreover, there is no implication of any ontological lack in God's being by such a desire any more than that God desires all to be saved (1 Tim 2:3–4). The psalmist calls out from this desire:

> Whom have I in heaven but you?
> And there is nothing on earth that I desire besides you.
> My flesh and my heart may fail,
> But God is the strength of my heart and my portion forever.
> (Ps 73:25–26)

The New Testament reflection and progression of the psalmist's heart and desire in response to God's heart and desire can be found in the Apostle Paul's words about Christ to the Philippians. In Christ one comes to know God the Father (John 14:7–11; Col 1:15–20). So then, to know Christ Jesus is to know God the Father and to satisfy God's and our own heart's desire. Indeed, everything should be seen as loss because of the incredible worth of knowing Christ Jesus the Lord. For his sake we should be willing to suffer the loss of everything and count it all as waste, in order to gain Christ and be found in him, not having our own inadequate righteousness, a righteousness that comes from the law, but a righteousness that comes through faith in Christ, the righteousness from God contingent on faith—that we may know him and the supremacy of his resurrection now, and that we may share his sufferings and tribulation now, becoming like him in his death, that by any means possible we may enjoy the resurrection from the dead (Phil 3:7–11).[50]

SPIRIT AND SPIRITUAL

A clear understanding about who or what God is, as discerned from God's self-revelation, is essential to any understanding or theology about human

---

49. Houston, *Heart's Desire*, 241–42.
50. Hooker, "Letter to the Phillippians," 526–29.

spirituality.[51] This notion is particularly important to us in these pages. An understanding of God as spirit and being spiritual is central. Additionally, God must ontologically be an entity capable, available, responsive, and desirous of relationship with humans for any reasonable hope of intimate encounter with him. This might seem troublesome since God is revealed as spirit, unsearchable, inscrutable, unseen, and as dwelling in unapproachable light (Ps 145:3; John 6:46; 2 Cor 3:17; 1 Tim 1:17; 6:16; Gen 1:2b; 1 Kgs 8:27; Isa 55:8; John 3:6, 8; 4:24; 1 John 4:12).

Further, God is not like any material, anti-material, energy, vapor, or space, but rather "the fullness or essence of being" or simply "pure being."[52] God's being is spiritual, and God acts from that center (1 Cor 2:13; 10:4). Moreover, God cannot be contained at any point of the created or uncreated (Ps 139:7–10; Isa 66:1) and forbids images and representations of himself to suggest he is limited by form or place or material things that are reflected by a body of some fashion (Exod 20:4; Isa 40:18, 25). God is "that being than which nothing greater can be conceived."[53]

As a spiritual being, God is invisible (John 1:18; 1 Tim 1:17; 6:16). Regarding spiritual matters, it more deeply has to do with his inaccessibility without his willed revelation and manifestation (incarnation) toward creatures that are capable of discerning his advances toward them. This does not suggest God as an obscurant being but rather above human self-willed scrutability.[54]

In discussing how Karl Barth was influenced by Søren Kierkegaard's thoughts about divine transcendence, Millard Erickson borrows the phrase "qualitative distinction and dimensional beyondness"[55] from Martin Heinecken, wherein this distinction and beyondness are the qualitative differences between God and humans and thus the inaccessibility of God by humans.[56] Such distinction exacerbates the inscrutability of God and assures God's invisibility. However, accepting this understanding does not negate the availability of a condescending and therefore immanent God. God is near and available (Job 12:10; Acts 17:28; Rom 10:8; Heb 7:25) notwithstanding his qualitative distinction.

---

51. Chan, *Spiritual Theology*, 40.
52. Grudem, *Systematic Theology*, 188.
53. Fairweather, *Scholastic Miscellany*, 75.
54. Moltmann, *Trinity and the Kingdom*, 220–21; Rad, *Genesis*, 25–26.
55. Erickson, *Christian Theology*.
56. Ibid., 284–85.

Trinitarian Perichoretic Relationship

Trinitarian theology demonstrates that God is not only spirit and spiritual but also, that God is three persons, Father, Son, and Spirit, who are in a perfect and unique relationship of divine love within the perichoretic union of the Trinity.[57] Borrowing from the Christian philosopher and martyr Boethius (c. 480–525) in that the nature of a person is its irreplaceable substance. Moltmann[58] juxtaposes this notion against Augustine's thoughts on relationship and concludes that each of the Trinity possess the "same individual, indivisible and one divine nature" in varied ways, the Father of himself and the Son and Spirit from the Father. So then, they are independent in their divinity but profoundly constrained and dependent on one another. It follows from this, Moltmann claims, that personality and relationships are connected and present simultaneously. The Trinity subsists in "the common divine nature" and the Trinity "exists in relations to one another."[59] In truth, to be a person, as is each of the Trinity, is to be in and molded by relationship "in accordance with the relational difference" and not constituted by the relationship but rather presupposed in it.[60]

In applying this concept to the Trinity, Moltmann speaks of that which is "noninterchangeable, untransferable individual existence in any particular case."[61] Moltmann brings Hegel into the discussion to join Boethius and Augustine in that the Trinity realizes within itself one another in love. By this third contribution, Moltmann speaks three terms into the doctrine of the Trinity: (1) person, (2) relations, and (3) history of God.[62] Moreover, God's "plural deliberation," that is in relation to himself, is singular in the plural and plural in the singular, and inferentially, humans are both singular and plural inversely. In this God has a correspondence of, or in human community individually and especially in unity.[63] Though Moltmann mistakenly limits this community to the male-female relationship. Van Huyssteen[64] presses that the image of God cannot be summed as the relationship between a man and woman. Male and female, in Genesis, simply indicate

---

57. Moltmann, *God in Creation*, 258.
58. Moltmann, *Trinity and the Kingdom*, 172.
59. Ibid., 173.
60. Ibid., 172.
61. Ibid., 171.
62. Ibid., 174.
63. Moltmann, *God in Creation*, 117–18.
64. Van Huyssteen, *Alone in the World?*, 138.

relationship. Moltmann[65] does allow that human likeness to God in the whole human existence as consisting in correspondence and relationship to the perichoretic God as revelation of the divine in earthly form. Although differing with Moltmann here in his insistence on the male-female image of God on earth, it is manifest that God's image can only fully be lived in full human expression in community as social beings.[66] Also as discussed below the male-female reality is necessary in reflection of continued creation by God's vice-regents. Incredibly, the perichoretic relationship reaches to all creation and includes it without necessitating creation's divinization although allowing creations influence upon the Godhead.[67] From this perichoretic relationship and human *imago Dei* flows "mutual need and mutual interpretation. The true human community is designed to be the *imago Trinitatis*."

As "plastic image" or "God's sovereign emblem"[68] humans not only function as God's representatives, but also reflect God in the ontology of being in which there is a draw to be in and express this perichoretic relationship. Not only should we (humans) be in relationship with one another, but also with God. God, as revealed in the Scriptures, is a personal being desirous of intimate relationship with his creation.[69] God desires and created humans to be like himself (Lev 11:44–45; John 17:11, 21; Rom 8:29; 1 Pet 1:14–16). In addition to created beings as *imago Dei*, God brings the fullness of this to fruition through a process of spiritual transformation in perichoretic relationship. Spiritual transformation is a determinant of material persons' ability to relate at some significant level with an immaterial and spiritual being and the ability of these material persons to "see" this self-same immaterial, spiritual, and invisible God, whoever may be initiating the encounter.[70]

Not arguing the filioque here, Moltmann[71] speaks of two movements of God in which the first, "the divine Trinity throws itself open" the Father having sent the Spirit of God through the Son, that is, the Spirit of God and the Spirit of Christ open to the world in time and to renew and unite in whole all of creation. The second movement is reversed from the first. In the transformation of the world in and through God the Spirit, all turns to God.

65. Moltmann, *God in Creation*, 220–21.
66. Ibid., 222–23.
67. Ibid., 258.
68. Rad, *Genesis*, 60.
69. Chan, *Spiritual Theology*, 41.
70. Pannenberg, *Systematic Theology*, 2:224.
71. Moltmann, *Trinity and the Kingdom*.

Being moved by the Spirit, all comes to the Father through Jesus Christ the Son. By the glorification of the Spirit, the world, times, people, and things are brought together before the Father and become his.[72]

In the first movement God reached out to creation, and in the second movement the creation is brought to God. Both movements are in the Son through and by the Spirit in full glorification of the Trinity. Later in this same work, Moltmann speaks of the manifestation of the Trinity in relationship (Gk. *perichōrēsis*) of divine life in glory as reaching further trinitarian manifestation or relations. It is the glorification of the Spirit of God in "the experience of salvation."[73] The depth of such an experience of salvation in the Trinity is enjoyed in the perichoretic relationship of Trinity drawing and welcoming humans into this same reality. Most fully, Moltmann says this salvation and relationship shall culminate as people becoming God's dwelling and home. The early church looked to an eschatological kingdom of glory in which all would be deified (Gk. *theōsis*). It is a kingdom in which people shall finally and completely be drawn into the eternal life of the triune God.[74]

Humans, constituted in part as spiritual beings, were created to experientially enjoy a spirituality that is living for God through Christ, in full communion, presence, and by the power of the Spirit of God.[75] Here in this perichoretic relationship, in the enjoyment of community, is found the true freedom in its truth of love for which persons were created—a "project of the future" which transcends the present and moves toward the direction of God's future—"the history of the kingdom of God"[76] which nurtures proleptic spiritual transformation (PrōST). Admittedly, these points are not all-inclusively developed here; however, they serve nicely to reflect the progressive Trinity in internal relationship and to humans especially his friends.

More is discussed in chapter 5 about the relatedness of spirituality within the perichoretic engagement of the Trinity and the effects of spirituality on the total person as he or she interacts with God, creation, and other humans. Also, more is considered about the effects of God's relationship on the being and attributes of humans as they are enjoyed and lived in real time and place especially in relationship to PrōST.

---

72. Ibid., 127.
73. Ibid., 176.
74. Ibid., 213.
75. Downey, *Upper Room Dictionary*, 258.
76. Heschel, "Holy Dimension," 120; Moltmann, *Trinity and the Kingdom*, 216–17, 221.

VERY GOOD

God's satisfaction and regard for the created universe, and humans particularly, was exceptional as noted at the end of the creation story in which God pronounced his doing in creation and the outcomes as "very good" (Gen 1:31). Pointing out the significance of human creation, Rad[77] notes that three times in verse twenty-seven, God created (Heb. *bara'*) in reference to humans, both singular and collective. This refrain points up "the fullest significance for that divine creativity which is absolutely without analogy."[78] The beauty of this enterprise is "completely perfect" in wonderful purpose and harmony.[79]

That which was very good, was inclusive of humans created very much like God. God formed the entire created order of things culminating as goodness inclusive of human beings created in God's image. This world, as "very good" is the environment into which we were conceived for God's intent of obedient, worshipful, and glorifying communion with himself. We were constituted with bodies as living souls inclusive of relationship, representation, and essence (Genesis 2:7 [Heb. *nepesh*]; 1 Corinthians 15:45 [Gk. *psuchēn*]). As argued herein, it is the best possible world in which to mature humans to a full expression of *imago Dei*.

No doubt, the goodness of God's creation is in part simply due to that God created it (Ps 119:68; 1 Tim 4:4). By definition whatever God does must be particularly, essentially, and consequentially or teleologically good if God is beneficent and in no way maleficent. Finally, that we have been created in God's image as the capstone to creation is to survey the whole in satisfaction, which brings a pronouncement of "very good" in reflection of God's heart.[80]

God communicated to us attributes such as love, mercy, grace, benevolence, and intellect. Even the physicality of humans seems to be included in this goodness, for we were given corporeal bodies and directed to rule over the physical earth in our bodies and to procreate in those same physical bodies (Gen 1:26–28; 2:7). Rad concurs, contrary to the arguments above, that the wonderment of the human physical appearance is not a development exempted from the domain and concept of God's image and should not be lessened by spiritualization or any kind of intellectual proclivity. The

---

77. Rad, *Genesis*.
78. Ibid., 57.
79. Ibid., 61.
80. Ibid.

whole human—our totality—is created in God's image.[81] It is not exact to speak of God in anthropomorphic terms, but rather to speak of humans as theomorphic.[82] Eventually, these worthy human bodies shall be resurrected into glory (1 Cor 15:52; 1 Thess 4:15–18). This goodness is shown below to be inclusive of God's image in humans as not simply one but complete expressions of God's full spectrum of communicable image, such as previously shown above, in the substantive, relational, and functional aspects of image. This is even shared in that we were created as male and female to share in God's creative ability in procreation as a special blessing.[83]

The goodness of God's creation and of humans within that creation is evident in God's thrice pronouncement of an incomparable creation (Heb. *bará*) in 1:27 culminating in humankind his intent and direction from the first verse.[84] The creation is God's, and we have been entrusted with its care (Gen 1:26, 28; Job 5:9; 37:14). Moreover, we are to continue the responsibility for creation as vice-regents for God (Ps 8:6).

This viceregency is more poignant when viewed through the agencies of genealogy and benefice. We are children, sons, heirs of God, fellow heirs with Christ, and eventually glorified with Christ (Rom 8:17; Gal 3:29; 4:7; Eph 3:6). God's intent is seen early in that he delegated his sovereign right to his first created human as a "worthy assistant" with a task to give names to the world's creatures and to rule over them (Gen 2:19).[85] As with powerful earthly sovereigns, we are God's sovereign emblems to represent God in relation with God in all earthly affairs.[86] Moreover, one might infer or receive a hint at the possibility of the fall in the free will that was given us in viceregency introducing rebellion into the created order. Included in this ground of goodness (or best possible world) is the opportunity for self-willed rebellion that as shown above also serves our transformation.[87]

Not only was creation declared very good in Scripture, but numerous philosophers and theologians have argued and debated that this is the "best of all possible worlds"[88] This best of all possible worlds has importance in that it is the environment into which God's creatures would be situated, tested, offered abundant life, and transformed into God's inclusive, unhin-

---

81. Ibid., 58–59.
82. Rad, *Old Testament Theology*, 145.
83. Rad, *Genesis*, 60–61.
84. Ibid., 57.
85. Ibid., 53, 59, 83.
86. Ibid., 60.
87. Plantinga, *God, Freedom, and Evil*, 29–30, 44; Willard, *Hearing God*, 10.
88. Steinberg, "Leibniz," 123–24.

dered expressed-image. Our nature is indeed wonderful and awesome.[89] If it were not so, God could not have become incarnate. It may even be that flesh was elevated by incarnation. In either case, God's remedy testifies to our nobility in the incarnation.[90]

IMAGO DEI

As addressed in chapter 1, the human image of God (L. *Homo imago Dei*), generally referred to in this study as *imago Dei*, is a discussion of great consequence not only to the premise of this study but also to anyone seeking understanding and meaning in this life. The *imago Dei* is foundational to all divine revelation.[91] A postfoundational strategy for revisionist interpretations that sympathizes and rings true with core scriptural texts, in a shift away from speculation and abstraction, ushers the understanding of *imago Dei* into a theological and interdisciplinary dialogue.[92] More specifically, God's image in us is central to the thesis of this study of proleptic spiritual transformation (PrōST). Since this is the case, it is vital that this study establish a coherent theory of the *imago Dei* before proceeding too far. It seems that Platonic, mediaeval, and Aristotelian beliefs may place the human parts in conflict with each pressing for supremacy and set against recognizing the whole human, spirit, soul, and body, as the full embodiment of the *imago Dei*.[93] This integrated-embodiment is the hoped-for consummation of the human life in reflection of the completed life of the God-man Jesus Christ.

Admittedly, such an embodiment is in its full transformation magnificent, and its effulgence emanates light making the sun seem dark in comparison.[94] The *imago Dei* is a sign of our gravitas, beauty, and original androgyny—the Adam Qadmon or Primordial human being.[95] We are, by this view, complete, integrated, and without partitioning. Such wholeness is animated by God's breath (Gen 2:7).

Yet, an exhaustive treatment of the vast proposals and arguments related to this subject are not necessary neither possible here except as begun in chapter 1 and in as much as the subject pertains to the central issues of this study. An understanding of our intended purpose in creation follows.

89. Rad, *Genesis*, 57–60.
90. Ranft, *How the Doctrine*, 5, 165–66.
91. Feinberg, "Image of God," 236.
92. Van Huyssteen, *Alone in the World?*, 151.
93. Moltmann, *God in Creation*, 245.
94. Gottstein, "Body as Image of God," 173–74.
95. Feinberg, "Image of God," 241.

The discussion includes what transpired in the fall and what expression and enjoyment may have been lost or damaged and whether it has or can be recovered.

Body And Spirit

There is a strong reluctance among rabbinic sources to define the concept "image of God."[96] However, among them a theory of God's image emerges as body or form that is similar to the human body.[97] According to rabbinic sources this body or form is the original homo *imago Dei*. Admittedly, as stated above, the human form is magnificent, and its effulgence or, emanating light would make the sun seem dark.[98] The *imago* is a display of human grandeur, beauty, and original androgyny—the Primordial human.[99]

Such a notion of body as God's image is lacking and inadequate alone. It leaves as created and material what of God's eternal being he has bestowed on or in us by his breath. Moreover, the vast gulf of meaning of "body" as image becomes almost impossible as the Christian theology of Christ, original sin (first sin), and the Trinity are introduced confounding any coherency among Theologies addressing this issue.[100] This problem is particularly highlighted if the human body solely is allowed to be God's image.

The Christian tradition has been more willing to directly challenge this difficulty. Origen[101] posited that God was invisible and therefore, that God's image in humans must be invisible. The general view coming out of the Middle Ages and based in Irenaeus, Augustine, and the Reformation supported by Luther, and Calvin, was that God's image is seated in the soul and reflected in our reason, rationality, intellect, and will; later adopted by Thomas Aquinas[102] and others, drawn from Aristotelianism, intellect and reason was thought more scientific.[103] The thought reasons that because we are intellectual creatures, we are the only ones of creation that contain God's image.[104] Though Western theology was first dominated by these substantive

---

96. Altmann, "Homo Imago Dei," 235.
97. Gottstein, "Body as Image of God," 171–72.
98. Ibid., 173–74.
99. Feinberg, "Image of God," 241.
100. Altmann, "Homo Imago Dei," 235.
101. Origen, *De Principiis*, II.6.3.
102. Aquinas, *Summa Theologia*, 470.
103. Erickson, *Christian Theology*, 409–502; Van Huyssteen, *Alone in the World?*, 126, 132.
104. Aquinas, *Summa Theologia*, 470.

interpretations of *imago* as intellect or reason, they are mostly unfavored by modern theologians today.[105]

More to the issue, and allowing something of the rabbinic proposal above, in the Gifford Lectures, van Huyssteen[106] argues that the *imago Dei* is not disembodied. Such a notion of disembodiment denigrates the wonder of God's creation in humans as *imago Dei*. What is more important, such a notion denigrates the incarnation of Christ implying that his body somehow was not included as God's image and thereby is not worthy of God's attention or salvation. This, not infrequently, leads to the belief in a bodiless, *post-mortem* existence with no allowance for physical resurrection. Rather, the whole person, including the body, as God's functional representative in relationship, van Huyssteen says is the *imago* in "enforcing God's claims as lord."[107] We are more than our discrete parts however they might be listed or defined. Those parts did not exist prior or independently of the whole person.[108]

Tertium Quid

Clearly, the image of God, that is in us, is a great mystery, and whether "similitude," "in similar fashion,"[109] or one of the many other translations or renderings is used, the fact remains that there is a scriptural basis that God is doing something unique with humans that was not done or given to any other part of creation. This something is the foundational place from which God reaches into our lives to invite us into full unhindered, communion and intimate fellowship. Such intimacy requires the *imago Dei* as requisite to full, open communication of what God is depositing or doing in us for all creation unto his expression and glory. This presses up against the very reason for being human—that is, to portray God's presence in the world.[110] So here there is transverse linkage between paleoanthropology and theology through our uniqueness of *imago Dei* as embodied.[111]

Although this book proposes that there is an element of the three (representative, substantive, and relational), the substantive is proposed as inherent in the very being of humans as breathed by God (Gen 2:7). The

105. Van Huyssteen, *Alone in the World?*, 133.
106. Ibid., 134.
107. Ibid., 134–37.
108. Heschel, "Holy Dimension," 123.
109. Altmann, "Homo Imago Dei," 236.
110. Van Huyssteen, *Alone in the World?*, 147.
111. Ibid., 148.

representative is presumed only in as much as an individual or a group corporately is in relationship with God, neighbor, and creation through love.

The *imago Dei* is active and lively; displaying many forms, and has variant interpretations.[112] For one, Welker[113] suggests *imago Dei* as possessing an understanding of what is favorable and unfavorable to life as a concept addressing the return to God's image.[114] Besides agreeing with Welker here, the initial position that drives this study is that the event of Genesis 3:22, in and of itself, is a referent to only one attribute (knowing) of the *imago Dei*. Any one-dimensional theory is wholly rejected by this study. The *imago Dei* is an inclusive *tertium quid*, a third way or a combination of "knowing," embodiment, and a larger array of communicable attributes born in relational love that reflect, represent, and are *imago Dei* to that degree.

More so than an inclusive definition of *imago Dei*, a leg of my investigation stands within, and heavily leans on, the Eastern Orthodox traditions that divinization is the goal and the full *imago Dei* in humanity. Specifically, this image culminates in full a perichoretic union of God and human beings and is, in unhindered relational terms, nothing less than perichoretic community.[115] Although not all theologians are willing to entertain, least of all defend, divinization or *theōsis*, Christian theology, particularly and uniquely, contends that there is some measure of God's essence that has been mysteriously shared with humans (Gen 6:7)—a "Divine DNA."

Regarding this "DNA" the Protestant and, more particularly, the Reformed position holds a relational theory of *imago Dei* in reflection of the divine. Although Martin Luther did not strictly and clearly label the *imago Dei* in humans, he has been understood to mean an original and dynamic righteousness in the human response to God that places him squarely in the relational camp.[116] Indeed, according to Luther, the image is lost as a result of this relationship having been broken.[117] However, John Calvin is usually given credit for setting Reformed doctrine of *imago Dei*.[118] Although Calvin[119] speaks of human beings as participating in God, he is referencing a pre-fall condition. Calvin further establishes his relational view as can be seen by a thorough review of his writings, rejecting any difference between

---

112. Van Huyssteen, *Alone in the World?*, 160.
113. Welker, *Creation and Reality*.
114. Ibid., 78.
115. Vishnevskaya, "Divinization as Perichoretic Embrace," 133–34.
116. Grenz, *Social God*, 165.
117. Ibid., 166.
118. Ibid.
119. Calvin, *Institutes*, II.II.1.

image and likeness (Gen 1:27) as a difference between substance and qualities[120] stating that humans are the "brightest mirror" of God's glory.[121] Canlis[122] reaches beyond "brightest mirror" and further into Calvin's thought in which Christ brings humanity into "obedient communion to the Father" by his descent from *koinōnia* with his Father, followed by his ascent back to the Father bringing with him, in ascension, all of the lost. It is in this *koinōnia* in Christ to God that *imago Dei* is born and enjoyed.[123]

The voice of Catholicism can be heard in Thomas Aquinas[124] and more closely touches a "Divine DNA" in which he postulates that image is a matter of "species," and intelligent creatures, humans, are most in God's image by virtue of their intellects.[125] This concept falls within the rubric of substantive *imago*. Moreover, leveraging Hilary, Thomas makes a clear case that Jesus Christ solely is the "species" of God as perfect and true image, while leaving room for us as the image of Christ, the Second of the Trinity, the human exemplar of Divine-human species.[126]

As seen above, this essence is variously spoken of as *imago Dei*. How this "essence" is defined, integrated, partitioned, expressed, and generally understood plays greatly on the relationship to God we may have and how our relationship with God, others, and creation is expressed. Expectations of this research, related to proleptic spiritual transformation (PrōST) hinge on what *imago Dei* is and to what degree it can be expressed in the present.

Rebranding

In its effects, the degree to which this image is obscured is the measure of hindrance of the manifestation of God's kingdom on earth as it is in heaven (Matt 6:10; 13:19; Rom 12:2). The "righteousness and peace and joy in the Holy Spirit," that is of the kingdom of God (Rom 14:17), is expressed by disciples who enjoy some measure of spiritual transformation, as is shown below as *imago Christi* (image of Christ), from which to spontaneously express these attributes of righteousness, peace, and joy in God's Spirit as

---

120. Grenz, *Social God*, 166–67.
121. Calvin, *Commentary on Psalms*, 85.
122. Canlis, *Calvin's Ladder*, 3, 80, 92.
123. Ibid., 3, 65, 82, 85.
124. Aquinas, *Summa Theologia*.
125. Ibid., 470.
126. Al- Bitar, "Critical Analysis," 29.

did Christ. This too-neglected movement of many formal churches (over 20 million believers) is at the heart of God's desire and intent.[127]

The dearth of direction and focus on spiritual transformation betrays a superficial ideal and branding of the Christian faith. Such spiritual realities or states, in their fullness, are typically reserved, in most theologies and popular preaching, for the eternal state in God's manifest presence.[128] Among these pages, we reexamine this conventional partitioning of the "now" and "not-yet" for a potential new balance and paradigm in expressed *imago Dei* expressed as PrōST.

Imago Christi

Foundational to this discussion is the baseline of what the human being is as *imago Dei* and into what we are to be transformed—from what to what. Jesus the Christ is presented as and shown to be the proto, fully expressed, *homo imago Dei*.[129] Missing this image in Christ (*imago Christi*) deflects seeing God's image in humans. In such cases the god of this world (Satan) has blinded the minds of those unbelievers that do not see, to prevent them from seeing the light of the Gospel of the glory of Christ—the image of God (Rom 8:29; 2 Cor 4:4; Col 1:5). The image of God, or icon (Gk. *eikón*), is not without resemblance or even a sharing or participating in the reality of what it represents—in this case Jesus manifested the reality of his father, God.[130] Humans, as created in the *imago Dei*, are nothing less than a new humanity created as *imago Christi*. This new humanity is the *telos* of which the Second Testament creation narrative speaks and points as the eschatological community of glorified humans.[131]

In this same narrative, Grenz continues by developing the thought that this new humanity is the very climax of the complete salvation-historical story, which is the culmination and explicative moment for the creation account of humans in the *imago Dei* as found in Genesis.[132] Christ could clearly claim that if one had seen him, one had seen his Father (John 14:7–9). To some debatable measure we can claim the same as Christ's disciples. In agreement with Grenz, here then is the fulfillment of God's intent and plan for humans as spiritual bodies (Gk. *pneumatikon sōma*) now in Christ clear-

---

127. Barna, "Faith Revolution."
128. Aquinas, *Summa Theologia*.
129. Bruce, *Epistle to the Hebrews*, 35–36; Lioy, *Evolutionary Creation*, 76.
130. Grenz, "Jesus as the Imago Dei," 619.
131. Ibid., 623.
132. Ibid.

ly shown in 2 Corinthians 3:18 in which beholding God's glory in Christ causes transformation in the beholder into the same image in progressing degrees of glory (PrōST).[133]

Jesus is the second person of the Trinity, the Son of God, the image of God, as well as God's presence in the world and now through his disciples, the church. Moreover, as shown in Christ, the value in human beings is not that humans hold a high value of themselves but that God gives us value. Christ is preeminent above the first human (Adam). He is both the manifestation of God and the true human being.[134] Our value does not come from being the highest accomplishment in the evolutionary process (though one might argue such), "but that the supreme eternal being has made [us] in his own image"[135]—in the image of Christ, the true human being as *imago Christi*.

As already discussed here, we were created in the "image and likeness" of God (Gen 1:26–27). God's image consists in spiritual, intellectual, and moral likeness to God from whom humanity's animating breath comes.[136] As such, contrary to traditional Roman Catholic and Protestant differences, humans are fully representational of God, in which image carries structural, essential, spiritual sameness, or possession of humans as God's image that brings forth representational, substantive, and relational positions for the human with God. There is no restriction to, in some manner, either sharing in the divine nature or relational realities as choices that must be made. In truth there is correlation. For example 2 Corinthians 3:18 speaks about a relationship that results in transformation into God's image. Moreover, the Eastern Orthodox view[137] argues through Irenaeus, Athanasius, Gregory of Nazianzus, and Gregory of Nyssa that the condescension of God into incarnation opens to us a path of ascent—the unimaginable reality of union of the mortal with the Divine. This uncreated grace is shed upon created humans. Thus the redeeming work of Christ, in his incarnation, is precisely related to God's penultimate goal for us, that is, to know union and thereby communion with God. According to Peter (2 Pet 1:4), if union has been accomplished in the divine person of the Son, who is God incarnate, it is necessary that each of us should become god by grace, or partaker of the divine nature.[138]

133. Ibid.; Moltmann, *God in Creation*, 219.
134. Grenz, "Jesus as the Imago Dei," 620.
135. Erickson, *Christian Theology*, 286–87.
136. Harris et al., *Theological Wordbook*, s.v. "děmuwth."
137. Lossky, *Image*, 97–98.
138. Ibid.

As stated in the introduction, the position of this study posits a scholastic similarity (at least as held by Thomas) to Orthodoxy[139] though route and methods may differ. I hold to the desired possibility of direct experiential fellowship with God by which deification "partaking of the Divine Nature"[140] is enjoyed by measures, as Paul says from glory to glory (2 Cor 3:18). Although admittedly "*deconstructive* concepts" intended to destroy gnostic "radical incompatibility [laid] between heaven and earth," this deification makes humans more like God in fellowship (Gk. *koinōnia*) or Triune, perichoretic-relationship with God and adoption as proof of such deification. Deification is not in any way an issue of receiving God's incommunicable essence (e.g., aseity, incomprehensibility, omnipotence, omniscience) but rather only God's communicable attributes such as righteousness, holiness, love, dominion, intellect, and glory (Gen 1:26; Deut 6:5; Eph 4:24; Col 3:10; 1 Cor 11:17).[141]

As already stated, while agreeing with Canlis[142] that deification is a matter of fellowship and relationship of *koinōnia*, with God, this work holds most closely to an Orthodox position that the image breathed (Gen 1:26; 2:7) into humans was the beginning, inviolate deposit of the divine communicable energies and nature of God ultimately resulting in grace in deification.[143] Thus, the transformation spoken of here is a coming into a fuller expression of that which is communicable and inherent to us, by removing the dross caused in the fall and protracted willful acts of defiance on display throughout human history, that opens one to fellowship or *koinōnia*. Thereby, removing that which may obscure, the *imago Dei* shall be more fully expressed in us, without limit to one particular human facet, but "the whole of human existence"[144] with an ontological eventuality of full, unhindered *imago Dei* as deification in relationship, energies of life, and expression of communicable attributes.

Along with the Genesis passage, Psalm 8:5–9 contains a central text for an inclusive dialogue on the *imago Dei* and mainly regarding the representational attributes of image. Here the psalmist queries God as to why he cares for humans by making them just a little lower than heavenly beings, which position may actually be understood as temporary (Heb 5:9), eventually

---

139. Plested, *Orthodox Readings of Aquinas*, 11, 27–28, 225.
140. Aquinas, *Summa Theologia*, 1140.
141. Kärkkäinen, *One with God*, 30–31.
142. Canlis, *Calvin's Ladder*, 236.
143. Lossky, *Image*, 110; Mantzaridis, *Deification of Man*, 15.
144. Ibid., 16.

leading to our elevation above the angels[145] and crowning us with glory and honor. Small but honored we have been given dominion over creation. The psalmist's consideration of this draws praises to God from him.

Representation is clear in the above passage; however, the substantive[146] and relational aspects are also present (cf. above, "Trinitarian Perichoretic Relationship"). To make humans in a way that they can represent God speaks to the substance of humans. From an Orthodox view, it is a *theōsis* or sharing in the life of God from which one's, and more so, humanity's being and acting arise.[147] Such a relationship between regent and vice-regents is vital, even paramount, to such a representation. What is more, it is now as a reflection of Christ's life that has enriched the *imago Dei*—the *imago Christi*. Despite and contrary to the judicial arguments for redemption by Anselm of Canterbury (L. *Cur Deus homo* [why was God a man?]), the thought of union with God should not be thought of as abnormal or restricted by preoccupation with redemptive salvation or a myopic focus on present human wretchedness.[148] Lossky[149] continues that Christ's passion neither can be separated from his resurrection, his glorified body seated at the right hand of the Father, nor from our life "below" (PrōST).

Christ: God's Self Address

As Jesus was God's "self-address,"[150] so are we all intended to be unhindered and in clear focus as God's address. We are to be God's address to others as well as to the creation and representationally of the creation and in worship back to God. Such an incarnational principle is at the root of the *imago Dei*. The *imago Dei*, seen as God's self-address, is deeper than the Genesis initiation. It, *imago Dei*, or God's self-address now carries something more—the God-man (*imago Christi*). God's image in Jesus the Christ, as bestowed to humans by the Spirit of God, now carries the existential realities of his incarnate life.[151] One might say that we are *ordained* to be Jesus' self-address (Eph 3:17–21; Col 2:9–10).

Christ's life now includes the reality of thirty-three and half years of all of his incarnated experiences including the details of his life, passion,

---

145. Lioy, *Evolutionary Creation*, 63.
146. Herzfeld, "Imago Dei," 363; Shults, *Reforming Theological Anthropology*, 220.
147. Ibid., 222.
148. Lossky, *Image*, 99, 101.
149. Ibid., 103.
150. Jenson, "Praying Animal," 320.
151. Shults, *Reforming Theological Anthropology*, 221–22.

death, resurrection, and ascension. Although we can learn a great deal, being created in God's image, one cannot sufficiently learn apart from God. More so, we discover who we are, not by studying just any other human, but by studying the superlative person of Jesus the Christ.[152] This is all the more the case when it comes to knowing something of what the image of God should look like played out in this life unhampered by internal sin. As is fully developed in these pages, this ontological, existential reality drives toward PrōST (proleptic spiritual transformation) as God's goal for humanity in full relationship with himself and creation in the now (John 14:23; 15:15; Rom 8:29; 2 Cor 4:4; Col 1:5; Rev 3:20).

Rational, Relational, and Depraved

Thomas Aquinas' and Calvin's holding that the image is in the human reason or intellect has more in common with Greek thought than scriptural truth.[153] Aristotle is a good example of this Greek influence. He spoke of the uniqueness of humans as being rational creatures and having vivacious faculties—rather, I would say spirited interior faculties. Among a number of posits, modern theory offers the distinction of *imago Dei* such things as chronic unreproductive sex and the ability to suffer inordinate amounts of pain for rewards perhaps not foreseeable or forthcoming.[154] Although the idea of too much sex and pain may seem creaturely and base, the idea of reason and intellect would only leave us with a partial or incomplete *imago Dei* versus the inclusive image proposed in this book.

Human uniqueness requires an intense "transversal, interdisciplinary dialogue" of science and theology, beyond the reach of my efforts here, to drive a conviction that the unique human is composed of the relationship of humans with God and humans with creation to God, and in this are animated representations of God.[155]

As discussed above Gadamer,[156] in an exchange with Hagel, propounds that humans gain a real sense of our selves by interaction and sacrifice for the universal. The *imago Dei* is found in a progressive expansion of relationship to God, the world, and creation in whole, wherein the heart of God is experienced and expressed. In such a relationship, we find particularity and ourselves in the largeness of the whole. It is a relational *imago Dei* in caring

---

152. Barth, *Church Dogmatics*, III.2.39–41.
153. Hoekema, *Created in God's Image*, 39.
154. Sapolsky, "Uniqueness of Humans."
155. Van Huyssteen, *Alone in the World?*, 163, 167.
156. Gadamer, *Century of Philosophy*, 7, 59.

for God's creation. Specifically, it is in relationship with Jesus Christ that we find our place in God and creation. Understanding God relationally is the critical factor by which we learn about ourselves and to do as God does.[157] It is more necessary specifically, however, to be in relationship with the God-man Jesus to experientially derive what human life is intended for in such a relationship with God and other human beings.[158] Jesus is the manifest image of God's nature and character already present[159] and the complete example for relational human living.

The Protestant and, more particularly, the Reformed tradition hold to a relational theory of *imago Dei* in reflection of God. Martin Luther has been understood to mean, by *imago Dei*, an original and dynamic righteousness in the human response to God placing Luther directly in the relational camp.[160] *Imago Dei* was created for and found in relationship and fellowship that is only fulfilled in Christ[161] that brings a likeness to those related to Christ in such things as growth in wisdom, grace, spirit, and in relationship to being human. Although here dominion or rule is not part of the definition of *imago Dei* but a consequence,[162] it is a clear capability for which responsibility attaches.

It seems that Karl Barth[163] approaches well the *imago Dei* in discussing who humans are in relationship. However, his proposal follows the misogynistic tendencies of an earlier era, in particular the Antiochene School of theologians, in misogynistically connecting males with God's image.[164] Such an approach is limiting in that *imago Dei* is expressed, for Barth, in a skewed polarity of male and female relationship. Not only is a "super- and subordination" image imposed in the male and female construct in Barth,[165] it is limiting in that the male and female relationship delimits a more full orbed and expansive expression. A broader expression is more inclusive even universal to God, the other (male and/or female), and the creation.

---

157. Power, "Imago Dei," 131.
158. Barth, *Church Dogmatics*, III.2.39–41.
159. Peacocke, *Theology for a Scientific Age*, 302.
160. Grenz, *Social God*, 165.
161. Pannenberg, *Systematic Theology*, 2:224–25, 227.
162. Rad, *Genesis*, 59.
163. Karl Barth, *Humanity of God*, 47.
164. Shults, *Reforming Theological Anthropology*, 224.
165. Barth, *Church Dogmatics*, III.2.287.

Barth is incorrect in his conjecture that the male and female relationship is the content of *imago Dei*.[166] Clark[167] challenges this thought in that gender relationships also occur in animals, and therefore, quizzes and ponders how such a relationship can be the image that shows humans as different from the rest of creation. Compounding this further there is that no sexual distinction is revealed in the Godhead. Then again, Barth's intent seems to be more beneficial, at least as it speaks to human inclusion in the trinitarian perichoretic relationship and humans reflecting of that relationship.

While John Calvin[168] believed that the *imago Dei* is reflected in the soul of humans and yet shattered by the Edenic fall, he left no room for unassisted unregenerate humanity to approach or know God. Moreover, Calvin[169] takes a strident stand against human ability. Human natural gifts were "corrupted," leaving only a corruption or residue of something of the understanding and judgment: strangled, weak and thrust into darkness. Calvin continues here, "Supernatural gifts were [totally] 'stripped,'" which, according to Calvin, removed any hope of salvation. The "mind is given over to blindness and the heart to depravity"; no part of the whole person is immune, and all that comes from humans is corrupt with sin.[170]

Calvin's "total depravity" affecting all that are the capabilities of *imago Dei* in humans is foundational to the modern construct of TULIP (Total Depravity, Unconditional Election, Limited Atonement, Irresistible Grace, Perseverance of the Saints).[171] While Calvin may not argue for the total loss of *imago Dei*, a measure of relational aspect has been impaired restricting knowledge and access to God in any synergistic construct, in opposition. However, Orthodoxy and others disagree with Calvin, especially total depravity, and argue that no function of the *imago Dei* is lost or in any aspect damaged.[172] Present enjoyment of the *imago Dei* in transformation is inclusive of the existential life of Christ as the *imago Christi*, reflected and represented by humans in relation to God and creation. That is, I argue here that PrōST, an experience of transformation is greatly available today. However, the enjoyment and expression, not its essence, has been greatly

---

166. Van Huyssteen, *Alone in the World?*, 138.
167. Clark, "Image of God in Man," 221.
168. Calvin, *Institutes*.
169. Ibid., 270–71.
170. Ibid., 253.
171. Ibid., II.I.9.
172. Dyrness and Kärkkäinen, *Global Dictionary of Theology*, 250; Shults, *Reforming Theological Anthropology*, 232–33; Rad, *Old Testament Theology*, 147.

blemished, marred, and damaged by a God-defying willfulness of humanity. Despite this rebellion, nothing of the *imago Dei* is lost.[173]

Shults and Rad, here, contend that the supporting passages of Genesis 5:1–3 and 9:6–7 do not give room for the historical position of original sin and damaged *imago Dei*. "Whoever sheds the blood of man, by man shall his blood be shed, for God made man in his own image" (Gen 1:26–27; 5:1; 9:6; 1 Cor 11:7; Col 3:10; Jas 3:9). Genesis is a sufficient defense, even if it stood alone; however, as shown, it is not the sole testimony. Also a topical word about Romans 3 may be helpful and set a different view of depravity of humans in sin. As the threat of death in Genesis was not immediate nor total, the condition of Romans no more necessitates an effect on the intrinsic *imago Dei*, that is, humans, than the cutting of a lily or even the damage or destruction of its whole structure, damages the bulb waiting underground for the requisite conditions to bring forth the flower into full bloom. The argument here is that the *imago Dei* is something of God's indestructible life breathed into humans and remains in the "soil" of humans, no matter human or creational action. Thereby, as I discuss below, removing that which obscures the *imago Dei* more fully expresses in us without limit to one particular human facet but "the whole of human existence"[174] with an ontological eventuality of fully bloomed, unhindered *imago Dei* as deification in relationship and expression not independent divine essence.

Nonetheless, without amassing volumes of data that would distract our purposes, let it satisfy that God announces the recompense penalty of humans for destruction of other humans created in God's image. To the point, this recognition of *imago Dei* in humans was also after the fall. Notwithstanding arguments of opposition from Calvin and Luther, this research stands on the subsequent obscuring of the human's expression and enjoyment of God's image in man, without damage to or loss of the *imago Dei* in essence. That is, we were created in the image of God; however, the enjoyment and *expression* of this *imago Dei* has been greatly blemished, and marred, not its essence, by a God-defying willfulness of humanity. Only the expression and enjoyment of God's image needed remedy and consequently Christ's incarnation and salvific work.[175]

In what may be an unpopular contention, my argument is that humans are not hindered in the reality of *imago Dei* by the notion of also *being*

---

173. Van Huyssteen, *Alone in the World?*, 135; Feinberg, "Image of God," 245; Schults, *Reforming Theological Anthropology*, 221.

174. Mantzaridis, *Deification of Man*, 16.

175. Grenz, "Jesus as the Imago Dei," 623; Kilner, "Humanity in God's Image," 611, 614; Schults, *Reforming Theological Anthropology*, 84–86.

sinners.[176] Although our actual sins do hinder us in relationship with God, sins become a blockage to divine communion. It is a violation of image bearing, limiting human reflection of God (2 Cor 3:18) and the nature of such a relationship that image bearing suggests and requires. Sin is a violation of loving God and others (Matt 22:36–40). The act of being human is unrelentingly in relationship to God.[177] Sin is a perversion of that relationship, but as a creation or gift from God, humanness cannot be annulled or rescinded except if God were to do it.[178] Since sins do not stop us from being human, relationship with God cannot be fully broken nor can the *imago Dei* be lost.[179] Following this, sin and righteousness is determined in the relationship of love of God and neighbor (Mark 12:30–31). This is the same love that drew God into incarnation and his sacrificial work. This is the *imago Dei* that Christ's disciples are called to live in unseating sins (not any notion of original sin except as the first sin) to freely live in relationship with God, others, and the creation.

As previously stated, Jesus Christ is God's "self-address."[180] As the perfect human prototype and example, we are meant to finally live unobstructed and in sharp focus as God's address. We are to be God's address to all of humanity, to creation, and representationally for the creation in full worship of God. This incarnational principle is at the ground of the *imago Dei*. The *imago Dei*, seen as God's self-address in Christ, is deeper and more accessible than the Genesis initiation. It, *imago Dei*, that is, God's self-address, carries something more than the Genesis account. It carries the God-man (*imago Christi*). God's image in Jesus Christ, as bestowed in us by the Spirit of God, now carries the existential realities of his incarnation and full life.[181] Humans are ordained to be Jesus' self-address (Eph 3:17–21; Col 2:9–10). More particularly, the relational aspect more deeply defines *imago Dei* (now *imago Christi*) not only in capacity but also in the reality of relationship with other persons including God.[182]

Moreover, as considered below, there is no ground to plant the seed of a lost or even distorted *imago Dei*.[183] Despite the conjecture that "by faith and obedience to the will of God as expressed in the Scriptures could [we]

---

176. Moltmann, *God in Creation*, 216, 219.
177. Brunner, *Man in Revolt*, 150; Moltmann, *God in Creation*, 220.
178. Ibid., 233.
179. Van Huyssteen, *Alone in the World?*, 135; Feinberg, "Image of God," 245.
180. Jenson, "Praying Animal," 320.
181. Shults, *Reforming Theological Anthropology*, 221–22.
182. Van Huyssteen, *Alone in the World?*, 135–37.
183. Ibid., 135; Feinberg, "Image of God," 245.

regain the lost status of *imago Dei*,"[184] I repeat, the *imago* is *not* lost but only obscured by the veil of sin. Central to this study, and my contention, is that people are restored, not the *imago Dei*. God's image in humans was not and cannot be lost; it is the status of all human beings.[185] Contrary to Feinberg,[186] the image is not in need of restoration or perfecting. Yes, conformation to God's image is the destination (Rom 8:29; 12:2), but that refers to the accidents and not the essential human which is inviolate. In either case, whether one holds to a lost or obscured paradigm, such a recovery of *imago* or experience and enjoyment of *imago* is not wanting for the feeble efforts of humans exercising untransformed attributes. It is the work of God (1 Cor 1:8; Phil 1:6; 1 Thess 3:13).

Essential and Accidental

In disagreement with my argument, Kilner[187] supports the orthodox position of original sin, but argues that *imago Dei* is the "status" of all humans while the spiritual transformation spoken of in this study is the "standard" from which one falls, a standard to be desired and sought. While this is a good distinction, Kilner's choice of "status" alone is inadequate to the task. Status is something that can change, whether by usurpation, erosion, or forfeiture. Status is not necessarily static.

Emil Brunner's formal (not lost) and material (damaged or lost) notion of image[188] and also Berkouwer[189] fail to understand the expression, and do not help. Berkouwer goes on to compare the formal and material proposal to the Reformed idea of image in human beings which is similar to describing a "wider aspect," which is not lost but retained, and the "narrower aspect," which is lost and not in anywise retained. This distinction does not help either, as it still leaves the *imago Dei* diminished and damaged. If "material" and "narrow aspect" can be construed not to be image at all, but the standard of righteousness and obedience required of humans, then they might serve well to describe what was damaged in the fall without impinging upon or impugning the *imago Dei*.

---

184. Altmann, "Homo Imago Dei," 257.
185. Kilner, "Humanity in God's Image," 611–12, 615.
186. Feinberg, "Image of God," 246.
187. Kilner, "Humanity in God's Image," 615.
188. Feinberg, "Image of God," 143.
189. Berkouwer, *Studies in Dogmatics*, 51–52.

As already discussed, despite Calvin and Berkouwer,[190] relationship with God is the reflection and profession of the essence of *imago Dei*. As damaged and negative as some might claim that relationship to be, the essential nature of humans, which is inclusive of the *imago Dei*, is something that cannot be changed or damaged,[191] or lost without a person ceasing to be a human. In an echo or call-and-response in Genesis 1:26 and associated passages, in which God creates humans in God's image and so places us as God's relational representatives, Psalm 8:5–9 speaks about humans in this image. It seems that the essential human is inclusive of the *imago Dei* that cannot be changed without obliterating humans so defined. This is, despite Feinberg's suggestion of "essential image" and "accidental image,"[192] which he claims respectively, what cannot be lost and what can be lost as helpful.

This *imago Dei* is neither a displacement by God in an obliteration of what is uniquely human and particular to the individual and the human discourse[193] nor a replacing with God's perichoretic relationship in the Trinity. The *imago Dei* is a continuation of personhood and discourse in a "kind of victory through time, occurring absolutely."[194] Moreover, this image is definable to being human and cannot be extracted from humanity without leaving humans as other than human.[195] The distinction is in the uplifting of the fallen condition of humanity by a restored expression and enjoyment of *imago Dei* that now includes the existential realities of the life lived by Christ. The prototypical living out of the *imago Dei* in Christ was the preeminent and supreme image of God.[196] This *imago Dei* perfectly lived-out as by Christ is now the intended unfolding of *imago Dei* in humanity. *Imago Dei*, as expressed in and through humans, is now included in the perichoretic relationship in the Trinity.

Deity Enclosing Humanity

Consulting Karl Barth[197] again, he argues that who humans and God are is less important than understanding that the truth of both resides in the

---

190. Ibid., 137, 139.
191. Erickson, *Christian Theology*, 465, 473; Kilner, "Humanity in God's Image," 615.
192. Feinberg, "Image of God," 245.
193. Jenson, "Praying Animal," 319.
194. Ibid.
195. Hoekema, *Created in God's Image*, 66.
196. Feinberg, "Image of God," 244.
197. Barth, *Humanity of God*, 47, 50.

"fullness of their togetherness." Jesus' "deity encloses humanity in itself," and so God cannot and does not exist without humans. Strongly agreeing with Barth here, this thesis concurs that God, in the incarnation, no longer exists without humanity. God has drawn humans into the perichoretic relationship of the Trinity.[198] However, it is still a profound importance to consider who humans and God are in this togetherness.

This often unattended reality of who God and humans are and their inviolate relationship is neglected to the detriment of an understanding of the goodness of human creation. Such neglect may denigrate any consideration of the worthiness of unfolding the human being in some present transformative availability (PrōST). Such neglect delays and defers transformation and full salvation and sanctification of a supposed unworthy vessel to the *eschaton*. Contrary to any suspension of human elevation for the future such an inclusion or enclosing of humanity in deity elevates even the present condition of every human. Created humans were already included in what was "very good" and are now mysteriously included in the very God—for the second person of the Trinity is eternally the God-man as noted below.

Moreover, the shared image in humans, now inclusive of the God-man, may only be fully realized as a corporate matter. This is "the great body of Adam . . . [the] cosmic form of Adam" as all future generations derived from that prototypical relationship which is the progressive plan of God for all of human beings.[199] This "cosmic Adam" is now inclusive as the body of Christ (Rom 12:4–5; 1 Cor 6:15; 12:12, 25, 27; Eph 3:6; 4:25; 5:30). Finally, and although here stated more firmly than Feinberg,[200] the *imago Dei* is at its irreducible foundation the intrinsic ability to know and love God in unhindered relationship and spontaneous, substantial, representation of the Trinity in and to the creation.

DISAFFECTION AND REBELLION

Like God

Aside from form criticism source debates regarding J and P (JEDP, the sources for what is most often attributed to Moses) it may be more important to understand what was said versus who said it. If "the knowledge of good and evil" (Heb. *Wā-rā', ṭō-wb had-da-'at* [Gen 2:17]), a prerogative and exercise

---

198. Moltmann, *God in Creation*, 218; Vishnevskaya, "Divinization as Perichoretic Embrace," 133–34.

199. Gottstein, "Body as Image," 192.

200. Feinberg, "Image of God," 246.

of God, can be understood as the contrast of a "negative response" or "no" and "favorable response" or "yes,"[201] then God's prohibition is above simple knowledge of choices between good and evil and is a prohibition against our wishes to act apart from and in place of God. This position, as represented by the tree of the knowledge of good and evil, provides both knowledge and action in human response of "no" and "yes" and usurps God's divine right and primacy.

Humans were created with the privilege of being God's agents, vice-regents, and representatives not to replace God in their own exercise of power unhinged from God. Clark[202] is correct, this event makes one like God (cf. Gen 3:5, 22; 2 Sam 14:17; 1 Kgs 3:22). It was evidently meant as a prohibition as shown in God's response in Genesis. God saw that Adam and Eve disobeyed him and took of the fruit from the tree of the knowledge of good and evil at which juncture God removed the opportunity for humans to eternally live in this state of rebellion (Gen 3:22). By this act humans became mortal[203] and lost the immortality that would have been secured in the tree of life. They were banished from the garden to work, hope, and die. The Levitical priesthood rightly illustrated this representative power for God, in the priests at the temple, in choosing a sacrifice as "good or bad" before God (Lev 27:12).

Contrariwise, Erickson[204] indicates human irreconcilable ontological difference from that of God and that humans shall never be God or like God. Nevertheless, it seems that this may have, indeed, been the trespass of humans—not only trying to become like God—but trying to be God without God, by making decisions reserved for God. By this humans usurped God's rightful position as sovereign, knowing and deciding, and found themselves alienated from God without his full and free benefit (Gen 3:22–24; Isa 47:8; Ezek 28:2, 9; Eph 2:12; 2 Thess 2:4).

So then, this discussion of the knowledge of good and evil weighs on the function and authority of God and of humans. It speaks to the intended relationship between God and the human being and the consequence of that relationship being damaged by human attempts to determine and exercise what is perceived as good and what is not apart from God. This is the message found in the Garden of Eden. God had forbidden such knowledge and activity (Gen 2:17). The first representative humans in Adam and Eve disobeyed, and estrangement from one another and God ensued. The privilege

---

201. Clark, "Legal Background," 272–74.
202. Ibid., 275.
203. Feinberg, "Image of God," 245.
204. Erickson, *Christian Theology*, 285–86.

of doing according to the God determined good was lost to ears that could no longer hear unhindered by the confusion of self-determination. The Levitical priesthood by God's mercy exampled and rightly illustrated this representative power for God, in the priests at the temple, in choosing a sacrifice as "good or bad" before God (Lev 27:12). As is shown below in this chapter, this usurped ability is restored in its rightful way and place in Christ as always intended[205] and in humans living the transformed Christ-life, not representatively by an elite priesthood.[206] Whereas, the first Adam took by force the knowledge of good and evil.

Human Freedom

A world that allows for the moral development of created human beings in *imago Dei*, allows for the error, fault, rebellion, and evil that might arise from such an exercise of genuine freedom.[207] It follows, then, that disaffection and rebellion are largely an indication of human free and consequential action in a best of all possible worlds. It is human free-action in a world where God's great and deep and care for the ultimate wellbeing of humans is inclusive of spiritual transformation in full expression of *imago Dei*.[208] It is a world in which all creation waits and yearns for the salvation of humans (Rom 8:18–25). The world has been created and equipped for the greatest degree of freedom and the greatest allowance for human development. This freedom and allowance makes necessary the possibility, and as it turns out, the realization of great rebellion and subsequent damage to God's creatures and creation.[209]

Although a fuller treatment of human freedom (free will defense) and theodicy is considered in chapter 4, a brief word may be in order here. Whether one uses John Hick's[210] concept of moral development through individual freedom by evolutionary means or Plantinga's notion of human free will,[211] it is a conjecture of my argument that God is interested in personal moral development for humans by such things as birth, constitution, environs, context, incidents, accidents, and milieus. Moreover, Plantinga's

---

205. Grenz, "Jesus as the Imago Dei," 618.
206. Lioy, *Evolutionary Creation*, 219.
207. Willard, "God and the Problem of Evil."
208. Moltmann, *Trinity and the Kingdom*, 216–17, 221.
209. Brunner, *Man in Revolt*, 262, 266; Hick, *Evil and the God of Love*, 240, 255–57; Plantinga, *God, Freedom, and Evil*, 29–30; Welker, *Creation and Reality*, 75–76.
210. Hick, *Evil and the God of Love*, 255–57.
211. Plantinga, *God, Freedom, and Evil*, 29–30.

"Free Will Defense" may have a better approach to the issue. That is, humans are free in respect to their actions, both, to do or not to do, outside of causal laws. According to Plantinga a world where such freedom is available is more valuable than a world without free will.[212] Plantinga is not exclusive from Hick's conjecture. Hick[213] following this thought rightly suggests, I further agree, that in order to be a whole human being, genuine free will of moral choice is necessary.

As we have already examined, humans, in legitimately exercising of genuine free will, rebelled against God both wrongly expressing *imago Dei* in choice and willfulness and thereby falling from God's intended purposes and in this falling away becoming like God (Gen 3:22).[214] This, unfortunately, is also on display in Christian culture as testified by cant and well-intentioned legalisms of living such as the popular phrase, "What would Jesus do?" Such an approach is symptomatic of trying to discern an ethical expression of God without God.

Such approaches are "soulless" and legalistic in that they are not driven from inside of an individual but from the outside by rules, regulations, and situational interpretations. This is expression of un-transformed living—trying to fly without being a "bird." Although God's Spirit is gracious to meet persons where they may be, and, therefore, honor someone's work, trying to emulate God without the benefit of the Spirit (Rom 8:28; Gal 3:1–9), to act from transformed being is the goal of the New Testament (Rom 8:29; 12:2; Gal 3:14; 4:4–7; Eph 1:5; Col 1:9).

Such efforts are simply eating from "the tree of the knowledge of good and evil" (Gen 2:17, 25; 3:7, 11), although admittedly with the good intent of living like Jesus. Nonetheless, trying to live like Jesus by rules and regulations, traditions, and any form of godless effort denies the life of Jesus provided by the Spirit. If the Spirit of Jesus lives within a person, it is to empower that one to express this life that is nothing less than the *imago Dei* now inclusive of the incarnation, life, death, resurrection, and ascension life of this superlative one—Jesus. With passion, the Apostle Paul made the point that we are now called to live differently. To live according to the tree of knowledge is to be foolish. It is an indication of being captivated by something other than God's life. Since the crucifixion of Christ, we are without excuse and foolish to live by the flesh. Having begun by the Spirit, we cannot be perfected by the flesh. We are only free to live by the Spirit (Gal 3:1–3).[215]

---

212. Ibid., 30.
213. Hick, *Evil and the God of Love*, 266.
214. Welker, *Creation and Reality*, 75–76.
215. Longenecker, *Galations*, 106–7.

Estrangement

Rebellion against God brings estrangement. It is not God's refusal of fellowship but our guilt that drives us from God's presence. God, as always, has had recourse for our sin and guilt if we are willing to be reconciled. Since we were created in relationship with God and one another, to be estranged in any measure leads to a dissatisfied and limited life, one that does not fulfill the calling and purposes of life in general and the individual in particular. Since relationship is the transformative space, such estrangement stunts, perhaps even halts, normal and progressive spiritual transformation,[216] to say nothing of prolepsis.

The reality of transgression from God in disobedience is clear in the judgments pronounced on Adam, Eve, their progeny, and the serpent (Gen 3:14–19). The results of this act of rebellion were immediately seen in the next generation as Abel showed his awareness of his own sin in sacrificing animals to God. Cain revealed his murderous heart by killing his brother, Abel—a clear demonstration of the rebellion recorded in Eden (Gen 4:8–16) played out by all who have followed since the great and tragic universal act.[217]

A turning from God was and still is necessary to disobey and rebel against God's wishes and commands (Gen 3:1–8). Moreover, humans must turn away from their own centers to commit sin against God as such an act is also an act against one's own integrity and integration in violation of the One (God) whose image we bear (Rom 7:7–25). If we are not in right relationship with God and self, there is no possibility of right relationship with other fellow human beings (2 Sam 12:13; Luke 15:21), and, therefore, no spiritual transformation without painful divine intervention.[218]

Instead of seeing God, we see ourselves. Our eyes have been opened (Gen 3:7). We perceive ourselves as uncoupled from God and from one another. Our nakedness leaves us vulnerable and exposed lacking the care and covering of God and fellow humans. This awareness of nakedness and separateness from our source brings shame. We suffer grief because of our estrangement from God and one another. Life, as intended and its completeness, has been sidelined.[219]

---

216. Bonheoffer, *Ethics*, 23–25; Clark, "Legal Background," 275; Welker, *Creation and Reality*, 75–76.

217. Chafer, *Systematic Theology*, 7:150; Lioy, *Evolutionary Creation*, 128.

218. Bonheoffer, *Ethics*, 23–24; Cooper, "Lutheran Response to Justification," 2–40.

219. Bonheoffer, *Ethics*, 23–24.

Bonheoffer[220] speaks of an estrangement brought on by humanity's own rebellion. This person's eyes are now, by disobedience, open and he or she sees his or her shame in causing separation from God by his or her revolt and usurpation by reason of misappropriated knowledge of good and evil (Gen 2:17; 3:22–24). We are now ashamed because of the rebellion represented by lost innocence, and obvious nakedness. We now feel exposed and vulnerable without "wholeness of life."

Veiled Imago

As discussed above, it is commonly thought by scholars and clergy alike that the *imago Dei* was either lost or at least damaged as a result of the fall. By this conjecture humans would be, to a degree, hindered from their created intent, and, therefore, could not clearly or fully express the *imago Dei*, if at all. This conflates two issues. One, the damage done in the fall was to the ability to live by the moral and ethical standard established and required by God and thereby the standard by which we may clearly represent God's image in human actions. Second, the essential or Kilner's "status"[221] (discussed above) of the definition of human beings created in God's image was not affected by the fall. That is, the *imago Dei* remains whole and vital within us although perhaps its expression may be diminished or obscured in the fall and not a pristine expression of God's intent for humans.

Although a distinction may not be defensible, in using a deferential concept between image and likeness, "image" as the essence of humans was not lost or affected, but "likeness" may be considered that which was lost.[222] I do not propose a difference between "image" (*tselem*) and "likeness" (Heb., *děmuwth*) as found in Genesis 1:26–27.[223] An imprecise luxury of parsing these two words might have briefly served the discussion but conflated its intent. The only real distinction required is that something of God's essence, here referred to as *imago Dei* is inviolate, and some part, attribute, or expression of the human is not exempt from harm and corruption that is in need of recovery.

Admittedly, this harm and corruption has especially obscured the moral and ethical expression of *imago Dei* in humans. Although no precise distinction is intended by the description, the expression and enjoyment of God's image, *not essence*, in humans was certainly damaged, diminished,

---

220. Ibid., 23–25.
221. Kilner, "Humanity in God's Image."
222. Feinberg, "Image of God," 237; Origen, *De Principiis*, II, 10.7.
223. Rad, *Genesis*, 58.

and obscured in the fall. However, God's essence or substance is unchangeable, and this distinction, as shared with humans, is here applied to the *imago Dei* of humans; whereas, the accidents of persons may be changeable.[224] The manifestation of God, which is his image in humans, to the extent that we "[allow it] to be penetrated by deifying grace," shows "by grace what God is by nature."[225]

Irenaeus[226] seems a bit muddled in claiming a loss of "likeness" without harm to the image signifying the person is left "carnal" and "imperfect." If Erickson's understanding and representation of Irenaeus is correct,[227] then Irenaeus' "the glory of God is living in humans" (L. *Gloria Dei est vivens homo*) theology is agreeable with this study in preserving the *imago Dei* while noting the "damage" of expression caused in the fall. As already clarified, the present work does not offer a difference between image and likeness; however, except as Irenaeus indicates that some part of humans is no more than God's moral qualities versus that which is a reflection of God in human natural attributes. So then, when the fall took place, the area of humans that reflects, expresses, and enjoys moral, ethical, and righteous action (by some referred to as likeness) was affected and even greatly damaged, but the image was entirely left unaffected as referenced in Lossky above. Although, holiness and goodness had been snatched from this once pristine human exemplar, the human essence given by God as his image was not.[228]

Continuing from Irenaeus,[229] Berkouwer asks whether the image of God in humans was totally corrupted and lost or if there is something left over as "remnants [traces] of the image."[230] In an attempt to clarify and limit such allowance, Berkouwer cites the Belgic Confession and the Canons of Dort which agree that "glimmerings of natural light"[231] remain after the fall but insufficient for saving knowledge. Conversely, he goes on to say that there is not anything that is left uncorrupted or untouched by sin and so whatever remains of God's goodness is also darkened—left in apostasy—humans are left fully and totally incapable of any good.[232]

---

224. Moltmann, *Trinity and the Kingdom*, 172–73.
225. Lossky, *Image*, 126, 139.
226. Irenaeus, *Against Heresies*, 5.6.1.
227. Erickson, *Christian Theology*.
228. Ibid., 461–64.
229. Irenaeus, *Against Heresies*, 5.6.1.
230. Berkouwer, *Studies in Dogmatics*, 119–20.
231. Canons of Dort, III, 4.
232. Berkouwer, *Studies in Dogmatics*, 126–28.

I disagree. Despite any contrary confessions, clearly humans are left with some sensibility and discernment (Ps 19:1; Rom 1:19–20). Although our focus is not centered on soteriology and humanity's salvific route, "remnants" and "glimmerings" of God's image in human beings present a view of humanity as, in reality, not left in total deprivation.

Berkouwer rightly points out that humans cannot be left sinful to the bone of their essence,[233] for Christ was born a man except sin. Otherwise this would have born him into sin, if God's work in creating human nature were totally corrupted without possible exception. Not only does this speak to God's mercy and grace, it suggests a created and inherent "family resemblance" that cannot be erased. Nevertheless, there does seems to be a clear loss of full expression and enjoyment of *imago Dei* in this "family."

Under thorough examination, no biblical support can be found to demonstrate damage or loss of *imago Dei*.[234] As already stated, only the expression and enjoyment of the image of God in humans was damaged, diminished, and obscured in the fall not the essence of the image. However, God's essence or substance is unchangeable, and this distinction is here applied to the *imago Dei* of humans, whereas the accidents of persons may be changeable.[235] Not only does the *imago Dei* continue in all humans, but it continues to be expressed, to some manner, by humans as can be seen in all that is good and beautiful in human cultures and relationships. In further emphasis, I contend that there is no lost, damaged, or marred image except that its expression and enjoyment are affected. I oppose any argument of loss as unsupportable. What is more, as I have already argued, there is not any scriptural support of any loss of the image of God in the fall.

The Bible seems to support the contention of image remaining in humans after the fall. In the book of James (3:9), for one, the Apostle James the Just, Jesus' brother (Jas 3:9–10), tells his audience that cursing any person (Gk. *anthrópos*) is forbidden because such a person is made in God's image or likeness (Gk. *homoiósis*). Earlier Genesis 9:6 stated this prohibition very clearly.

Additionally, without becoming entangled in the debate about Paul's intent and alleged misogyny, he says in 1 Corinthians 11:7a, that a man should not cover his head, because he is the image and glory of God. This, too, demonstrates Paul's mind in that he believed that God's image was not

---

233. Ibid., 133.
234. Kilner, "Humanity in God's Image," 615.
235. Moltmann, *Trinity and the Kingdom*, 172–73.

lost or damaged in humans. Moreover, Shults[236] posits, and Rad[237] agrees that absolutely no function of the *imago Dei* is lost or in any manner damaged.

To press the point further, Kilner[238] uses the analogy of a worn denarius with the image of Caesar on its face was no less representative of Caesar because of its poor condition. It would not be diminished in value any more than a quarter (USA) would now only be worth twenty-two cents because of its worn and poor condition. Similarly, humans do not lose "value" as God's image due to the fall or "wear." So then, whether the Hebrew Scriptures or the Christian Scriptures, the image of God remains (present tense) intact after the Edenic fall no matter the interpretations of appearances and actions to the contrary.

Discussed above, Genesis 9:6, in particular, is founded in the reality of the *imago Dei* remaining in humans after the fall. Because of this abiding image, God forbids the killing of a human being, and in the Hebrew Scriptures, finds it so egregious that the life of the murderer must be yielded in reciprocity or as payment.

Deaf and Blind

The guilt that arises and follows from disobedience and estrangement from God, self, and others leads to limited access to God, self, and others if there is any reasonable access remaining. The limitations reach to an inability to see or hear regarding spiritual matters. In a recurring motif, Scripture speaks of the human condition in rebellion as not being able to hear or see rightly (Exod 4:11; Deut 32:1; Isa 6:10; 29:18; 42:7; Mark 4:9, 12; 10:49, 51; Rom 2:19; 2 Pet 1:9; Rev 2:7; 3:17). This is why Christ spoke in parables, because seeing they did not see, hearing they did not hear, and in either case they did not understand (Matt 13:13).

When Paul spoke about beholding God's face as the means to transformation into the same image as God (2 Cor 3:18), it appears to be the "narrow aspect" or "standard" of image. He is speaking about the expression and enjoyment that was damaged or lost. Paul, in the same thought, recognized that some persons are blinded and therefore cannot see this face of God as Jesus Christ who is his image (4:4). God, nevertheless, has actively shone in the faces to make beatific vision possible (4:6). Willful inability to behold Christ is the bane of humanity; notwithstanding, God declares the magnificence of his son in humanity and determined his incarnation before

236. Shults, *Reforming Theological Anthropology*, 232–33.
237. Rad, *Old Testament Theology*, 147.
238. Kilner, "Humanity in God's Image," 610.

any "fall" was to come. It was not a fallback plan. It was always the primary, magnificent plan and intent of God (John 1:1–18; Rom 8:29; Eph 1:4; 1 Tim 3:16; 1 Pet 1:20).

Jesus Christ is the image of the invisible God. He is the preeminent of all creation. By him all things, whether in heaven on earth, visible or invisible were brought into being through him and by him. This includes thrones, dominions, rulers, and authorities. All things hold together in him. Christ is the head of the body, the church. He is the beginning and the firstborn from the dead, that he might be preeminent in everything. For in him all the fullness of the Godhead dwells with pleasure. Through Christ God reconciled all things to himself including the inhabited earth and heaven. He made peace in all of this by shedding his blood on his cross (Col 1:15–20).[239]

Lawlessness

Goldstein[240] focuses on lawlessness or sin as inordinate concern for oneself, power, and prestige. This overreaching and imposing effort is an attempt to bridge the space between individuals by diminishing them to mere objects that can then be treated with objectifying, depersonalization. It is the same objectifying we might give our appendages, and thereby freely manipulating and dominating them with impunity.

Although this may not be an exhaustive definition of sin, it speaks much about the treatment of humans toward one another and God. From the first record of lawlessness in Scripture at the tree of the knowledge of good and evil, God's top creation has been rebelling against him and living against the letter and spirit of God's heart. A brief review of history testifies to this terrible reality. However, it is not only the acts of Adam and Eve, King David, the Crusaders, Stalin, Hitler, Pol Pot, Jewish and Rwandan genocides, and an unfortunate host of other atrocities, but the lawlessness reaches into the secret places of home and heart all over the world in every time and situation. Jesus spoke about the heart and it as the place of sins no matter the outward action or verification (Matt 5:20–44).[241]

As was noted above in Matthew 5, Hagner, and Willard, the most ignominious acts and histories began in the heart. The guilt of the heart has created whole belief systems, disciplines, and penal and correctional infrastructures in an attempt to remedy the problem. Religious counseling

---

239. Bruce, *Epistle to the Colossians*, 62–63, 66, 74–75.
240. Goldstein, "Human Situation," 100.
241. Hagner, *Matthew 1–13*, 116; Willard, *Divine Conspiracy*, 129–36.

and psychiatry are but two that are strained under the burden and hope to help those crushed under the weight of guilt and despair from lawlessness.

How we treat a single human being is how we treat the whole world, for in a manner, the world was created for that one person.[242] Yet, Kilner[243] presents a critical issue: If we view one another as less than ourselves, "damaged goods" so to speak or more precisely damaged *imago Dei* or perhaps even people who have fully lost the image of God in the fall, then we may feel free to treat or mistreat one an "other" with impunity in whatever manner we choose.

In Moses one can see both intimacy with God and the resultant and even required responsibility and response and the resultant attempt to escape from God.[244] This sympathy toward God is a natural result of creatures created in God's image; however, ruling oneself and vying for power and position in the world drives one to rebel against and escape from God.

PUTTING DOWN THE REBELLION

To restore humans to right relationship with one another and God is necessary but not sufficient for spiritual transformation. The process and events began in eternity past and transpire in time (1 Pet 1:20–21). The story and events are well known. The fall took place in Eden, and the corporate human, as represented by Adam and Eve, was desperately estranged from God. All of humanity was at odds with God in this fall. God's created humans turned from him as their source and sufficiency to their own devices as represented by the tree and the serpent in the Garden of Eden. From that time onward, the Hebrew and Christian Scriptures have recorded God's movement toward fallen humans and creation. God's "arms," like the father to the prodigal, remained open and filled with loving embrace to any who would turn for home. The law was introduced as a taskmaster and to show everyone how far they had fallen from righteousness and God's holiness. Covenants and conditions were given over and again to chronically be broken and leave guilt and shame in the people making an effort to live rightly and obey God.[245]

God, himself, came in the person of Jesus the Christ to live the life that no one until then had been capable of as satisfaction toward God. The incarnation, which had been determined before time, was God's ultimate and

242. Altmann, "Homo Imago Dei," 242.
243. Kilner, "Humanity in God's Image," 516.
244. Richardson, "God's Search for Man," 11.
245. Goldstein, "Human Situation," 100.

loving solution to the rebellion. Jesus lived the sinless example, provided himself as the solution for sin and sins[246] and opened the way back to God the Father in his own flesh by his life, death, resurrection, and ascension. He was and is triumphant.

I do not the intend to provide an apologetic for the theology of "Christ is victorious" (L. *Christus Victor*), in these pages, but only to make use of it for support of my argument. Greg Boyd,[247] in a more extended discussion not represented here, put it nicely in describing the atonement theory of *Christus Victor*. Following his assessment, simply put, is that Christ revealed the truth about himself (Rom 5:8; cf. John 14:7–10), accomplished reconciliation (2 Cor 5:18–19; Col 1:20–22), forgave sins (Acts 13:38; Eph 1:7), healed the human nature (1 Pet 2:24), gave his Spirit (Rom 8:2–16), provided himself as an example (Eph 5:1–2; 1 Pet 2:21), and finally defeated evil (Heb 2:14; 1 John 3:8).

In an echo of Isaiah 42:6b–7 and 61:1–2, the Apostle Paul is commissioned by Jesus. Paul put it very succinctly in describing that God was sending him (Paul) for this purpose of putting down the rebellion, that is, to work for the Gospel. Paul was to partner with God "to open [our] eyes, so that [we] may turn from darkness and from the power of Satan to God, that [we] may receive forgiveness of sins and a place among those who are sanctified by faith in [God]" (Acts 26:18). The sequence to put down the rebellion begins with opening one's eyes, to receive light, to then be put under God's power, to receive forgiveness, and to be sanctified (Acts 26:18; 2 Cor 4:4, 6; Eph 1:8; 1 John 3:2).[248]

Whether this sequence would survive a thorough argument, there is a progression from Satan and sins to forgiveness and sanctification. An argument can be made that God has provided the light from which to turn from darkness, by which we may see God and be freed of sin's power, which allows us to be forgiven of sins and to be found as sanctified with those others who are also being sanctified by faith in Jesus.[249]

Freedom from the bondage of sins comes first, eventually leading to sanctification. This setting apart is inclusive of spiritual transformation as said by "sanctification." Freedom from sins frees the disciples of Christ to indulge in and enjoy relationships that are vital, intimate, and thereby

---

246. Grenz, "Jesus as the Imago Dei," 617.

247. Boyd, "'Christus Victor' View of Atonement."

248. Brunner, *Man in Revolt*, 266–67; Grenz, "Jesus as the Imago Dei," 617; Willimon, *Who Will Be Saved?*, 84.

249. Boyd, "Christus Victor View," 35; Boyd, "'Christus Victor' View of Atonement"; Greathouse, "Sanctification and the Christus Victor," 219.

transformative among themselves, God, and the creation (Col 2:13–15; Heb 2:14–15).

Restraining and Consuming Love

Greek philosophical influences have produced a Judeo-Christian God that is impassable and thereby unfeeling and unsympathetic to the plight of humans.[250] Such a God would not—cannot—be involved in the affairs of humans least of all love from shared suffering or empathy. On the other hand, Heschel[251] posits a God exuding pathos. This is a God who is intimately involved and caring for the issues of all creation especially the creatures found in his image. The Judeo-Christian God is one who can be moved (passibility) by the call and response of his creation. This issue of passibility is treated more fully in chapter 4. Nevertheless, God has a constraining love for humans ("For the love of Christ controls us," 2 Cor 5:14a; cf. Rom 8:37 and Eph 5:2) that is foundational to his passibility as prompted by the human plight.

Not only is God's love constraining or controlling, but, at its core, love is also the *imago Dei* in a manner of embodied availability to God and others through an act of communication with God through prayer.[252] This manifest love is a reflection of God's love in those who embody his image. God's love is not evanescent and impotent. By God's love, we are constrained to a living and responsiveness to God and our neighbor in a way that is fully reflective of an icon of God lived out from Christ with all that life has become (2 Cor 5:14–15). Living by this love is a matter of putting on the "new self, created after the likeness of God in true righteousness and holiness" (Eph 4:24).

Dallas Willard[253] warns that the present interest in spirituality versus religion must find a foundation within the human personality and God's salvific work, or it shall be found as nothing more than a "passing fad." This is where a living relationship with Christ comes into the soul and total human being to constrain and generally, organically influence the disciple to complete "filling up what is lacking in Christ's afflictions for the sake of his body" (Col 1:24b) in the salvific work of Christ.

---

250. Power, "Imago Dei," 136–37.
251. Heschel, "Holy Dimension," 120.
252. Van Huyssteen, *Alone in the World?*, 146–47.
253. Willard, "Spiritual Disciplines."

Incarnation for Liberation

Mondzain[254] argues that a large and critical contribution of Christian theology is that only the image can be incarnated. He goes on to contend that this image is not one sign among others but that it has a specific power to make visible, to form, to wield space, and to make bodies that are made present to the fixed gaze of others. This incarnation is nothing less than God's face becoming visible through Christ's incarnation. It is the "unrepresentable" represented in image. This image is able to transform the violence of rebellion into freedom.

The image is a reality that, at its root, is found in admonitions like Paul's to the Corinthians to behold Jesus's face to remove the hindering dross (flesh) over God's intended expression in humanity and bring transformation (Job 19:26; 2 Cor 3:18; 1 Cor 13:12). Everything about his incarnation brings liberation. To the point of this book, all that is contained in the incarnation is transformative, and to behold his face, or to be in his presence, causes one to be progressively transformed into the same image living forth the Christ-life as he would live it today inclusive of adversity leading to prolepsis.[255]

Caputo[256] interacting with Emmanuel Levinas speaks of the face of the "other" with whom we encounter as being the trace of God that God leaves behind as he withdraws. The allusion is enticing and lovely; however, although God does implant himself and provide a trace of himself that can be seen by the attentive observer in one in whom the *imago Dei* is less obscured, God does not withdraw. Perception of withdrawal is nothing more than that—a perception. God uses such imperceptible times, where presence is not discerned, for the purposes of maturing and transforming the disciple (2 Cor 2:10). John of the Cross,[257] speaks about the purgation and light that shines into the soul because of this "dark night of the soul." These times of darkness are in truth liberating in that we are taught to freely move within the realm God has given without self-reliance but with full, dedicated dependence on God. God desires his children to mature into independence, living out the life that he has prepared before the foundation of the earth (Eph 1:4; 2:10).

---

254. Mondzain, "Can Images Kill?," 28–29.

255. Moltmann, *God in Creation*, 273–75; Pannenberg, *Systematic Theology*, 2:224–25.

256. Caputo, *Deconstruction in a Nutshell*, 98.

257. Cross, *Dark Night of the Soul*, 127–35.

Restored Enjoyment of Imago Dei

The presence of ancient sovereigns was strictly controlled, and unless one was summoned or forgiven intrusion because of prior relationship and intimacy, death was certain. However, in both Hebrew and Christian Scriptures, examples are given of not only admittance to God being granted, but, most importantly, God initiating the encounter and approaching, even condescending, to the non-royal to commune with him or her (Adam and Eve, Abraham, Moses, David, Daniel, Mary, Paul). The list is almost exhaustless.

The present state of human life throughout a too-often-troubled world seems to most often present as something less than transformed and in many instances as ruinous defeat. Yet, Jesus proclaimed a different interpretation in which the kingdom has arrived (Mark 1:15). Moreover, Jesus promised that those who believe in him would do greater things than he (John 14:12). This is a clear reflection of the arrival of the kingdom of God into which we, created as *imago Dei*, are best suited to live, move, and have our being.[258]

Jesus' divine power has granted to us, his children, all things that pertain to life and godliness through the knowledge of God who called us to his own glory and excellence. By this knowledge of God, he has granted to us his precious and very great promises. It is through these promises that we may become partakers of his divine nature, having escaped from the corruption that is in the world (2 Pet 1:4).[259]

God restored, in Christ, the full expression and enjoyment of his image to us as partakers of the divine nature. Moreover, God not only brought the life that he had already communicated to humans as something of God's spiritual nature[260] in creation (Gen 1:26–27), but God gave an image that is now constituted with the incarnation, life, death, resurrection, and ascension of the God-man (Gk. *Theos-anthrōpos*) Jesus. It is the *imago Christi*.

So then, doing comes from being.[261] If we are to represent God as his image, then we must first fully express and enjoy his being to some measure to organically and spontaneously act for him as his representatives. Additionally, the relational aspect more deeply defines *imago Dei* (now *imago Christi*) not only in capacity but also in the reality of relationship with other persons including God.[262]

---

258. Boyd, "Christus Victor View," 35, 47; Pannenberg, *Systematic Theology*, 2:224.
259. Bauckman, "2 Peter," 184; Watson, "Second Letter of Peter," 336.
260. Grudem, *Systematic Theology*, 188.
261. Van Huyssteen, *Alone in the World?*, 134.
262. Ibid., 135–37.

There is no ground to plant the seed of a lost or even distorted *imago Dei*.²⁶³ Despite the conjecture that "by faith and obedience to the will of God as expressed in the scriptures could [humans] regain the lost status of *imago Dei*";²⁶⁴ the *imago* is not lost but only obscured. Central to this study and point, is that we are restored not the *imago Dei*. God's image in humans was not and cannot be lost; it is the status of all human beings.²⁶⁵ Standing against Feinberg,²⁶⁶ I argue that the image is not in need of restoration or perfecting. Conformation to God's image is the destination (Rom 8:29; 12:2), but that refers to the accidents and not the essential human which is inviolate. Whether one holds to a lost or obscured paradigm, the recovery of *imago* or experience and enjoyment of *imago* is not dependent on the frail efforts of humans exercising immature attributes. It is God's work (1 Cor 1:8; Phil 1:6; 1 Thess 3:13).

CONCLUSIONS

This chapter set forth foundational considerations on which the following chapters build. This chapter spoke to the very good world into which God created and made humans with an ineffaceable drive within them as God's children and vice-regents of this planet to find, serve, worship and love God, and to care for the creation. God created the very best possible world with the means for human seeking and transformation. As a result of the lawlessness of sins brought on through human freedom, God needed to intervene (incarnation) in order to put down the rebellion that had, to some measure, veiled the *imago Dei* in human beings and created estrangement of humans from God. It, *imago Dei*, or God's self-address now carries something more—the God-man (*imago Christi*). God's image in Jesus the Christ, as bestowed to humans by the Spirit of God, now carries the existential realities of his incarnate life, passion, resurrection, and ascension. Although surely not the final word in this study, this chapter discussed God as Spirit and spiritual by whom humans have been created as *imago Dei*. It spoke about God's heart in seeking to fully recover and express his image in humanity as proleptic spiritual transformation (PrōST) in perichoretic relationship as the remedy to the spiritual effects of the fall. It is a reciprocated drive—a response from humans to God who first sought and continues to seek humans—a correlate and concomitant seeking in response to God.

263. Ibid., 135; Feinberg, "Image of God," 245.
264. Altmann, "Homo Imago Dei," 257.
265. Kilner, "Humanity in God's Image," 611–12, 615.
266. Feinberg, "Image of God," 246.

3

Transforming-Salvation

PREFATORY

The introductory chapter 1 briefly laid out the thesis background and problem, the aims and objectives in pursuing the present focus of these pages, the theoretical argument, and the means and methods of pursuit. Chapter 2, in particular, set forth foundational considerations for the entire work. It discussed God's heart regarding the eternal plan in light of the fall and its remedy through incarnation. More to the point of the study, chapter 2 spoke about God's seeking to fully recover and express God's image in humanity as proleptic spiritual transformation (PrōST) in perichoretic relationship with God the Trinity. The present chapter takes a more focused look at soteriology, especially in relation to spiritual transformation. While this work is neither focused on soteriology nor able to exhaust the subject, there is a clear linkage between soteriology and spiritual transformation. In particular, the concept of sin as generally understood is of great import for PrōST.

These pages, at this juncture, consider two lines of reason that greatly affect salvific presuppositions. The first has to do with the intent and broadness of God's heart: Receiving God's salvation and who may not, creates broad spiritual effects. The second reasoning has to do with the human heart, especially in reflection of God's heart. Soteriological constructs cannot here be exhaustively developed, but some amount of discussion is necessarily given for the full intent of the present work.

Although this study is not a polemic, a defense, or an apology for a particular soteriological construct, a brief consideration or précis of some key theological concepts that may affect the objectives and goals of this work is in order. As in Schleiermacher[1] taking care not to do violence to individual scriptural passages by wrenching them from contextual considerations, reference is made with the larger support of contextual and dogmatic considerations. Yet the necessary limited survey or gloss, and wanting of further details of these considerations, is only in support of the more specific and primary aim of this study. The aim is to investigate whether individuals must wait for the afterlife to have purification and spiritual transformation fully or largely "worked out"—that is, the possible opportunity to greatly "work out [one's transformation] with fear and trembling [now]" (Phil 2:12–13).

The assessment of Finney[2] and others, guided by reformational lights like Calvin and Luther—in fact Augustinian soteriology—is most often unquestionably accepted as canon or rule. This obedience is to inherited, irrevocable, and constitutional sin even after Christ's work, contrary to some arguments.[3] As discussed below, such an inescapable judgment militates against human change and any large hope of approaching unqualified sanctification or any prodigious or substantial measure of spiritual transformation in this life (PrōST), as proposed in this book. The hope of thorough PrōST may be fettered, frustrated, and simply turned aside. An infused and inexorable sin within human nature fights and contends against PrōST and frustrates its existential reality.

LEBENSFORM

In examining salvation, Alister McGrath[4] discusses the philosopher Ludwig Wittgenstein and his affect on theologians and their sensitivity to *Lebensform* (form of living) in determining the use, application, and meaning of a particular word. In what might now seem obvious, Wittgenstein asks if it would be accurate to suggest that concepts reflect one's life. He concludes with what most philosophies and theologies know today as foundational, with a resounding yes, collectively "they [concepts] stand in the middle of it

---

1. Schleiermacher, *Christian Faith*, 116.
2. Finney, "Accounting for Moral Depravity," 190, 192.
3. Pannenberg, *Systematic Theology*, 2:232–33; Shults, *Reforming Theological Anthropology*, 192, 200–201, 232–33.
4. McGrath, "Particularist View," 173–74.

[one's life]."[5] The importance of this is of large import for this study's conjectures about spiritual transformation. Christian *Lebensform* is particularly important in informing enculturation and presuppositions. Following this notion, our understanding of salvation and transformation shall open or close its horizons, decide who is included, and to what degrees they might be included. Words and concepts are examined and often defined throughout this work in a particular desire to look at spiritual transformation from a different facet than is typically discussed, that is, proleptic, spiritual transformation (PrōST).

Although John Hick[6] stands with an acceptance and defense of religious pluralism, with which I disagree, it shall not do for Hick to name pluralism as sufficient proof of parity between religions based, in part, on the moral testimony of their major representatives.[7] Moral goodness among adherents of a given religion does not provide conclusion to the religion's worthiness for them to stand next to Christianity as equal for the souls of humanity.[8] Hick does not account for the reality of Christ's work in any sufficiency to restore the human condition from self imposed alienation from God.[9] Moreover, Hick's idea of the "Real [God] as undifferentiated,"[10] leaves no room for a central contention of this book that *theōsis* is inherent to human creation and, in truth, is the destination of all humanity in full expression.

Hick does, however, provide a rational theory from which to interpret religions and their distinctions. Without favoring one religion over or against another, he argues that all human experience is "concept-laden"; and therefore, the major world religions have different ways of perceiving and participating in reality.[11] This concept-laden, human experience plays from Wittgenstein's *Lebensform*.[12] From this an argument against inherited sin is set.

More basic than inherited sin (present before transgression), some, and I, argue that there is no original sin whatsoever (except the first transgression in the garden).[13] However, there is no logical necessity, except

5. Wittgenstein, *Remarks on Colour*, 57e.
6. Hick, "Response to Alister E. McGrath," 183.
7. Hick, "Pluralist View," 39–41.
8. Pinnock, "Response to John Hick," 61–62, 78.
9. Geivett and Phillips, "Response to John Hick," 76.
10. Hick, "Pluralist View," 47; Geivett and Phillips, "Response to John Hick," 76.
11. Hick, "Response to Alister E. McGrath," 183.
12. Wittgenstein, *Remarks on Colour*, 57e.
13. Brunner, *Man in Revolt*, 145–47; Pannenberg, *Systematic Theology*, 2:231–33;

ingrained "orthodox" Western theology, translational error (Rom 5:12),[14] and a primitive scientific understanding by Augustine, driving a traducianism interpretation,[15] that inherited Augustinian sin was infused into and remains in the nature of Adam's federated progeny. Even the great philosophical theologian Jonathan Edwards, along with others,[16] questioned such a concept. He questioned that there was any causality between Adam and Eve's colossal blunder and their descendants' inherited compunction to the same. Wyman[17] rightly points out that one cannot clearly discern the fall of the first couple as irreversible changes of human nature. Neither does it hold that a single couple could change the course of the entire human race, present and future, and yet themselves remain the same. An individual can act according to his or her nature but not upon that nature without the argument supporting some form of heretical Manichaeism.[18] The proposition that the first sin changed human nature forever may have no place within the Christian consciousness except to say that our ancestors "re-present" the sin model to their descendants which are culpable in consonant or reflective, same will.[19]

Moreover, the proposition of an original pair of ancestors cannot be based in a prescientific community's "deepest intuition," predetermined worldview, symbology, or "imaginative descriptions"[20] in direct conflict with accepted science no matter the biblical convictions one may have. This point, however, does not nullify the truth that myth can present, in a creative manner, fact of an historical event.[21] The position of the present work, however, is that Adam and Eve, as an original and singular pair of universal ancestors, are not wholly, scientifically tenable.[22] For one, in support of collective creation the Hebrew *ādām* is collective—mankind/humanity, not a single couple but derives from a ~10,000 member group.[23] Scripture, "as

---

Wiley, *Original Sin*, 206–8.

14. Shults, *Reforming Theological Anthropology*, 192.

15. Ibid., 204–6; Meyendorff, *Byzantine Theology*, 144.

16. Pannenberg, *Systematic Theology*, 2:232–33; Shults, *Reforming Theological Anthropology*, 192, 200–201, 232–33.

17. Wyman, "Rethinking the Christian Doctrine of Sin," 206.

18. Ibid., 206–7.

19. Schleiermacher, *Christian Faith*, 298; Wyman, "Rethinking the Christian Doctrine of Sin," 210–11.

20. Lioy, "Two Contrasting Views," 196–97, 204.

21. Ibid., 197.

22. Venema, "Mitochondrial Eve."

23. Rad, *Genesis*, 57; Anderson, *Understanding the Old Testament*, 148; Venema, "Mitochondrial Eve."

bold ahistorical theological declarations" must be read, understood, and rightly honored in light of scientific discovery and evidence of irrefutable evolutionary proofs.[24] Since there was no original couple as historical theology stands, then there is no original sin (except a first sin) transferable except the well documented historical proclivities to sin found in all humans still leaving the need for Christ's salvific accomplishment.

Moreover, the nature of humanity has been liberated in Christ's salvific work.[25] Although this all may not be common Western orthodoxy, it is not a Pelagian argument either, rightly understood. The "original sin" problem was still Adam's impetus of troubles, continues on for his progeny, and the remedy is found in the grace of Christ (Acts 4:12; 1 Cor 15:21–22; 1 Tim 2:5). Yes, it is all due to sin but not because of a Manichean or gnostic skewed concept in which nature requires it.[26] God is not the author and sustainer of sin.[27] Nevertheless, because creaturely life is changeable and defectible, error and sin have followed.[28] Clearly, the contest over original and inherited sin still plays out. I do not propose a transmission of any type of genetic sin intrinsic to humans but choice. Moreover for Calvin[29] this process of sin transmission is a mystery. The modern concept of the transmission of sin raises further questions about human evolution, the original human pair, and science's affect upon theology's understanding of sin as still a mystery.[30]

UNION

Contrary to Govett,[31] sin is not a quality, a state, or a substance resident in persons; it is an actual iterative decision against God.[32] Understanding that to be "a sinner" is not a quality that is unsolvable or limited due to an intrinsically fallen human nature but an act, that assists the potentiality or possibility of PrōST. In what may be an unpopular argument, and although humans are *imago Dei*, I contend that humans are not hindered in this reality by the notion of also *being* sinners,[33] although their actual sins do hinder.

24. Lioy, "Two Contrasting Views," 208–9, 217; Venema, "Mitochondrial Eve."
25. Lossky, *Image*, 102–5.
26. Brunner, *Man in Revolt*, 145–47.
27. Shults, *Reforming Theological Anthropology*, 206, 210.
28. Govett, *Calvinism by Calvin*, 13–14.
29. Calvin, *Commentary on Psalms*, 250–53; Vorster, "Calvin's Modification," 54.
30. Masi, "Credo of Paul VI"; De Duve and Patterson, *Genetics of Original Sin*.
31. Govett, *Calvinism by Calvin*, 13–15.
32. Brunner, *Man in Revolt*, 147–48.
33. Moltmann, *God in Creation*, 216, 219.

Tennant[34] argues that collectively humans have "propensities which are both neutral in value and non-moral in character, necessary and essential also to human nature as God purposed it to be." He continues, in other words, advancing self-directed proclivities, once considered sinful, are in fact simply natural. Clearly, this does not eliminate actual sins as a category. Although responsibility is not averted in this proposal, the problem of antinomy between universal and individual sin is not necessarily obdurate and unsolvable as we move toward spiritual transformation in the now (PrōST). The necessary and contentious claim is that no irreparable sin is intractably innate to human beings.

Finney[35] references 1 John 3:4 and says that all sin is a violation of the law, and it, law, is the only measure of what is right and wrong. Sin here is unrighteousness[36] through lawlessness, and as such the law is that which, if violated, ushers in unrighteousness. Law in the context of the present examination refers to the 613 *mitzvah* including moral law, the ceremonial law, and the civil law or any specific rules, statutes, commandments, or regulations that may attach as Judeo-Christian strictures. So certainly sins are a violation of God's law; however, at the deepest level, and for the meaning required in this study, sins are a violation of the *imago Dei* in both God and humans. That is, as humans are *imago Dei* in relationship with God, sins become a blockage to that communion. It is a violation of image bearing, limiting human reflection of God and the nature of such a relationship that image bearing suggests and requires. It is a violation of loving God and others (Matt 22:36–40). The act of being human is in relation to God.[37] Sins are a perversion of that relationship, and as a creation or gift from God, and it cannot be annulled or rescinded except if God were to do it.[38] Since sins do not stop us from being human beings, relationship with God cannot be fully broken nor can the *imago Dei* be lost. Following this, right and wrong in Christ is determined in the relationship of love of God and neighbor (Mark 12:30–31). This is the same love that drew God into incarnation and his sacrificial work. This is the *imago Dei* that Christ's disciples are called to live in unseating sins.

The soteriological discussion, as it speaks to who is included in Christ's salvific work, is often divisive and contentious, especially as considerations cross the grain of orthodoxy. Although, as already stated, this study, by far,

---

34. Tennant, *Evolutionary Theory*, 120.
35. Finney, "Accounting for Moral Depravity," 184.
36. Ibid.
37. Brunner, *Man in Revolt*, 150; Moltmann, *God in Creation*, 220.
38. Ibid., 233.

is not a thorough treatment of soteriology; some measure of examination seems necessary to the considerations of spiritual transformation especially as it applies to spiritual prolepsis. That is, who is being transformed and in what manner sets expectations and processes to be taught, pursued, and perhaps observed.

Kärkkäinen,[39] as well, cautions that it is difficult to derive a coherent, common soteriology from the various traditions, all colored or contextualized by their respective milieus. However, a "dominant motif" emerges as "union with God," and that this postulate may be common to all religious expressions. Admittedly, this common ground is often walked with different vistas in view or definitions guiding in deriving what one tradition versus another means by union. It seems, nevertheless, that at least main Catholic and Orthodox positions concede minimally a theology in which something essential takes place within humans as a result of this union brought on in justification and deification.[40] Such a union, though more rare in Protestant minds, is the intent and result of the salvific process and the atonement Christ gained in his incarnational experience. This is not to be confused with the heretical *apotheosis* (deification in God's essence). Deification is not in any way an issue of receiving God's essence (incommunicable), but rather only God's energies—communicable attributes.[41]

JUSTIFICATION

Justification is a forensic term indicating to pronounce, regard, and receive as not liable for legal transgressions and grant all the same privileges of those living legally without any legal violation.[42] While Packer speaks of a single or legal-facet-Calvinistic view of justification, it includes both regenerative and transformative elements by participating in Christ in an ontic union.[43] This transformative work is an ontological change to those justified by Christ's work. Although it is "eschatological vindication" and reality invading the present, it is an accomplishment that needs cooperation, discipline, and nurturing by the redeemed for present and progressive existential enjoyment and growth.[44]

---

39. Kärkkäinen, *One with God*, 116–17.
40. Ibid., 119–20.
41. Ibid., 30–31.
42. Packer, "Justification," 593–97.
43. Cooper, "Lutheran Response to Justification," 2–4.
44. Ibid., 3, 6.

Setting aside these distinctions for the moment, Kärkkäinen[45] lists six areas that New Testament scholarship is presently debating concerning justification two (5 and 6) of which play directly upon the subject of this book:

1. Justification is one of many legitimate biblical salvation images, but *not* the *hermeneutical key*.

2. Paul uses *dikaiosyne* (justice) not to mean legal imputation. He uses a legal image only as one facet of his doctrine.

3. Justification is about making justice—putting a person in *right relationship* with God and others. Moreover, justification and sanctification cannot be differentiated from each other in the way the Reformational (i.e., Calvinistic) theology has been separated from both Catholic and Orthodox theologies.

4. Christian interpretation of the Jewish *religion and law* must be *reassessed* considering Jesus' teachings (breaking in of the kingdom) and Paul's teachings (end/goal of the law, fulfilled in Christ). All of which leads to faith.

5. *Union* with God, the creator, by faith in Christ, through the Spirit, is the new status of justification.

6. Justification is *not individualist*, but rather for the purpose of saving the *community* and the kingdom come. Therefore, righteousness is a relational concept in right relationship with God and others.

As they play upon the present discussion, this study is mainly concerned with the last two: (5) Union of the humans with God, and (6) justification is particularly concerned with community and God's coming kingdom. Central to this discussion is God's nature as succinctly and poignantly posed by Kosuke Koyama:[46] "[We] need to decide whether the God of the Scriptures is a generous God or a stingy one." This decision is explored below in the "Soteriological Construct" section. Whether God is generous or restrictive in his gifting plays heavily on an understanding of soteriology and more particularly an understanding regarding who is being transformed and when. Proleptic spiritual transformation (PrōST) posits a munificent, merciful, just, unconstrained, and satiating God.

Again, although some salvific constructs are discussed herein, none are exhaustively defended. The ecumenical councils, in their efforts to produce and defend orthodoxy, in their pronouncements and creeds, never

---

45. Kärkkäinen, *One with God*, 16, 121–22.
46. Mouw, "More Thoughts."

announced one interpretation of salvation as definitive.[47] However, without putting the full case here for *Christus Victor* (ch. 2), such a paradigm rightly understood is helpful for our freeing into full transformational engagement with God. We are not only justified in this notion, but sanctification (transformation) is delivered in the reality of a victorious Christ.[48] Concurring with this viewpoint, Greathouse[49] says, that *Christus Victor* is the notion that Christ's work spotlights the atonement as the eradication of sin making possible real, complete sanctification and perfection. It is a cosmic victory first for all of creation, which frees humans for an individual encounter of salvific work.[50]

This victory brings sanctification bound to justification without possibility of divorce.[51] Everyone has been freed from the cosmic demonic possession.[52] Pointedly, sin no longer has right of rule. Although one may commit acts of unlawfulness, no devil has any right to exact payment or punishment. In God's kingdom only God may carry out the dealings of the reign.

Kärkkäinen[53] also gives support to this idea where he says Christ was victorious over death and accomplished sanctified life. This life is grand. It is more than salvation; it is inclusive of the God-man and his accomplishments to enable the same life in humans in a transformative process of growth and intimacy with God. Said more directly, though more controversially, salvation is to become like God[54] in unhindered expression of the *imago Dei* as exampled in *imago Christi*.

Moreover, I extend such considerations further to a non-competitive but supportive incarnational theory or model of the atonement that more fully supports the contentions of this book. By the incarnational theory I attempt to explain how the atonement is brought about in human sharing in Jesus' life, death, resurrection, and thereby his communicable virtues that could not have been transmitted without Jesus having lived them as a human.[55] It is in this that we become God's address to others and the creation. This theory does not attempt to present a new doctrine that God's

---

47. Green, "Kaleidoscopic View," 168.
48. Boyd, "'Christus Victor' View of Atonement."
49. Greathouse, "Sanctification and the Christus Victor," 219.
50. Boyd, "Christus Victor View," 35.
51. Ibid., 47.
52. Ibid., 35.
53. Kärkkäinen, *One with God*, 22–23.
54. Ibid., 123.
55. Collins, "Incarnational Theory," 5–6.

work saved humanity from sin bringing reconciliation, but simply a theory of *how* the atonement is especially important to the argument of these pages regarding proleptic spiritual transformation (PrōST).

Of critical import, we must come to understand, what is too often left unsaid, that salvation itself is integrally connected with transformation, and, in fact, transformation, not only justification, naturally follows salvation.[56] Therefore, justification cannot be divorced from transformation and sanctification. This is further supported by righteousness being of God's character inclusive of an inseparable justification and sanctification.[57] Moreover, relationship with God is the reflection and profession of the essence of *imago Dei*, as damaged and negative as Berkouwer[58] and others wrongly claim that relationship to be. Such a damaged and negative relationship is an antecedent to spiritual transformation and in particular PrōST.

NOT WITHOUT RESEMBLANCE

In the prior chapter, partitioning of the human being into a dichotomy, trichotomy, or monism was briefly discussed. The danger of such considerations, however, creates "acts of domination" abstracting spirit, soul, and body making one part superior to another and thereby separate.[59] Such separation assures no possibility of integration of humans in reflection of God's salvific work and the (Gk. *perichōrēsis*) into which human beings are intentioned in relationship.

This is all the more important when we consider that the goal of all God's work, including reconciliation, is embodiment versus a form of partition of spirit, soul, and body.[60] Platonic, mediaeval, and Aristotelian beliefs put the human parts at war with each positioning for supremacy set against recognizing the whole human, spirit, soul, and body as the full embodiment of the *imago Dei*.[61] This integrated-embodiment is the consummation of the human life in reflection of the completed life of the God-man Jesus.

Altmann[62] speaks about the clear reluctance among rabbinic sources to define the concept "image of God." God's image emerges as body or form

---

56. Willard, "Spiritual Formation."
57. Kärkkäinen, *One with God*, 122.
58. Berkouwer, *Studies in Dogmatics*, 137, 139.
59. Moltmann, *God in Creation*, 244.
60. Ibid., 244–45.
61. Ibid., 245.
62. Altmann, "Homo Imago Dei," 235.

that is similar to the human body.[63] As already addressed, rabbinic sources posit this body or form as the original *homo imago Dei*. Admittedly, such a body is finally magnificent, and its effulgence emanates light making the sun seem dark in comparison.[64] The *imago Dei* is a sign of humans' gravitas, beauty, and original androgyny—the Adam Qadmon or Primordial Man.[65] We are, by this view, complete, integrated, and without partitioning into spirit, soul, and body. Such wholeness is animated by God's breath (Gen 2:7).

Who God Is

It seems that without a beginning or measure of understanding as to who God is, even to speak of the draw and desire of persons to clearly express the *imago Dei* is nothing more than chimera. To use William Power's phrase, "[Without a] literal affirmative or positive understanding of God"[66] there can be no dependable and trusted interpretation of the meaning of *imago Dei* or how *imago Dei* is expressed, that is, *imitatio Dei*. As the discussion already began in the prior chapter, what *imago Dei* looks like, how to express *imago Dei*, and what it is to enjoy *imago Dei* is fully related to a proper, clear understanding of who God is. As a child enjoys the genetics of its parents, it must also, to a degree, observe his or her parents for imitation.

Proleptic spiritual transformation (PrōST) is especially dependent upon an understanding of who God is in Christ. It is he, Christ, of which PrōST is a reflection. Christ lived the example of what God intends for humanity to the greatest extent possible in the now not to be delayed to an eternal state. The magnificent life of Christ is to be repeated by his followers in the now, but in greater measure (John 14:12) driven by the Spirit of God (John 7:39; 14:16; 16:7, 26). More importantly, although we are often moving forward without balance and clarity, our resemblance to Christ cannot be denied when we express his communicable attributes especially love (Matt 5:16).[67]

A sampling of communicable attributes brings to consideration love, righteousness, peace, joy, mercy, endurance, affection, patience, kindness, virtue, steadfastness, holiness, knowledge, self control, veracity, wisdom, insight, faithfulness, benevolence, purity, truth, truthful speech, spirituality,

---

63. Gottstein, "Body as Image," 171–72.
64. Ibid., 173–74.
65. Feinberg, "Image of God," 241.
66. Power, "Imago Dei," 134.
67. Lossky, *Orthodox Theology*, 72; Willard, "Living a Transformed Life."

justice, gentleness, rejoicing, godliness, patience, goodness, beauty, and the mind of Christ (cf. Matt 7:16; Rom 14:17; 1 Cor 2:16; 2 Cor 6:4–12; Gal 5:22; Eph 1:1–4, 8–9; 4:1–7, 22–24; Col 3:12–17; Phil 2:2–8; 2 Pet 1:1–11). Although one might be able to make a complete scriptural listing, it would still only be a select representative and not an exhaustive, full-orbed description of the person living in full proleptic spiritual expression.[68]

True Human

The fall of humanity as recorded in Genesis is instructive whether we believe in an archetypical Adam and Eve, a literal pair of disobedient first humans, or an initial group of prehistoric humans from which modern humans descend. As discussed earlier, the fall records both a becoming and a fall in that becoming. Moreover, in that this image, according to Welker,[69] has been expressed, damaged, and started toward recovery, the image bearing and image-violation were in fact, incredibly, both brought on by a God-defying willfulness of humanity (Gen 3). In this present work, I disagree that the image bearing is damaged but posit an obscuring of the expression and enjoyment of image. Nevertheless, I do agree that such hubris greatly wounded the communion and intimacy between God and humans introducing an alienation from God and the "other" that has warped the perceptions, desires, and directions of humanity and creation. Yet, remaining in us and yearning for expression, is an overwhelming resonance for full expression and enjoyment of image and relationship to God, one another, and creation as a whole.

Whether one accepts him as merely human or divine, the great minds of this world have fervently tried to describe and represent Christ as the perfect life that affects all of humanity.[70] He is not only both human and divine but the perfect example of human integration for which we were called and desire to live. Bushnell[71] continues, that once we become aware of Christ, the grandeur of his eternity returns upon the transgression and we tremble in awe of himself—himself the power of an endless life. Unfortunately, this drive is unrecognized by most of us and remains frustrated in such things as false gods, concupiscence, power, materialism, and other impotent and

---

68. Willard, *Divine Conspiracy*, 366; Willard, *Spirit of the Disciplines*, 156–57.
69. Welker, *Creation and Reality*, 75.
70. Bushnell, "Protestant Views," 345.
71. Ibid., 348.

dissipates of the world. Christ is the ideal, true human as God intended and created us to be.[72] Christ is the real and ideal for which we yearn and reach.

The *imago Dei* as expressed and enjoyed was obscured, although not marred or lost, in a number of ways already discussed above. That is to say, the image may be, in some small or large part, hidden from view in its expression, but it is never marred or lost. Although rather limited, rabbinic literature seems to agree with the possibility that the divine image in humans may be diminished but never lost.[73] Disagreeing here, humans are not and cannot be left without resemblance to their creator, because to be a human is to bear God's image. Pannenberg,[74] too, argues that the *imago Dei* in humans was not destroyed or annihilated nor left without expression. Continuing on in support, Bratt[75] rightly cites and discusses Pannenberg in that the *imago Dei* cannot be lost. We have the capacity and are disposed toward transcendence in fellowship, even for those of us who are mentally and physically handicapped, vegetative, sociopathic, or nonfunctioning as normal human beings.[76] These disadvantaged humans do not cease to be our kind although the full, healthy human expression is obscured.

This suggests that the *imago Dei* is not limited to intellectual expression or "higher" faculties of reason. Habermas, Moreland,[77] and others posit the possibility of mind not being dependent on the physical health of the body and brain distinctly and that "mind is a causal power independent of brain activity."[78] In light of such a truth, higher faculties of the mind would remain independent of the brain. Although the human being is not complete in this independence, to whatever measure or linkage, mind is not diminished by material affect or handicap, and in this neither is the *imago Dei* to that measure.

Neither is this *imago Dei* exclusive and restricted to a single group of chosen people. It is not limited to those who make a confession of faith or call on God's name. Rather, it is present even in those who have rejected God and whose futures are as yet not known.[79] The goodness in this world, such as charity, kindness, love, sacrifice, the arts, philosophy, joy, and the seeking heart in each of us testifies to the *imago Dei* trying to break forth

72. Barth, *Church Dogmatics*, III.2.155.
73. Gottstein, "Body as Image," 186–89.
74. Pannenberg, *Systematic Theology*, 2:228.
75. Bratt, "Wolfhart Pannenberg."
76. Ibid., 18.
77. Habermas and Moreland, *Immortality*, 77–83.
78. Ibid., 82
79. Bratt, "Wolfhart Pannenberg," 19.

in full expression, but its enjoyment is simply hindered by the fall. Humans cannot evade this relationship to God to a realm beyond human being and imperative.[80]

Some 1800 years ago, Origen[81] variously wrote of this reality exampled in that God clearly works in both transgressors and the virtuous as testified by all "rational beings" partaking of the germ of reason and thereby displaying proofs such as wisdom and justice, which are nothing less than Christ (Rom 10:8). By this germ or seed, Christ is in all humans since he is the word or reason participating in rational beings, and all human beings have communion with God (Gen 2:7; Luke 17:20–21) and share in him.[82] If salvation is a receipt of "life in hope," then it is a hope of proleptic engagement in divine and eternal glory with God.[83] Salvation is not only and simply being secured from a future separation from God but a present enjoyment of God in an ever-increasing glory (Ps 84:7; John 1:16; 1 Cor 15:49; 2 Cor 3:18).

Although I hold, within these pages, a more expansive view of *imago Dei* than Origen's "rational beings," the value of Origen's statement for this section comes in that all persons have communion with and sharing in God. From this communion comes some measure of relational reflection of *imago Dei* no matter the decline or condition of a particular individual.

Presence and Free Will

Gadamer,[84] in speaking of symbols and copies, is helpful with an application that can be made to the subject of this research. He refers to a copy as that which I refer to as image representing what it contains. That is, what a copy or image contains, in this case, God, is represented and made present even though *not* present. Moreover, I propose that not only do humans make God present—but also that God *is in fact* present. The lack of perception in most of us is often simply due to an immature expression that can begin its remedy in PrōST.

Along with Eastern Orthodoxy, the present writing rejects Calvin's total depravity[85] and exclusive determinism to leave place for human free will although enabled by God's prevenient grace (Ezek 18:1–4; 18:19–20,

---

80. Berkouwer, *Studies in Dogmatics*, 135.
81. Origen, *De Principiis*, I.3.6.
82. Ibid.
83. Shults, *Reforming Theological Anthropology*, 241.
84. Gadamer, "Truth and Method," 413–14.
85. Calvin, *Institutes*, II.I.9.

30–31) avoiding incompatibilism. As addressed above, although he holds to total corruption, Calvin does not argue for a total corruption of *imago Dei*, and rather that a measure of relational aspect has been impaired restricting knowledge and access to God in any synergistic construct. In opposition, Shults[86] argues, and Rad[87] concurs, that no function of the *imago Dei* is lost or in any manner damaged.

More clearly, free will, not to be confused with libertarianism without constraints, has restraints or constructs within which it must be exercised. This should not appear as a surprise or contradiction. Even God has such restraints and constraints. For example, God is free to act as he wills within the limits of love, holiness, righteousness, and sovereignty. Inversely, God is restrained from willing or acting outside of these attributes. McGrath[88] speaks about these "two powers of God" to act, as ordained power (L. *potentia Dei ordinata*) and absolute power (L. *potentia Dei absoluta*). The usage of these concepts by Duns Scotus, that is, *potentia Dei absoluta et ordinata*, plays a clarifying role regarding God's powers in acting. There is the entirely-free, absolutely, powerful God in natural creation (things that might have been) balanced with the stability derived from the reliability of God's ordained power (as things are) stabilizing the contingent order in God's relationship with creation.[89] So then, while God cannot be limited by creation, except by his design, he has freely limited himself to certain dealings. For considerations of the limitations of this book they are such as love, holiness, righteousness, and sovereignty.

To speak of such free will in humans, is to speak of the inner person's ability to choose and to be held morally culpable for deficient decisions.[90] If prevenient grace is perspicacious, then we cannot be culpable and we are not truly free in our decisions to accept or reject Christ's offer of salvation.[91] My position here, as further discussed below, is most closely within a Monist view that in God's providence humans have free will and are thereby culpable. God knows all things as well as human contingencies (L. *scientia media* [middle knowledge]). Nevertheless, free will is never separated from God's grace[92] and yet requires our free participation.

---

86. Shults, *Reforming Theological Anthropology*, 232–33.
87. Rad, *Old Testament Theology*, 147.
88. McGrath, *Intellectual Origins*, 20.
89. Oakley, "Absolute and Ordained Power," 441–42, 445.
90. Campbell, *Self and Free-Will*, 360.
91. Myers, "Exclusivism," 416.
92. Kärkkäinen, *One with God*, 31.

How this issue is parsed may also be viewed from a psychological perspective especially as discussed by the attribution theory's *Motivational Bias Hypothesis*, assigning blameworthiness and justification. First, I disagree with Nietzsche[93] that free will is nothing more than an invention to assign guilt in order to justify punishing malefactors. That is, Stalin, Hitler, or Pol Pot would not be culpable without free will. I do not agree, however, with the thought that humans excuse themselves, while finding blame in others who commit no worse transgressions, unless they have done well which is not to be reckoned to their will.[94]

Govett, in beginning his interaction with John Calvin and the theology named for him as opposed to Arminius's theology, suggests that to reject facts that seem at odds with other facts is not to follow a "doctrine of sound philosophy and reason."[95] He argues that both grace and responsibility (free will) should be accepted. Unlike the unconditional, absolute, and independent freedom of God (within his attributes and the constraints he placed within his creation), human freedom is conditional, relative, and dependent—willing obedience in communion with God.[96] This restrained freedom is qualified and elevated by the *imago Dei* in perichoretic relationship with God.

Finally, we all enjoy some measure of God's image no matter the extent of willed distortion. And no human can break with God no matter the degree of errant-will, sin, or "stupidity."[97] So, God's children, created in God's image, are never disowned, nor is our receipt of God's image recalled. No matter the damage by sin and sinfulness, we, God's children, continue to look like our Father who is in heaven as exampled by the God-man Jesus.

SOTERIOLOGICAL CONSTRUCTS

Whatever the salvific construct, this study stands squarely on the belief that no matter the human effort, salvation cannot be won by toil and endeavor. Lossky[98] rightly points out that we do not look for God like we might look for an object; rather, we are captured by the person of God in revelation, and because of this capture we can now, in response, search for God with

---

93. Nietzsche, *Twilight of Idols*, 64.
94. Earp, "Do I Have More Free Will," 21.
95. Govett, *Calvinism by Calvin*, 3–4.
96. Brunner, *Man in Revolt*, 262, 266.
97. Heschel, "Holy Dimension," 121.
98. Lossky, *Orthodox Theology*, 27.

all of our strength. Salvation is a work of God.[99] It is God reaching out that brings our reconciliation. God's ceaseless and iterative actions in movement toward us is the catalyst that pursues and woos every human to seek for God and thereby not find full satisfaction without this draw being fulfilled. God's absolute power, coupled with the very power of his nature, allows God to accomplish his will beyond what is known or predetermined. This ensures his success and satisfaction regarding our salvation.

Even Augustine argues for our will in God's reaching. Before we come into being, Augustine[100] says, God knows all things. Moreover, Augustine continues that God's knowledge does not nullify our free will from doing what is felt to be done driven by the will to do it, but our free will in nowise excludes God's order and causes, and therefore God does not depend on our free will to accomplish his purposes. Moreover, our free will is included in God's will, causes, and purposes. Consequent human will and actions are in God's foreknowledge[101] arguing here for *scientia media* (middle knowledge).

More recently on this issue, John Laing[102] writes about Luis Molina's *scientia media* and how it ensures that not only does God's sovereign arm reach to all extents, but also that free agents are guaranteed free will in our decisions and responsibility. Although God is eternally omniscient, *scientia media* is how God's need for knowledge of contingent action, that is, that which to a finite view may or may not obtain (occur). *Scientia media* stands between Aquinas' natural knowledge (God's nature and essence) and free knowledge (God's knowledge of his own will). *Scientia media*, or counterfactual knowledge, is exercised by God as a pre-volitional knowledge of all true counterfactuals of free will. This middle knowledge of God is necessary in that we have choice and free response to God (Josh 24:15; Deut 30:15–18; John 15:6–7; 3:16, 36; Rom 1:20), as it must be for us to rightly respond in love toward our maker and to freely assume or walk in God's image and nature.[103]

Open Theism takes such consideration further and proposes that God's give-and-receive relationship with humans requires that we have free will and that God's actions are contingent upon human unknown actions. It is free will that may change God's flexible strategies making macro predestination viable but micro predestination contingent, a bit like improvisational

---

99. Aquinas, *Summa Theologia*, 139–40.
100. Augustine, *City of God and Christian Doctrine*.
101. Ibid.
102. Laing, "Middle Knowledge."
103. Lossky, *Orthodox Theology*, 72.

jazz solos within an overriding melody.[104] In other words, there is an unstructured or unknown polyphonic, improvisational element to our existence for which God accounts and responds, in real time, in harmonic kind.

Clearly, the constructs briefly considered here do not have a *prima facie* "winner" for which this study can argue without debate. Kärkkäinen[105] underscores the African conjecture that perceives salvation as divisible into three concepts: deification, liberation, and justification. Pressing an inference, the division can be applied to a greater part of the world. The Eastern Church holds deification as a salvific concept. The Western Church has typically favored justification by judicial models. Finally, the church in Latin America has been home for liberation theology and therein salvation.

Liberation is peripheral to the present discussion and only addressed in reflection of God's movement in disciples as to how we are to treat others and the world. Justification, briefly discussed above, is more forcefully considered since it cannot be separated from transformation. While getting less attention as an ancient representation of salvation within the Christian church, deification is considered throughout this work, especially as expressed in the East. Some Protestant academicians and more so Catholics scholars have produced work in this area. Nevertheless, there is no room for "different salvations."[106] Christian dialogue, especially in the West, would be assisted in the wider world by discussion based in the concept of deification. Such a dialogue would also provide common ground on which to engage and pursue God's transformative work in the now (PrōST).

Although, as is shown below, this work stands on one soteriological construct, this section does not attempt a rigorous defense of salvific constructs. I only attempt to assist an understanding of PrōST in discerning salvation as subsequent sanctification expressed as transformation. So constructs are merely used to label or categorize perceived scriptural teachings on the subject to support and place proleptic spiritual transformation (PrōST).

Exclusive and Limited

The supposition of an exclusive salvation is the traditional Christian theology.[107] It is scripturally defensible by a supportive exegesis of a number of biblical passages (Matt 7:13–28; 25:31–46; Mark 9:45–48; Luke 16:23; John

---

104. Sanders, *God Who Risks*, 245.
105. Kärkkäinen, *One with God*, 8.
106. Ibid., 8–9.
107. McGrath, "Particularist View," 163–64.

3:36). Its foundation, by this, allows only a few into God's heaven—a chosen few. Not many shall be saved; the rest are damned to eternal punishment (Matt 7:13; Luke 13:24). This horror raises the soteriological problem of evil. This soteriological problem questions not only how a fully-benevolent God can allow evil, but be party to the damnation of some large number of his creatures because of their sin: (A) God is omnipresent, omniscient, and omnibenevolent seems contrary to (B) Some humans do not receive Christ (salvation) and therefore are damned. One often proposed argument easily follows, since (A) is necessary and essential to Christian theism, then (B) must be denied. This is discussed further below, and the "traditional problem of evil" is further examined in chapter 4 (Theodicy and Other Trials).

More particularly, Reformed theology, exclusivism, or negatively interpreted "restrictionism" holds sway over a vast portion of Christendom and leaves most of humanity lost to eternal perdition and a few, or remnant, destined to glory.[108] Large numbers of Christians further argue mistakenly that this binodal choice of God is God's inescapable, sovereign prerogative *without* human involvement.[109] In its most radical expression, it is a kind marginal, non-historical, ultra-, or hyper-Calvinism. In hyper-Calvinism, God's sovereignty is exercised at the exclusion of any human responsibility versus historic Calvinism or Reformed theology in which the Spirit's enlightenment or effectual calling is so that God's elect may welcome the Gospel.[110]

The hyper-extreme expression is coupled with, but goes beyond, historical Limited Atonement or Limited Redemption, which is simply atonement limited to the elect.[111] That is, the so-called hyper-Calvinism propounds that humans have absolutely no option or involvement in the process of salvation beyond God's sovereign activity and choice. Favored verses are John 14:6; Acts 14:12; Romans 3:10; 6:23; 2 Thessalonians 1:8–9.

The Narrow Way

Furthermore, regarding exclusivism, there is a traditional belief, especially held among the Catholic and Orthodox churches, of outside the church there is no salvation (L. *extra ecclesiam nulla salus*). Clearly, debates about institutional claims aside, if the church is Christ's body (and it is), then indeed there is not any salvation outside of the church as stated by *ecclesiam*

---

108. Calvin, *Institutes*, 2.XXI.7.
109. Grudem, *Systematic Theology*, 679–81.
110. Reid, "Calvinism," 187.
111. Boettner, *Reformed Doctrine*, 150–51.

nulla salus (John 10:9; 14:6; Eph 2:18; Heb 10:20). Again, this understanding does not speak to exclusive, exceptionalistic, institutional claims.

God has made his awarded choice through irresistible prevenient grace from which one cannot escape (Calvinism) or prevenient grace which can be resisted (Arminianism), which seems to nullify preordination[112] before anyone's physical conception and despite any possible developments or changes. Additionally, this contention—arguably, by definition, not fully endorsed by John Calvin or John Wesley as pressed today—excludes the need for spiritual transformation. Eventual salvation is guaranteed to the chosen and withheld from those not chosen or predestined to such mercy and grace.[113] If transformation, proleptic or otherwise, is allowed as salvation, it is limited to that small number.

People are less willing today to accept the "abhorrent notion" that a select number are saved while the larger rest is lost in never ending perdition.[114] The single focused theology of exclusivism, practiced by some, besides any nefarious intent, often expresses a single and shallow focused effort of saving souls. Although vital, this myopic approach may simply be the result of shallow teaching from some pulpits. Neither do too many superficial, unenlightened books and other media, which crowd the bookshelves of too many stores and libraries and the accessible memory of too many computer servers, help this condition of single-minded focus on "saving souls." Although many speak about saving souls, and this is necessary in the scheme of missions, few speak of any form of spiritual transformation after salvation. There is an abundant list of so-called "Christian books" that mirror this societal myopia at large. Spiritual and theological study found in popular books, magazines, and blogs is either superficial, or if having any depth or weight heeded only by the few willing to dig deep for the "gold and precious stones." Popular Christian teaching is too often too much about how to be wealthy, healthy, and generally successful as defined by the Western world and, especially, in North America. According to survey data,[115] when considered, spiritual quests are seen as too much of an abstruse effort—too far from understanding, reach, ability, or even will (Matt 13:22; Rom 12:2; Eph 4:23; 1 Pet 1:14).

Again, since a general exclusive view of salvation (only a select few shall be saved) holds sway in the larger part of Christian theology, preaching and teaching, initial salvation is the main, slavish focus of most of what

---

112. Talbott, "Christ Victorious," 5.
113. Boettner, *Reformed Doctrine*, 152–53.
114. Pinnock, "Response to John Hick," 97.
115. Barna, "Self-Described Christians."

occupies Christian churches. Some top Christian apologists[116] rigorously argue in defense of God's best possible world as his best ability through *scientia media* to save as many humans as possible (although that may be few), minimizing the numbers to be damned no matter what possible world.[117] This seemingly hobbled God is doing as best as he can.

When triaging church focus and effort, saving souls is the top priority. Worsening the problem is a half-hearted effort, which is to the neglect of making disciples that reflect God's image. However, *imago Dei* best shows forth God's love, mercy, and grace to creation, making the Christian faith desirable and transformative (Matt 5:16).[118] Such gifts cause the gifted to love the giver, God. God's image in us is better able to offer devotion and praise to God in return, pleasing God. If such transformation is what attracts people to God and satisfies God's heart, and if most North Americans and others are not being transformed,[119] then a vital need for the fullest extent of proleptic, spiritual transformation (PrōST) pleads to be experienced by us and the world.

Allowing that spiritual transformation is reserved for God's destined individuals (Matt 22:14) who shall be with him throughout eternity highly restricts the numbers who can be expected for transformation. So then, exclusivism says that spiritual transformation driven by God's presence does not happen for any except the chosen. That is, it is a broad view speaking about a narrow way (Matt 7:13–14).

Inclusive and Affirming

Alternatively to an exclusive theology is the notion of God as unsparingly inclusive. Although various definitions can be given, inclusivism, here, is not to be confused with pluralism, universalism (considered below), or that all religions are equal. Rather, it is the belief that God works within the cultural, religious, and societal milieu of the given era, as well as all of creation to prepare and draw humans to the Gospel of Jesus Christ thereby the salvific reality only found in him.[120]

If God is not compelled to accept the extent of loss as exclusive theology proposes with "an optimal balance between saved and unsaved,"[121] then

---

116. Craig, *No Other Name*, 4–5.
117. Ibid.
118. Willard, "Living a Transformed Life."
119. Kinnaman and Lyons, *Unchristian*, 79–83.
120. Pinnock, "Response to John Hick," 96, 98.
121. Craig, *No Other Name*, 7.

perhaps God's salvific work may be further reaching than usually expressed. Many passages, as exampled in Scripture (Matt 20:15; John 3:17; Rom 2:4; 2 Pet 3:9; 1 Tim 2:4; 1 John 2:2), speak of the testimony of God being available to all people and that no one has an excuse. We should note that such passages are also used for exclusive and universal arguments. This seems to mean that everyone, no matter time or place, is given more than sufficient testimony of God to rely upon him for all that is necessary for life. This does not necessitate a stipulated belief system, although the Christian Gospel is, I believe, uniquely suited for the revelation and task. As with exclusivism above, the position of this study holds to a particularistic view of salvation: Whatever construct of salvation is discussed, whatever the means, the way is through Jesus Christ only (John 10:9; 14:6; Heb 10:20).[122]

Even Augustine[123] leaves room for caution when he says that since no one can determine who is predestined versus those who are not, then because of this we ought to desire all persons to be saved. The inclusivism from the love of God and the work of Christ is to secure salvation for all; except, according to inclusivism, there are those who apparently, finally insist upon not having it.[124]

God's grace, mercy, and love, and thereby salvation is greater and more inclusive than often thought. If all have sinned in Adam, then all that have been saved in Christ is as an inclusive view (Rom 5:10–12; 18–19). Commenting about this issue over a century past, Hodge[125] wrote, that all of Adam's descendants are condemned, but that all are saved except those that the Scripture has explicitly said they cannot be saved. Punt[126] concurs that those who continue to resist God's grace and salvific work in the final judgment shall be eternally lost. Moreover, he goes on to agree with the Apostle Paul (Rom 5:20) saying that where sin abounds, grace abounds even much more and that redemption far exceeds all evils of the fall, and that there shall be more saved than lost.[127] It is a large, generous, and perhaps frightening proposition that Christ's salvific work is efficacious for everyone but that some insist in the final analysis on rejecting such powerful love that has reached out with all measures to draw in the person sought.

---

122. McGrath, "Particularist View," 163–64; Origen, *De Principiis*, I.3.6; Pinnock, "Response to John Hick," 96, 98.

123. Augustine, *On Christian Doctrine* (NPNF¹ 14).

124. Punt, *Theology of Inclusivism*, 10, 215, 241.

125. Hodge, *Systematic Theology*, 26.

126. Punt, *Theology of Inclusivism*, 29, 37–38.

127. Hodge, *Systematic Theology*, 26.

The main pertinence of this theology for the present discussion has to do with the attitude of disciples of Christ and the breadth of Christ's work. John Stott[128] leaves room for this viewpoint where he says that he can never contrive the horrible vision of millions of people perishing, but neither can he, by this horror, become a universalist. Rather standing against both extremes, and on biblical grounds, he hopes the majority of humans shall be saved.

To be inclusive is an effort to widely embrace God's heart of love and acceptance to be all encompassing. The effect of death upon God's creation in the fall was inclusive of all people and all creation. In response God's sacrificial death was also inclusive of all people (Ezek 18:23; John 6:37; 1 Tim 2:4; 4:10; 2 Pet 3:9). An inclusive construct of salvation holds that if the sacrificial death of Jesus only saved a small selected number of people, his triumph is small. If, however, his salvation brought life to the largest number of people and the creation, then his salvation is great. By this, according to an inclusive view, his large love is best testified and manifest compared to an exclusive or restrictive interpretation. So then, inclusivism allows for a larger umbrella than exclusivism under which large numbers may be spiritually transformed and thereby PrōST only excluding those who in the final analysis refuse God's salvific offer.

Universal and Encompassing

At the risk of appearing to oversimplify a complicated and even contentious subject, I present universalism here as a viable construct that does not need to violate any orthodox doctrine. However, because of its questioned heterodox theology, universalism receives a longer, though not exhaustive, treatment here than exclusivism or inclusivism above. As addressed for exclusivism and inclusivism, the intent in discussing Christian universalism is only in support of the present proposal on proleptic spiritual transformation (PrōST).

Christian universalism denies eternal punishment for the non-confessing and salvation for only an elect few, and rather, contends that everyone shall be saved from any and all penalties of sin and suffer no eternal punishment and eventually be fully restored to God.[129] According to Talbott,[130] Christian universalism is both the Augustinian idea of God's complete sovereignty in assuring salvation for the predestined and the Ar-

---

128. Edwards and Stott, *Evangelical Essentials*, 327.
129. Eller, "Universalism," 849.
130. Talbott, "Towards a Better Understanding," 7.

minian notion that God died and resurrected to provide salvation for all. The implication is that this universalist benefit is bestowed on everyone no matter beliefs or works, or lack of beliefs or works. Central to the Christian version of universalism is particularity of salvation only in Christ and is thereby non-negotiable to any dialogue about universalism.[131] Christian universalism rightly shares with exclusivism this argument for particularism that salvation is only found in Christ.[132] Furthermore, the Christian or trinitarian universalism argument posits, as do I, that such an event does not necessarily have to occur in a traditional community, particular cultus, or manner.

God's Intent

In this study, universalism is reserved for the belief that all paths, religions, and beliefs, though not equally efficacious, may end in final salvation only through Christ. God is generous, but any reasoning, not withstanding, it must be seen in the *eschaton* whether God allows or planned universal salvation or restoration (Gk. *apocatastasis*).[133] If so, it shall have been through Christ. This particularism is illustrated in the parables of the workers in the field, the lost sheep, and the lost coin which all suggest such a generosity (Luke 15:1–10; 20). Many of these same "universal verses" along with other "exclusive verses" (Matt 7:13–28; 25:31–46; Mark 9:45–48; Luke 16:23; and John 3:36) used by theologies to support exclusivism are viewed through the prism and presuppositions of exclusivist theology. Nonetheless, as discussed herein the contention for universalism is not easily sidelined.

God declared his intent that all should be saved (Acts 3:21; Rom 6:18–19; 1 Cor 15:22; Eph 1:9–10; 1 Tim 2:4; 4:10; Titus 2:11; 2 Pet 3:9), and in support, that his intent shall always be fulfilled (Matt 24:35; Isa 45:23; 46:10; 55:11). Paul's first epistle to Timothy affirms God's desire to save all, especially those who believe (1 Tim 2:3–4a; 4:10). Lest it be thought an aberration, Paul also writes in Titus 2:11 about God's wish. Both (Gk. *pantas anthrōpous* and *pasin anthrōpous*) 1 Timothy 2:4 and Titus 2:11 leave no room for exception. However, as argued by Mounce[134] and Dunn,[135] leaving allowance for both God's determinative will and permissive will, eliminating any form of universalism (God's desire), salvation requires belief and as-

---

131. Greggs, *Barth, Origen*, 86–87; Parry and Partridge, *Universal Salvation?*, xvii.
132. Wright, "Towards a Biblical View," 57–58.
133. Neuhaus, "Will All Be Saved?"; Balthasar, *Dare We Hope*, 237.
134. Mounce, *Pastoral Epistles*, 84–85.
135. Dunn, "First and Second Letters to Timothy," 798 (1 Tim 2:1–7).

sent (Rom 10:9) both on the intellectual and existential levels, with not only an awareness but also including personal acknowledgement. According to Mounce,[136] Paul's concern to Timothy here, accordingly therefore, by this point, appears to only be against any sectarianism against "sinners" versus "the righteous." Although that argument is made, Paul can easily be joined by other of his words and owned by the universalist (Rom 5:18–19; 11:32) as furthered below.[137]

As I have already said, many of the so-called universal texts (Acts 4:12; Rom 5:15, 18; 11:32–36; 1 Cor 15:22; 1 Tim 2:4; 4:10; Titus 2:11–12) often used to defend universalism or restoration of all things (Gk. *apocatastasis pantós*) contrarily can also support exclusive theology. Origin's supportive position on this subject has met with great opposition.[138] Particularly, the Council of Constantinople in 553 ostensibly tried to condemn Origin, and although the account was not an interpolation, it was perhaps no more than in passing (Fr. *en passant*).[139] Based in scriptural reasoning (e.g., Col 1:19–20; 1 Cor 15:22, 28; Rom 5:18; 11:33–36; Phil 2:10–11) as well as Hellenistic philosophy, Origen's thought was unoriginal but the most important concept in his philosophy, while attacked as heresy but not anathematized. Restoration (Gk. *apocatastasis*) is the light by which Origin judged all theories.[140] As an example, Origen argued *apocatastasis* from 1 Corinthians 15:25–28 in which all shall be subjected to Christ that God may be "all in all" (Gk. *panta en pasin*). While a scriptural assault against his contention may be made, Origen's logical defense does not allow his systematic ideas to simply be swept aside.[141] Both heavily influenced by Christian and pagan Hellenist philosophy, Gregory of Nyssa followed closely behind Origin beginning a long historical list or proponents of all shall eventually be saved as God's intent.[142]

---

136. Ibid., 85.

137. McDonald, *Creation in Christ*, 78; Talbott, *Inescapable Love of God*, 57–59, 62, 78–79.

138. Neuhaus, "Will All Be Saved?"

139. Shahan, "Second Council of Constantinople."

140. Greggs, *Barth, Origen*, 51–53, 68–71; Moore, "Origen of Alexandria."

141. Ludlow, "Universalism," 191; Moore, "Origen of Alexandria."

142. Ludlow, "Universalism," 191, 215.

The Hope

Contrary to his detractors, Balthasar has been a notable supporter of Origin's ideas about universalism.[143] Including Origin's arguments on his own, Balthasar[144] leaves open the horrible possibility of eternal loss and therein is careful to distinguish between universal salvation as hope versus doctrine. God alone knows, he says, fashioned creatures may only hope, and this hope must be found only in Christ's love. Under much criticism Neuhaus[145] supports Balthasar in this thought in his "poetic-devotional reflection," *Death on a Friday Afternoon*,[146] and his research article, "Will All Be Saved?"[147] He points out the evident need for hope in order to intercede with God for souls as believers are commanded (Matt 28:16–20).

Bauckham[148] presents Friedrich Schleiermacher as a nineteenth-century champion of universalism in opposition to Augustine and Calvin. Schleiermacher is perhaps the first great theologian of modern times to defend universalism. He rejects any interpretation or type of double-predestination (hell or heaven). Boettner[149] contends that Luther, corroborated by his friend and supporter, Melanchthon, believed in single predestination. Luther[150] said, that the true God foreordains and foreknows all things, and that God cannot be deceived nor held back in his foreknowledge or predestined choice. Everything, according to Luther, takes place by God's will. Universal grace did not lead Luther to universalism. As Florian Berndt[151] demonstrates, while some would put Luther in a universalist camp, his supposed *post-mortem* allowance for necessary salvific faith is mostly from a mistranslation of the original German. Although Romans 5:18 is one of the scriptures used to support universalism, the counter argument says that this does not apply to those who die before confessing Christ (Luke 12:8; Rom 10:9). Even so, there is no necessary requirement outside of polemic (and there is much) that believing confession must occur before a particular human age or even before death. Talbott[152] offers an algebraic observation in

---

143. Neuhaus, "Will All Be Saved?"
144. Balthasar, *Dare We Hope*, 237.
145. Neuhaus, "Will All Be Saved?"
146. Neuhaus, *Death on a Friday*.
147. Neuhaus, "Will All Be Saved?"
148. Bauckham, *Universalism*, 49–51.
149. Boettner, *Reformed Doctrine*, 15.
150. Luther, *Bondage of the Will*, sect. CLXVII.
151. Berndt, "Did Martin Luther."
152. Talbott, *Inescapable Love of God*, 78–79.

that (1) the Bible declares *all* shall be saved (Rom 5:18), and (2) *some* shall be eternally lost in punishment and destruction (2 Thess 1:8–9), and (3) if Paul wrote both texts, and if (4) there is no error in either, then (5) interpretation of one of the texts are suspect. So, although one interpretation leaves a universal solution (all are saved), and the other interpretation leaves an exclusive solution (damnation for some), hope of universal salvation is left and not destroyed in the incongruity.

As is shown below, judgment verses may refer to discipline as God works to restore creation. Although strictly referring to the restoration to the original things or condition (Gk. *apocatastasis pantós*), I continue to argue here that God is interested in something beyond restoration whatever soteriological construct it is within.[153] Moreover, I contend that any restoration must include an eschatological eventuality of humanity in the image of God in Christ also constituted as perfect man or, that is, truly human.[154]

Extra Ecclesiam Nulla Salus

After the Bible and the writings of St. Augustine, Martin Luther found no work more helpful than the *Theologia Germanica*.[155] Written of Catholic parentage, Luther discovered and published this mystical work in 1516 to better help believers to righteous living. The unknown author of the *Theologia Germanica*[156] speaks about the enlightened human's common desire to reflect back to God what his blessings are to humans. It is to dedicate oneself to God but more so in desiring to be closer to God with clear knowledge, love, assurance, obedience, and subjection so that one might reflect God's desire that all people be saved. Although Stuart Hackett[157] would surely not argue for universalism, he speaks of the richness and depth of God's provisions for salvific opportunity for everyone as he provides object and unique remedy through Jesus Christ. This provision is above time, place, cultural milieu, or any other circumstances.

As I previously stated, in particularism, whether universalism or exclusivism is considered, Christ is the only means of salvation (Acts 4:12; 10:43). That is, the body of Christ is the church and he is its head placing him as the only means of salvation since there is no salvation outside of the

---

153. Ludlow, "Universalism," 192.
154. Greggs, *Barth, Origen*, 44–45.
155. Anon, *Theologia Germanica*.
156. Ibid., ch. 10.
157. Hackett, *Reconstruction*, 244.

church (Rom 12:5; 1 Cor 12:27; Eph 5:23; Col 1:18, 24).[158] Although most often used by the Roman Catholic Church as self-promotion, it is appropriate to make the tautological claim, *extra Christi nulla salus* (L.), "no salvation outside of Christ [church]." Christ, his body the church here, is not to be limited to an institution or edifice but to that mystical body of Christ—all the saved and restored—that are in Christ.

Leaning on the Catechism of the Catholic Church, Hryniewicz[159] argues for an eventual all-encompassing eternal salvation that includes those who, by no fault of their own, do not know anything of the Gospel but have still sought God as God's grace efforts them to do his bidding as they best can see driven by their consciences. In this *extra Christi nulla salus* is included those who, by no intention at the end of their course, do not know anything of the Gospel but sought God as God's grace helped them to do his will as they were best informed by their circumstances and consciences.

Hick[160] argues for many images in Christ's representation as fatherhood of God, brotherhood of man, apocalyptic preacher, gentle Jesus, radical, cosmic Christ, presence, and other titles. Not surprisingly due to his pluralism, Hick[161] and many non-pluralists,[162] argue that the loving fatherhood of God proceeds and seems to necessitate a universal salvation of all people. The idea of "soteriological spaces," within which there is opportunity for salvation, freedom, and complete fulfillment,[163] supports the conjecture that God honors the good faith effort of people to do God's will as best they can. Again, this is not to be confused with any suggested equality or plurality between Christianity and other religions. Pluralism is not usually argued as compatible with Christian theology.[164]

Although salvation, as I discuss here, is not shared by all other religions, philosophies, and psychologies, this does not preclude the possibility of salvation, universal or otherwise. That a particular belief system does not include salvation in its constructs as discussed here does not limit it or, for that matter, posit universalism. Such an exercise does not of necessity convince, dissuade, or disabuse any system, belief construct, group, or individual to modify, accept, or reject any argument I put forward by this contention or any other about universal salvation.

---

158. McGrath, "Particularist View," 163, 166.
159. Hryniewicz, *Challenge of Our Hope*, 54–55.
160. Hick, *God Has Many Names*, 98.
161. Hick, *God and the Universe of Faiths*, 120–32.
162. Chan, *Spiritual Theology*, 46.
163. Hick, *Interpretation of Religion*, 240.
164. Geivett and Phillips, "Response to John Hick," 79.

Relatedness

It follows, that in a common human destiny, in the reality of the *imago Dei*, humans are destined for fellowship with God as the "inner *teleos*" of the relatedness of the *imago Dei* toward encompassing humans into God's kingdom.[165] The whole of humanity is of necessity born of such an intimate relatedness to God and destined to experience, eventuality, unhindered divine communion evinced as an existential reality.

Nevertheless, in agreement with Stott, in his interview with Barnes,[166] in which Stott speaks about guarding against what seems to be a Christ-less pluralism, Stott responds that Christ is unique in his incarnation, atonement, resurrection, and his gift of the Holy Spirit.[167] My position is that Jesus is unique and without competition, and his finality is without successors. His all, and more, makes Christ uniquely qualified to bring salvation to the world. Salvation is found solely and particularly in Christ. By this, and other means, many theologians hope, and even presume universal salvation as dogma.[168] Surely many representative scriptural proofs can be brought to bear (Lam 3:31, 32; Isa 54:7, 8; 57:16–18; John 12:32–33; 1 John 1:21; 1 Cor 15:22; Heb 2:9; 12:7–11; Ps 89:30–35; 119:67; 1 Tim 2:4; Rom 5:12–21; 8:38–39; 11:32; Phil 2:10–11; 1 Tim 4:10; Titus 2:11; 2 Pet 2:8–9; 3:9). Exclusivism's adherents supported by non-universal leaning exegesis, can provide equal testimony.

Universally Triumphant

Although there is no proof of appeal to the people (L. *ad populum*) or even in consensus, there is attestation and testimony that may weigh against the issue that universalism is a non-Christian notion. It holds testimony of both Scripture and person that should not be ignored. These venerables, in no particular order, have all held to a form of Christian or trinitarian universalism: Athanasius, Gregory of Nyssa, John Cassian, Therese of Avila, John Chrysostum, Amalric of Bena, Julian of Norwich, Origen, John Scotus Erigena and moderns such as George MacDonald, Karl Barth, Hans Urs von Balthasar, William Barclay, William Law, Keith DeRose, Thomas Talbott, William Barclay, John Hick, Karl Rahner, Elhanan Winchester, John Murray, John Paul II, Robin Parry, F. D. E. Schleiermacher, J. A. T. Robinson,

---

165. Pannenberg, *Systematic Theology*, 2:224.
166. Barnes, "Why Don't They Listen?"
167. Ibid.
168. Bauckham, *Universalism*, 47.

and Thomas Torrance. I also accept Barth as a universalist as argued by Greggs.[169] Universalists have also adopted Robinson, and Torrance often without full theological consensus.

Lewis[170] poignantly and rightly points out that salvation is only through Christ but not without explicit acceptance of Christ. Lewis accepts that in other religions whatever is true is "consummated and perfected" in Christ. Yet we cannot classify Lewis as a universalist in any pluralist sense in which all religions and beliefs would be held as true. Nonetheless, Lewis, on many occasions, as above, has left vast space for the possibility of the truth of Christ grabbing an individual from within the beliefs of a non-confessing or non-Christian mode.

Protestants shall most likely not accept the conclusions of the Roman Second Vatican Council, or may not be in agreement with its inclusive pronouncement that allows for the possibility of salvation outside of traditional church constructs as secured by Christ.[171] However, salvation, in this allowance, would extend to uninformed non-believers, informed, conventional non-believers, and informed, reflective non-believers.[172] That is, those who never heard the Gospel, those who heard but follow another faith, and those who heard and decide not to follow any faith (agnostics and atheists).

Early Christians believed in this exclusive way of Christ and still many of them were universalists not to be conflated with pluralists. MacDonald's series of *Unspoken Sermons*[173] delivered a message, "Justice," in which he equaled justice and mercy. He argued for an undivided God who is not confounded by conflicting offices in which justice fights against mercy. He spoke of any putative action by God as only for the purpose of purifying his children being freed to rush into the arms of God and Jesus Christ. Of note is the "hyper-Calvinist" moves among universalism, in the 1700s, and the "Ultra Universalism" of the 1800s, ending at the end of the nineteenth century with death of Ballou.[174] These extreme views were against putative or purifying *post-mortem* actions by God and for an ontological unity by which all people are saved in that ontological unity; cleansing and readying for God's presence was accomplished by Christ's complete victory in incarnation, death, and resurrection.[175]

169. Greggs, *Barth, Origen*, 23.
170. Lewis, *God in the Dock*, 102.
171. Myers, "Exclusivism," 409.
172. Ibid., 407.
173. MacDonald, *Unspoken Sermons*.
174. Ludlow, "Universalism," 205–6.
175. Ibid.

As noted above in Origen and as echoed by Gross,[176] there is the eternal truth that God is willing, compelled by himself to not abandon his creatures to the triumph of evil. Barclay[177] says that if one person were to be left out from God's love in the end, it would mean that one person has defeated God's relentless, universal love and triumph, and such a defeat is impossible. Without minimizing evil's actuality or the guilt of those who cause harm to others diminishing their victims, and without eliminating a need of retributive punishment, the New Testament presents a view more vast than base retribution.

God's justice is fulfilled only by full victory over evil and the restoration of all its victims along with hope and peace in the newness of all creation.[178] Moreover, the soteriological problem of evil presents a conundrum. If in Christ God's knowledge, power, and goodness are on display, then his full, triumphant accomplishment of salvation that extends beyond human rejection is required even if this allows salient parts of Vatican II or pluralism.[179]

Contrary to any argument otherwise,[180] it seems plausible that (A) God is omnipotent and can create a world in which all humans eventually, freely believe in Christ (Isa 40:26–31; Ps 147:5; Jer 32:17; Luke 1:37), and (B) since God desires such a world (1 Tim 2:4; Titus 2:11; 2 Pet 3:9), then (C) through omniscience and omnipotence, God, utilizing *scientia media* (Ezek 3:6–7; Matt 11:23; 23:27–32; John 15:22–24; 1 Cor 2:8), can arrange such a world in which eventually all willing receive him even if a large amount of time is required—counterfactuals not withstanding (2 Cor 9:8; Eph 3:20;). So then, by this (D) God can, and I believe did, fashion a world in which counterfactuals and free will cannot frustrate his desire that all would be saved and shall triumph (Heb 7:25; 2 Tim 1:12). Moreover, such a world may encompass *post-mortem* realities.[181] John 7:17 may provide a basis from which to argue for those who are involuntarily ignorant or prejudiced that have by these faults been kept from adequate understanding of the revealed truth in Christ.

The above views are in no way rigorous or a thorough presentation of a logical method to a thorough theodicy. It is only meant as a defense or postulate to the possibility of a world in which universal salvation is a reality; further development remains. A *post-mortem* opportunity would be one

---

176. Gross, *Divinization of the Christian*, 268.
177. Barclay, *William Barclay*, 65–67.
178. Marshall, *Beyond Retribution*, 284.
179. Myers, "Exclusivism," 408.
180. Craig, *No Other Name*.
181. Hick, "D Z Phillips"; Plumptre, *Spirits in Prison*, 403.

in which eyes shall be unclouded, deaf ears shall hear, stammering tongues shall speak plainly, and purgation shall be completed.[182]

Barth and Lewis

In speaking of God's humanity, Barth[183] addresses the acceptance of all humans as those whom Jesus, as their Brother and God and as their Father, has exalted as his "covenant partner" as distinct. This acceptance carries no concern for appearance or state, no matter how wretched or iniquitous. In fairness to his theology, according to Greggs,[184] Barth speaks about salvation for all only in the context of particularity in Christ; Greggs claims that Barth outright jettisons universalism as an open principle. Similarly, Crisp[185] claims Barth did not teach universalism and lists Eberhard Jüngel, Joseph D. Bettis, and John Colwell as solid examples of those who deny that Barth taught universalism. Crisp claims that Barth was either "disingenuous," "muddled," or simply, though unlikely, "did not see the logical implications of his position." Clarity on this point may still be debated. Even so, other of Barth's statements surely called for a greater openness to God's grace than is usually allowed.

Barth[186] appeared to reach for something supportive of universalism when he said, there is no theological basis to limit God's loving-kindness as manifest by Christ, but that one's theological requirement is to see this loving-kindness as greater still. More supportive than above, Greggs[187] convincingly argues for universal salvation as seen by both Origin and Barth. More fairly, Barth might better be characterized as affirming *Christus Victor* rejecting universalism as a principle and embracing it within particularism.[188] Nevertheless, Christ's victory is not complete if any are not reconciled including sin completely destroyed.[189]

As already stated Lewis was not a universalist; nevertheless, he had great space for his universalist mentor George MacDonald. Lewis[190] said there was something that puzzled him, that it seemed terribly unfair that

---

182. Plumptre, *Spirits in Prison*, 403; Ludlow, "Universalism," 204–5.
183. Barth, *Humanity of God*, 52–53.
184. Greggs, *Barth, Origen*, 31.
185. Crisp, "On Barth's Denial," 19–20.
186. Barth, *Humanity of God*, 61.
187. Greggs, *Barth, Origen*, 51–53, 68–71.
188. Ibid., 30–31, 41.
189. Talbott, "Christ Victorious," 22.
190. Lewis, *Mere Christianity*, 65.

eternal life would be limited only to people who have heard and believed in Christ. Paul (Rom 10:9; 14:11) does assert a need for active intellectual and emotional involvement. In fact, however, despite shouts for eternal damnation, it is not readily clear what is the outcome for those others who have not confessed and believed. It is, however, clear by Scripture, Lewis continues, that no one can be saved except through Christ, but it is not clear that only those who know him can be saved through Christ. Contrary to the contention of Craig[191] and others, such testimony that no one comes to God without Jesus or that eternal life is found only in Christ (John 14:6 and 1 John 5:11) does not of necessity require intellectual ascent to the person or a doctrine of Christ's salvific work. It means, however, that whatever the tributary or how one comes, such travel must lead through Christ.

God is truly ecumenical in his mercy and generosity, and does not refuse assistance to anyone. This book does not propose that a formal conversion experience is required or even precedes human inherent, elemental, and inexpungible propensity for transformation.[192] Potential is intrinsic to humans and proper to relationship with God as fully recovered by the incarnation and work of Christ has secured the means to this. In the inclusive eschatological nature of this reality and God's transformative work universal restoration shall not be frustrated or interrupted (2 Pet 2:9).

More space has been given here to universalism since it is less received in Western theologies than exclusivism or inclusivism. In the final analysis, universalism purports or professes a restoration altogether (Gk. *apocatastasis pantós*) of God's creation especially human beings as relates to this study. Moreover, this restoration includes that we be elevated in the image of the God-man, Jesus Christ, short of his non-communicable attributes. It facilitates an all-inclusive and universal proleptic spiritual transformation (PrōST).

Hell and Annihilation

Whatever the theological, philosophical, or ethical arguments regarding life after death and judgment, they should be measured by God's revealed mind and heart and through God's mercy and generosity (Rom 2:4; 2 Pet 3:9).[193] Although mercy is sometimes experienced as sever, purifying punishment, mercy and justice are not conflicting attributes, but mercy is to save from

---

191. Craig, *No Other Name*, 2–3.
192. Mahoney and Pargament, "Sacred Changes," 481.
193. Mouw, "More Thoughts"; Pinnock, *Wideness in God's Mercy*, 18.

sin not God's justice, which is about forgiveness to establish righteousness that is God's mercy.[194]

Various theologies and popular concepts on judgment in the afterlife circulate in the church and other religious discussions. Three major thoughts on judgment are presently important to the conjectures of our discussion on proleptic spiritual transformation (PrōST). Hell, purgation, and annihilation have already entered the discussion above; however, a further discussion presents as appropriate to present needs. The etymology of such words as hell, hadesm, Abaddon, Gehenna, Tartarus, abyss, and Sheol do not receive investigation in these pages but are referred to as synonyms for a place of punishment, trial, or purification of debated duration and severity.

To question, moreover, whether hell or annihilation, by any name, exists, is displaced by the query of whether such a conjecture as an eternal sentence can be given to any person created in the image of God. In consideration of exclusivism, inclusivism, and universalism, an evident issue presents regarding the afterlife and what happens to any not redeemed. Setting aside Eastern concepts of reincarnation and endless cycles of paying the karmic debt, problems loom as to whether persons reside in an eternal hell, are annihilated, or pass through some form of purgation.[195]

If there is an after-life punishment, it might not be anything more repugnant or grisly than a purifying and completion of what God began and has promised to complete (1 Cor 1:8; Phil 1:6; Heb 12:2). Separation seems clearly taught by Scripture (e.g., Matt 7:13–28; 25:31–46; Mark 9:45–48; Luke 16:23; John 3:36). Nonetheless, other scriptures (Lam 3:31, 32; Isa 54:7, 8; 57:16–18; Heb 12:7–11; Ps 89:30–35; 119:67) and adding Plumptre[196] and Ludlow[197] to the scholars listed in the prior paragraph, any separation is not forever.

If hell is the destination of those who are the objects of the "sovereign hatred, grounded in [God's] divine good pleasure" regulating his objects of wrath to everlasting destruction,[198] then escape is an empty notion (Dan 12:2). The view that sin, in opposition to God, has the ability to create a never-ending world, gives sin power on par with God. In such a world, persons whom God died for shall spend eternity in a place of unrelenting torment

---

194. Talbott, "Pauline Interpretation," 33, 48.

195. Hick, *Dialogues in the Philosophy of Religion*, 183; Steeves, "Othodox Tradition," 806; Talbott, "Universalism."

196. Plumptre, *Spirits in Prison*, 403.

197. Ludlow, "Universalism," 204–5.

198. Hoeksema, "Scriptural Presentation of God's Hatred," 32–33.

brought about by sin and subsisted by sin and the Devil.[199] This seems abhorrent to the reasoning mind. Concedingly, the human mind alone is not the measure of divine truth.

As discussed above under Exclusivism and Inclusivism, there is a widely held assumption that most people shall ultimately end life in separation from God whether by God's sovereign choice or human insistence.[200] This place of separation is either thought to be in annihilation or, more commonly, some type of unending, conscious hell. This presupposition has been generally established as orthodox teaching from seminary and pulpit for the last fifteen hundred years with the possible exception of the early years of the church and other minor thought.[201] In fact, this assumption has been integrally woven into the fabric of what has come to be thought of as the Gospel message and Christian orthodoxy. Moreover, the dominant doctrine for this position asserts that the mass of humanity shall not be saved from these horrors and rather ends in an eternity of conscious hell (Matt 25:41; 2 Thess 1:8–9). That would contend that the majority of one-hundred-and-eight-billion people who have lived to date are destined for hell (Matt 7:13–14).[202]

Although up until the nineteenth century, most theologians believed in eternal damnation and punishment in hell, except those few outside of mainstream orthodoxy that believed in annihilation, which consequentially and necessarily spelled out a conditional immortality.[203] Even fewer theologians, though arguably of more import, stated a belief in universalism (ἀποκατάστασις) until the church creeds anathematized universalism and consigned the unbelievers to a conscious, eternal hell (Athanasian Creed, Fourth Lateran Council, Augsburg Confession, Second Helvetic Confession, Westminster Confession, Dordrecht Confession). A turn developed in the 1800s, and by some accounts[204] the majority of English-speaking believers and growing number of theologians believed in at least an un-defended, non-dogmatic form of universalism leaving behind eternal punishment.

While Bell's popular book *Love Wins*[205] denied hell (at least its enduring), and stirred up large numbers of Christians, especially American

---

199. Jukes, *Second Death*, 114.
200. Punt, *Theology of Inclusivism*, 61, 64.
201. Ludlow, "Universalism," 191, 194–95.
202. Haub, "How Many People"; Punt, *Theology of Inclusivism*, 217.
203. Bauckham, *Universalism*, 48.
204. Ludlow, "Universalism," 204; Mackintosh, *Immortality and the Future*, 197.
205. Bell, *Love Wins*, 109.

Evangelicals,[206] Neuhaus[207] and orthodoxy firmly leave no room for eliminating the concept of hell. He warns that no one should make any mistake that hell is real and that it involves separation from God. God only knows who are damned, but they *are* damned.[208]

Even if one cannot dismiss a never-ending hell, an argument can be made that hell is metaphorical, as many believe heaven to be a metaphor for an unimaginable state or place of wonder and enjoyment in God's presence. Metaphor is a common biblical devise: "rock" of salvation (2 Sam 22:32); "light" of one's path (Ps 119:105); God "sitting" and "standing" (Ps 139:2); "I am the door" (John 10:9); "I am the good shepherd" (John 10:11). Most do not think that heaven has literal streets of gold, gates of pearl, or that the walls are layers of precious jewels (Rev 21:11–19, 21). These represent something unimaginably splendid that awaits those "going" to heaven. In the same metaphorical manner, hell can be thought to represent the results of horrible sins waiting for those who in the end find themselves so punished, away from God's presence. *The Great Divorce*[209] is an allegorical and metaphorical account of heaven and hell imaginatively presented by Lewis. Although an argument can be made for a literal place, Lewis, in his fictional account, illustrates something beyond a literal understanding.

Bauckham[210] discusses Origen as enigmatically known for his denial of hell. Some have argued that his views on this subject are, at root, Platonic. But for Origen such a concept as hell merely posits the marvelous work of God's grace bringing his human creatures to repentance and transformation. Both Origen and Gregory of Nyssa held that hell is educative and restorative; it is a matter of God's goodness requiring his severity.[211] In this same discussion, Bauckham[212] compares Origin's theology on this point to Darwinian evolution in which humans are nothing more than en route, up an evolutionary ladder. As with Origen, the final restoration of humans was held by Gregory of Nyssa, Diodore of Tarsus, Theodore of Mopsuestia, and a few Nestorian theologians all of the fourth and fifth centuries. Augustine rejected such positions. The First Council of Ephesus, 431 CE, condemned the Nestorians for monophysitism. Nor should it be forgotten that Origin's

---

206. Galli, "Heaven, Hell."

207. Neuhaus, *Death on a Friday Afternoon*.

208. Ibid.

209. Lewis, *Great Divorce*, 67–71.

210. Bauckham, *Universalism*, 48.

211. Gregory, "On the Soul"; Origen, *De Principiis*, II.3.6; Ludlow, "Universalism," 192, 215n.

212. Bauckham, *Universalism*, 48.

position was severely opposed. In fact Emperor Justinian tried, without success, to get Origen condemned at the Second Council of Constantinople in 553 CE.[213]

Hellish Heaven

Willard[214] speaks of heaven being a kind of hell and too much heat for those who insist against God's love to exist apart from him. They shall, according to Willard, eventually be given their insistent desires. Heaven shall be too "hot" for them. They were not predestined to damnation and hell but insist on separation from God and his provisions. Yet further, I submit that in the final accounting, after perhaps much dealing from God, all the intransigent holdouts shall come around after seeing and experiencing the love and provision of God. For pain is not for punishment but for rehabilitation and transformation (Heb 12:8–11).[215]

I take a tentative contrarian position to exclusive theologies and suggest most, no, all of humanity is in fact saved from such extreme punishment and suffering and rather is redeemed and destined for salvation, transformation, and a blessed eternity with God. This is a universally inclusive argument, and if it is correct, then necessary faith, by that larger mercy, is facilitated for some by the Spirit's work even into *post-mortem* realms.[216] Holiness before such a loving God is also facilitated for creatures that are enamored with such a great and loving God. If we can believe that God has saved everyone by his merciful work, then we can understand God as truly of love in larger dimensions than most of modern history's theologians and churchmen and women have allowed. I propose God as capable of rescuing all of his creation and transforming his objects of love into the image of his Son following his example of holy living as revealed in Matthew 5–7 excluding any hell. Gross[217] points out the eternal truth that God was bound to his essence and cannot abandon his masterpiece and leave the devil victorious ruling over even a minimally populated hell in God's creation.

In speculating of life after death, Plumptre[218] says that repentance after death in those with the capacity may be more deep and terrible than if repented in life. The worm that does not die and the flame that is not

---

213. Shahan, "Second Council of Constantinople."
214. Willard, "Spiritual Formation."
215. Lewis, *Mere Christianity*, 176.
216. Hick, "D Z Phillips."
217. Gross, *Divinization of the Christian*, 268.
218. Plumptre, *Spirits in Prison*, 402.

quenched (Mark 9:48), I offer, will begin an efficacious work and lead to repentance and the consequent forgiveness and sense of having been forgiven. This large and furthest reaching mercy is versus humanity's inveterate sin and rebellion. By this, the enemy loses in the largest, deepest, and most complete measures. Sin and hell are defeated before God's munificent and victorious accomplishment to redeem his creation in total. This is rather than relegating a large number of people to the torments of conscious hell in eternal separation from God's presence. Athanasius[219] argues against hell or annihilation when he says that it would be monstrous that creatures created in God's image should parish due to their own fault, deception, or that corruption and death should have their way. Such creatures were not created for neglect, and to leave his creature to it would be unworthy of God. The hint in Ecclesiastes (12:5-8) suggests the connection of people to God in that the silver chord of physical life from God is broken at death and one's soul seeks home with God not hell.

Necrology

Necrology, or the possible intermediate state of those who have died,[220] is of interest here. However, a full treatment is neither possible nor necessary for this subject. Parts of the Orthodox Church, while rejecting the Catholic belief in purgatory, accepts an intermediate state which purpose is the purging, through temporary suffering, of what was not worked out in the present life in those destined for heaven.[221] Presenting an argument against the designation "anonymous Christians," Hick[222] also looks at the possibility of becoming a Christian and transformation that may happen spontaneously upon death or through purgation *post-mortem*. Elsewhere Hick[223] says that we must gradually grow toward "future perfection beyond this world"—a *post-mortem* eschatological theodicy. Moreover, within this same argument, Hick suggests that humans must be given a world as if there were no God (L. *etsi deus non daretur*), in which to exercise autonomy in this uncomfortable process of transformation that includes pain and suffering for self and others often without discernible, apparent reason. Talbott[224] speaks about a temporary casting into outer darkness for teaching and remedial punish-

219. Athanasius, *De Incarnatione Verbi Dei*.
220. Cromhout, *Dead in Christ*, 83.
221. Steeves, "Othodox Tradition," 806.
222. Hick, *Death and Eternal Life*, 183.
223. Hick, "D Z Phillips."
224. Talbott, "Universalism."

ment regarding one's sinful or selfish actions. Such a cleansing is necessary so that rational agents can receive full and unhindered revelation of God and eventual union (Talbott).[225] Talbott continues that the choices we make determine this remedial condition not whether one goes to heaven or hell. God has already decided that.

Although warning of final judgment, Augustine[226] speaking on this subject said, "But if the Last Day finds us advancing, there we shall learn what we could not learn here." One might argue that this sentiment by Augustine should be restricted to knowledge limited by Greek philosophy. However, Augustine's words should not be limited to some type of scholastic interpretation but left in the broader context that Jesus would have intended. That is, this knowledge is not limited to intellectual understanding but that which comes to a clear, transformed soul. Moreover, the implication is that something shall be accomplished "there" perhaps after this present life is over. Christ suffered for the unrighteous to bring them to God. He delivered them from prison those who were disobedient during the Noahic period and preached or proclaimed victory to the dead (1 Pet 3:18–20; 4:6).[227] Bartlett[228] discusses the various interpretations of these passages in that Peter's words here are complicated for which their meaning is unclear without consensus. The verses are a highly suggestive model for all regarding Christ's eschatological victory over all who were disobedient whether angels or human souls and perhaps a *post-mortem* solution.

It is a work that does not exclude, disallow, or leave behind one person. This would include those that have too often been judged as outside the veil of Christian orthodoxy and orthopraxy. Heresy or who is a heretic is an issue of the powers so naming it.[229] Explicitly, all are saved from eternal hell: inclusively the non-confessing, the various gender orientations, the heretic, the agnostic. Even the atheist senses the presence of God's shining through the distractions and sin of this life.[230] This and more demonstrate the strength and efficacy of God's salvific work. If all were lost because of the one man, Adam, and all are saved through the one man, Jesus, then everyone must receive eventual spiritual transformation (Rom 5:12–21). That which does not transpire in this life shall continue after death. The Catholics refer to this process as purgatory. The Orthodox refers to this as a

225. Ibid.
226. Augustine, Tractate 53.
227. Bauckham, *Universalism*.
228. Bartlett, "First Letter of Peter," 293–95.
229. Schwartz, *All Can Be Saved*, 11.
230. Bushnell, "Protestant Views," 347.

"condition of waiting"[231] or "toll-houses" wherein a soul moves *post-mortem* from obstacle to obstacle in the hope of escaping *Gehenna*. Maximovitch[232] invokes Ephesians 6:12 as support for the concept. Most Protestants do not refer to such a process and rather speak of hell without reprieve. I consider any perspectives of *post-mortem* states within the pale of Christian thought.

It may be that afterlife or *post-mortem* purification or transformation has nothing to do with salvation or relegation to any hell, since, as already proposed by universalism, salvation has already been accomplished for all by Christ. Since justification in salvation has been accomplished, the afterlife question may only refer to sanctification or transformation, which cannot be partitioned from justification,[233] but is included in a full and unhindered image and likeness of God. So while the Roman Catholic view of purgatory is that a saved person who has not been perfected must be purged to ready himself or herself for heaven and God's holy presence,[234] the Orthodox view is that *post-mortem* tests may determine individual eternity. What I, in this book, propose is that any supposed purgatory, limbo, or after-life purification is to complete the work God has begun and not a matter of salvation or eternal perishing or recompense.

Working It Out

Notwithstanding such possibility, no one should wait for the afterlife to have full sanctification or transformation worked out. Moreover, we have the marvelous opportunity to work out our transformative salvation with a quivering angst in the now (1 Cor 2:2–3; PrōST). This is the proleptic experience greatly available today if we but cooperate with the Spirit of God by his grace and mercy (Titus 2:11–12). It is a reality in tension. That is, everyone is fully dependent on God and yet needs to work as those we were only cheering on to the accomplishment. God's strength is perfected in us through our weaknesses (2 Cor 3:5; 12:5, 9–10). Doing this work in building on Christ's foundation burns away the seditious proclivities and brings transformation and rewards determined by God after surviving the present and *post-mortem* "fire" (1 Cor 3:14–15).

Relegating our present, earthly life to an unexacting staging or waiting place for heaven is a first order mistake. Earthly life is not independent of life in the *eschaton* but is the critical beginning of God's transformational

---

231. Azkoul, "What Are the Differences."
232. Maximovitch, "Life after Death."
233. Walls, "Purgatory for Everyone."
234. Catechism of the Catholic Church [CCC 1030].

activities without which we would not be sufficiently suited for full revelation of God.[235] This is part of the reason for God not placing us in such a condition presented after earthly life from the beginning (L. *ab initio*). Such a beginning in the *post-mortem* derails the intended benefit of transformational activity in the now (Phil 2:12) and the honor of caring for others and God's creation. It removes the opportunity to represent God to the creation and the creation in praise to God. Talbott[236] speculates about the place of hell, purgatory, banishment to outer darkness, or any other supposed *post-mortem* activity as a redemptive (sanctification/transformation) activity not as reciprocity but experience in a teaching and refining process of the terror one might have caused in life.

Since no one, except Christ, dies in perfection, where or how purification is accomplished *post-mortem*, without which no one can enter God's presence, is mysterious. Many die not confessing Christ but are still saved through him, because he is the only way to the Father (John 14:6; Acts 4:12; Heb 7:25). Even if universalism or inclusivism is denied, according to Talbott[237] and Lewis[238] those chosen need to have completed what God began in them and come to the Father through the Son.

Whatever the theology, God's compassion and all-encompassing love is in time resistible, yet in the end it is relentless and cannot be conquered or defeated.[239] So then, whether some form of hell or purgation is the required process, God shall not abandon his *imago* (Lam 3:31, 32; Isa 54:7, 8; 57:16–18; Heb 12:7–11; Ps 89:30–35; 119:67). God's love is triumphant and shall deliver.

OUTSIDE THE PALE AND UNTOUCHABLE

I agree with Gomes[240] that God is large and generous and the God of everyone and everything and that no one is outside of God's providence. God's generosity is diminished by the argument of the predominant belief in a separatist eschatological view of dual human destiny. While trying to sort out separatist views, particularity considerations often manifest in prejudices,

---

235. Talbott, "Universalism."
236. Ibid.
237. Ibid.
238. Lewis, *Mere Christianity*, 176.
239. Power, "Imago Dei," 140.
240. Gomes, *Scandalous Gospel of Jesus*, 154.

a sense of superiority, and expressions of enmity to others not in the select group but destined to eternal damnation in separation from God.[241]

The need to remove separatist thought, not simply to soften the edges with numbers adjustment for those saved versus lost,[242] is in large measure necessary in order to be inclusive of those most often excluded. A generous God lives among the downtrodden, disenfranchised, untouchable, distasteful, marginalized, and heretics who cannot be lost as God's very image. All have the capacity and are disposed toward transcendence in fellowship, even those who are mentally and physically handicapped, vegetative, sociopathic, or none-functioning as normal humans.[243] Our destiny is found within the incarnation of Christ because we are the "same species," who is God on earth lifting humanity above the natural world and the social relationships of the world.[244] Our dignity, Pannenberg continues, derives from the destiny of fellowship with the Triune God. Such dignity leaves no one outside the pale as untouchable. Jesus demonstrated this on many occasions as represented by the leper, the paralytic, the demon possessed, and the woman with twelve years of feminine bleeding (Mark 1:40–42; 2:5; 5:14–20; 5:25–34).

The process of spiritual transformation leads us outside of our own singular concerns to the social community in which we live. It is a concern that eventually reaches out to the greater world. It manifests in the requirement to redress all forms of "unjust dominance and exploitation."[245] There is "transformative union with the Holy Spirit" which empowered the apostles to put aside their own fears and insecurities and journey into the world to help others in need.[246] This sense and understanding to unrestricted love of our neighbor in practical matters draws in those considered outside the pale.

We were created for fellowship with one another.[247] Having been so created is the point of *imago Dei* as Christ's incarnated life examples in human destiny.[248] This *imago Dei* is a work that does *not* exclude, disallow, or leave behind one person. This includes those that have too often been judged as outside the veil of Christian orthodoxy and orthopraxy. Again, it should be remembered that heresy or who is the heretic is an issue of the powers so

---

241. Greggs, *Barth, Origen*, vii.
242. Ibid., x.
243. Bratt, "Wolfhart Pannenberg," 18.
244. Pannenberg, *Systematic Theology*, 2:175–76.
245. Mahoney and Pargament, "Sacred Changes," 486–87.
246. Ibid.
247. Moltmann, *God in Creation*, 223.
248. Pannenberg, *Systematic Theology*, 2:176, 224–25, 227.

naming it.²⁴⁹ Explicitly, all are saved and transformed: inclusively the non-confessing, the various gender orientations, the heretic, the agnostic and atheist—the list is inexhaustive. This demonstrates the strength and efficacy of God's salvific work. If all were lost because of the one man, Adam, and all are saved through the one man, Jesus, then everyone must receive eventual spiritual transformation (Rom 5:12–21). That which does not transpire in this life shall continue after death in purgation.

Neuhaus²⁵⁰ speaks about the unseemly thought that Hitler and Mao Zedong would finally arrive in heaven without full reciprocity or recompense for their earthly wrongs. He cites Lewis and Methodist theologian Walls to speak for those who believe a long and painful purgation is appropriate but still journeying to the beatific vision. Perhaps to the railing dismay and even revulsion of most, Hitler, in this notion, is a candidate for such a *post-mortem* mercy, remediable purgation though interminable, and eventual reconciliation. Lewis²⁵¹ indirectly assures God's completing work in his creatures in that God says be perfect (Matt 5:48). Furthermore, Lewis says that God shall make humans creatures that can obey this seemingly impossible command: the apparently feeblest and filthiest of God's children shall be made into a "god or goddess, a dazzling, radiant, immortal creature, pulsating all through with energy and joy and wisdom and love as we cannot now image."²⁵² Lewis appears to allude to an after-death process of transformation here that shall take a long and painful process to realize this promise.²⁵³ In light of such sentiments, no human can, in the final day, be left outside the pale, and untouchable. They shall be bright mirrors with no stain, perfectly reflecting to creation and back to God, while on a smaller scale, God's limitless power, savor, and goodness.

The connection between humans and God is not limited or only something that occurred in the beginnings of nascent humanity to be lost in the fall. What is the relationship between humans and God is a permanent connection that cannot be interrupted or deleted by any event no matter how horrible and debilitating or how thoroughly based in rebellion or ignorance.²⁵⁴

As we discussed in chapter 2, sins are overblown concerns for one's own control and reputation; it compels us to attempt to close the separation

---

249. Schwartz, *All Can Be Saved*, 11.
250. Neuhaus, *Death on a Friday Afternoon*.
251. Lewis, *Mere Christianity*, 176.
252. Ibid.
253. Ibid.
254. Heschel, "Holy Dimension," 119, 121.

between ourselves and others by minimizing them to nothing more than objects, so that they can be thought of and acted upon as mere rags or excess of ourselves and therefore manipulated without guilt.[255] God put down the satanic rebellion and freed creation to an unhindered relationship with God-self. Jesus lived the sinless life of intimacy and reflection of God as the example he desires for us and incorporated that life into the gift of the Holy Spirit, who blows into humanity all that Christ is (John 3:6–8; Gal 5:22), which now includes a victorious, transformed, triumphant humanity.

Exacerbating this often dismayed and frustrated desire to express and enjoy the image of God is the usual exclusion of the purportedly "unchosen," "unclean," or "unqualified" persons: The persons who have not confessed Christ, the degenerate, the homosexual, the atheist, the stranger, widow, poor, orphan, prisoner, disenfranchised, alien, off-cast, outcast, and a long list of those said not to be fit to enter into the kingdom of God and heaven. Nevertheless, no one is left outside the pale. As discussed above, the numbers on this list of the supposedly excluded and even damned people apparently far outnumbers those supposedly destined for glory with God in eternity. Inflating the list is facilitated by an often held theology, discussed above, that *imago Dei* in human beings was either damaged or even lost as a result of the fall along with the tragedy of mistreatment, even torture, damning, and killing of those thought not to bare God's image.[256]

Such an exclusionary inventory accuses God of failing to maximally accomplish his goal and heart's desire toward the vast majority of his created beings, the zenith of his creation (1 Tim 2:4; Titus 2:11; 2 Pet 3:9). So, driven by this exclusionary theology of very Limited Atonement, rather than the focus and energy that might be used toward the PrōST of everyone without consideration to his or her qualifications and worthiness, inordinate energy is wasted to exclude and disqualify the mass of humanity through tests of predestination and a restricted version of orthodoxy. This approach is utilized rather than the inclusion used by Jesus, who in love and without condemnation, partook with the poor, the blind, the drunkards, the unclean, the prostitutes, the thieves, the sick, the outcasts, the downtrodden, the disenfranchised, the alien, the unorthodox, the *persona non grata*, and the generally un-chosen. It is this open display of love that seems to be inclusive of any who might be absented by an exclusionary theology.

Consider the picture of a commanding military officer given the mission to save a large group of prisoners from an island heavily guarded by an elite guard of Special Forces holding this group hostage under threat of

---

255. Goldstein, "Human Situation," 100.
256. Kilner, "Humanity in God's Image," 617.

death. If the commander tasked with their rescue was to only rescue a small select group of these and the majority were left behind in mortal danger, then it would not be considered a successful rescue mission. No amount of consoling would satisfy the commander or his superior officer or the families of those lost. A rescue mission of a "chosen few" is not laudable.

The *imago Dei* fully expressed as destiny, not yet realized, is present even in us who have rejected God and whose futures are as yet not known, and so God cannot abandon his own image in us although the full process and means are not known or understood.[257] Moreover, through Jesus, God now offers PrōST to everyone including the poor, the blind, the orphaned, the heretic, the drunkards, degenerate, the homosexual, and atheist. Persons that explicitly reject Christ are also included in salvation according to the particularistic view (in Christ): stranger, widow, poor, orphan, prisoner, disenfranchised, alien, off-cast, outcast, unclean, prostitutes, thieves, diseased, downtrodden, disenfranchised, unorthodox, persona non grata, un-chosen, and the dead.

CHRIST PARTICULARISM

Whether exclusivism, inclusivism, or universalism is appraised, particularism in Christ (Acts 4:12; 10:43) is the means of salvation from a Christocentric position as is held in orthodox Christianity and this book. Particularism states that salvation comes through only one way, and that way is the person Jesus Christ, his life, death, and resurrection (John 16:6; Heb 10:20).[258] Since the body of Christ is the church and he its head (Rom 12:5; 1 Cor 12:27; Eph 5:23; Col 1:18, 24),[259] only those who are saved as members of Christ, are his body or the church. Any who could be excluded from such a relationship with Christ would, according to particularism, not be of his.

The New Testament presents Jesus as the only savior of humanity through the life, death, and resurrection of Christ (John 3:17; 4:2; 12:47; 1 John 4:14).[260] The high Christology of traditional Christianity, although, often seen as offensive by pluralistic thought, resists any homogenization of soteriology across religious lines.[261] This resistance against pluralist thought excludes other none Christological ways to salvation (John 14:6–7a).[262]

257. Bratt, "Wolfhart Pannenberg," 19.
258. McGath, "Particularist View," 163, 166.
259. Ibid.
260. Ibid., 163.
261. Ibid., 166.
262. Ibid., 67.

A favored selection often used to prove exclusive theory is Matthew 7:13–14. Without trying to defeat this passage or the many that can be marshaled to the debate, one small point of different understanding might be presented to indicate such proof texts are not inviolate. The "narrow gate" of this warning may be understood, not as the missed gate of only opportunity, but rather meaning, the right gate.[263] Having such a discussion does not in a short time prove or defeat any of these positions, but merely suggest that there are other legitimate interpretations and exegeses of these and other passages that enter the ring of conflicting theologies.

McDonald[264] affirmed his belief in Christ as the world's atonement. Through God we are reconciled to God and not God to us. Following this care for his creatures, and that transformation is connected to this salvific work as its natural following, it is God's work that develops transformation past, present, future, and proleptically. Paul (Acts 4:12) spoke the same thing when he spoke of Christ's name alone being given for salvation, as did Luke's record after Paul (Acts 10:43). Salvation is found solely, uniquely, and particularly in Christ. Since a central tenet to Christianity is particularity of salvation only in Christ, it is thereby nonnegotiable to any dialogue about Christ's life, work, and, victory.[265]

Human beings are called to enjoy eternal, heavenly existence. No religion, self-efforts, or pleading sacrifices can lift us to such a state. Fulfilling legal requirements secures no surety (Heb 7:19). It is only by the heavenly priesthood of Christ that opens these marvelous possibilities.[266] Christ is victor and brings the victory by which it is now possible to live in him, through him, and with him in the heavenly realms (Eph 1:3; 2:6).

The particularity of Christ is foundation to our goals and objectives. Without Christ as central, necessary, and sufficient, no transformation into his image by beholding his glory is possible (2 Cor 3:18). The image of God in humans is not an allusion to royal theology; a prince is not the focus of bearing this image but all and every one of us.[267] This bears upon the present discussion in that all who have this image are included in proleptic spiritual transformation (PrōST) as per God's intent. Soteriology as Christ is a critical and central doctrine for the Christian church. The heart of God is revealed in a proper understanding and enjoyment of the full extent of salvation in

---

263. Punt, *Theology of Inclusivism*, 219.
264. McDonald, *Creation in Christ*, 78.
265. Greggs, *Barth, Origen*, 86–87.
266. Aulén, *Christus Victor*, 78.
267. Moltmann, *God in Creation*, 219.

Christ. Salvation burgeoning as spiritual transformation is found as the meaning and purpose of Christ's incarnation to bring life (1 John 5:12).[268]

The Apostle John's claim of Jesus as the only way to his Father and God (John 14:6; 1 Tim 2:5–6) is a truth of great joy to those who claim Jesus as Savior and Lord. However, this same verse is one of great contention from those outside of the Christian tradition. Even some within the Christian tradition as well as the pluralist outside feel any one way to God is myopic and ignores the diversity of religions and the reality that such an exclusive claim is puerile and parochial at best and maliciously eviscerating to the human soul at worst. However, "through Christ" does not, of necessity, indicate a particular religion or system by which one might come to God the Father through Christ. An agnostic Christian universalism would then mean that although one is not certain regarding the claims of Christianity and its heralds but has been saved, that it was nevertheless through Christ that salvation was secured (Rev 5:9–14). If one is saved or secured, by this verse and belief, then it is indicated that it is somehow through Christ.[269]

John 15 is a famous chapter in which Jesus speaks about abiding in him and being one with him and the Father. To be in Christ suggests some measure of proleptic enjoyment of Christ's accomplishments (John 13:15; 1 John 2:6). The life of victory in expression of God's image (John 14:10–11) is available in the now. This is his promise (John 14:12; Phil 2:12).[270]

CHRISTOSIS AS IMAGO DEI

Christ lived a life in full expression of the intent of God in human creation. Where the first Adam failed, the last Adam (Jesus Christ) was successful. The life of the last Adam and his expression is what is intended as our "final destiny."[271] Moreover, Christ is the human eschatological hope lived now proleptically.[272] In this Pannenberg seems to suggest that while this eschatological reality, or "arriving future," is introduced in Christ, and although it is intended for all persons now, it can only be partly realized this side of eternity. I agree that it does not seem to reach perfectionism this side

---

268. Chan, *Spiritual Theology*, 167; Grenz, "Jesus as the Imago Dei," 617, 621; Lossky, *Orthodox Theology*, 70–71.

269. McGrath, "Particularist View," 163–64; Origen, *De Principiis*, I.3.6; Pinnock, "Response to John Hick," 96, 98.

270. Bartlett, "First Letter of Peter," 293–95; Pannenberg, *Systematic Theology*, 2:220.

271. Ibid.

272. Ibid., 220, 240.

of eschatological completions, but presses that such a reality is exceedingly more available in the present than commonly believed or lived.

Regarding such a perfecting, it appears that we were created in a way that makes us open to and curious about the finite as new experiences; and actually in this openness comes an awareness of the infinite and an openness to God that is pointed to by the finite.[273] This "exocentricity" is a human awareness of the transcendent beyond all things finite.[274] Such openness is our destiny as expressed already in Christ as the eschatological new man according to Shults,[275] and is the proleptic experience in and expression of the divine as *Christosis* ("Christification" of a human).

Jesus showed the way of fellowship and communion in expressing God's likeness in his relationship to humans even wherein our personalities are developed.[276] As Luke put it, Jesus grew in wisdom, grace, and spirit (Luke 1:80; 2:40, 52). Herein is the point of *imago Dei* created for relationship and fellowship that is only fulfilled in Christ[277] that brings a likeness to those related to Christ in such things as growth in wisdom, grace, and spirit.

The notion of divinization, deification, or *Christosis* as touched above and discussed below, lost any prominent support after the first five centuries of the church, to be kept alive predominantly by the Orthodox Church and found its present expression in the fourteenth century as supported by Gregory Palamas.[278] Although hints of divinization or deification can be found in both Catholicism and Protestantism, Catholic theologians were willing to repeat Athanasius' famous words that God became human that the human might become god. Gross[279] represents Protestant scholars F. W. Norris and Robert V. Rakestraw and their willingness to argue for divinization or deification. What was and still is allowed is an unfortunate theology of loss of God's image in humans.

Imago Dei Glorified

Many theologians argue that the marvel of Genesis (*imago Dei*) was destroyed or extremely marred and even lost (cf. the discussion by Van

---

273. Ibid., 229.
274. Shults, *Reforming Theological Anthropology*, 237.
275. Ibid.
276. Moltmann, *God in Creation*, 223.
277. Pannenberg, *Systematic Theology*, 2:224–25, 227.
278. Gross, *Divinization of the Christian*, x.
279. Ibid.

Huyssteen).[280] A contrary opinion regarding the inviolate nature of *imago Dei* was considered above. In agreement with such pillars as Aquinas, Luther and Calvin, Atmann contends that Christ restores the image of God in humans.[281] Departing from this conjecture already in the prior chapter, I contend that the image of God (*imago Dei*) was never and can never be lost or even damaged; it is the "status" of the human being[282] or our very essence. Moreover, such an image is glorified in Christ who brings the existential realities of his incarnation, life, death, resurrection, and ascension to bear within the image. So now, as proposed by Kilner,[283] the *imago Dei* became the *imago Christi*. It carries the reality of a new capacity in the life of the God-man who is perfect God and perfect man. Lossky,[284] furthermore and nicely, asserts the very goal, salvation, hope, and purpose of humans as nothing less than *theōsis* and the restoration of the cosmos. It is a participation in a creation that is set free from bondage to corruption to its yearning freedom in the glory of God's children (Rom 8:21).

The fulfillment of our destiny as God's image is a growing representation of its fulfillment as modeled in Jesus Christ proleptically. It is regarding or representing all humanity by the man Jesus Christ and a life that cannot be exceeded by any other model of intimacy between God and humans.[285] Although what is too often only seen as humans in the image of the man of dust, we shall, one day, in full expression bear forth the image of the man of heaven in full manifest *Christosis* (1 Cor 15:47, 49).

As briefly touched on earlier, the premise of this work is inclusive of a spiritual transformation that is higher and beyond the life enjoyed in Eden. This transforming opportunity is especially offered to those that behold God's face in Christ (2 Cor 3:18). According to Kärkkäinen,[286] *Christosis* may be thought of as a Christological complex within humans, and that this is human destiny. It reads as though Kärkkäinen here is referring to a status of humans before the first advent of Christ. If this is the case, then difference might be argued here. Rather, such a *Christosis* does not seem likely before the incarnation as first displayed in the man Jesus and therefrom subsequently by his followers. Although God desires to restore what was lost in the garden, his solution includes an *imago Dei* that is now inclusive

---

280. Van Huyssteen, *Alone in the World?*, 127.
281. Atmann, *Homo Imago Dei*, 247.
282. Kilner, "Humanity in God's Image," 611, 614.
283. Ibid., 611–12.
284. Lossky, *Orthodox Theology*, 70–71.
285. Pannenberg, *Systematic Theology*, 2:225.
286. Kärkkäinen, *One with God*, 25.

of the experiential realities of the God-man Jesus Christ—the *imago Christi*. It is now possible for humans to live a life like Jesus lived in his incarnation—of course without being God. Bratt[287] hints at this in her paper as she speaks about God's true image as embodied in his Son. More particularly, I argue that others may approach this same reality in the now in the reality of spiritual transformation into the *imago Dei* that is inclusive of the life and experiences of Jesus Christ (L. *imago Christi*).

The image bearing like the "man of heaven" (1 Cor 15:49) is not to be reserved only for the eternal state when all things shall be restored and even made new (Rev 21:1–5). Gordon Fee[288] positions the Apostle Paul as limiting this eventuality to the *eschaton*. Conversely, the context and full testimony of Scripture does not necessitate such a limitation. In this same passage, Fee, himself, curiously portrays Paul as encouraging the Corinthians to "press on to *eschaton*" now. The *eschaton* shall arrive without pressing toward it. One might be encouraged to do something in light of the *eschaton* and judgment but not to "press on" toward it. Not to make too much of Fee's choice of words here, he goes on to say on the same page, "So that as believers now behold him as the risen One, they are themselves being 'transformed' *back* into that image/likeness"[289] (emphasis added), an indication of Fee's belief in the image's loss.

Paul's full testimony and experience posits at least a beginning experience of the not-yet now. This glimpse of present potentiality begins to crack open a window to the *imago Christi* as the standard goal. Blackwell[290] suggests *Christosis* as a designation here since disciples are being formed into such an image as provided by and in Christ in an encounter with the Trinity. There is no confusion or mingling of the human nature and the divine essence (Gk. *ousia*); they remain distinct.[291] Lossky[292] speaks of an oneness and uniqueness in the Trinity that does not diminish or give one-upmanship of one of the Trinity over another of the Trinity. This suggests the space and possibility for an oneness among humans and yet also uniqueness that is reflective of purpose as created and an expression of *imago Dei* that is amazingly seen within the Trinity.[293] In this same analysis of Lossky, Harrison assertively questions whether the irreducible distinctiveness of each

---

287. Bratt, "Wolfhart Pannenberg," 5.
288. Fee, *Pauline Christology*, 185.
289. Ibid.
290. Blackwell, *Christosis*, 253.
291. Kärkkäinen, *One with God*, 31.
292. Lossky, *Mystical Theology*, 54–55.
293. Harrison, "God's Many-Splendored Image," 175–77.

individual could not be an expression of the Trinity in uniqueness. Building on Harrison's examination, the implication of this value of human uniqueness as a reality of intrinsic worth remains in the completion of the full expression of God's image as *Christosis* as a result of spiritual transformation (cf. 2 Cor 3:18; 4:6).

Following on this transformation is a facilitation of love for one's neighbor as one with whom eternity shall be enjoyed. "The Word of God, our Lord Jesus Christ, who did, through His transcendent love, become what we are, that He might bring us to be even what He is Himself."[294] God's intent is perfect humans (Matt 5:48; Jas 1:2–3). We shall be like gods and goddesses, magnificent, brilliant, ablaze, undying creatures that pulsate with energy, ecstasy, wisdom, and love that cannot presently be imagined; we shall be like bright unstained mirrors reflecting to the world and to God perfectly his own inexhaustible power, joy, and goodness.[295]

Christ is the image of God (Col 1:15; Heb 1:3). In this Christ is intended as the firstborn from whom we also are intended to conform as *imago Christi* as mediated through Christ.[296] Moltmann further suggests that Christology is the end and fulfillment of anthropology as the preparation for Christology. We represent God on earth; it is a "divine mode of appearance." Wherever we appear, it is God's indirect manifestation among creation revealing something of God.[297]

Significance for Whom

Talbott,[298] along with many popular preachers and theologians, provides a common foil contrary to a Gospel of hope, in which God's universe ends in the tragedy of most humans being eternally lost. More tragically, they are lost in unrelenting punishment and hideous conscious torture due to sins against God, in which no consolation can be found in the midst of such horror. In contrast, if the end is found in the glorious inclusive and universal reality of the restoration of all things (Gk. ἀποκατάστασις πάντως) then the anxious fretting that plague too many Christians is vanished for God's munificence and largess in restoration.

---

294. Irenaeus, preface to *Against Heresies*, V.
295. Lewis, *Mere Christianity*, 176.
296. Moltmann, *God in Creation*, 218.
297. Ibid., 219.
298. Talbott, "Christ Victorious," 18.

Human dignity, Pannenberg[299] says, derives from the destiny of fellowship with the Triune God. As I have already argued, all humans enjoy some measure of this fellowship despite an often-profound lack of awareness or expression (Gen 1:26–27; 2:7; 5:3; 9:6). Such dignity leaves no one outside the pale or untouchable. If Jesus believed this (Mark 1:40–42; 2:5; 5:25–34; Luke 10:37), then his disciples cannot live otherwise.

It appears, as already noted, that sanctification (transformation) is tied to salvation through Christ alone. If transformation is an expression of a part or measure of salvation, then one's opinion about who is saved has a major bearing on one's expectations of and opportunity for transformation. We might be convinced that everyone should be treated well even equitably. However, if we believe the other is most likely destined to eternal damnation and conscious torment outside of the awareness of the select redeemed and community under God's care and eternal blessings, then we shall have great difficulty treating every individual as worthy. If everyone is presumed to be God's child, through Christ redeemed, and eventual heavenly subject as the greatest and most lauded saint, then the treatment of every individual takes up a care and honor rightfully due a child of God and representative of God in Christ's life and image (Matt 25:43–45). So then, despite the doctrinal stance or outcome, this should be the hope of all for all.[300]

Neuhaus[301] lists scripture examples that support separation from God (Matt 7:13–28; 25:31–46; Mark 9:45–48; Luke 16:23; John 3:36) and then the apparently contrary scriptures that give hope that all shall be redeemed (Col 1:19–20; 1 Cor 15:22, 28; Rom 5:18; 11:33–36; Phil 2:10–11). He suggests that if one gives priority to the redemption scriptures, then the separation verses would be considered as giving caution and admonishment so one may not face the terrible possibility. Contrastingly, if the scriptures on separation are given priority, then those apparently supporting universal salvation are admittedly not dealt with so easily. As with Arminian and Calvinistic positions,[302] conclude that the Christian Church historically has not settled such issues, and that this lack of required doctrine may be a wise response by not locking in a nonessential.

If to have real, loving, and vital relationship with God indicates that God can be affected by humans, as held by Open Theism,[303] then God can be moved by our prayers, petitions, dilemmas, and situations. Many

---

299. Pannenberg, *Systematic Theology*, 2:175–76.
300. Fee, *God's Empowering Presence*, 570–72.
301. Neuhaus, "Will All Be Saved?"
302. Ibid.
303. Sanders, *God Who Risks*, 245.

erudite minds, like Augustine, Pannnenberg, Power, and Sanders, all listed here, exceeding the breadth and depth of the present work, have focused on this issue with both defense and rebuttal. Nonetheless, it appears that only within a human relationship to God, and especially in relationship to eschatological destiny, does any moral self-determination and ethical freedom find place.[304] In this relationship is the reality of God's all embracing and irresistible love, and in the final analysis, it is unassailable and inviolable.[305] Following on this is a facilitation of love for one's neighbor as one with whom eternity shall be enjoyed. It is key to know and remember that God's intent is perfect humans (Matt 5:48; Jas 1:2–3), people who shall be like gods, magnificent, not held by death, reflecting God's image to the world and God.[306] Augustine[307] agrees, that God makes his disciples gods by participation in himself. Admittedly, Augustine makes this claim without universalistic overtones.

Following this thought, if one would stay in Christ's embrace, he or she must also become and remain availably and lavishly inclusive. One must be an agent for the sanctifying mantle of the church. Obeying God shall unarm the world's powers with the keys of the kingdom of God through preaching the councils of God.[308] It is this prophetic voice of the transformed and empowered church living out the *imago Christi*. This is being transformed (Gk. *metamorphoumetha*) through the power of the Spirit of God in the present[309] from which God can destroy these powers and have open expression of his kingdom in and through his people to a needful world.

Accordingly, Jesus did not only die for this or that house and clan or another's. He died for all and in particular the house and clan of those who might most be marginalized for their sin, their differences, their "bad" theology and company, their different cultural expressions. To lay one's head on Christ's bosom is to be mindful for whom he was and is available: the prostitute, the thief, the adulterer, the alien and sojourner, the murderer, the disenfranchised, the blasphemer, and the dead and good as dead. His love circumscribes all in need (Matt 5:16).[310]

So often Christians reserve any grace or joy for their fellow Christians of the same belief-set, or community leaving out many other Christians

---

304. Pannenberg, *Systematic Theology*, 2:224.
305. Power, "Imago Dei," 140.
306. Lewis, *Mere Christianity*, 176.
307. Augustine, *City of God* (NPNF1-02).
308. Vorster, "Transformation in South Africa," 735–36.
309. Ibid., 737.
310. Willard, "Living a Transformed Life."

and surely non-Christians from any real God-given grace, encounter, joy, and peace in this life let alone eternity. This poverty of God is too often preached from the pulpits, written in books, and spoken in the public and private conversations of the "knowledgeable and wise." This is contrary to the largess of God. It is contrary to the vast love of God. As we have already discussed, such an exclusive interpretation is contrary to Scripture. Finally, by such a reading, it is seen as contrary to the experiential knowledge of human history (Acts, 17:26–27).[311]

The Hope

The hope, as de Chardin[312] believes, as do many Christians, that humans shall one day come face to face with God. But he says, that the ultimate vision Christ has for the world is an inseparable connectedness to God through the "elevating and illuminating action of Christ." He goes on by stating, one's "mystical effort" shall receive "essential completion" in union, rewarded in its union with the mystical effort of all other humans.[313]

As the notional chart below depicts, this vision implies and hopes that an often unseen work is being accomplished in us all by Christ to finish the work he has begun, one that is not frustrated by human condition, time, place, belief, theology, or death (1 Cor 1:8; Gal 3:3; Phil 1:6). The chart shows the particularity of Christ as center; while those coming through him are all people, whether they have heard the Gospel, are heterodox or even heretical, outcast, or otherwise. Transformation takes place in the now and in the last times (Gk. *eschaton*) through purgation if necessary.[314] This destination of *Christosis* (or "Christification") is the hope for all God's children. However, God is holy and requires a spotless bride (1 Cor 5:5; Eph 5:27; Col 1:22). The completion of his good work shall not be frustrated (1 Cor 1:8; Phil 1:6).

---

311. Pannenberg, *Systematic Theology*, 2:175–76; Talbott, "Christ Victorious," 18.
312. De Chardin, *Divine Milieu*, 119.
313. Ibid.
314. Talbott, "Essential Role of Free Will."

Notional Chart of Spiritual Transformation

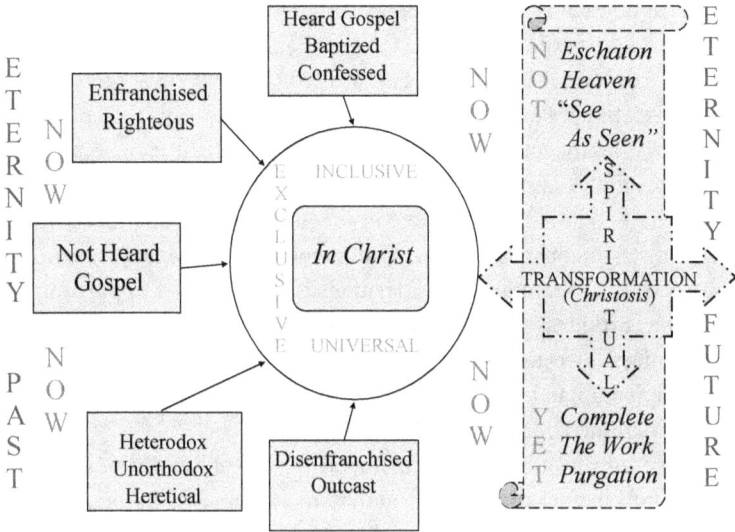

Figure 1

One's ultimate destiny is not his or her decision to make. Talbott[315] says God's disciplines as well as his mercy are means of grace. Human free choice does not decide eternal destiny, which God has already secured, but only the means or the road to its accomplishment. Talbott continues that the more one holds onto false belief and fleshly desires the harder and rougher the road to transformation by the shattering of delusions and flesh to separate one from sins.

On several occasions I have tied sanctification and transformation together as part of the same work of God in humans. When one has an attitude of "having arrived" or being chosen ahead of others or even instead of others, it is unkind and lacks love, that is, an attitude of exclusive position frustrates the fruit of the Spirit (Gal 5:22), and spiritual growth is hindered. Further, it becomes probable that a superior attitude over those who have not been chosen shall develop. If a large group of people is preordained to perdition and hell, then to look at them as *them*, beyond pity, is difficult to resist. It is a type of Elysian Fields, a heaven where some few are comforted

---

315. Ibid.

versus the idea of one's starless destiny as an embodied, dark shade or vapor that is banished to hades never to be released or reprieved.[316]

This Greek image appears to drive the Christian interpretation of the afterlife as an exclusive arrangement even predestination leaving only a very few with the hope of heaven and eternal joy and presence with God. Any exclusive form seems to perpetuate an individualistic view of salvation. Contrary to relational justification one shall find in the Apostle Paul, Western soteriology has in fact supported such an individualistic view of salvation.[317] In fact this follows from the posits of some theologians,[318] in that the saved shall be able to look upon the lost in torment and not be moved but glory God in his righteousness for such judgment. How we view others is critical to how we treat them and consider their transformative opportunity. This is why war produces pejorative references to the enemy. Once the enemy is dehumanized—treating him or her without the compassion and deference due a fellow human being created in God's image—extreme prejudice (killing) is sanctioned, forgiven, and even honored.

When an awareness of transformation actually presents within us, a quantum change, that is the catalyst to habitual paths being radically changed, leads to a new understanding of significance which drives us to a place of peace, tranquility, joyfulness, and a manner of life that is a stranger to the prior means that were mundane, and ruinous patterns.[319] Such change, Mahoney and Pargament continue, may bring with it immediate and effortless, immense breakthrough in awareness, a transformation which changes what we consider important or critical and worthy of attention.

Moreover, in Christ not only are all of the promises of the past fulfilled; but as important, the future is in Christ as well as the perfect God-man who has restored and elevated the human condition into the accomplishments of his life, death, and resurrection. In him is the possibility and reality of proleptic spirituality transformation (PrōST). He lived the completely transformed life in loving communion with God and others despite the age or conditions in which he contended. His followers are called to such a glorious and God-glorifying life and visible expression as his (Matt 5:16).[320]

---

316. Gross, *Divinization of the Christian*, 13, 15.

317. Kärkkäinen, *One with God*, 11–12.

318. Spurgeon, "Hope of Future Bliss"; Packer, "Hell's Final Enigma," 2002; Augustine, *City of God* (NPNF).

319. Mahoney and Pargament, "Sacred Changes," 487.

320. Moltmann, *God in Creation*, 273–75; Pannenberg, *Systematic Theology*, 2:224–25; Willard, "Living a Transformed Life"; Willard, *Divine Conspiracy*, 366; Willard, *Spirit of Disciplines*, 156–57.

In the book of Romans, the apostle begins to open a vista into the inauguration of "the freedom of the glory of the children of God" (Rom 8:21b) who have the first fruits of the Spirit and are looking for bodily salvation, however, being conformed to Christ's image (Rom 8:23, 29). The tension between present adoption and future adoption is shown in the sharing of present suffering and hope for future identifying with Christ in his glorification now.[321] Moreover, I have argued that Christ's present glorification is, to a measure, enjoyable now as the not-yet by the gift of the Spirit. Clendenin[322] supports in saying salvation, including transformation, is through deification and that this process is not completed until the *eschaton*, the "third birth," but must be started now. For Paul and the early church the resurrection of Christ and the outflowing of Spirit signaled the arrival of the future in some measure even if only a dawning.[323] Ludlow's words[324] further the contention that God's salvific and restorative work is not merely a return to the beginning a cycle begun in the garden but a fulfillment or even a perfection of creation.

CONCLUSIONS

A gloss of soteriological constructs was briefly considered in this chapter. We did not argue for a pluralistic theology in which all religions are equal. Christian Exclusivism was shown to present a salvation found only in and through Christ (John 14:6; 1 John 5:12) but under that concept there are only a limited number that shall be saved in the final judgment. Giving more room, Christian Inclusivism argued that most would, in fact, be saved except those who remain intransigently hardened and intent to resist all of God's graces to save them. Christian Universalism, as presented here, posited both that Christ is the only way to God (particularism) and that all shall be saved and redeemed through Christ perhaps after some respective or required time of purgation. Karl Barth, along with others, was shown to hold such a universal hope.[325] Barth, as representative, was shown to hold salvation as found in none other than Jesus Christ; that is, Christian Universalism is particularism that remains in the Christian fold.[326]

---

321. Fee, *God's Empowering Presence*, 570–72.
322. Clendenin, "Partakers of Divinity," 377.
323. Fee, *God's Empowering Presence*, 573.
324. Ludlow, "Universalism," 192–93.
325. Greggs, *Barth, Origen*, 30–31, 41.
326. Ibid., 310.

An understanding and belief about salvation and subsequent transformation opens horizons to human destiny, which are included, and to what degrees they are included. Nevertheless, despite various conflicting doctrinal assertions and popular testimonies, this study cannot say with certainty, which salvific construct is correct. Any possible, falsifiable understanding would surely present as distraction and challenge to the objectives of this study. Nevertheless, it is my belief and hope that Christian universal salvation founded in the particularity of Christ wins out in the eschatological end. The presumption of such a hope presents all people with the dignity and deference of a destined magnificent of God's choosing who shall be made into radiant gods or goddesses.[327] Such a conceptualization or vision provides a particular view of oneself and all others that in turn fuel an attitude and response that facilitates communion and open fellowship with God and others. As I have argued thus far, such fellowship makes available God's transformative activity in all persons.

As already considered above but with no theological consensus, there seem to be several reasons why Christian or trinitarian universalism may be the best reflection of the Gospel. Among them, the Scripture can be shown to support such a view in that God's love for all of us cannot be defeated. Additionally, Jesus Christ's salvific work cannot be defeated in the smallest degree. Existentially, there is a witness, an instinct deep in the soul of every person to everlasting life in a better condition in rest. As already reviewed, there is an early historical testimony to this view. And importantly, philosophical reasons support the continued existence of the human soul.

Moreover, lacking the full expression of a universal image hinders the manifestation of God's kingdom on earth as it is in heaven (Matt 6:10; 13:19; Rom 12:2). That is, if one holds to an exclusive belief of salvation, results in fewer souls attracted to the Gospel as it is impotently lived out. The "righteousness and peace and joy in the Holy Spirit," that is of the kingdom of God (Rom 14:17), is expressed by disciples who enjoy some measure of spiritual transformation from which to spontaneously express these attributes of righteousness, peace and joy in God's Spirit. This too-neglected movement was shown to be at the heart of God's desire and intent opening to PrōST.

The Christian, analytic philosopher Alvin Plantinga[328] shares the same hope, and although he does not quite believe universalism, he does not disbelieve it either and rather thinks universalism is something for which

---

327. Lewis, *Mere Christianity*, 176.
328. Plantinga, "Can a Person Be a Soul?"

Christians should at least hope. Lewis[329] envisions what God is doing as nothing less than making his people gods and goddesses who are such beautiful creatures, radiant, and filled with the love that can be seen in Christ. Although this has been a brief chapter on transformational-salvation, it was foundationally necessary and sufficient for what follows. Exclusive, Inclusive, and Universal salvation were considered with a view to proleptic spiritual transformation (PrōST).

God is ecumenical, merciful, generous, and does not refuse assistance to anyone. A formal conversion experience is not required or needed to proceed to human inherent, elemental, and inexpungible propensity for transformation.[330] Potential is intrinsic to humans and proper to a relationship with God as fully recovered and experienced by Christ's incarnation and work in securing the means to a transformed life for the rest of God's children. In this inclusive eschatological nature of the reality and God's transformative work, universal restoration shall not be frustrated or interrupted (2 Pet 2:9).

The *imago Dei* in humans is not an allusion to royal theology. A prince is not the focus of bearing this image but all and every human being is.[331] This bears upon the present discussion in that all who have this image are included in proleptic spiritual transformation (PrōST) as per God's intent. The fulfillment of human destiny as *imago Dei* is a growing representation of its fulfillment as it was modeled in Jesus Christ proleptically, regarding or representing all humanity by the man Jesus. It is a life that cannot be exceeded by any other model of intimacy between God and humans.[332] Although what is too often only seen as humans in the image of the man of dust, we shall, one day, be the full expression and bear forth the image of the man of heaven in full manifest *Christosis* (1 Cor 15:47, 49).

More space has been given to universalism because it is less received in Western theologies than exclusivism and inclusivism. In the final analysis, universalism offers a restoration of all things (Gk. *apocatastasis pantós*) of God's creation and especially humans. Finally, restoration includes elevated humans in the image of the God-man, Jesus Christ, minus his divine noncommunicable attributes. Universalism facilitates an all inclusive and universal proleptic spiritual transformation (PrōST).

---

329. Lewis, *Mere Christianity*, 176.
330. Mahoney and Pargament, "Sacred Changes," 481.
331. Moltmann, *God in Creation*, 219.
332. Pannenberg, *Systematic Theology*, 2:225.

4

Devices in the Unveiling

PREFATORY

WE CONSIDERED APPLICABLE SOTERIOLOGICAL constructs in the prior chapter by a gloss in support of the focus of proleptic spiritual transformation (PrōST). A short review of those ideas is in order here. God's salvation is greater than human limitations and the hermeneutics of exclusivity in Christian tradition. The prior chapter briefly examined that, while hoped for, universalism is not essential for the present study. Christian universalism was presented as the best and most inclusive salvific argument for a fuller population of those eligible for PrōST. I hope for universalism, as expressed in this book. But we must remember, such universalism is found only in the particularism of Christ as the exclusive and necessary way of salvation provided by God. The realization of such a hope presents all people with the dignity and deference of the destined magnificence of God's choosing. Since all humans are created in God's image and destined for eventual reconciliation (Gk. *apocatastasis pantós*) to God, and if Christian Universalism is true, then all will be included in spiritual transformation as per God's intent.

In the prior chapter, I proposed the fulfillment of human destiny as *imago Dei* finding its fulfillment as modeled in Jesus Christ as *imago Christi*. Pannenberg[1] rightly argues that such a destiny plays both on the present and the future eschatological life. Agreeing with Paul (1 Cor 15:49), Pannenberg[2]

---

1. Pannenberg, *Systematic Theology*, 2:222–23.
2. Ibid., 163.

further says that Christ, as the new human, is the completion of creation. Since God is ecumenical, merciful, and generous he does not refuse this glorious reality to anyone. This potential for transformation is intrinsic to humans and proper to a relationship with God as fully recovered, experienced, and exalted by Christ's incarnation, accomplishments, and triumph. According to Pannenberg,[3] the reality of God's transformative work, universal restoration (Gk. *apocatastasis pantós*), discussed earlier, shall not be frustrated or interrupted as is testified by human constitutional openness. Further, in view of the finite, Pannenberg continues, the infinite is beheld by us, in which the finite is transcended in the light of the infinite.

In the present chapter, we move to important beginning considerations as to how PrōST can be entered and enjoyed. While these considerations are not exhaustive, they are touch points from which a practical understanding might begin in focusing us towards some practical considerations regarding PrōST. The objectives and intents of this book, as stated in chapter 1, shall be advanced in the present chapter by looking at how God reveals or unveils his heart, truth, and intents toward creation and humanity in particular in the plan of spiritual recovery (PrōST).

We review here God's communication with creation and especially human beings. We briefly, further examine the mystery of human suffering under the view of an all-beneficent God. We also evaluate here how sentient beings proceed through story, allegory, and parable in a relationship toward spirituality requiring God's grace[4] with an unknowable God in light of God's often-enigmatic communication. Finally, we discuss the ends or teleological intent or destination in leading from PrōST.

REVELATION

With Milbank[5] I hold that revelation is the intersection of human and divine interaction. Also in support, Pannenberg[6] more pointedly says, revelation in Christianity is definitive of the reality of God, which would be hidden without the revelation of God in Christ (John 1:14; 8:19; 12:45; 14:9). Although revelation might be well considered in its holistic sense in the interaction between humans and God, especially as revealed in Christ, without partition into categories, general and special revelation may prove unhelpful to the present study. Before consideration of revelation in hu-

3. Ibid., 229.
4. Dunn, "Justice of God," 1–2, 8.
5. Milbank, *Word Made Strange*, 130.
6. Pannenberg, *Systematic Theology*, 2:225.

mans as part of special revelation, general revelation in creation needs brief attention.

General Revelation

God is both revealed in general and accessible ways to all of his creation.[7] According to Scriptures, no one can be excused for not knowing that much of God's revelation (Ps 19:1–4; Rom 1:20). He is witnessed in nature and human hearts and consciences and is displayed in us (Gen 1:26–27; Acts 14:17; Rom 2:14–16). In the book of Romans, the Apostle Paul points to nature as a revealer of God's heart. The apostle stood in the Areopagus of Athens and spoke of such a reality to the philosophers present. In fact, to demonstrate that the reality of God is clear to all without respect to special revelation or religion, Paul quoted from contemporary writers that the philosophers of the day would have recognized. He recited from a hymn to Zeus by Epimenides of Crete (c. 600 BCE) and the poem *Phainomena* by the Stoic poet Aratus (c. 315–240 BCE), "'In him we live and move and have our being'; as even some of your own poets have said, 'For we are indeed his offspring'" (Acts 17:28). Further, Paul suggests that God uses history and times to drive human seeking for God (Acts, 17:26–27). Paul, here, is affirming the oneness of humanity against the supposed elite, Athenian philosophies of his day that are not adequate from which to come to know God.[8] With all of the allusions to Greek poets, Paul is "simply [presenting] the Galilean Gospel" in which God has decided when and where someone should live to best "seek him and find him."[9] God has not abandoned human beings to stumble along seeking God "in a *kosmos* without coherent pattern or purpose"; he orders life for humanity for his purposes.[10] This should not surprise the readers of this passage, but it seems amazing, moreover, and perhaps unacceptable to most Christians that union with God and deification are spoken in some form by all religious expressions[11] and as perceptible in creation. God is forever and everywhere present to his creation, and when awareness of God is keen, revelation is the result.[12] Calvin[13] makes it clear, however, that although God has manifested himself by such mercies, they shall not "lead us

---

7. Grudem, *Systematic Theology*, 121–24, 1243, 1255.
8. Longenecker, "Acts," 476–77; Wall, "Acts of the Apostles," 247.
9. Longenecker, "Acts," 476.
10. Wall, "Acts of the Apostles," 274.
11. Kärkkäinen, *One with God*, 2.
12. Hick, "Pluralist View," 34.
13. Calvin, *Institutes*, I.V.9, 14.

into the right path." The divine invisible, through creation, still requires that we receive an inner revelation or illumination from God by contemplating his works that we may be restored by God's goodness.

However, whatever benefit naturalism (versus theistic realism) may have to understanding the workings of nature at some level, it does not, and this study does not, support naturalism as a sufficient means to truth and knowledge as required to an adequate understanding and high assessment of humans in light of God's intent and work.[14] Specific revelation is required. Einstein[15] said that he could see a pattern or a clock but not the maker of the pattern nor the clock maker. His point, he said, was that the human mind cannot conceive of four dimensions, and therefore cannot conceive of God for whom a thousand years and a thousand dimensions are one. Here Einstein speaks of a logical consequence or conclusion of an inference (L. *sequitur*). That is, the mind cannot conceive (L. *non sequitur*) of the maker of what it first does not have the ability to conceive. Or one cannot understand the most complicated and mysterious universal if one cannot first grasp the making.

Used here as an expansion on this thought, Milbank[16] speaks about God's revelation in the order of the creation, but that there is no awareness of this reality if God does not go before us in the "objective spirit" that is the human culture. Here, Milbank says, is where God confronts us. In light of humans being made in the image of God, there does seem to be a measure of discernment retained within each of us. Interacting with Brunner and Barth, McGrath[17] proposes that there must be an innate concept of God as a "point of contact" in order for us to relate or appropriate any revelation of God. Such preconceptions may then be supplanted for the real of the revelation. Building on this, Erickson[18] boldly notes that even without special revelation, there is some possibility of gaining true knowledge and understanding of God through natural means and natural theology, whether one recognizes the reality of God or his handy work. Harrison[19] finds a further insight in that the interaction with, and in, the physical universe is what manifests the image of God in persons. Moreover, the image of God is not

---

14. Milbank, *Theology and Social Theory*, 328; Moreland, *Kingdom Triangle*, 41, 59, 193.
15. Einstein, *Expanded Quotable Einstein*, 208.
16. Milbank, *Word Made Strange*, 130.
17. McGrath, *Luther's Theology of the Cross*, 163.
18. Erickson, *Christian Theology*, 462.
19. Harrison, "God's Many-Splendored Image," 159.

a passive attribute that is without a foil against which it might be expressed and developed.

As gifted as we have been created to be, many with brilliant intellects and vast abilities of perception, others with amazing skill and talent, it is not possible for the greatest genius to fathom all of the depths of the universe, its foundations, workings, and teleologies. It is necessary that God give special revelation to humans to overcome our limitations to knowledge and experience. Whether those limitations were inherent or the fault of the fall, it is a reality that must be addressed (Rom 6:6; Gal 5:24; Eph 4:22).[20]

Special Revelation

Whatever may be known of specifics and specifically of what God might desire of his creatures, is a matter of God's self-revelation and not any of human investigative-discovery of God's desire.[21] God reveals himself in special ways and means to particular individuals, using holy writ, literature, visions, dreams, preaching, and even earthly creatures of nature for more specific telling of God's self, attributes and intents (Num 12:6; 22:27–30; Joel 2:28; John 5:17, 19; Luke 19:40; 2 Tim 3:16; Heb 1:1). Orthodoxy is sometimes accused of taking Scripture out of context in freely spiritualizing its meanings.[22] Admittedly, spiritualizing Scripture is a precarious act, and yet special revelation often opens the deeper spiritual meanings within God's word. Kärkkäinen[23] further characterizes Orthodox theology as a "lived theology rather than analytical speculation" bringing special revelation into the finite world of practice or doing (L. *praxy*). That may be the experience of the Orthodox Church, but it is a need for all desirous of spiritual transformation in communion with God no matter their church affiliation.

The Scriptures reveal that it is God who made humans with the potential for communication (Gen 1:28a; 2:16a; 18a; 3:8–10). Not only so, but God provides all human capability and defers to no one (Exod 4:11 and Luke 1:20, 64). Human capacity is given and withheld by the self-existent, eternal God of creation. Psalm 8 speaks of the importance of humans to God in how he has created them. We have been uniquely created in such a way that they can directly commune with God (Gen 3:8–10). Then, no

---

20. Ibid., 86–87; Schneiders, "Christian Spirituality," 5.
21. Erickson, *Christian Theology*, 286–87.
22. Kärkkäinen, *One with God*, 19.
23. Ibid., 19.

matter our capacity or capability, it is God that must still bring the revelation (Matt 16:17; Rom 16:26; 1 Tim 3:16; 1 Pet 1:12).[24]

God is progressively revealed in Scripture and especially in Jesus the Christ as warranted by human intellectual ability.[25] To dig out the essential revelation, one must, moved by God, gently sift off the accumulated textualization or un-peel and deconstruct the text from its many layers and out from boxes within boxes.[26] This "event" revealed in the un-peeling is already present within the work needing to be un-peeled or deconstructed.[27] Of critical importance, science continues to look for demonstrable, objective reasons and repeatable designed experimentation for subjective religious experiences often, *a priori*, nullifying any divine or supernatural variables or involvement. In fact, the National Academy of Sciences says, "Science is a way of knowing about the natural world. It is limited to explaining the natural world through natural causes. Science can say nothing about the supernatural. Whether God exists or not is a question about which science is neutral."[28]

As mentioned above in the introduction, in this work "deconstruction is treated as an hermeneutic of the *kingdom* of God" as an approach to interpretation that assists in seeing the prophetic spirit of the unpredictable and sometimes dissonant outsider—Jesus—who took a stand with the marginalized, disenfranchised, and downtrodden.[29] Within this work, it is the underlying method buoying much of the contentions in these pages such as prolepsis, *post-mortem* transformation, *imago Dei* status, and the possibility of universalism though not always directly referenced. Presently, we will look at near death experience (NDE).

Newberg and D'Aquili[30] propose two classes of neuropsychological mechanisms or "operators" which are simply housed in the human brain as "nerve tissues" with functionality in the brain that is thought to address and explain how religious experiences have developed in the brain. These mechanisms allow a brain to (1) perceive causally and (2) to perceive wholeness within diversity and thereby to fulfill transcendently total human needs

---

24. Erickson, *Christian Theology*, 286–87; McGrath, *Luther's Theology*, 163; Milbank, *Word Made Strange*, 130.
25. Lioy, *Evolutionary Creation*, 55.
26. Caputo, *Deconstruction in a Nutshell*, 88.
27. Derrida, "Structure, Sign, and Play," 223.
28. National Academy of Sciences, *Teaching about Evolution*, 58.
29. Caputo, *What Would Jesus Deconstruct?*, 26.
30. Newberg and D'Aquili, "Wired for the Ultimate Reality."

in whole states of human experience. Newberg and D'Aquili[31] further argue that the mildest anesthetics to the most profound states may simply "have their basis [sic] in neuroanatomy, neurophysiology, and the flux of neurotransmitters." However, Newberg and D'Aquili[32] leave room for the need of a way or process to go beyond the perception of the materialistic reality, as the human brain perceives it.

Chris Carter[33] has done recent work into NDE. He has researched scientific developments and has found empirical support for NDE. Additionally to NDEs other psychical phenomena have also been found to corroborate the mind's survival independent of the human brain and body, despite the resistance of materialists and areas of the scientific community. Siding with Wilder Penfield, John Eccles, and Gary Edwards, prominent neurosurgeon, neuroscientist, and neurologist respectively, Carter[34] claims that two elements of brain and mind is more demonstrable than one, in which the brain controls and manifests the mind. Moreover, a dualist understanding of mind-brain reality corresponds better with the best understanding of quantum mechanics according to Carter's[35] investigations. These observations argue for the mind's existence apart from and independent of a need for a physical brain to create or animate it. This phenomenon argues for something beyond naturalism and classic physics. According to Carter,[36] such outdated science is inadequate to the task when dealing with mind-brain connection and thereby, as held by this work, also inadequate when dealing with revelation to humans from God's mind.

Quantum mechanics suggests the possibility for experience, understanding, and revelation that are not simply linear chemical or mechanical reactions deterministically created in and by the brain as in classical physics. Although Ludwig[37] argues against Stapp[38] that the two positions of quantum and classical physics both can be used to sufficiently answer the mind/body problem. Quantum mechanics moves past materialistic reductionism, inclusive of God not being chemical or mechanical; and therefore, neither God's mind or communicated thought can be considered on materialistic,

---

31. Ibid., 198.
32. Ibid., 200.
33. Carter, *Science and the Near-Death Experience*, 238.
34. Ibid., 27–28, 30.
35. Ibid., 60–64, 77.
36. Ibid., 60.
37. Ludwig, "Why the Difference."
38. Stapp, "Why Classical Mechanics."

reductionist bases. According to Greyson,[39] such reality as the mind as separate and above the brain can be inferred by "enhanced mentation and memory during cerebral impairment [and] accurate perceptions from a perspective outside the body" not relatable to expected brain functions which have ceased. This "terminal lucidity," which often includes an increased cognitive capability, memory, and speed, has been widely documented.[40] The mind/body problem is better answered by postclassical physics, that is, quantum mechanics.[41] Contrary to any form of mysterianism, old or new, according to quantum mechanics the mind seems to be something other than brain chemistry and activity. Thereby special revelation, while perhaps using electrons to communicate or "tunnel across synaptic gaps,"[42] is something more or beyond special brain chemistry or processes as mind.

Minimally, the science of all of this suggests that humans have been created sufficiently capable of receiving supra-materialistic revelation and communication directly from God (Matt 16:17). In a real sense, all revelation is singular and superlative in that God actively accommodates himself to the needs, capacities, and milieu in which he desires to communicate.[43] The Apostle John speaks about God's action as the Word expressed in Jesus Christ making all of creation (John 1:1–3). This is special revelation of God of himself in historical action. Cullmann[44] points to the Word, Logos, which is Christ as God's revelation in action. This Word of God is fullness of creative action in the history of human kind, and is God's manifest love. The incarnation is God's highest form of self-revelation.[45]

Whether God utilizes the brain and/or mind is less important than that he communicates both general revelation through what all sentient beings can experience and special revelation to us who have been selected for whatever reason. This is inclusive of those who have positioned themselves by God's operative grace, to receive such revelation. The aseity of God does not create any dependence whereby God would be required to reveal anything of himself, and yet God deigns to communicate in a relatable manner of special means something of himself to his creatures—special revelation.

---

39. Greyson, "Implications of Near-Death Experiences," 37.
40. Ibid., 38, 40, 41.
41. Ibid., 43.
42. Carter, *Science and the Near-Death Experience*, 64.
43. Gamble, "Calvin as Theologian and Exegete," 182.
44. Cullmann, *Christ and Time*, 24–25.
45. Geivett and Phillips, "Response to John Hick," 76.

This communication has been recorded as visions, theophanies, and dreams, both through angels and prophecy and especially self-revelation in Christ.[46]

The rich and often obscure character of Scripture leaves large space for conflating or conflicting interpretations most noted in the various church councils, denominations, anathemas, excommunications, various theologies from Calvinism to Arminianism to Lutheranism to Orthodoxy, eschatologies, and cults. Since all Scripture is *theopneustos* (breathed out by God [2 Tim 3:16]) and of God's being, God's revelation is needed to see, understand, and experience something of himself. God reveals himself in special ways and means to particular individuals, using Scripture, literature, speaking, preaching, and even earthly creatures' natures (Num 22:27–30; Luke 19:40; John 5:17, 19; 2 Tim 3:16; 2 Pet 1:20–21; Heb 1:1) for more specific telling of God's self, attributes and intents.

DISCIPLINE

A discipline is a natural activity within human power, which facilitates, to a point, what we, at present, cannot do by direct unaided effort.[47] Although not abandoned in this process, it seems that our developed participation in *imago Dei* must progress and mature by free and focused effort empowered by grace. This participation brings about, in our will, what is essential to human nature—becoming what we already are—in the vital relationship with God driven from within human origins.[48] While a great focus is brought to bear on the supremacy of God's will,[49] in balance Lossky[50] speaks of a single will for creation and two for deification. That is, God's will alone was required for creation, but both divine and human will are required for spiritual transformation (deification). More to the point of human will, Willard[51] argues that humans are not to be passive but to "learn and accept the responsibility" through spiritual disciplines in cooperation with God for transformation to live within the freedom of God's kingdom. Although disciplines are not the sole means for spiritual transformation, the goal of disciplines is transformation of the human being in progressive movement. Marcus Borg[52] rightly cites paying attention to the relationship with God

---

46. Ibid.
47. Willard, "Spiritual Disciplines," 106.
48. Pannenberg, *Systematic Theology*, 2:223, 228–29.
49. Wilkins, *Following the Master*, 135.
50. Lossky, *Orthodox Theology*, 73.
51. Willard, "Spiritual Disciplines," 106.
52. Borg, "Religious Pluralism."

as the simple and essential process or discipline in spiritual transformation from God. However, most disciples are better served by a more structured approach. Human will is required in cooperation with God's will. Along with such influences as environment, circumstances, nature, and nurture the process is most often facilitated through spiritual disciplines.

Evangelism Not Discipleship

However there has developed, it seems to me, a proclivity toward superficial Gospel presentations and against all things spiritual that seem blinded to the very words of Jesus Christ to "make *disciples* of all nations" (Matt 28:18–20, emphasis added). It appears to me, that most Christians use this passage singularly as a main proof text to drive them into the noble effort of evangelization and missions. However, the main emphasis here is the single transitive verb μαθητεύσατε translated "make disciples."[53] Yet, it seems that discipleship and disciplines that change the souls of individuals and the consequent spiritual transformation are endemically missing among most Christian communities and individuals. Focusing on conversion at the expense of discipleship shall only lead to "diverse legalisms and vacuous 'spiritualities.'"[54] There is a vital need among us to heed the call and behold the face of the one who leads into a Christ-like transformation and response (2 Cor 3:18).[55]

As statistics show below, where excluding people is not the focus, large swaths of Christendom merely pursue salvation from hell for as many people as possible. By this myopic focus on saving from hell, most individual Christians seem to be regrettably complacent about any focus on discipleship, sanctification, and spiritual transformation. And yet, one representative example shows that this effort toward "saving souls" is wanting. While 80 percent of believers say they believe they are responsible to the Gospel, only 39 percent of US churchgoers actually share the Gospel. In fact it is the lowest of biblical markers of maturing Christians, according to Wilke.[56] His survey shows that most new disciples find it natural to share their faith. However, the study continues, that those who have been Christians longer are more intentional in their sharing. Three-quarters (3/4) feel comfortable that they are able to share the Gospel, and 12 percent do not feel comfortable with this task at all. Over a six month period, only 25 percent of that

---

53. Carson, "Matthew," in *Matthew, Mark, Luke*, 595.
54. Willard, "Spiritual Formation."
55. Wilkins, *Following the Master*, 107.
56. Wilke, "Churchgoers Believe."

group has actually shared the Gospel once or twice while 14 percent have talked to someone about the Gospel three or more times. Additionally, almost half (48 percent) of churchgoers said they have not invited anyone to a church meeting. While 33 percent said they have made the invitation once or twice, and 19 percent claimed three or more invitations over the last six-month period. So then, not only is discipleship sidelined, but also the focus on evangelism seems desultory and ineffectual at best.

Proceeding toward God

When not fully distracted and instead desiring to gain what was lost, people are too often at a loss as to how to proceed in order to gain or recover a right relationship with God. It says nothing of what more is offered in the reality of the God-man's (Jesus Christ) accomplishments and provisions. Rarely is a Christian disciple seen who is engaged in, aware, or has any hope of transformation any time before heaven's advent. According to Willard,[57] the act of salvation is nothing more than a matter of justification and sadly not of spiritual transformation. While this may be true for many believers, it is not for others, especially some Wesleyan, holiness, and confessional Lutheran groups. Not withstanding exceptions, most at least are not even aware of the need and privilege (John 5:39; Eph 4:13; 2 Pet 1:4; 1 John 3:2). The world is filled with a confounding and confusing array of means and methods to a promised-spirituality often superficial and poorly defined. A dire problem remains as to how one discerns these means and methods to what achingly calls from within the pit of humanity's yearning soul. The calling need is restoration into a full expression and enjoyment of the same image of God and transformed more richly into the fullness of the God-man, Jesus the Christ.

Without focusing on any distinct faith group, and without distinction or normalizing for particular religious groups or denominations, one study[58] carried out a random sample in the United States shows that spiritual disciplines are rarely practiced. While 78 percent of self-identifying Christians say spirituality is very important, only 18 percent claim to be committed to investing the appropriate time to any effort. The same survey found that less than 10 percent have specifically practiced spiritual disciplines such as prayer, meditation, silence, service, sacrifice, or solitude.

Moreover, the US Bureau of Labor Statistics, American Time Use Survey Summary[59] shows that Americans, in particular, are manifestly busy and

---

57. Willard, "Spiritual Formation."
58. Barna, "Self-Described Christians."
59. US Bureau of Labor Statistics, American Time Use Survey Summary.

distracted people with such things as work, children, eldercare, households, and leisure activities. According to an accompanying survey,[60] lamentably, Americans claim they do not have enough time to balance the various areas of their lives.

By this lack of focus or follow-through, one can generally conclude that most self-identifying Christian Americans, outside of particular pockets of spiritual excellence, and perhaps the broader Christian world by inference, have no conscious plan for spiritual growth and do not seem interested in matters of faith. This most often leaves such individuals to today's *Zeitgeist* (John 12:31; 2 Cor 4:4) through the demagoguery of the loudest voices, focus marketing, and the strongest lobbies to persuade and secure their devotions. Such a lack leaves them helpless "against the rulers, against the authorities, against the cosmic powers over this present darkness, against the spiritual forces of evil in the heavenly places" (Eph 6:12).

Rigor through Christ

It is noteworthy that the Orthodox lead the church in proposing and even believing in a form of divinization, deification, or *theōsis* as is variously referred to, it, and most others, are wary of saying as much about practical approaches to such lofty theology.[61] This general reluctance is mirrored in the lack of rigor among disciples desirous of life change. That is, this evangelistic effort, to even begin, requires some number of Christians that can reach beyond the self-satisfaction of our own salvation. We must jettison the hindering belief that only a few shall be effectually reached thoroughly rejecting non-confessing salvation before death as fatally troublesome.[62] In this, there must be sufficient concern nurtured for the kind of Christ-reflective life that might develop in those saved souls. Moreover, these Christians must be helped to an idea and thirst for the means to spiritual transformation.

Traditional means in salvation and transformation must enter from outside of human systems.[63] Prayer, as one discipline, is, at its foundation, about communion, encounter, and conversation between God and his creatures in mutual desire. Change and transformation, by this encounter, is available in the now. It is a reality based in the present structure of reality.[64]

---

60. Ibid.
61. Finlan and Vladimir, *Theosis*, 8; Gross, *Divinization of the Christian*, xii.
62. Nash, "Is Belief in Jesus Necessary?," 1–2.
63. Willard, "Spiritual Disciplines," 105–6.
64. Hick, "Pluralist View," 43.

As doctrinally understood, Jesus lived as a man of flesh and blood with all the vagaries that beset human beings, minus the actual committing of sin (Heb 2:17; 4:15; 7:26). Here is a key to present transformation for his disciples. The incarnation, passion, and resurrection are literally of eternal importance. However, to marginalize, minimize, even to forget the life of the man Jesus Christ is to miss seeing the human being in action as God intended such a life to be lived. It is in the daily living that spiritual transformation organically rises in the soil of life's troubles, challenges, tests, and temptations. The New Testament records that Jesus developed and grew, became weary and thirsty, was sorrowful and anguished, struggled with God's will, and was tempted in every way as all humans (Heb 4:15).[65] In this same section, Kärkkäinen presents his own translation of Ephesians 1 in that by Christ's passing through all of these stages of life, he was restoring all of human experience to communion with God: "that he might kill sin, deprive death of its power, and vivify man; and therefore his works are true."[66]

Gracious Disciplines

Disciplines, although not the goal, are necessary means, but not the cause to spiritual transformation in the now. We are dependent upon the work of the Holy Spirit for intentioned, spontaneous spiritual growth.[67] The Holy Spirit's work is foundational to drawing us into this primordial fellowship first recorded in Eden. A discipline is only good or beneficial when it serves to unite, receive, and accept divine grace.[68] This divine grace brings measures of *theōsis* in the present—PrōST. As discussed above, two wills are involved. According to Stavropoulos,[69] the early fathers and Eastern Orthodox tradition, spoke about such grace and cooperative works, concurrently and respectively delivered from God and humans.

One must be cautioned against any form of Pelagianism and self-sufficiency apart from God. However, human will is not dead but unhealthy and fully dependent upon God's grace. Working through the contentious debates embroiling Augustine, Pelagius, and their historical surrogates, this study stands with the Orthodox theology on this issue. Ware[70] speaking for the Orthodox Church and my position taken in this book, says that human

65. Kärkkäinen, "Human Prototype," 30.
66. Ibid.
67. Wilkins, *Following the Master*, 135.
68. Stavropoulos, *Partakers of the Divine Nature*, 33–34.
69. Ibid., 34, 37.
70. Ware, *Orthodox Church*, 221–22, 224.

free will, in *imago Dei*, in cooperation with God, is sufficiently intact and that culpability can fairly follow (Rev 3:20). As Lossky[71] rightly states, it is a matter of "simultaneity in the synergy of divine grace and human freedom." Good works, however, driven by an agent, independent from God's grace, is of no benefit to any real spiritual transformation or PrōST. We are not, in ourselves, sufficient to work out our own salvation (Phil 2:12).

According to Mahoney and Pargament[72] quantum change or radical transformation is preceded one third of the time by prayer and is the most common activity or discipline before a sudden spiritual change. In table 1 below, I list prayer as the primary discipline toward transformation. Jenson[73] rightly points to prayer, in its simplest definition, as nothing less than dialogue and communion with God. It is direct conversation with the causeless cause and creator of all, who enters time-space to an intimate arrangement with his "praying animal." Another example of disciplines is Scripture reading, rightly directed through Christ, which is, as Origen claimed, nothing less than the divine *logos* embodied drawing all persons to himself (Jesus) in a spiritual journey to the highest goal of love of God (John 12:32).[74]

Foundational to this as indispensable, grace, is a requisite, without which movement toward God and kingdom living is not possible. As one strives to exercise spiritual disciplines, "means of grace" from God by his Spirit are essential, by which the spiritual life, outside of the disciple's power, is made possible. Grace is "an active agency in the psychological and biological reality of the disciple."[75] Willard goes on, in this same paper, to rightly note that grace is not in opposition to effort but that it is in opposition to earning. However, Willard[76] wrongly states that the disciple can, by his or her own efforts, "increase the amount of grace" that is in one's life. Grace, as with *imago Dei*, is not increased but enjoyed as the full grace already given. We may have other experiences of grace as in Paul's comments to the Corinthians: "Because I was sure of this, I wanted to come to you first, so that you might have a second experience of grace" (2 Cor 1:15).

Examining the book of Jude, the translation "May mercy, peace, and love be multiplied *to* you" (Jude 1:2, emphasis added), the Greek word *humin* may be rendered alternatively "with" or "by you." This would give a possible translation as, "May mercy, peace, and love be yours in abundance!"

71. Lossky, *Orthodox Theology*, 199.
72. Mahoney and Pargament, "Sacred Changes," 490.
73. Jenson, "Praying Animal," 319.
74. Decock, *Origen of Alexandria*, 3–4.
75. Willard, "Spiritual Formation."
76. Ibid.

(NIV). This rendering implies that these attributes increase in enjoyment and experience in the disciple. In either case, and to limit the risk of becoming mired in a full exegesis of this issue, the preponderance of biblical testimony is that the mercy of God is not withheld or given in less than full measure (Jas 2:13).[77]

Although this presses against the edges of semi-Pelagian thought, God, as the initiator of faith, has given the objective conditions and means to attain the marvelous goal of spiritual transformation in union with God. Lossky[78] rightly says, God's creatures must avail themselves to the subjective conditions to synergistically work with God to accomplish such marvelous realities as union with God. This, however, cannot be accomplished without God's grace.

So then, it is by special revelation that God facilitates spiritual transformation. God reveals or unveils something of himself in communion with his creation—humans—and by this communion or speaking brings to being something transformed in the communicant. The intimacy of being in God's presence is the foundational catalyst to change; prayer simply ushers into presence the praying one, where intimacy in beholding God brings about the transformation from one degree of glory to the next (2 Cor 3:18). Automatically, our praying, in intimacy with God and beholding this superlative One, will usher us into spontaneous and responsive worship.[79] Beholding God is reflected in worship, and worship draws us into a deep, loving relationship that desires to please the One who holds us.[80]

Activation

Gregory of Nyssa[81] claims that prayer's effect is union with God. He says that through prayer temperament is controlled against vanity, envy, sin, and with it intimacy with God is gained. Prayer, Gregory argues, defeats injustice, finds wellbeing, gives courage, and brings refreshing. If prayer were nothing more than an exercise in words of, perhaps, psychological import with no metaphysical result, then no one in critical need would invest in

---

77. Burridge, "Jesus and the Origins," 19, 21; Harrison, "God's Many-Splendored Image," 86–87; Milligan, *Elijah*, 36.

78. Lossky, *Mystical Theology*, 196.

79. Richardson, "God's Search for Man," 10.

80. Mann, "Every Now and Then," 41–48; Harrison, "God's Many-Splendored Image," 20–21; Tyson, *Invitation to Christian Spirituality*, 132–33.

81. Gregory, *Lord's Prayer, the Beatitudes*, 24.

such an empty effort or venture.[82] As noted above, prayer is not primarily about positive responses to petitions and intercessions. More importantly, foundationally prayer is about communion, encounter, and conversation between God and his creatures in mutual desire and satisfaction. As we become more intimate with God, a desire to spend more time in God's specific presence grows. Although one may live a disjointed life that does not cohere, in prayer is found all that we are and have done.[83] We cannot lead a life of dissimilitude and falsehood in genuine prayer. All is brought into the encounter and eventually exposed and transformed:

> Search me, O God, and know my heart!
> Try me and know my thoughts!
> And see if there be any grievous way in me,
> and lead me in the way everlasting!
> (Ps 139:23-24).

Old Testament discipleship was a communal matter, perhaps to avoid individual forms, unique to individuals following masters, leaders, and teachers, from disrupting a relationship with God.[84] Especially today many disciples follow celebrated preachers, charismatic leaders, and other admired persons perhaps missing God in the distraction. Whether corporate disciplines or ones guided by a pastor or spiritual director, the call is to a vital, intimate relationship with God based in grace.[85]

This grace issues in divine likeness as human destiny, and each of us is inclined toward this destiny in fellowship with God.[86] Inclination must find its fulfillment in this destiny through development by some form of "activation."[87] Pannenberg continues, that it is not development of the inclination but activation of the inclination already inherent. More clearly, it seems that we are inclined to or destined to intimate fellowship with God. The divine breath, in each of us, draws its vitality from God's life in experiential enjoyment. Disciplines are nothing more than facilitations of this reality, a positioning for "activation."

Being in Christ and Christ being in someone is clear, real relationship (John 10:34-35; 14:20; 17:20-26; Acts 17: 28-29). I am not proposing that one can acquire such a relationship by effort alone. Disciplines, fuelled by

---

82. Heschel, "Holy Dimension," 119.
83. Ibid.
84. Wilkins, *Following the Master*, 60.
85. Dunn, "Justice of God," 1-2, 8.
86. Pannenberg, *Systematic Theology*, 2:227.
87. Ibid., 228.

God's grace, only have place for improving an already existing relationship. It is a matter of, Lossky[88] claims, concurrent synergy of God's grace and human freedom. According to Brunner,[89] "The highest discipline is that of belonging to God." In this belonging is found a synergistic work with God and human freedom. As in any relationship, disciplines are helpful in forming an individual and therefore how that individual relates. The closeness of a person to God is not really improved without belonging to God. God, in fact, dwells with the disciple (Job 20:10; Acts 17:28). The reality of Christ's accomplishments is sought in all of this for us to be freed from what hinders enjoyment of that which is already completed through and by Christ's indwelling by the Spirit of God.

Even if all of the disciplines that one might find in the Scriptures were catalogued, it still would not exhaust the possible disciplines including opportunities creatively available to us. Though biblically supportable, or at least not disallowed, an extrabiblical list might include journaling, pauses (from occupation), and expectation (exercised attitude of hope). Therefore, the following list is not claimed as exhaustive neither all-inclusive. It is only a beginning point from which we can examine proleptic spiritual transformation (PrōST) and its means by vivisection. Although we can make an argument that each discipline includes and affects all categories, they are listed in primary columns for clarity and ease of analysis.

Table 1. Selected Spiritual Disciplines

	Biblical Disciplines	Common Disciplines	Minimal Required Disciplines	Proposed PrōST Disciplines	Example Support: Biblical/ Extra-Biblical*
Stillness/ Inaction				Love, Pure Selfless	Mark 12:30–33; 1 Cor 13; Gal 5:13; Eph 4:15; 1 John 3–4
		Meditation		Meditation	Josh 8:35; 2 Kgs 23:2; Neh 8:8, 18; 9:3; Ps 119:103; Matt 12:3, 5; 19:4; 21:42; Acts 8: 28, 32; 15:31; Eph 3:4; Col 4:16; 2 Tim 2:15; Rev 1:3

---

88. Lossky, *Orthodox Theology*, 199.
89. Brunner, *Man in Revolt*, 267.

Devices in the Unveiling 137

Biblical Disciplines	Common Disciplines	Minimal Required Disciplines	Proposed PrōST Disciplines	Example Support: Biblical/Extra-Biblical*
Silence			Silence	Matt 6:7; Job 29:2; Ps 3:2–3; 62:5; 131:3; Lam 3:26
Contemplation			Contemplation	Ps 119:103; Matt 6:7; 11:28
Prayer	Prayer	Prayer	Prayer	Ps 119:4–11; Ezek 7:10; Eccl 12:9; John 5:39; Acts 8:30; 2 Tim 2:15
Solitude				Exod 25:2; Deut 15:7–11; Matt 6:4; Rom 12:5; 2 Cor 8:12; 9:7
Perseverance				Rom 6:16, 17; 2 Cor 2:9; Titus 3:1; 1 Pet 1:14
Worship		Worship	Worship	Gen 2:5, 15; 3:23; Exod 20:9; 23:12; Ps 62:12; 104:23; Prov 16:3; 31:13; Eccl 3:22; Matt 5:16; Luke 13:14; Acts 18:3; Eph 2:10; 4:28
Secrecy				Rom 13:13; 1 Cor 6:9; Eph 5:5; Col 3:5; Phil 4:8; 1 Tim 5:22; 1 Pet 3:1–2
Simplicity				Matt 18:2–3; 2 Cor 1:12; 11:3; Rom 12:8
Submission				Mark 14:36; Eph 5:22; Jas 4:7; Heb 5:8; Heb 13:17
Chastity				Rom 13:13; 1 Cor 6:18–29; Col 3:5; 1 Thess 4:3, 7
Pauses			Pauses	Rev 8:1; Job 2:13; 6:24; Prov 29:11
Expectations			Expectations	Prov 23:18; Matt 24:44, 50; Acts 3:5; Phil 1:10

	Biblical Disciplines	Common Disciplines	Minimal Required Disciplines	Proposed PrōST Disciplines	Example Support: Biblical/ Extra-Biblical*
Action	Fasting	Fasting			Ps 77:12; 104:34; 143:5; Josh 18:8
	Sacrifice				Job 31:24–28; Matt 6:19–21; Acts 2:46; Rom 12:8; 2 Cor 1:12; Phil 4:12; Col 3:22; Heb 13:5
	Confession	Confession	Confession	Confession	Exod 14:14; Job 6:24; Ps 4:4; Zeph 1:7; Zech 2:13; Matt 26:63; Acts 15:12; 1 Cor 14:28, 30, 34; Rev 8:1
	Celebration			Celebration	Ps 143:10; Mark 8:34; Eph 5:21; Jas 4:7; 1 Pet 5:5
	Worship	Worship	Worship	Worship	Gen 2:5, 15; 3:23; Exod 20:9; 23:12; Ps 62:12; 104:23; Prov 16:3; 31:13; Eccl 3:22; Matt 5:16; Luke 13:14; Acts 18:3; Eph 2:10; 4:28
	Study				Ps 119:103; Eccl 1:13; 7:25; Acts 17:11; 2 Tim 2:15; 3:14–15
		Journaling			Isa 8:1; Hab 2:2; Rev 1:19
		Stewardship			Prov 16:3; 1 Cor 6:19–20; 1 Pet 4:10
		Simplicity			Matt 18:2–3; 2 Cor 1:12; 11:3; Rom 12:8
	Scripture Reading	Scripture Reading	Scripture Reading	Scripture Reading	Josh 1:8; Ps 119:103; John 8:31; 14:23–24; Rom 15:5; 2 Tim 3:16; Heb 4:12

Devices in the Unveiling 139

	Biblical Disciplines	Common Disciplines	Minimal Required Disciplines	Proposed PrōST Disciplines	Example Support: Biblical/Extra-Biblical*
	Giving	Giving			Prov 3:27; Mark 9:41; Acts 10:35; 1 Cor 8:14; 2 Cor 9:6–7; Titus 2:7–8
	Obedience				John 14:15; Acts 5:29; Phil 2:12; 1 Pet 1:14; 1 John 5:3
	Work	Work			Gen 1:28; 2:15; Eccl 9:10; Gal 6:4–5; Eph 2:10; 4:28; 6:7; Col 3:23; 1 Cor 15:10
Spirit			Love, Pure Selfless		Mark 12:30–33; 1 Cor 13; Gal 5:13; Eph 4:15; 1 John 3–4
	Meditation			Meditation	Josh 8:35; 2 Kgs 23:2; Neh 8:8, 18; 9:3; Ps 119:103; Matt 12:3, 5; 19:4; 21:42; Acts 8: 28, 32; 15:31; Eph 3:4; Col 4:16; 2 Tim 2:15; Rev 1:3
	Prayer	Prayer	Prayer	Prayer	Ps 119:4–11; Ezek 7:10; Eccl 12:9; John 5:39; Acts 8:30; 2 Tim 2:15
	Solitude			Solitude	Exod 25:2; Deut 15:7–11; Matt 6:4; Rom 12:5; 2 Cor 8:12; 9:7
	Confession		Confession	Confession	Exod 14:14; Job 6:24; Ps 4:4; Zeph 1:7; Zech 2:13; Matt 26:63; Acts 15:12; 1 Cor 14:28, 30, 34; Rev 8:1

	Biblical Disciplines	Common Disciplines	Minimal Required Disciplines	Proposed PrōST Disciplines	Example Support: Biblical/ Extra-Biblical*
	Worship			Worship	Gen 2:5, 15; 3:23; Exod 20:9; 23:12; Ps 62:12; 104:23; Prov 16:3; 31:13; Eccl 3:22; Matt 5:16; Luke 13:14; Acts 18:3; Eph 2:10; 4:28
	Scripture Reading			Scripture Reading	Josh 1:8; Ps 119:103; John 8:31; 14:23–24; Rom 15:5; 2 Tim 3:16; Heb 4:12
	Pauses			Pauses	Rev 8:1; Job 2:13; 6:24; Prov 29:11
	Expectations			Expectations	Prov 23:18; Matt 24:44, 50; Acts 3:5; Phil 1:10
Soul			Love, Pure Selfless		Mark 12:30–33; 1 Cor 13; Gal 5:13; Eph 4:15; 1 John 3–4
	Contemplation			Contemplation	Ps 119:103; Matt 6:7; 11:28
	Silence			Silence	Matt 6:7; Job 29:2; Ps 3:2–3; 62:5; 131:3; Lam 3:26
	Prayer	Prayer	Prayer	Prayer	Ps 119:4–11; Ezek 7:10; Eccl 12:9; John 5:39; Ac 8:30; 2 Tim 2:15
	Fasting				Ps 77:12; 104:34; 143:5; Josh 18:8
	Sacrifice				Job 31:24–28; Matt 6:19–21; Acts 2:46; Rom 12:8; 2 Cor 1:12; Phil 4:12; Col 3:22; Heb 13:5
	Solitude			Solitude	Exod 25:2; Deut 15:7–11; Matt 6:4; Rom 12:5; 2 Cor 8:12; 9:7

Devices in the Unveiling 141

Biblical Disciplines	Common Disciplines	Minimal Required Disciplines	Proposed PrōST Disciplines	Example Support: Biblical/ Extra-Biblical*
Confession	Confession	Confession	Confession	Prov 18:21; 28:13; Rom 10:9–11; 1 John 1:9; 4:2, 15
Celebration	Celebration		Celebration	Ps 143:10; Mark 8:34; Eph 5:21; Jas 4:7; 1 Pet 5:5
Perseverance				Rom 6:16, 17; 2 Cor 2:9; Titus 3:1; 1 Pet 1:14
Worship	Worship	Worship	Worship	Gen 2:5, 15; 3:23; Exod 20:9; 23:12; Ps 62:12; 104:23; Prov 16:3; 31:13; Eccl 3:22; Matt 5:16; Luke 13:14; Acts 18:3; Eph 2:10; 4:28
Secrecy				Rom 13:13; 1 Cor 6:9; Eph 5:5; Col 3:5; Phil 4:8; 1 Tim 5:22; 1 Pet 3:1–2
Study				Ps 119:103; Eccl 1:13; 7:25; Acts 17:11; 2 Tim 2:15; 3:14–15
Journaling				Isa 8:1; Hab 2:2; Rev 1:19
Stewardship				Prov 16:3; 1 Cor 6:19–20; 1 Pet 4:10
Simplicity				Matt 18:2–3; 2 Cor 1:12; 11:3; Rom 12:8
Scripture Reading	Scripture Reading		Scripture Reading	Josh 1:8; Ps 119:103; John 8:31; 14:23–24; Rom 15:5; 2 Tim 3:16; Heb 4:12
Scripture Memorization	Scripture Memorization			Josh 1:8; Ps 119:9, 11, 103, 105; John 8:31; 14:23–24; Rom 15:5; 2 Tim 3:16; Heb 4:12

	Biblical Disciplines	Common Disciplines	Minimal Required Disciplines	Proposed PrōST Disciplines	Example Support: Biblical/ Extra-Biblical*
	Giving	Giving		Giving	Prov 3:27; Mark 9:41; Acts 10:35; 1 Cor 8:14; 2 Cor 9:6–7; Titus 2:7–8
	Submission				Mark 14:36; Eph 5:22; Jas 4:7; Heb 5:8; Heb 13:17
	Obedience				John 14:15; Acts 5:29; Phil 2:12; 1 Pet 1:14; 1 John 5:3
	Work	Work			Gen 1:28; 2:15; Eccl 9:10; Gal 6:4–5; Eph 2:10; 4:28; 6:7; Col 3:23; 1 Cor 15:10
	Chastity				Rom 13:13; 1 Cor 6:18–29; Col 3:5; 1 Thess 4:3, 7
	Pauses			Pauses	Rev 8:1; Job 2:13; 6:24; Prov 29:11
	Expectations			Expectations	Prov 23:18; Matt 24:44, 50; Acts 3:5; Phil 1:10
Body			Love, Pure Selfless		Mark 12:30–33; 1 Cor 13; Gal 5:13; Eph 4:15; 1 John 3–4
	Silence			Silence	Matt 6:7; Job 29:2; Ps 3:2–3; 62:5; 131:3; Lam 3:26;
	Fasting	Fasting			Ps 77:12; 104:34; 143:5; Josh 18:8;
	Serving		Serving	Serving	Matt 25:26–27; Luke 16:2, 10–13; 1 Cor 3:8; 4:1–2; 9:17; Eph 3:2; Col 1:5; 1 Tim 1:4

Devices in the Unveiling 143

Biblical Disciplines	Common Disciplines	Minimal Required Disciplines	Proposed PröST Disciplines	Example Support: Biblical/ Extra-Biblical*
Sacrifice				Job 31:24–28; Matt 6:19–21; Acts 2:46; Rom 12:8; 2 Cor 1:12; Phil 4:12; Col 3:22; Heb 13:5
Solitude				Exod 25:2; Deut 15:7–11; Matt 6:4; Rom 12:5; 2 Cor 8:12; 9:7
Celebration	Celebration		Celebration	Ps 143:10; Mark 8:34; Eph 5:21; Jas 4:7; 1 Pet 5:5
Worship		Worship	Worship	Gen 2:5, 15; 3:23; Exod 20:9; 23:12; Ps 62:12; 104:23; Prov 16:3; 31:13; Eccl 3:22; Matt 5:16; Luke 13:14; Acts 18:3; Eph 2:10; 4:28
Secrecy				Rom 13:13; 1 Cor 6:9; Eph 5:5; Col 3:5; Phil 4:8; 1 Tim 5:22; 1 Pet 3:1–2
Study				Ps 119:103; Eccl 1:13; 7:25; Acts 17:11; 2 Tim 2:15; 3:14–15
Journaling				Isa 8:1; Hab 2:2; Rev 1:19;
Simplicity				Matt 18:2–3; 2 Cor 1:12; 11:3; Rom 12:8
Scripture Reading	Scripture Reading	Scripture Reading	Scripture Reading	Josh 1:8; Ps 119:103; John 8:31; 14:23–24; Rom 15:5; 2 Tim 3:16; Heb 4:12
Submission				Mark 14:36; Eph 5:22; Jas 4:7; Heb 5:8; Heb 13:17

	Biblical Disciplines	Common Disciplines	Minimal Required Disciplines	Proposed PrōST Disciplines	Example Support: Biblical/Extra-Biblical*
	Work	Work			Gen 1:28; 2:15; Eccl 9:10; Gal 6:4–5; Eph 2:10; 4:28; 6:7; Col 3:23; 1 Cor 15:10
	Chastity				Rom 13:13; 1 Cor 6:18–29; Col 3:5; 1 Thess 4:3, 7

* Augustine (NPNF1-06); Banks, 2001; Barton, 2004; Bonheoffer, 1995b; Bruce, 1988; De Caussade, 1982; Decock, 2011; Foster, 1992; Foster, 1998; McGinn, 2006; Guyon, 1975; Murray, 1984; Peterson, 2000; Peterson, 2007; Willard 1988; Willard, 1998; Whitney, 1991

We might sound caution that disciplines practiced over long periods of time without living engagement can fall into longstanding routine of little benefit.[90] Admittedly, most of us do not even practice such disciplines. As Sandra Schneiders[91] says, one cannot defend "religious life." Translating this life as the spiritual life, those who choose it are driven, compelled to it and they cannot be dissuaded. To accomplish the divine vocation I have spoken of in the pages of this book, disciplines cannot be ignored. This study claims it is this life that manifests as a result of the inclination rising up or being "activated" to meet its divine siren.

Proposed PrōST Disciplines

Since I propose that God is interested in every person's spiritual development and God-related intimacy with himself and other humans, the "PrōST disciplines" below (table 2), a short list of table 1, are proposed to be inclusive for all without regard for ability, giftedness, or specific faith tradition. They are meditation, silence, contemplation, prayer, worship, confession, celebration, Scripture reading, solitude, giving, serving, pauses, and expectation.

Table 2. Proposed PrōST Disciplines

Meditation	Scripture Reading
Silence	Solitude

90. Schneiders, "Religious Life."
91. Ibid.

Contemplation	Giving
Prayer	Serving
Worship	Pauses
Confession	Expectations
Celebration	

As is broadly cited, the greatest two commandments, according to Jesus, are to love God with full commitment, nothing being withheld and to love others as oneself (Mark 12:28b–31). The practice of the "PrōST Disciplines" shall position one "in-front" of God and open one's heart and spirit toward God and humanity. Beginning disciplines shall spontaneously, progressively develop one's ability and desire for a wider range of disciplines as God works in the individual through this selective set. Willard[92] states that such an exercise and enjoyed reality shall be manifest in many ways, chief among them is a spontaneous love for God and neighbor. A short, select survey may be in order, as to how discipling-practitioners use and develop new disciplines.

Friendship with God is found preeminently in prayer and such disciplines develop through fellowship with other persons.[93] Prayer is nothing less than fellowship issuing in love for God and others. Such activity produces fruit. Love, manifested in Jesus Christ, is his activity showing us how to live.[94] It is the beginning manifestation of kingdom life by setting our minds on heavenly eventualities in Christ where we are hidden (Col 3:1–4). It is a movement in that we open to the Spirit's work in Christ. Jesus works in and through the Spirit of God to affect this transformation. He does not leave us alone for such heavy work (John 14:16). The Spirit of God works into us sanctification, in part, by the trials of this present life. This comes about by spending intimate time with God in Christ ushered by the Spirit. The fruit of the Spirit exhibits in the now in such glorious things as "love, joy, peace, patience, kindness, goodness, faithfulness, gentleness, and self-control" (Gal 5:22–23). The value of one-sided discipline, though arguably possible and of benefit is not sufficient or adequate. Discipline requires the intimate involvement of the Holy Spirit of God enabling us to work out our salvation (Phil 2:12).[95]

For those looking for powerful transformed living, disciplines, as many involved in the field of psychology are discovering, such as solitude,

---

92. Willard, "Spiritual Formation."
93. Moltmann, *God in Creation*, 220–21, 223.
94. Shults, *Reforming Theological Anthropology*, 215–16.
95. Power, "Imago Dei," 140; Talbott, "Universalism."

silence, fasting, and Scripture memorization, are found in the new life of the Spirit of God.[96] As briefly addressed above, God is giving form and expression in the world to his intent in setting in motion his desire and showing its potency in relationship to us.[97] Pannenberg asserts that it is an inward motion, an inherent inclination to this movement and goal created for relationship and fellowship fulfilled in Christ. It is the "free activation" of such a movement and inclination that had its vital beginning in human creation and was saved and advanced in Christ's accomplishment. This book aligns here with Pannenberg[98] in that we are innately aware and eventually fully open to participation and actualization in becoming what God has already determined that we actually are as God's creation found in Christ.

If prayer is open communication in communion with God, then solitude might be considered the place were this encounter often occurs in focus. Schneiders[99] observes from a Catholic perspective that solitude is clearly at the center of the "religious life" because it is essentially the vow of "consecrated celibacy." This solitude ushers one into a place of immediacy with God and marginality regarding the cultural milieu.[100] Consecrated celibacy, herein, is expanded to mean a focused and dedicated abstinence from what distracts us from devotion to God and full love for God and our neighbors. This expression of celibacy is service to others and the creation, no matter the dictates and cautions of church and society. It is especially in response to the immediacy of our relationship with God, and it is directly applicable to spiritual development and can be owned by all of God's disciples.

The influences of Jan Rysbroeck (1293–1381), sometimes referred to as John Ruusbroec, can be seen in such as the Beguines of Flanders, Gerard Grote, and the devotees of Thomas à Kempis, and thereby have far reaching influence for those interested in closeness to God. Ruusbroec[101] sought to guide his listeners to an "interior coming of Christ." One was directed to go out and meet Christ in his coming as the five wise virgins in Matthew 25. First, we must depend upon the unity of God for being. Second, we must avail higher powers from which understanding and will rise and thereby the ability to perform spiritual disciplines. Third, the powers are found in the body from which bodily disciplines can only arise. The point at issue,

---

96. Willard, "Spiritual Disciplines," 101.
97. Pannenberg, *Systematic Theology*, 2:224–25, 227–29.
98. Ibid., 227–29.
99. Schneiders, "Religious Life."
100. Ibid.
101. Ruusbroec, *Spiritual Espousals*, 286–87.

whether one agrees with Ruusbroec's assessment or not, is that we are dependent on God for being, will, and ability to respond to God's availability. This is directly applicable in practicing disciplines to facilitate transformation in fellowship for proleptic spiritual transformation (PrōST).

THEODICY AND OTHER TRIALS

Although an exhaustive treatment of theodicy is outside the scope of our discussion, a couple of comments and considerations, regarding the traditional problem of evil, which may prove helpful, are in order to assist the developing thoughts. Evil and affliction have been unrelentingly troublesome for many trying to prove the existence of an omni-benevolent and omnipotent God, leading to the self-evident conundrum of goodness versus omnipotence.[102] As presented by Collins,[103] the concepts of good and the problem of evil—theodicy—clash in theological constructs. The traditional or soteriological problem of evil theorizes about the suffering of those, apparently innocent persons, especially children, and sees them as undeserving of pain and suffering often not consequent of sin.[104] Moreover, contrary to Collins'[105] claim, God desires and has obligated himself to rescue them. This rescue is in the cross of Christ. Christ's life, passion, and death respond to the problem of evil and God's often-thought silence on the bane. Christ nailed the problem of sin, its commandments, and every one's sins to the cross (Col 2:14; Eph 4:15; 1 Pet 2:24). So, although theodicy may be unresolved and debated, its ultimate solution is found in Christ's work.

One must distinguish between real (intrinsic) evil, that which is existentially "real" from what merely seems or is interim (instrumental) evil or as Barth say, "*das Nichtige*," or vain or void, defeated in Christ.[106] Although Hick argues that the effect of the event shall determine the judgment, Mesle[107] presses against one of Hick's antagonists, David Griffin,[108] in attempting to clarify the misunderstanding between Griffin and Hick that it (instrumental evil), too, is real but leading to good. Although various arguments can be

---

102. Vorster, *Created in the Image of God*, 25.
103. Collins, *God of Miracles*, 156–57.
104. Pannenberg, *Systematic Theology*, 2:165–66.
105. Collins, *God of Miracles*, 157.
106. Hick, *Evil and the God of Love*, 137–44, 291.
107. Mesle, "Problem of Genuine Evil," 418, 420.
108. Griffin, *God, Power and Evil*, 22.

made regarding evil, it still remains an unsolved concern as to why God did not create a world without evil.[109]

As proposed above, I do not hold to the "Leibniz Lapse" that God could have created any possible world he might have wished.[110] Contrary to a deterministic idea, "natural causal" or otherwise, humans have free will.[111] It is a truth held as foundational to these pages. We can, by our free-actions, unlike God, introduce evil, pain, and suffering. Also important to the issue of sin, pain, and life's vicissitudes is the demonstrable reality of a "malfunctioning of evolutionary systems and randomness."[112] If the first couple was created righteous and still chose an unrighteous rebellion, then God is made responsible, having created them thusly just as if God created them as foolish requiring the foolish choice.[113] Neither is God absolved, Shults continues, from the choice of God's perfect angel, Lucifer, falling. A world in which the "malfunctioning of evolutionary systems" is consequential even inevitable seems to be the reality of human life and does not necessitate intention or full culpability.

Admittedly, whatever its cause, it is first helpful for us to consider such evil, pain, and suffering or difficult situations as transformative opportunities for persons.[114] The solution is in the incarnation and cross of Christ, which open to a progressive relationship with God (1 Cor 1:18, 23, 30). It ushers in not only salvation, but also access to God and the benefits of transformation that organically and spontaneously presses forward from such intimacy. It is this, from a utilitarian view, which makes difficulty and affliction so valuable. Further, MacDonald[115] claims that the terror of God is "the other side of his love." MacDonald presses further that difficulties are God's love being exercised outside of a person dwelling with God. It is God removing things that frustrate our souls and the truth they must enter making it possible to dwell with God. In Hick's words, it is soul-making.[116] Vorster[117] argues that the pain and suffering so prevalent in this world are not directed soul-making but consequential to evolutionary processes corrupted by sin. Vorster continues *creatio continua* (continuous creation) pre-

---

109. Pannenberg, *Systematic Theology*, 2:165.
110. Plantinga, *God, Freedom, and Evil*, 44.
111. Brunner, *Man in Revolt*, 147.
112. Vorster, *Created in the Image of God*, 47.
113. Shults, *Reforming Theological Anthropology*, 210–11.
114. Lewis, *Mere Christianity*, 176; Wyman, "Rethinking," 212.
115. MacDonald, *Unspoken Sermons*, 122.
116. Hick, *Evil and the God of Love*, 333–36.
117. Vorster, *Created in the Image of God*, 47.

senting another option from God's intentionality in pain, suffering, and sin. Although the complete sin problem cannot be answered in this, I agree, it is the progressive movement upward to more complex systems that causes and exposes difficulties, even causing "sin, suffering, and chaos."[118]

Humans are justified by grace; suffering is, in no way, for appeasing God but to expresses God and displays God's unconquerable love.[119] By this, besides our own sinful and often-tragic devices, God-arranged situations may be determined to place persons in difficulty for transformational means. However, all should admit, along with Vorster's solution[120] that some difficulties, and outright tragedies, cannot easily be found in the heart of a loving God. Although considering the world's creation and Jesus' crucifixion, one cannot absolve God.[121] Nevertheless, Augustine[122] protests, no fault can be found in God regarding sin in creation, simply because God is creator. His judgments are as a "great deep"; God is unsearchable (Rom 11:33).[123] However, seeing no right to judge the creator of the universe, neither Israel nor primitive Christianity dared to accuse God of evil (Isa 45:9; Jer 18:6; Rom 9:20).[124] Contrary to usual Augustinian thought, we are capable of will and directed to workout transformational ends (Phil 1:6; 2:12).[125] This capability to workout our salvation must not be allowed frustration by churning on irreconcilable struggles and misery of this life that might wrongly even cause accusations that God is maleficent or at least neglectful.

Wyman,[126] in his reevaluation of Hick and Irenaeus, argues for spiritual transformation as a gradual process beginning in the now. He claims it is by our will and the power of the Spirit of God in this "appointed environment" inclusive of the unresolved sin problem. Hick rests in Irenaeus for his theodicy in that we are capable and well served by often-inexplicable difficulty, and he speaks of pain and the value of its emotional response, and that "sin is inevitable."[127] The best possible world does not necessitate a world *without* evil, sin, or hardship. Allowing for evil, sin, and hardship may be the best possible world in light of the purpose and intent of creation as

118. Ibid.
119. Bushnell, "Protestant Views," 350.
120. Vorster, *Created in the Image of God*, 47.
121. Pannenberg, *Systematic Theology*, 2:166.
122. Augustine, Tractate 53.
123. Ibid.
124. Pannenberg, *Systematic Theology*, 2:163.
125. Irenaeus, *Against Heresies*, 4.37.6–7; Willard, "Spiritual Disciplines," 106.
126. Wyman, "Rethinking the Christian Doctrine of Sin," 202, 210.
127. Hick, *Evil and the God of Love*, 59, 298; Wyman, "Rethinking," 212, 214.

set in evolutionary motion. If something better could be willed and chosen, then that will and choice would be better or best compared to the world in which God created humans and placed us. Such a will and actor would have bested the biblical God of creation. Clearly, that would be a contradiction of God, since God is *omnitudo realitatis* (sum-total of reality) and therefore chooses what is best.[128]

It seems clear that whatever the theodical argument, evil, sin, and hardship are good servants or catalysts to spiritual transformation (Rom 8:28; Eph 1:11; 1 Pet 3:9). Bringing hope to the conundrum, Lewis[129] proposes an eternal reality of suffering culminating and working backwards to make even agony into a glory. The human soul is of great worth, and if trouble were not of great value in its development, then allowing suffering and sin would be wrong.[130] Such an allowance would impinge upon God's best possible world and his benevolence. It would contradict his revealed heart. God would not be that being than which nothing greater can be conceived.[131] So then, in light of God's heart desire, this best of possible worlds must avail its structure, now inclusive of evil, sin, and hardship, as a perfect ground for spiritual transformation in the full revelation of *imago Dei* in humans.

Lewis,[132] in a fictional way, presses the point being made here, that God seems to leave his creatures alone to their own devices and will, to do what has often lost its taste and luster. In doing this, growing, being transformed into that which God intends for us, is accomplished. Prayer, or fellowship with God, during such moments of dryness, even apparent abandoned-ness, is most pleasing to God. Concluding, Lewis asserts, through his antagonist, Screwtape (a devil and tempter), that God wants his creatures to grow in maturity without holding "His hand."

To attempt the development of the human soul, inclusive of character, without allowing choice is impossible since choice is part of our soul and character.[133] Whatever the reason(s) and allowance(s) involved in suffering and even evil, what is demonstrable is the reality of God's help in the trouble.[134] Although the fourth adversary of Job, the interloper and loquacious Elihu (whoever he was is debated) beginning in Job 32, spoke for six chapters but did not address the issues any better than Eliphaz, Bildad, or

---

128. Kant, *Lectures on Philosophical Theology*, 137.
129. Lewis, *Great Divorce*, 67.
130. Willard, "God and the Problem of Evil."
131. Fairweather, *Scholastic Miscellany*, 75.
132. Lewis, *Screwtape Letters*, 39–40.
133. Willard, "God and the Problem of Evil."
134. Richardson, "God's Search for Man," 10.

Zophar (e.g., Job 32). Elihu was not right, but rather confusing in his assessment of Job's condition, prescription, and prognosis. The observation that we are instructed and ultimately delivered through affliction is applicable in this.[135] It is noteworthy that suffering is no respecter of persons. Though it may be correct to interject oneself into such a dialogue and consideration, as did Elihu, the final word of understanding cannot be found simply in the face of God's sovereignty.[136]

It seems, as stated by Abba Anthony, that without temptation one cannot enter in the kingdom of heaven or be saved.[137] There is the possibility of a perfecting and maturing that can only result from such temptation from a world in which the problem of sin arises. Although the above point does not address all of the complications and difficulties regarding theodicy or suffering and a benevolent God, it speaks to some measure of human suffering and its possible value as particularly applicable to this study. So much suffering is found in the temptations and potential faults and sins of humans when we fall to these temptations and bring upon ourselves the vagaries and entanglements of the ensuing results that cling to our lives (Heb 12:1). This suffering in, what often seems to be, inescapable sin has the potential to create a desperateness from which we throw ourselves on the mercy and grace of God and develop the habit of not leaving this place of comfort and sustenance.[138] This is within the place of spiritual transformation and, rightfully addressed, PrōST. In the finality, natural, evolutionary, or human efforts apparently against God's accomplishment leading to the full manifestation of his kingdom, cannot prevail (Rom 8:28; 1 Cor 1:9; 2 Cor 4:7–18; Eph 1:11).[139]

Passibility

Simoni[140] rightly points out that proposals regarding God that exclude experiences of evil and a strong passibility, cannot be coherently conjectured or allowed. If this is so, then it leaves the problem of how God might really know about and be compassionate in the face of evil without directly and intimately experiencing it. Scriptures testify to God as thoroughly compassionate for his suffering creatures; and therefore, a passibility (feelings of

---

135. Ibid., 13.
136. Newsome, "Book of Job."
137. Harrison, "God's Many-Splendored Image," 86.
138. Ibid., 86–87.
139. Eichrodt, *Theology of the Old Testament*, 107.
140. Simoni, "Divine Passibility," 329.

pain and pleasure) of God must be allowed. Although an argument for empathy and compassion can be made, the problem of simultaneously feeling the pain of the victim and the thrill of the sadist is unthinkable according to Simoni.[141] Therefore, a "radical particularity" of the variant feelings of individuals stands in the way of a strong passibilty, as well as an ability of God to both feel with the persons who are experiencing opposed emotions and conditions.[142] Notwithstanding, the Scriptures portray an omnipresent and omniscient God, who in fact, does feel, know, and empathize with the needy and abused as well as having full response to the errant feelings and actions of the stray and willfully, defiant malfeasant. It does not seem necessary, however, that God become radically passible and become mired in the filth of evil, death, and torture in knowing and feeling.

The tension between a strong passibility and a weak passibility need not be resolved here for our purposes. That is, the divine *paschein* (suffering) is involved in a strong passibility in which, according to Bauckham,[143] God is under a "fateful subjection to suffering" is versus a passibility in which God only identifies with the pain of the world. Bauckham goes on to rightly say that a God, who only rules over suffering with compassion, is a "cosmic monster." It suffices here to offer that God relates and feels with us for whom he is drawing into a deeper reality of his presence and transforming work. Moreover, it is helpful to accept Bauckham's strong passibility, to assert again that this world reflects a caring God. And that it is best suited for spiritual transformation making PrōST possible. God does not need to or have to feel all things, nor does God need to feel with equal intensities[144] to empathize with us toward full maturity. All that transpires, as painful and ugly as it often is, is supportive of redemption and transformation of human beings. It is not a charade; God does in fact feel and empathize in falsehood with the creatures of this world especially humans.

As the highest good, God must be moved by the sufferings of his creatures and must respond to their cries of pain and prayers for assistance as an omni-passible God.[145] If God were not compassionate to the suffering of his creatures and moved to response by us created in his image, then God would not be the kind of being with whom intelligent creatures would wish to be related. No rational, emotionally healthy being would be attracted to an unloving being that is proposed as God that cannot affect a response

---

141. Ibid., 343
142. Ibid., 332, 328.
143. Bauckham, "Only the Suffering God."
144. Simoni, "Divine Passibility," 342.
145. Power, "Imago Dei," 137–38.

of loving compassion for his creatures. Disciples cannot be allowed to patently and frigidity fall back upon the superficial, isolated interpretations of a verse that suggest God is the maker, and human creatures are the made, and, therefore, God can, in unfocused fiat, simply do as he wishes without complaint from his creatures (Rom 9:21). Such isolated exegesis seems to make God heartless and a monster. Rather, the whole council of God speaks to his compassion and desire to rescue his creatures from calamity. God is lovingly and compassionately passible and shall be moved by us even to changing our destiny (Jer 18:8; 26:3; Matt 11:23; Mark 7:27; 2 Tim 2:20–21).

More particularly, influencing God as friends, not only being God's non-contributing children, implies God's passiblity and allows for free will and freedom in growing human maturity inclusive of error.[146] God is desirous of progressive freedom in maturity for his human creation in relationships that move from servants, to children, to friends of God, and ultimately to knowing God face to face in "unhindered participation in the eternal life of the Triune God himself, in his inexhaustible fullness and glory."[147]

If health can be defined, in part, as the ability to live with "malfunctions," to live in either wellbeing or ill, it is then what is, in part, the strength of being human. More clearly, health, in its broadest sense, is the strength to be human as defined in *imago Dei*. The meaning of life is found and not changed in well being of adversity or its absences, even despite the prospect of life or death.[148] In these crises, the prolepsis of a future reality is often experienced more clearly than any theology and brings about an existential reality in the now (PrōST) far in excess of orthodoxy or orthopraxy.

Finally, suffering and difficulty is eventually the door to fellowship with the ineffable God and spiritual transformation both in the now and the not-yet. The problem of evil shall ultimately be answered looking past the present world, its origin, and its evil, to the world's consummation and the open manifestation of God's kingdom in creation as already begun in Christ.[149]

RELATIONSHIP AND BEING

In his message, "Justice," MacDonald[150] said, "I believe that to be the disciple of Christ is the end of being; that to persuade men to be his disciples is the

---

146. Moltmann, *Trinity and the Kingdom*, 220–21.
147. Ibid., 221–22.
148. Moltmann, *God in Creation*, 273.
149. Pannenberg, *Systematic Theology*, 2:164–65.
150. MacDonald, *Unspoken Sermons*, 156.

end of teaching." This is a good devotional, perhaps even hyperbolic word or consideration; however, God, in progressive revelation,[151] continues in the process of "teaching" and elevating his creatures in "being." This progression includes renewal of an evolving creation and the development of world history driving toward God's eschatological goals and purposes.[152] It also may be problematic for MacDonald to say, "end." We are in determined, progressing relationships with God. Our destinies are decided in the image of God, and in this, we are destined for a relationship in increasing fellowship and life with God.[153] Moreover, such a relationship ultimately finds its *teleos* in fellowship with God. Even now this future destiny manifests itself. Pannenberg continues that it is in this fellowship where the present life and one's personality is understood.

Community

Additionally, the image of God cannot be lived apart from others in isolation, but must be lived in community.[154] Relationship requires the involvement of two or more persons, and God, too, is a person in relationship (Gk. *perichōrēsis*). We, as *imago Dei*, are social creatures and grow in fellowship with other persons in differentiated relationship that is a reflection of and corresponds to the Trinity.[155] Moreover, there is an inclination in humans toward an expression of this image and destiny.[156]

The God of tri-unity, who is differentiated in himself, in triune, perichoretic relationship, finds correspondence in human community.[157] Such a *relationship* (Gk. *perichōrēsis*) inclusive of humans, in the same relationship, has great implications for theology and orthopraxy. Jesus, in *perichōrēsis*, is the one who, like Adam before him, defines the relationship between humans and God, and what is known about God and relationship is revealed through and in Jesus Christ as reflected and understood in natural being of God's self-communication (John 1:18; 17:25–26; Col 1:15).[158] This sug-

---

151. Lioy, *Evolutionary Creation*, 55; Saucy, *Case for Progressive Dispensationalism*, 13, 32–33.
152. Vorster, *Created in the Image of God*, 47.
153. Pannenberg, *Systematic Theology*, 2:224.
154. Moltmann, *God in Creation*, 222.
155. Ibid., 223.
156. Pannenberg, *Systematic Theology*, 2:227.
157. Moltmann, *God in Creation*, 218.
158. Van Huyssteen, *Alone in the World?*, 160–61; Peacocke, *Theology for a Scientific Age*, 300.

gests such a reality, as expressed in Christ, is a potential for all persons[159] in *perichōrēsis*.

It is in relationship that the greatest movement toward God in transformation is found. An intimate relationship is the transformative ground.[160] Although manifestly not on the level of Scripture, such relationship gives special revelation to the heart. Moses exemplifies the physical manifestation of this reality in his encounters with God on Mount Sinai. His very countenance was changed as a result of this encounter. So much transformation and glory resulted that the Israelites could not look on his face (Exod 34:33–35; Num 12:8; 2 Cor 3:13). This is as it is with God: no one can behold him directly and live except by a resurrection event (Exod 33:20; 1 Tim 6:16). Moreover, a person must behold him in the face of Jesus Christ (John 14:1–14).[161]

Nothing Known Outside of Conversation

Calvin[162] rightly argues that if one were left only to nature (general revelation), as was Simonides, to understand God, then nothing "certain or solid" or definite could be known. The Scriptures speak of a hidden and un-seeable God (Isa 45:15; John 1:18). Following this revelation, one can see Martin Luther's firm hold on *Deus absconditus* (hiddenness of God) as recorded in the Heidelberg Disputation (1518). Lohse[163] offers the concept of *absconditus* (hidden) as Luther's greatest contribution to theology. Not all, admittedly, may agree with the concept (ref. salvation by faith alone by grace alone). It is also noteworthy, according to Gerrish[164] that Luther speaks of God's hiddenness and not an "unknown" God. However, more expansive than Lohse's assessment, McGrath[165] points to Luther's contribution of the more full-orbed "riddle of the crucified and hidden God," and as a simple tool of Luther's, *Deus absconditus* (hidden God). Particularly, God is hidden in his revelation as theology. Moreover, McGrath[166] suggests the cross is a "theology of revelation," and continues that Luther strongly says to look elsewhere should be dismissed without discussion. Nevertheless, ac-

---

159. Ibid., 306.
160. Cooper, "Lutheran Response to Justification," 2–4.
161. Barrett, *Gospel according to St. John*, 458–60.
162. Calvin, *Institutes*, I.V.12.
163. Lohse, *Martin Luther's Theology*, 217.
164. Gerrish, "To the Unknown God," 265.
165. McGrath, *Luther's Theology of the Cross*, 161, 164.
166. Ibid., 163.

cording to Luther's later writings *Deus revelatus* (revealed God) seems to be in permanent tension with *Deus absconditus*, and so the final word of God is not found in the cross or Scripture because of his intransigent hiddenness according to McGrath's[167] and my understanding of Luther.

Christ made present virtues such as courage, faith, and love in the earthly human life of vicissitudes, displaying "inner potency or powers,"[168] as we should now express in enjoyment of the *imago Dei*. Love is manifested in Jesus Christ's activity, which was inclusive of community, love, and suffering in goodness (L. *sub ratione boni*) showing the world how to live.[169] If God's very "being is specifiable as conversation,"[170] then to be in relationship with the Triune God is to be in conversation with God. All creation is a result of conversation by God to God as the spoken and received word. To the degree and goodness of this pattern being repeated, is the degree of *imago Dei* being lived out by his creatures. This conversation and communication is a direct reflection of God in his creation and particularly his vice-regents—human beings.

Peacocke[171] proposes that the emergent capabilities of humans are inclusive of mental, personal, and spiritual abilities. The later by which humans are uniquely equipped to relate to God. This speaks something of the height of human activity. Conversation with God in relationship is the fullest experience of *imago Dei*. From this conversation comes the image bearing and outworking to the creation in which we live and thereby the clearest representation of *imago Dei*. Communion changes the nature of a thing.

Gadamer,[172] in an exchange with Hagel, suggests that as we interact with, even sacrifice for the universal, we gain a sense of ourselves. It is in this progressive expansion of relationship to the world and creation in whole that the heart of God is experienced and expressed putting on display the expansiveness of *imago Dei*. Here, in such a relationship, we find particularity and our self in the largeness of the whole. It is a relational *imago Dei* in caring for God's creation. More specifically, it is in relationship with the God-man, Jesus, in which we find our place in God and the world. Understanding God in relationship is the defining factor in learning about ourselves and from this to do as God does.[173] It is more specific and necessary to the point,

---

167. Ibid., 166.
168. Collins, "Incarnational Theory," 3.
169. Shults, *Reforming Theological Anthropology*, 215–16.
170. Jenson, "Praying Animal," 319.
171. Peacocke, *Evolution*, 76–77.
172. Gadamer, *Century of Philosophy*, 7, 59.
173. Power, "Imago Dei," 131.

however, to be in relationship with the God-man Jesus to learn and derive what human life was intended for in such a relationship with God and other human beings.[174] Jesus is the manifestation of God's nature and character already present[175] and the model for triumphant living.

Jesus spoke of the truth setting us free (John 8:32). It can be argued, as does Moltmann,[176] at this juncture, that this freedom is freedom to have relationship with God. Truth here is something more than an epistemological consideration. Rollins[177] is correct; as Moltmann says it is a matter of freedom to be in relationship with God and working out such a relationship within the world in which we find ourselves. I disagree with Barrett's[178] comment that John 14:6 strictly shows the way to the Father as the same road that Jesus would take, several hours hence, through crucifixion and resurrection. Carson[179] says it better, that Jesus is the way to the Father in his "uniqueness and sufficiency." This distinction is important in that Jesus was not simply a symbol or way-shower, but that Jesus is, in reality, the incarnation of the way, the truth, and the life to and in God the Father in and of himself (John 14:6; Heb 10:20). The process does not weigh against the person.

This truth, in relationship, is poking at the reality of a transformed mind (Rom 12:2). Borrowing Turner's[180] use of "*intellectus*," I suggest that to ask about an unknown or unknowable God rises from, one, the human experience but also from one's inability to comprehend the unknowable. In this *intellectus*, in *imago Dei*, is the meeting with God or knowing beyond knowing.

Working, whether the mind or body, is not the way to relationship. The idea that if we study hard the Torah or law,[181] or any other recommended text or practice, we might find resistance to temptation and an opening to transformation is simply unattested and indemonstrable. As Lioy[182] notes, seekers can easily establish the false gods of doing, praying, and sacrificing enough. Moreover the testimony of Scripture and the great saints of the church demonstrate the very contrary to works (Gen 2:17; Gal 3:2; 3:3); it

---

174. Barth, *Church Dogmatics*, III.2.39–41.
175. Peacocke, *Theology for a Scientific Age*, 302.
176. Moltmann, *Trinity and the Kingdom*, 212–13.
177. Rollins, *How Not to Speak to God*, 133.
178. Barrett, *Gospel according to St. John*, 458.
179. Carson, "Gospel of John," 570.
180. Turner, *Faith, Reason*, 16.
181. Altmann, "Homo Imago Dei," 248–49.
182. Lioy, *Jesus as Torah in John 1–12*, 210.

is a matter of seeing and being in relationship with God in Christ (Matt 5:8; 2 Cor 3:18; Col 3:4; 1 John 3:2). Moreover, as Lioy[183] rightly clarifies, Jesus threw over the old temple and its requirement of the law, including the law's consequence of "entitlement" and "merit" (Torah). Jesus brought the "new order represented by the temple of his body." Lioy continues that in Christ, as God's final expression, are all of God's blessings such as enjoyment of an uninterrupted fellowship with God removing any need of works. Adam's original absorption in a contemplative relationship with God negated any awareness of good and evil, any understanding of truth against the false, until he succumb to the temptation of partaking of this knowledge of good and evil.[184] Such a fall introduced the need for the law and ultimately Christ's fulfillment of that law in his body.

Unknowing

The relation of origin is the only attribute that can be said to be proper and exclusive to each in the hypostases of the Triune God.[185] To be properly understood, Lossky continues, this can only be viewed from an apophatic sense. Although a negation, the Father is not the Son nor is he the Spirit. Neither is the Son the Father nor is he the Spirit. Finally, the Spirit is neither the Father nor the Son. Not considered this way, it would submit the Trinity to the fourth category of relation in Aristotelian logic,[186] attempting to attribute specific properties, or primary substance in God to secondary substances or hypostasis. An Aristotelian approach would be an attempt at presuming language to be isomorphic with one's understood reality. However, understood apophatically or negatively, the relation of origin describes the difference but nevertheless does not indicate the manner of the divine processions.[187]

The theological understanding of hypostasis can be compared to the apparent enigmatic behavior seen in attempting to observe quantum mechanics' waves-particles duality, demonstrating two natures integrated into a single entity echoing the theological formulation, God-man.[188] The inseparableness of the two properties (complementarity), Bozack continues, seems to be, in one perspective, incompatible. However, the hypostasis, or

183. Ibid., 84–85, 209.
184. Altmann, "Homo Imago Dei," 254.
185. Lossky, *Mystical Theology*, 54.
186. Aristotle, *Categories and De Interpretatione*, 4.1b 25–2a4.
187. Lossky, *Mystical Theology*, 54–55.
188. Bozack, "Conjugate Properties."

synergy of the God-man transcends the individual properties as comprised by and in themselves—without this mystery of two natures, in Christ, sin's atonement would not be possible.[189] This might explain how Jesus walked on water, changed water into wine, and resurrected from the dead. Each attribute of either God or man is on display as the situation calls. Thus, the two natures, without corruption, are not incompatible but fully complementary.[190]

The German philosopher and Renaissance humanist, Nicholas of Cusa,[191] said, God, the creator, is both three and one, but as the infinite one, God is neither three nor one nor anything of which one can speak. Further, Nicholas claims, the names given to God are simply taken from creatures, because God is "ineffable" and thereby beyond the reach of naming or speaking. In disagreement, I conjecture something must be knowable about God, or we cannot have an informed relationship with our creator. As already offered, humans were created for relationship/fellowship fulfilled in Christ.[192] To know something of good and evil (Gen 3:22; 2 Sam 14:17, 20; 1 Kgs 3:9), at least as God views it, one must know something of God's heart. Such an understanding reveals something about God.

Khôra

In Badiou's[193] extreme claims of the unknowable, he speaks of language and the veridical of subject being beyond one's usual verification with any meaning "under [its] condition." That is, he is speaking about language being constrained to what is presented by a particular situation. It is bounded to a future anterior of something indiscernible. By this surreptitious pronouncement, the future verification can only pronounce the veracity of the thing presently spoken.

Moreover, Jacques Derrida, in a conversation with Caputo,[194] speaks about region or country (Gk. *khôra*) possibly meaning God unknown. The term as used and confounding Badiou, resists attempts at labeling and logic. Caputo deconstructs khora indicating Plato's philosophical usage in Timaeus to mean receptacle, space, or interval. It is alleged to be neither being nor nonbeing. It is an interval in between. It is where Plato's forms were

189. Ibid.
190. Ibid.
191. Nicholas of Cusa, *On the Peace of Earth*, 7.21.
192. Pannenberg, *Systematic Theology*, 2:224–25, 227.
193. Badiou, *Being and Event*, 400–406.
194. Caputo, *Deconstruction in a Nutshell*, 18, 92.

held from the beginning. Khora, deconstructed, has maternal overtones and provides space as in a womb or matrix. Heidegger addresses khora referring to it as "clearing," the place where being happens.[195] Derrida[196] uses khora, more recently, to name a radical otherness in which place for being is found.

To stridently press a theology or simple practice toward God in unknowing or extreme apophatic approach to God, is unhelpful. To even have a proper name such as God, even if it is only "god" is to speak of some unique individual person whose thought to be known, although admittedly, if only in a limited fashion.[197] Power seems to respond to Cusa,[198] when he rightly points out that if one cannot know God and therefore say nothing about God that one cannot even say that nothing about God can be said.[199] Giving room to the concept that God is a mystery and therefore cannot be fully known is not only understandable but also perhaps philosophically true and laudable. And yet, to deny the hope of knowing anything about God including experience is unnecessary and premature.

Hick,[200] while not agreeing with khora or an ineffable god, speaks of God in a pluralistic vein as the "Real," as it is in itself and what is conceived and experienced by humans, especially as the absolutes of world religions. By such a conjecture of God as the absolute of any given religion, knowable worship would appear confounded and troublesome if even possible. The cataphatic way or positive approach to God, in which it is claimed something about God can be known and followed in experience, may not leave as much room for the mystery of God and the unknowable God. However, it is a more hopeful and less a theology of negation and resignation as with an apophatic approach. The basis of this book stands firmly on the ground that God is a mystery and ineffably obscured from the soul of humans unless God deigns to be made known. The Judeo-Christian tradition has promulgated the orthodoxy of God's revelation in creation, special revelation, and personally to humans. Power[201] aptly quotes Augustine's use of *Theologia Germanica*, but then in the translation uses the word "ineffable" versus "unspeakable" to indicate the greatness that causes the inconceivable nature of God.

---

195. Nader El-Bizri.
196. Caputo, *Deconstruction in a Nutshell*.
197. Power, "Imago Dei," 132.
198. Nicholas, *Peace of Earth*, 7.21.
199. Power, "Imago Dei," 133.
200. Hick, "Pluralist View," 49–51.
201. Power, "Imago Dei," 133.

DEVICES IN THE UNVEILING   161

Augustine[202] says it differently with a question, as to whether speaking of God or giving God praise can be done in a worthy manner. He (Augustine) posits that all that he has done from a simple desire to speak does not speak what he desires, because God is "unspeakable." Augustine further says that if he could have spoken the unspeakable it, in fact, could not be spoken. Therefore God should not be spoken of as unspeakable, because that even is to speak of God. Therefore silence is better than explanation. Yet God has condescended to be worshiped and praised by a creature unable to comprehend. God is a "nature supreme in excellence and eternal in existence."

The significance in the usage of "unspeakable" rather than "ineffable" for this discussion is that to know something is to speak it, to communicate the thing known, especially when speaking of something so great as the very God of the universe. Whether one speaks in word (spoken or written) or deed, to know God is to speak out God. The existential reality of this knowing cannot be escaped. There is no unknowing the known. Such a knowing is transformative and "transportive." The life of one who knows is forever altered and ushered into a new experience and place of existence.

A passage in the *Theologia Germanica*[203] points to the evident truth that wee are far from perfect. This ineffable God is working to deliver us to a higher place often by withdrawing his "comfort and sweetness" by which most become distressed, withdraw from any disciplines that might have been practiced, and believe that God has forsaken them to an eternal loss. However, the *Theologia Germanica* continues, the disciple should not faint and grow weary, but love God and continue forward despite one's feelings or senses about God's presence and care. God's honor, by this, whether having or not is thus being proven.

Hick[204] refers to Pseudo-Dionysius[205] and his apophatic proposal of God such as indescribable, beyond all being and knowledge, not soul or mind. That is, God cannot be grasped by understanding or being labeled as one, nor oneness, against which a contrary argument can be brought. Hick[206] interprets Pseudo-Dionysius and the above attributes as not applicable to God in the positive or negative, stating that such an application is a category mistake. Hick argues that God is not the kind of being that such things as oneness or goodness can be applied, since God is not part of a reality in which such attributes can apply. It seems that Hick is partial to

202. Augustine, Sermon LXVII.
203. Anon, *Theologia Germanica*, ch. 10.
204. Hick, "Who or What Is God?"
205. Pseudo-Dionysius, *Dionysius the Areopagite*, 143.
206. Hick, "Who or What Is God?"

ineffable but prefers "transcategorial," which supports his conjecture that God is beyond the range of human systems, concepts, or mental categories.[207] Hick concludes that persons can only speak about God's effect and humans' experience on themselves and the world. Of course, such an argument negates years of Judeo-Christian belief and doctrine and is contrary to the present research.

The position of this study is, as Augustine says, that God may be "unspeakable" or "ineffable," that he desires to reveal something of himself to his creation. As considered below, this is often through story, allegory, and parable as is most commonly read in Scripture and other extra biblical writings. God makes something of God-self knowable in humanly accessible means such as writing, speaking, and nature.

STORY, ALLEGORY, AND PARABLE

Bauckham[208] writes a fictional series about English speaking, adventurous bears. Although a theological scholar, in these stories Bauckham presents no apparent message, moral, or deep theological meaning. At least there is none readily discernible. Whereas others such as C. S. Lewis have written fictional works in which parable and message is just below the surface if not screaming for acknowledgment. The very popular, self-published modern fiction, *The Shack*,[209] by Young, grabbed the imaginations of over eighteen million readers. It has been contested, on literary and doctrinal grounds, and yet its story has drawn many people into deeper recesses and questions of the soul and of God.[210]

Messaging within fiction is as old as human culture. Some have argued for much of the Bible's method, beginning with the creation story, as metaphor. There is something deeper and greater in literary devices than a poorly attempted scientific account of how the universe allegedly came into being with all of its constituents, parts, and population.[211] Among Christian writers using fictional story, allegory, and parable to great effect, in addition to Lewis and Young, are Tolkien, Milton, Bunyan, Dostoyevsky, Alighieri, Hurnard, Macdonald, Chesterton, Updike, and Rowling.

---

207. Ibid.
208. Bauckham, *Macbears of Bearloch*.
209. Young, *Shack*.
210. Alcorn, "Reflections on *The Shack*"; Rauser, *Finding God in "The Shack."*
211. Lam, "Biblical Creation"; Rad, *Genesis*, 48–49.

In speaking of the visible and invisible in metaphor, truth is revealed about who Jesus is to the world.[212] Clearly, Jesus is not a literal road on the way (John 14:6). Natural science and literalism alone cannot give adequate ontological truth.[213] Rather than myopically struggling to make a literal case for all scriptural story, whatever amount can be "proven," a cooperation with literary devices is needed to receive divine, self, and the other revelation.

Unlike the faculty psychology of Aquinas and others, this book supports an integrated and holistic view of humans. The faculties or constituents of spirit, soul, or body are not separated here except artificially for ease of discussion. As stated earlier, we are singular beings determined, in part, as whole persons and so composed by a totality. This understanding is important to present considerations regarding fiction, story, allegory, and parable. As is the case that the whole person is affected by stirring one part, reaching through to persons by the imagination and emotions generated by fiction, story, allegory, and parable, affects our whole person.

Narrative theology shows how embroiled the individual is in community, and such a concept that is a challenge to the usual focus on individualism, privatization, and "substances."[214] Further, Shults says that it is in this place of relationship that the self is found, oriented, and expressed. The communal experience found in narrative and especially story, fictional or otherwise, is tied into the heavenly community in trinitarian experience as a reflection of that communal reality in *perichōrēsis*. The argument here is that story, as found throughout the biblical narrative, is not as dependent on historical fact as the central intent to speak of and lead one into spiritual truth and experience.

In an internal review of a book by Russell Rathbone,[215] McLaren cites Kierkegaard as purportedly saying, "People held in the grip of an illusion cannot be directly reasoned with. One must assault them with appealing but apparently absurd stories and even contradictions in the desperate hope that indirect communication can accomplish what direct communication cannot." Although the primary source of Kierkegaard cannot be found, the words nicely speak to the sentiment of these pages. That is, story, allegory, and parable are some of the means to break through the conscious resistance that often blocks hearing.

---

212. Peterson, *Jesus Way*, 24–25.
213. Milbank, *Theology and Social Theory*, 259.
214. Dunn, "Justice of God," 4; Shults, *Reforming Theological Anthropology*, 213.
215. Rathbone, *Post-Rapture Radio*.

"The King and the Maiden"[216] is a beautiful example of the use of parable to illustrate the truth of God's love in condescension for his human creatures through incarnation. As valuable as direct, unhindered truth is, it is often missed, unaccepted, or misunderstood. Story, among a small number of approaches, is a means to break through the preconceptions and presuppositions that hinder our minds from seeing different perspectives and truths. Our tremendous capacity is limited by packed-in, received knowledge. Story disarms our minds, draws in our souls, and allows the assault of counter-grain views and visions. This is often the meaning of story in the Scriptures. But human proclivity looks for facts and twists the story into science and western concepts of linear history thereby missing the intent and splendor of the affect of story, which is often called myth. We further examine only these preliminary thoughts. Whole books have been dedicated to this consideration, but this section shall have to suffice.

Demonstrably, in his scholarly exegesis of Genesis, Rad[217] understands some measure of this truth of indirect telling. The Genesis narrators do not give an outright explanation to their readers, says Rad,[218] but simply guide us through experiences without an explanation or assessment. The thought is that the Genesis events can speak for themselves, and reflections may be found in multiple directions. This suggests a theopoetic or evocative articulation of the experiential, creating fluid interpretations and responses (Gk. *praxis*) to divine narrative.

"If the reader of today raises the question of 'historicity' of the events, he must first realize that the ancient narrators were simply not aware of this question that so often troubles modern man."[219] Rad further explains that we must give up finding a direct answer in such writings because we are found in the indirect telling of the ancient story. This thought challenges any of its own kind (L. *sui generis*) approach and rather suggests the possibility of a polysemous of meanings.

Peter Rollins[220] is a young philosophical whose voice echoes the likes of Anselm, Barth, Marx, Nietzsche, and the Bible itself (in the use of the unnamed name Yahweh [Heb. *YHWH*]) in reminding his readers that concepts of God are in danger of becoming "conceptual [idols] made from the conceptual materials of the human imagination." The Eastern Church has said such things for millennia, and we cannot ignore this reality.

216. Kierkegaard, *Parables of Kierkegaard*.
217. Rad, *Genesis*.
218. Ibid., 39–40.
219. Ibid., 40.
220. Rollins, *How Not to Speak to God*, 127.

DEVICES IN THE UNVEILING   165

Chesterton[221] poignantly describes what myth and art are about. He says that mythology "belongs to the poetic man" and that myth is about imagination and by that imagination a work of art. Myth is about imagination, but that does not mean imaginary or false. In the same thought, Chesterton rightly notes that every real artist touches transcendental truths. The artist's works are shadows of the real seen through veils. Human imagination is the "incantation" that calls up the real and beauty.

Among the various genres Scripture uses, are such devices as story, allegory, and parable, in seeking to break through the intransigent ways of thinking that enslave individuals and communities to processing thought as comfortably expected. Christ's mission is more of a poem and less of its common use as treatise, more art than science, using feelings and sensibilities to reach the mind to share sympathy, love, and life—it is about God's beauty.[222]

However, humans are not blank slates (L. *tabula rasa*); rather, they all come to an understanding or interpretation with a full burden of prior knowledge, understanding, prejudgments, and preferences. Deconstruction attempts to address this entrenched conundrum. Humans build on what has already been known; however, if revelation has space to break forth it must often, somehow, circumvent the known to present the unknown—the "unknowable." Such devises, which can simply be called signs, do not limit thinking only to themselves.[223]

"New language" is often found being utilized in political movements to help people think what they are not supposed to think,[224] and it is new language that must be employed to break through the intransigent thoughts, beliefs, and presuppositions of the person being sought by God (Isa 65; Rom 3:11).

Although, as already noted, some do not think God can be spoken of at all; Power[225] proposes that God can only be spoken of metaphorically. Certainly Moses used metaphor and symbol to speak about eternal truths with spiritual and ethical meaning and consequence.[226] Additional to metaphor, Luther[227] taught that God is known in the revelation of the apparent weakness and folly of the cross although not God's final word. For

---

221. Chesterton, *Everlasting Man*, 101, 105.
222. Bushnell, "Protestant Views," 344.
223. Willard, "Absurdity of Thinking in Language.'"
224. Schneiders, "Religious Life."
225. Power, "Imago Dei," 133.
226. Lioy, *Evolutionary Creation*, 94.
227. McGrath, *Luther's Theology of the Cross*, 161, 163, 165–66.

the purposes of reaching through human imagination, we might even say the "fiction" of the cross.

Howard Thurman[228] said that, by nature, the human mind must find sense in experience to reduce large amounts of experienced data into comprehensible propositions, ideologies, and abstractions. Religious experience is in motion, and the human mind, in an effort to find order and sense, must put it into neat packages from which to garner "concepts, notions, dogmas." Of course, any motion after such settling is then incomprehensible and must be subjected to the same euhemeristic method or left unknown.

TELEOLOGICAL MOTIF

While Scripture must be understood in ethical, logical, and historical ways, it must also be understood in its "aesthetic"[229]—a beauty expressed in story, allegory, and parable. Scriptural materials can be said to be, in some parts, less of an ethical, logical, and historical focus and more of a teleological pointer even escort. Scriptural meanings and messages support spiritual transformational development toward the eventual goal of living in unobscured *imago Dei* in unhindered divine presence expressing God in creation. It is an experiential reality that can begin its enjoyment in the present (PrōST).

God is revealed in Scripture through metaphorical and poetic devices to draw forward the pilgrim's progress and uplift the human mind.[230] It arrests the imagination. What of the spiritual disciplines, that have been discussed above, that might be seen or practiced as "manipulative," can be found rather as an internal act or *praxis* if practical instructions are exceeded for "poetic [Gk.] *mimesis*" that is imitation[231] of the reality shown in story, parable, and allegory found in the Scriptures. It is a kind of meme, or intergenerational idea in relationship from the inner message and meaning of Scripture to the reader and on from him or her, as Milbank,[232] continues, as of "*virtus* [L. excellence] or active potency" changing the inner person. It is "selfhood in relation to *teleos*" but not exhausted by the produce of its *virtus* and actions. Jesus' incarnation was showing forth the distinctive possibility

---

228. Thurman and Eyre, "Interview," 211.
229. Milbank, *Word Made Strange*, 123.
230. Hick, "Who or What Is God?"
231. Milbank, *Word Made Strange*, 124.
232. Ibid.

of human life always intended in continuity and emergence within us[233] of the elevation delivered by the life of Christ.

CONCLUSIONS

The objectives and intents of this book were further advanced in this chapter, in part, by considering the means by which God reveals and unveils his heart, truth, and purposes toward creation including humanity. In this, God utilizing both general and special revelation, with a view to spiritual recovery (PrōST), was shown to communicate through creation and especially humans by various means. It was shown thereby, that we do not have any excuse for not knowing what God has made accessible through general revelation (Ps 19:1–4; Rom 1:20).

Moreover, God was also shown as revelatory in special ways and means for more specific telling of his self, attributes and intents communicating to particular individuals, using holy writ, literature, visions, dreams, preaching, and even earthly creatures and nature (Gen 1:26–27; Num 12:6; 22:27–30; Matt 16:17; John 5:17, 19; Luke 19:40; 2 Tim 3:16; Heb 1:1). God uses various means to accomplish the intent of revelation in his desire to draw us into an intimate relationship with himself now (PrōST). Particularly, this chapter examined how God communicates himself to humans.

Examined above were facilitations of this communication. Specifically, beginning entrance into spiritual disciplines was presented by which we might avail ourselves to God in spiritual growth. God was shown to speak into the harmonizing, sympathetic, and resonating heart of humans. A category of these means includes disciplines such as prayer, fasting, confession, and meditation. Although we saw that there is an apparent general weak interest and practice among disciples, I postulated these disciplines as opening one to God's presence and transformative in-working to humans inclusive of spirit, soul, and body. These disciplines, however, are only means and should not be confused with goals, ends, or warrant for God's grace.

In this chapter I also forwarded the concept that sentient beings proceed through mind shifting and transforming through such as scriptural story, allegory, and parable toward a spiritual relationship issuing in God's unwarranted grace. This relationship was shown to be with the "unknowable" God despite God's apparent, often enigmatic communication. We also examined the teleological intent in leading from PrōST to unobscured *imago Dei* in unhindered divine presence expressing God in creation.

---

233. Peacock, *Theology for a Scientific Age*, 302.

Finally, we briefly examined theodicy, or particularly the mystery of human suffering under the eye of an omnipotent, all-beneficent God as means for God's transformative work no matter suffering's causes. It seems important to consider that whatever the full reasons of suffering in the world, God's heart is inclined to the best environment for spiritual transformation of his human creatures. Particularly, this chapter continued the argument that God is especially interested in spiritual transformation in the now (PrōST) availing present suffering. Theodicy is a complicated and contested area of theology with wide reaching implications. I have not attempted a thorough review of the historical and personal implications of the full subject but suggested that suffering, whatever its causes, is used by God for ultimate purposes in creation.

Scriptures were discussed as putting on display an omnipresent, omniscient God, who feels, knows, and empathizes with the needy and abused as well as having full response to the errant feelings and actions of the stray and willfully, defiant person. We considered the passibility of God as shown in Scripture to be God offering to change his "mind" and to withhold judgment if his creatures listen to his warnings and heed his direction. God, I argued, can be influenced by the will of human vice-regents.

Moreover, the commonly held belief that God is ineffable and unknowable would seem to frustrate any hope of enjoying God in any measure of perichoretic relationship. God, however, as we have seen, has made whatever of himself is needful for spiritual transformation manifest and knowable in Christ. The communal experience found in narrative and especially story, fictional or otherwise, is found into the heavenly community as trinitarian experience in reflection of that communal reality in *perichōrēsis*. As I have already forwarded, story, as found throughout the biblical narrative, is not dependent on linear historical fact as the central intent to speak of and lead us into spiritual truth and experience. God uses various literary devices to press past the ingrained mental habits of persons. Story, allegory, and parable, we considered, as common devices found in Scripture by which God speaks of deeper and higher truths than are readily seen by simple propositions and historical accounts. This is dressed in the beauty and pleasure of story pointing and reaching for the teleological goals of the creator of the universe particularly the spiritual maturation of humans beginning now.

5

Enculturation and Presuppositions

PREFATORY

BRIEFLY, CHAPTER 4 FURTHERED our objectives and intents by presenting God as revealed in creation by general revelation, removing the excuse from everyone of not knowing about and coming into intimacy with God. We also examined special revelation as a method and means of God in revealing a reality fully dependent upon God's self revelation, which is a far more specific telling of God's heart, attributes, intents, and, actions. Both general and special revelations were examined as intents and methods to spiritual recovery or transformation in the now (PrōST). Also examined were other means such as Scripture, and spiritual disciplines including prayer, fasting, confession, and meditation. The mysterious and the beautiful dress of truth in narrative, story, and fiction, displaying suffering in the process exposing God's passibility were also reviewed.

In the present chapter, foundational limitations that interrupt proleptic spiritual transformation (PrōST) are considered. Especially examined are such scriptural constraints and decrees, wrongly applied that are shown to hinder spiritual growth of loving intimacy with God. We also address the phantom pains that keep people in the shadows due to false beliefs. This chapter shows how phantom pains create false beliefs such as materialism and specifically physicalism, which obstruct efforts to spiritual transformation. Based in the phenomenon phantom-limb pain seen in amputees (a sense of pain in a severed limb) and particularly the work done by Schleifer[1] phantom pain has been implied as a spiritual, illusionary fixation.

Foundational limitations, even when falling into doctrinal lines, often restrain the believers' transformation and prevent us from living the fullest enjoyment of what the church can be in the now especially regarding proleptic spiritual transformation (PrōST). These are considered in this chapter, along with the problem of misunderstanding God that subsequently derails pursuit of God based on such misunderstandings that produce inclinations, constancies, and endeavors that miss God's divine will.

This chapter also examines the cycles and epochs involved in Christian history and their affects on spiritual development. They are shown below as contrived human periods to understand world events. These cycles and epochs are constructed for an analysis and better understanding of human past, present, and future life. It is history driven and unfolding as God's image in creation. The development and promises of postmodern thought are also examined below against human spiritual transformation. The tensions created by postmodern, deconstruction studies, within this present period, especially as they are used as interpretive methods for Christianity, are at best tenuous, and so what is offered is only to further the aims of this book.

Finally, in an aim to demonstrate that PrōST (proleptic spirituality transformation)—an experience usually reserved for the afterlife—is greatly available today through the influence that humans have with God in intimate relationship as friends in a maturity that allows for free will. Such an open relationship engenders freedom in growing human maturity including allowances for human error. God has arranged a world of progressive freedom for the maturing of his human creatures in relationships that, as examined below, move ultimately in un-frustrated partaking in the eternal life of God himself in unbounded depth, profundity, and glory as furthered in chapter 6.

There is a future hope and fullness that does not discount the present intimate, spiritual experience as friends of God. Important to chapter 6, the now is available and facilitated by a clear conscience in God's forgiveness. In tension, the followers of Christ now represent the kingdom, although not fully so; and therefore, we must live with a sense of urgency. This urgency against the paralyzing affects of enculturation and presupposition discussed in this chapter is drawn into chapter 6 in which human glory is experienced in reflection of God's glory. The exposed misapprehensions and misunderstandings about God and human relationship and the wrongly applied,

---

1. Schleifer, "Intangible Materialism," 152–54.

scriptural constraints, directives, decrees, and physicalism hinder expression of God's glory as discussed in the next chapter.

Moreover, the arguments of this chapter regarding the limitations of enculturation and unchallenged presupposition better position the discussion following in chapter 6 which argues for the God intended glory available to humans. Especially helpful in this chapter is the understanding of the forgiveness and clear conscience provided by the work of Christ's love that is shown to free the disciple to unhindered relationship with God and others in expression of *imago Dei*.

FOUNDATIONAL LIMITATIONS

What follows are a few of the trenchant issues hindering proleptic spiritual transformation (PrōST). Normative, Christian spirituality is generally walled within supposed scriptural constraints, boundaries, and directives. These are, expectantly, within historical orthodoxy in faith and practice. However, Schneiders[2] poignantly notes, as experiential examples or paradigm shifts play out, these spiritualities are often varied and escape attempts to neatly package them into an obedient codification or genus. Not unexpectedly, what has fallen into doctrinal lines about the present and future, develops foundational limitations in the believers against living the fullest enjoyment of what the church can be in the now (PrōST). Grenz[3] draws on Luther, Cairns, and Hall to speak of a supposed lost *imago Dei* (original righteousness) as defective response to God or a fallen relationship that has been totally abrogated while looking for its restoration in a future life through a gradual progress in this life. As I thoroughly addressed earlier in this research, this concept, foundational limitation, if it were so, would erect an impossible wall of separation from the truth of the created nobility of humans in God's irrevocable image that cannot be lost but can only be obscured or remain un-exercised.

Yet-To-Be

Eschatological constructs can also be foundational hindrances. Although not in full, Hoekema,[4] and a large supporting witness, testify that the eschatological hope of the Old Testament is, especially in Christ's sacrifice,

---

2. Schneiders, "Christian Spirituality," 5.
3. Grenz, *Social God*, 165–66.
4. Hoekema, *Created in God's Image*, 13–15.

seen fulfilled in the New Testament. There are, nevertheless, Hoekema reminds, still not-yet eschatological fulfillments waiting in the next age. This yet-to-be completed reality is part of the limitations seen in proleptic spiritual transformation (PrōST). It suggests that such a hope may not yet be fully realizable. Nonetheless, admitting that there is still a future hope and fullness does not delete the present, or now, that is available (Matt 3:2; Mark 1:15; Luke 10:9). In tension the Christian disciples are, in the present, an expression of the kingdom although not fully so and, therefore, we must live with a sense of urgency (Matt 6:10).[5] The first-century believers viewed reality as an already and a not-yet eschatological reality anticipated by Jew and Christian alike.[6] This reality allowed the followers of Christ to enjoy the reality and down payment of the Spirit and yet not slip into triumphalism by overextending the not-yet.

While Walvoord,[7] in the main, would limit the presence of the kingdom to the activities of Christ, I contend this has been and remains that Christ's disciples are, although not fully or perfectly, presently living a measure of the principles and reality of the kingdom (Acts 2:33b, 38b; Rom 14:17; 2 Cor 5:17; Gal 5:22; 6:15; Eph 2:10). Shults[8] points out, while not providing an excuse that the environmental and biological conditions with which humans must contend to survive and evolve, such as "sexual possessiveness and aggression," reflect the great difficulty humans experience when trying to live the transformed life. So too, it is a restraining concept that continues to hold the human imagination from entering the realms of possible, personal development and must be considered as a foundational limitation.

Physicalism

An intransigent and seemingly inviolate materialism and specifically physicalism hinders thoughts and efforts to spiritual transformation since such transformation is mostly thought to be in the ideas beyond demonstrable scientific procedure. In *The Human Person in Science and Theology*, Hefner[9] speaks about humans emerging within a process of "physical and biological evolution." Human personhood is, he says, simply as a result of interaction of "physical, biological and cultural materials." Humans, according

---

5. Ibid., 52.
6. Fee, *God's Empowering Presence*, 803–4.
7. Walvoord, "Realized Eschatology."
8. Shults, *Reforming Theological Anthropology*, 209.
9. Hefner, "Imago Dei," 73–74, 82.

to his paradigm, are "biocultural creature[s]" simply in need of a "moral concept" in which an understanding of self is supposed to emerge, and it is all of this, in the body and brain, according to Hefner, that personhood is "constrained." No mention of spiritual influences are made until Hefner[10] interacts with Tillich and Pannenberg in defining the dynamics of personhood as equivalent to "spiritual individuality" (undefined) apparently on a trajectory to scientific causal explanation or dismissal. Ostensibly, while physics, biology, neuroscience, psychology, and sociology are welcomed to the discussion, the thought is that the spiritual is not scientifically demonstrable and thereby ruled out from consideration except as pseudo-scientific conjecture in physicalism or materialism as properties of neurons.[11]

As discussed in the prior chapter, a materialist view of humans is only partial at best and certainly not sufficient or exhaustive. If physicalism is accepted as a sole thesis, then a block of inability is set up. Moltmann[12] suggests that evolution and creation need not be thought of as opposing theories of concepts. He claims that the spirit is evolving to "higher awareness of its self in the human being." This is within the evolution of creation driving toward God's kingdom of glory transcending its present self.

Forgiveness

Above we considered soteriology and its import on spiritual transformation. The particularity of forgiveness is in need of address here as it specifically plays upon spiritual transformation, or more precisely as unforgiveness hinders PrōST. Unforgiveness creates a spiritual prison in which we are confined in the brine of brackish, spiritual poison and darkness pressing us into self-banished solitude from God and others. Not only is there plenty of scriptural testimony for the need of forgiveness (Job 5:2; Matt 5:44; 6:12, 14–15; 18:21–35; Luke 13:3; 2 Cor 5:19, 20) but academic research also shows its critical nature. According to Jankélévitch,[13] any allowance for the unforgivable would be hell. Jankélévitch continues that even the inexcusable is forgivable. Contrary to a traditional Christian reading, Derrida[14] seemingly contradictorily suggests that forgiveness, if it exists, is only possible if there is the unforgivable and forgiveness is exempt from "the law of the possible." Contrarily, it seems clear to me that forgiveness is not only possible

    10. Ibid., 81–82.
    11. National Academy of Sciences, *Teaching About Evolution*, 58.
    12. Moltmann, *God in Creation*, 18–19.
    13. Jankélévitch , *Forgiveness*, 106, 162.
    14. Derrida, "Forgive," 48.

but also necessary for the disciple seeking intimacy with God and others. God's work makes forgiveness possible.

In order to approach God with a clear conscience, knowing unhindered receipt of one's person is assured, it must be in the forgiveness secured by the work of Christ. This clear conscience is foundational to any healthy relationship. I side with Peters[15] here, and expand on his assessment, that when we are forgiven we may "borrow the goodness of the forgiver" versus working to create the delusion of our own goodness. In this Peters continues we are released to rely on the life of the giver (Christ) who has the power of forgiveness. This truth must be expanded to our forgiving others and self for full release from guilt that hinders relationship. The power to forgive is concomitant with the power to love according to King.[16] Such forgiveness is in itself transformative. The mercy of forgiveness trumps judgment (Jas 2:13) freeing the forgiven to intimacy with God and others.

God of the Gaps

The Lukan narrative presents ignorance as misunderstanding. According to Green,[17] it is a fault in missing the purpose of God. This misunderstanding presents God in an untrue perspective and is trying in this misconstrual, Green continues, to follow but actually misses the plain will of God. This is important here in that to misunderstand God and to pursue God according to this misunderstanding produces inclinations, devotions, and endeavors that are outside of divine will, a misrepresentation of God's person and attributes, and often counter to spiritual transformation as we can deduce from Green's assertions.

Küng[18] talks about living under a false idea of what he calls the "God of the gaps." A god, who is placed only in the inexplicable, presently unknown or seemingly unknowable about the universe, is nothing more than a creation of none rigorous thought and misused scientific method. Such an attitude fights against scientific progression as exampled regarding such facts as heliocentricity and evolution. The idea that Christ followers do not yet know what they shall be or when Christ is coming (Rom 8:19; Col 3:4; 1 John 3:2) excuses too many to the future and thereby limits spiritual development in the present.

15. Peters, *Sin*, 20.
16. King, "Loving Your Enemies," 427.
17. Green, "Kaleidoscopic View," 182.
18. Küng, *Beginning of All Things*, 80.

Focus and Diffuse

Jenson[19] says that ritual, or more precisely ritual as in prayer, is a dialogue with God making persons visible, embodied persons. Even so, partaking only in the usual sense of emptying meditation before an "ineffable eternity" leaves one with a god alien to Christianity. The foundational problem, however, is that a Christian habit of ritual prayer is not sufficient and this meditation is not per Christian tenets. Practicing disciplines either way in empty ritual or empty non-focused prayer leaves a gap and perhaps misdirection for the disciple.

Whether prayer, worship, or soteriology, the memes of traditional theologies regarding salvation have been a severe division between the various Christian bodies over the centuries. What is surprising is that the doctrine of salvation may now be emerging as a uniting factor or "bridge between the East and West, between Catholics and Protestants, and finally, between the older and younger churches."[20] How this salvation forms and guides, as we discussed above in chapter 3, plays a great deal on the present subject and specifically the viability of PrōST.

Of course, there is the obvious sin and rebellion that frustrate spiritual transformation that has already been reviewed above. Such hindrance was not only considered but it is manifestly evident and only requires the reminder that sin and rebellion cause us to hide from God (Gen 3:8; Job 31:33; Rev 6:15) and thereby anything that might draw us close such as the disciplines of spiritual transformation. Moreover, if Goldstein[21] is even partly correct, and "masculinity is an endless process of *becoming*, while in femininity the emphasis is on *being*," then to that fact men and women face a measure of different challenges on the way to spiritual transformation. Indeed, the disquiet common to men must be rested, Goldstein continues, while a woman must find freedom from acculturated bondage. While perhaps dissonant, sin of man, at its root, *is* pride, woman's "sin" is "a failure to acquire a strong sense of self" according to Mahoney and Pargament,[22] albeit no male disavowal or responsibility is allowable.

Goldstein[23] correlates this becoming and being to "pride" and "will-to-power" for men and for women respectively such as triviality, distractibility, diffuseness, and dependence on others for a sense self-worth. So

---

19. Jenson, "Praying Animal," 317.
20. Kärkkäinen, *One with God*, 120.
21. Goldstein, "Human Situation," 105.
22. Mahoney and Pargament, "Sacred Changes," 485.
23. Goldstein, "Human Situation," 109.

then, although people, both men and women, are being wooed to intimate relationship with God and the others in their world, there are these unique behaviors, along with others not examined here that must be accounted for on the sometimes-bumpy road toward spiritual transformation. My intent here is not to venture into a debate about gender roles or differences. There is commonality in the sin situation of all humans. There are, however, foundational difference that create unique areas of temptation and need for resistance and growth. One might be right in arguing that Goldstein's observations were made in 1960 and that women have moved on from those generalizations. To whatever degree that can be demonstrated, the problem still anecdotally subsists in the societies of the world. Moreover, there remains a need, beginning within the academy, that assists the church in knowing what Scripture is cultural and what is transcultural. That is, one should discriminate from a scriptural understanding what is limited to an understanding that has cultural roots.[24]

Additionally, although it is of critical importance that some exercise extreme energy in examining and discerning the spiritual reality that may be available, Heschel[25] suggests at some point study must be displaced, or at least set to the side, to make obvious by existential enjoyment what is too often left in the test tubes of speculation and theory. This experience of the divine, however, cannot be left in the breast of the communicant, but must be presented to those outside such reality. Heschel, in the same breath, insightfully goes on to present his case as, "Only those will apprehend religion who can probe its depth with unmalting precision, who can combine the intuition of love with [the] rigor of method, who are able to translate the ineffable into thought and to forge the imponderable into words."

Imagining God

By some accounts, as reported by Schneiders,[26] spirituality may be gaining interest in small parts of civil society as social activism was in the 1960s even if it is adulterated with pretentious egocentrism rather than a contemplative expression. Disagreeing with Schneiders point that the reticence of the 1960s to the contemplative life has been left behind, Barna's[27] research shows that contemplative life still meets a need for justification entering the twenty-first century.

24. Webb, *Slaves, Women & Homosexuals*, 245.
25. Heschel, "Holy Dimension," 117.
26. Schneiders, "Religious Life."
27. Barna, "Self-Described Christians."

The mythologist, Joseph Campbell,[28] said that for the primitive world, in which most of the understanding of the origins of mythology must be found, "gods and demons are not conceived in the way of hard and fast, positive realities. A god can simultaneously be two or more places—like a melody, or like the form of a traditional mask." And whenever or wherever God is found or comes, God's impact and presence is the same. God is not reduced by multiplication. For us what can be garnered from Campbell here is that God is not diminished by questionable conceptions. As Lewis[29] pointedly shows in his *Screwtape Letters*, humans seem to have a tendency to locate God in communicating with him in prayer. Locating God "up and to the left at the corner of the bedroom ceiling, or inside his own head, or in a crucifix on the wall," Screwtape encourages Wormwood to keep his apprentice "praying to *it*–to the thing that he has made, not to the Person who has made him." God's grace is larger, greater than our errors and foibles. God is not changed by even what is classified as orthodox theology and perceptions. In any case, God exceeds our conceptions, even when they seem to closely reflect biblical constructs, which are peppered with anthropomorphisms and allegory and to add further harm tragically *eisegeted*. Even viewing God in the face of Jesus Christ is inexact, since no one actually knows what he looked like or how he related and behaved.

PHANTOM PAINS

As addressed in the prefatory of this chapter, phantom pain is drawn from physiological/psychological phenomenon in which brain-commands cause pain when the source of pain is no longer present. This phenomenon is attributed to Teresa of Avila's shared pain of the suffering Christ[30] to become one with the one who, of course, is no longer suffering. Christ has overcome pain and death, and so any claimed "shared pain" with him is but a phantom and not actual. The phantom pains of sins (Rom 6:11; 1 John 1:9),[31] long ago dealt with by the redemptive, regenerative, victorious work of Christ, can be allowed to interrupt the expression of a transformed life.

Liminal positions toward transformation are intransigent, in part, because the traveller holds onto past conditioning and states when confronted by the new status presenting in progressive transformation. They are states and conditions that have in God's assessment changed (Rom 6:4, 8; 2 Cor

28. Campbell, *Masks of God*, 21.
29. Lewis, *Screwtape Letters*, 18.
30. Schleifer, "Intangible Materialism," 154.
31. Farley, *Naked Gospel*, 151.

5:17; Eph 4:17–24). As was presented in the prior chapter,[32] story, allegory, and parable are used to tell truth and break through staid, stagnant, formalistic-views and beliefs whether they are present in biblical myth or history.

Supernatural and Natural

The philosopher Žižek,[33] an admitted atheist, says that Chesterton preferred prosaics to deliver his message rather than a magical or mystical account. Furthermore, Chesterton[34] himself speaks through one of his fictional characters about the drowning of rationalism and skepticism, by superstition. He says it is the result of not believing in God and rather gullibly believing anything presented. Consequently, Chesterton says in the same passage, "Reeling back to the bestial gods of the beginning, escaping into elephants and snakes and crocodiles; and all because you are frightened of four words: 'He was made Man.'"

Žižek,[35] however, goes beyond Chesterton's words that humans are too easily persuaded to the magical of various religions and explanations in holding to a supernatural explanation of the world. Žižek supports John Wesley's earlier recorded arguments regarding perfectionism.

In his monograph, *A Plain Account of Christian Perfectionism*, the champion of perfectionism, John Wesley[36] said, that humans willfully grant and pronounce that perfection in this life is not possible. This position, he argued, was used to relieve them from good works or following the ruling of God. This argument would agree with Žižek's accusation that rather than "now" magical (perfection, transformation, unfolding) waits for a supernatural intervention in the *eschaton*. It is something progressively within the natural that is "now." Wesley continues that the protest is held by a strong objection to any full release from ignorance, error, tempting the multitude of vagaries attributed to human existence in this age. But the truth is that, according to Wesley[37] in this same monograph, "there is no *absolute perfection*. There is no perfection which does not admit of a *continual increase*" (emphasis original).

---

32. Chesterton, *Everlasting Man*, 101, 105; Lam, "Biblical Creation"; Lioy, *Evolutionary Creation*, 94; Rathbone, *Post-Rapture Radio*.
33. Žižek, and Milbank, *Monstrosity of Christ*, 25.
34. Chesterton, *Incredulity of Father Brown*, 72.
35. Žižek and Milbank. *Monstrosity of Christ*, 25.
36. Wesley, *Works of the Reverend*, 494.
37. Ibid., 489.

This is a softening of the idea of moral perfectionism and sinless existence in the present life before the *eschaton*. However, there is a contrary, pernicious belief, heard in common conversations, that humans must live in a place of defeat; after all, "I'm only human, and to err is human," goes the refrain. This caliginous view is perpetuated from pulpits, pews, and cultural converse, giving unwarranted excuse, as so much rehearsed pious cant polluting the souls of humans created in God's image.

Heschel,[38] in speaking about the construals of religion, makes an observation that is directly applicable to this discussion. That is, the impressions given by a thing are not necessarily equal or reflective in our imaginations. The place of the experiential reality and objective reality are not found on the same footing.

Not only are our perceptions of the other often askew from objective reality, but also, it seems, we most often produce impressions that speak contrariwise to an essential reality of *imago Dei* or anything that might hint of the divine. Most particularly, as discussed above, perceptible, spiritual transformation for any age seems to be lacking in most individuals and communities.

Not understanding that sin has been dealt a death blow and firmly holding beliefs of other limitations interrupt the reality of God's heart toward us created in his image who have been freed from subjugating sin into the kingdom of his son. We too often have believed a fabrication and turned away from the reality of the kingdom having arrived and thereby refuse to walk in its presence, offers, and realities. Moreover, continuing with Heschel's[39] insight, the pains suffered by us in time are not a true reflection of the inner reality or the essence of the human being created in the image of God. The *imago Dei* is enjoyed without diminishing, and that which too often seems obscured, in nowise changes the reality of the truth and shining of this image. The essential *imago* is striving to press through in full expression to the world and God having been liberated from the dross and mendacity that sometimes obscures its view and brilliance. The disbelief of its possibility and the phantom pains of unrequited sin hold back *imago Dei*, as the standard of the expressed life. Bushnell[40] agrees, God must become the focus of love and replace those sinful habits once held and insisting on attention although they have lost their hold by Christ's freeing work.

The kingdom has come and yet its full manifestation and fulfillment is still future. And yet, the present or now reality is greater than usually

---

38. Heschel, "Holy Dimension," 118.
39. Ibid.
40. Bushnell, "Protestant Views," 347.

thought or entertained. Such a fuller understanding about the present is liberation to expectations about what of spiritual transformation might presently be experienced and enjoyed. When God accepted the life of Christ, through resurrection and ascension, the kingdom life, inclusive of a life that is a clear, unhindered *imago Dei*, became available to the rest of humanity. The phantom pains of the prior condition of humanity before the Second Adam, Christ, trouble most of us to such an extent that we cannot possibly accept the possibility of a proleptic spiritual transformation (PrōST). Of no help, as a search shows, most theological discussions are laconic regarding prolepsis in any form especially as used in this book. O'Collins[41] cites prolepsis as anticipation regarding "OT history of divine promise and human hope." He then cites a couple of names mostly associated, that is, Pannenberg, in his theology of revelation and Christology and Moltmann regarding the Christ event as anticipation of future history within the present. However, a new age has already begun in which such a life is possible as exemplified by Christ. Yes, the gifts of the Spirit are present as well as the fruit of the Spirit in a reflection of the image of God as manifest by communicable attributes such as "love, joy, peace, patience, kindness, goodness, faithfulness, gentleness, self-control" (Gal 5:22–23; cf. Eph 4:24; Col 3:12).

CYCLES AND EPOCHS

Whether yugas, epochs, cycles, or ages, humans have incessantly and understandably tried to fit world events and future prognostications into neat compartments that can be analyzed and discussed for a better understanding of human past, present, and future life. Universal histories, from a Western tradition, were established by Christian historians and writers and spoke about equality and a shared destiny underlying events.[42] Fukuyama presses further that a luminary like Augustine (owned by the West) was not concerned with Greek or Jewish history, but with the story of redemption as God's intent in history on earth. Augustine was perhaps a bit myopic or insular implying God's redemptive activity as radically limited. By this approach, whatever epochs, cycles, or periods are discernibly classified, they are animated by such a noble purpose as God's redemptive history. In the following descriptions they are particularly directed to Christian spiritual developments.

---

41. O'Collins, *Westminster Dictionary*, 472.
42. Fukuyama, *End of History*, 56.

The advent of Christ was a new epoch into the fallen history of God-alienated humans, a "vital force that cannot die," Bushnell says,[43] and from it is manifest a "kingdom of life, and reign." In this kingdom the sin problem is remedied. Christ's advent was a universal epoch. Clearly, this is the most important epoch in the history of the universe. There can be nothing higher, more incredible, or more magnificent than the incarnation into creation, of the very God who is creator of all, with the express purpose of reconciling it in love. The reign and epoch of evil was defeated and crushed under the foot of Christ (Gen 3:15; John 12:31; 19:30; Rom 16:20).

If eternity is an immeasurable future duration of time or "endless extended time," as Cullmann[44] claims, into which God's goals are complete, then, as already proposed, the work that all are called to, regarding maturation and transformation in time, may be possible into the "eternity" after death. In fact, there is only record of a few (e.g., Enoch, Elijah, Jesus) who have translated from this life perhaps having completed all earthly "requirements" for perhaps complete transformation no matter how well most have run the race (1 Cor 9:26–27; 1 Tim 6:12; 2 Tim 4:7; Heb 12:1).

Whether time, as measured in past, present, or future events, is simply created and eventually ends or folds into eternity future, the present time of our lives and sojourns is allotted for the "work" of transformation in reflecting God, the work of preparation for entering into the *eschaton*. So there is tension between the now of incompleteness and the future accomplishment. Surely this suggests that, although there is a possibility, most disciples shall not largely experience proleptic spiritual transformation (PrōST). To pull down the kingdom by force (Matt 11:12; Luke 16:16) is not for the delicate and squeamish recalcitrant who does not even entertain such a measure and cost. As Bonheoffer[45] said, the lives of disciples of Christ must be conformed to his crucifixion and death on the cross; that is, we must be baptized, conformed to a life of crucifixion (Phil 3:10; Rom 6:4; Gal 2:19), and live in the strength of Christ's death. Continuing with Bonheoffer, in this is an expression of the entire, tempered humanity that Christ bore.

It seems that Van Huyssteen[46] is correct in his critique of *imago Dei* and its expression in humans, that is, "we are in fact the theme of history in which we become, through Christ, what we already are." Furthermore, if the self-transcendence or exocentricity of the human soul is in expression of *imago Dei*, then history and the epochs of history are driven and an un-

---

43. Bushnell, "Protestant Views," 346–47.
44. Cullmann, *Christ and Time*, 65, 69.
45. Bonheoffer, *Cost of Discipleship*, 302.
46. Van Huyssteen, *Alone in the World?*, 140.

folding of God's image in creation through his vice-regents—humans. This unfolding is an eschatological expression in the now of persons through the life of Christ as the "new human being in them."[47]

Playing off of Moltmann[48] and reaching further, into this need of God's appointed Sabbath is the rest of the human soul in God's accomplishments in Christ, and "history is sanctified with the divine measure and blessed with the measure of true humanity." This rest comes in, as Van Huyssteen again describes as, "becoming through Christ, what we already are."

Shifts

Although there are many proposed historical periods, Schaff[49] speaks of his well known nine historical church periods spanning the time of Jesus through the French Revolution to 1880. More concisely, here we look at five major paradigm shifts in church history. This is not an historical treatise but a cursory look at some few of the spiritual activities and luminaries by period as they are germane to the present work and best serve present intents. These paradigm shifts illustrate the historical, cyclical nature of church community that changes and disrupts everything affecting human life in the church and thereby tangent institutions. Again, what follows is but an attenuated review as supportive of the present effort and by design leaves out large parts of historical records and personalities for a few select events in support of church spiritual development.

Jesus

The first great shift began with the rise of early Christianity and saw a tremendous amount of paradigm-shifting greenfield activity beginning in the soil of Judaism. Christ and the church took primacy. Spiritual activity was ubiquitous among the disciples under Christ and the Apostles. By way of clarification, spiritual here does not imply asceticism or other-worldly positions, but the early church was infused with the fresh activity of God's Spirit and accordingly responded spontaneously. As Kärkkäinen[50] points out, the early church routinely experienced and even celebrated charismata (1 Cor

---

47. Ibid., 141.
48. Moltmann, *God in Creation*, 139.
49. Schaff, *History of the Christian Church*, 18–19.
50. Kärkkäinen, *Pneumatology*, 39.

1:4–7).⁵¹ According to Stronstad,⁵² the day of Pentecost was an historically pivotal-event in the salvific theology particularly in Luke's understanding. Although charismata were necessary for the work and testimony of the church, a "clothing, a baptizing, an empowering, a filling, and an outpouring of the Spirit,"⁵³ it does not always clearly nor directly result in spiritual fruit such as love, joy, peace, patience, kindness, goodness, faith, that is, transformation. Paul spent much time addressing this issue (1 Cor 13:1–13; 2 Cor 3:18; Eph 5:9; Gal 5:16–17, 22; Phil 1:11).

The embroiling debate surrounding cessation or continuation was not a first consideration in the early church. Charismata were expected and required for empowering the early Christians for service.⁵⁴ The early church was, Fee⁵⁵ argues, in an "already" and a "not-yet" regarding the eschatological reality anticipated by Jew and Christian alike. This allowed the follower of Christ to enjoy the reality of the Spirit as a down payment, Fee continues, and yet not slip into triumphalism by overextending to the not-yet. The Spirit's outpouring was proof of the arrival of the messianic age and a guarantee of its not-yet eventuality.

As today, then also, many disciples mistook charismatic gifts for spiritual fruit borne of spiritual transformation. Kärkkäinen⁵⁶ comments that from this "beginning charismatic, enthusiastic Christian expressions" were experienced differently than the extant universal church at the time. The goal was to fan the flame of early church charismatic experience. Kärkkäinen rightly posits that such behavior was normative in the early centuries of the church and not a minority voice.

The developing charismatic practices and the anticipation of Christ's immediate return fuelled a desire for spiritual reality in transformed lives in the now (Luke 13:9; Rom 13:12; Gal 5:22; Phil 4:5; 1 Pet 4:7–11; Jas 5:8; 2 Thess 3:5). Although introducing its own problems, according to Mursell,⁵⁷ Platonism, while dualistic, supported the early believers toward seeing a beautiful world in which desire was fulfilled and thereby gave "Christian spirituality a dynamism and energy that it might otherwise have lost."

---

51. Fee, *God's Empowering Presence*, xxi, 2, 84–85; Stronstad, *Charismatic Theology*, 2, 5, 12.
52. Ibid., 49.
53. Ibid., 50.
54. Ibid., 60.
55. Fee, *God's Empowering Presence*, 803–4.
56. Kärkkäinen, *Pneumatology*, 39.
57. Mursell, *Story of Christian Spirituality*, 10.

During this beginning period, Jesus, including his prayer life and teachings, forever changed the worship of billions of seekers throughout the ages and placed justice and mercy above the ritual and legalistic demands of religion.[58] However, as Burridge[59] explains, care must be exercised not to read back into this period present spiritual practices and realities. He does acknowledge, however, that Jesus' life, spirituality, and example deeply influenced the early disciples.

Tertullian of Carthage (c. 160–220) sought the Christian life and morality leading to spirituality through the Rule of Faith.[60] As Tyson notes this drove Tertullian to join the "puritanical sect called Montanism" eventually rejecting the Catholic Church. Origen of Alexandria (185–251) from this period, is one of the most influential personalities. His *De Principis* is required reading. It is rich with allegorical readings of the Scripture.[61] His method would last as a "methodological foundation" that later mystics would use to this day. According to Tyson,[62] Origen leaned heavily on worldly renunciation, purification, and prayer as a means to entering God's presence and gaining spiritual transformation.

Although often maligned for his theocratic, institutional affects on the church, Emperor Constantine (c. 272–337) opened an opportunity for the church to freely practice its faith in both words and images, which made Constantinople the Byzantine Empire's artistic center and a place of freedom for such as Basil the Great, Gregory the Theologian, John Chrysostom, Athanasius, and Cyril of Alexandria.[63]

While Athanasius of Alexandria (c. 296–373) may be known best for his polemic against Arianism, his introduction of spiritual biography served well as a means to not only teach orthodoxy but holy living. As Tyson[64] argues, Athanasius's biography *The Life of Antony* (c. 356) served as a model for Christian spirituality that even Augustine of Hippo (354–430) attempted to follow. Athanasius' influence was very great on Augustine. Best known for *Confessions*, *City of God*, and *On the Trinity*, Augustine was painfully self-aware of his spiritual shortcomings and sin.[65] Consequently, Augustine

---

58. Burridge, "Jesus and the Origins," 19, 21.
59. Ibid., 25.
60. Tyson, *Invitation to Christian Spirituality*, 63.
61. Ibid., 73.
62. Ibid., 74, 76–77.
63. Ouspensky, "Icon and Art," 385.
64. Tyson, *Invitation to Christian Spirituality*, 87.
65. Ibid., 104–5.

ENCULTURATION AND PRESUPPOSITIONS   185

approached God in this contrite position waiting for God's cleansing and mercy.

Cyril of Alexandria (d. 444 [*That the Christ Is One*]), together with Athanasius, also had a great influence on Christian spiritual life during this period. According to Mursell,[66] Cyril directed disciples away from an invisible and immaterial Christ to one who was God incarnate and an example of human, godly living—the new Adam and the expected authentic life on display. Mursell states it is an "intimate and mystical union with the divine presence." Also from this period John Cassian's (c. 365–435) impactful work, *Conference* (c. 240) compiled wisdom from the desert fathers representing their discussions of spiritual matters. Cassian popularized Egyptian monastic life and Christian spirituality including disciplines, especially ceaseless prayer, as spiritual means that were later found in the monastic rules of Benedict of Nursia.[67]

Gregory the Great

Gregory the Great (c. 540–604) is used as a pivotal point as one of the notable individuals to identify this period. This period is often referred to as "The Fall of the Roman Empire" or "The Coming of the Dark Ages."[68] Though not great himself, Gregory simplified and made accessible Augustine's works.[69] Mursell notes that Gregory left guidance to clergy to live a spiritual model and to share the Scriptures in a simplified way that all levels of society would aspire to live by, thus possibly pointing to the Protestant Reformation. Building upon St. Benedict (b. 480) in the wake of the decline of the Roman Empire, Gregory helped to establish monasticism, which would in turn act to preserve the Christian faith through the Dark Ages.

Just prior (451) to this time, the Council of Chalcedon determined Mary's place as the *Theotókos* (Mother of God) and Jesus as one person with two natures. By then the Rules of Pachomius and cenobitic life had been well established.[70] A number of early church fathers and mothers strove for spiritual life and practice most often within the monastery. Maximus the Confessor (580–662) worked to explain the Christian mysteries. Tyson[71] notes that Maximus sought to lead disciples into deep Christian experience

---

66. Mursell, *Story of Christian Spirituality*, 127–28.
67. Tyson, *Invitation to Christian Spirituality*, 113, 115–17.
68. Tickel, *Great Emergence*, 21.
69. Mursell, *Story of Christian Spirituality*, 70–72.
70. McGuckin, "Eastern Christian Tradition," 133.
71. Tyson, *Invitation to Christian Spirituality*, 132.

using symbolism of Christian worship as a means to incite disciples into the life and liturgy of the church of the time. Tyson[72] also represents Maximus as saying in his *Holy Assembly* that the purpose of divine chants is for leading the soul into virtues and "spiritual delight." It is by reading the Gospels, according to Tyson, that one brings the end of earthly thinking or the world of sense.

Through to the eighth century, the Syrian spiritual writers brought a large spiritual influence. Isaac of Nineveh (d. c. 700) bears note. He synthesized the intellectual, mystical traditions of Evagrius of Pontus (c. 346–99), the ascent of the mind of God, and Egyptian and Assyrian traditions that speak about the descent of God's mind into the heart where humans meet God.[73] Also, of tangential note, Islam, beginning with Muhammad's visions starting in 610 CE, enters world history during this period, and up to the present moment, introduced a point of contention and conflict to Christendom.

Pseudo-Dionysius (c. 500), as one of the most celebrated mystical writers of the time, blended Christian and Platonic mysticism. According to Tyson,[74] he saw the spiritual life in three parts: purification (purgative way), meditation on God's word (illuminative way), and union with God (unitive way). His work was carried forward by Meister Eckart and the Rhineland mystics up until the sixteenth century, when the spurious authorship was shown, questioning its importance.

The Great Schism

The Great Schism toward its end is best known as the monumental church split into Roman Catholicism and Greek Orthodoxy. In particular, the Middle Ages (1095–1145) brought a crisis that grew from monasticism. Particularly the growth of the Benedictine order brought prosperity, which created a conflict between the world and asceticism.[75] However, the Scholasticism that burgeoned during this era supported a deductive-allegorization of the Bible. The spirituality that arose during this time, according to Tyson,[76] was represented by Anselm's (c. 1033–1109) intellectual, philosophical, and psychological depth. It also drove Thomas Aquinas (1225–1274) to a synthetic and inclusive spirituality, according to Tyson. This period spills into

72. Ibid., 133
73. McGuckin, "Eastern Christian Tradition," 140.
74. Tyson, *Invitation to Christian Spirituality*, 128.
75. Ibid., 141.
76. Ibid.

the next as considered in the section below. Beginning in the fourteenth through to the late sixteenth century, which is most popularly associated with Luther, Wycliffe, Muntzer, Zwingli, Knox, Calvin, and Hooker, according to Tickle.[77]

John Wycliff (d. 1384), who preceded Gutenberg, was the pivotal figure in beginning access of Scriptures in the language of the people. This period also saw Francis of Assisi (1181–1226) who experienced God's presence through nature as famously named "Brother Sun," "Sister Moon," "Brother Wind," Sister Water," and "Sister Bodily Death." Although, according to Tyson,[78] Francis was ambivalent to the material world, owning nothing.

Thomas á Kempis (1380–1471) must be included in this brief review of the period. He was a member of the Brethren of the Common Life who were firmly Christocentric—to live in Christ and have Christ live in them.[79] As Tyson continues, reading Scripture in reverence was central to their discipline. Perhaps best known for his *Imitation of Christ*, á Kempis focused on the virtuous life against the learned life. The love and grace of God is of more importance than the memorization of Scripture. Moreover, simplicity, purity, pleasing God, and caring for one's neighbor shall bring inner freedom are among the many focuses á Kempis made in imitating Christ.

The Great Reformation

While the names are too many for this short section, the Great Reformation is best and popularly identified with Martin Luther's (1483–1546) nailing of the 95 theses to the door of the Wittenberg church, *sola scriptura*, and the priesthood of all believers. Furthermore, science continued to question long-held doctrine, which introduced dissonance to the Christian soul. The challenge was driven by such as Copernicus (1473–1543), Galileo (1584–1642), Kepler (1571–1630), and Newton (1643–1727). Along with this scientific movement came, according to Fukuyama,[80] the important beginnings of secular universal history penned by Pascal, Galileo, Bacon, Descartes and others connecting to the growing identification of universal laws.

The emerging literacy and access to the Bible birthed large numbers of interpretations and growing denominationalism that found over 34,000

77. Tickle, *Great Emergence*, 20.
78. Tyson, *Invitation to Christian Spirituality*, 5.
79. Ibid., 195–97.
80. Fukuyama, *End of History*, 56–57.

sects by the end of the twentieth century.[81] Although the exact numbers can be adjusted, the point remaining is the high numbers (even reduced by a large factor) of divergent theology driving differing practice or doing (L. *praxy*), in part energized by literacy. Although a great confidence in human ability was on the rise, piety was also finding prominence according to Tyson.[82]

Luther's "bound conscience," Calvin's "teachable mind," and Loyola's "exercises" pressed for the spirituality in the personal, and even with the laity, religious and secular according to Tyson. The Catholic Reformation, or the so-called Counter-Reformation, was good for both Catholics and Protestants. According to Tickle,[83] it brought such benefits as the Spanish mystics like Teresa of Avila (1515–1582) whose *Interior Castle* metaphorically led followers through the character of spiritual life.[84] Ignatius of Loyola (1491–1556), heading the Jesuits, helped to elevate Western history. His famous writing *Spiritual Exercises* (published 1548) stressed both physical and mental discipline and self-examination.[85] Not left behind, Tyson reflects on Loyola's contributions as prayer, meditation, and reflection on Christ's passion. Additionally, the Sikh movement in Hinduism (1489–1538) developed as another major contender for missionaries seeking to gain the hearts of the multitudes. Calvin (1509–1564) said in *Institutes*[86] that one could not contemplate oneself without "immediately turning his thoughts to contemplation of God." Although this pronouncement might be contested by postmoderns, his further statement cannot be biblically contested: that humans cannot gain a "clear knowledge" of themselves without first beholding God's face from which one might then "scrutinize himself."[87] As discussed earlier this beholding of God's face leads to spiritual transformation in the now ([PrōST] 2 Cor 3:18). In support, the claim is made, argues Tyson,[88] that "the heart of Calvin's spirituality" is "*unio mystica* [L.] 'mystical union with Christ.'"

Agreeing with Tyson,[89] this study argues that John of the Cross (1542–1591) is perhaps best known for his *Dark Night of the Soul*, in

81. Barrett et al., *World Christian Encyclopedia*, 10.
82. Tyson, *Invitation to Christian Spirituality*, 205.
83. Tickle, *Great Emergence*, 58.
84. Tyson, *Invitation to Christian Spirituality*, 255.
85. Ibid., 245.
86. Calvin, *Institutes*, I.I.1.
87. Ibid., I.I.2.
88. Tyson, *Invitation to Christian Spirituality*, 230.
89. Ibid., 262–63.

which he wrote of the need for such an experience for the human soul to be unburdened from worldly affections and possessed of God's light. The friend of Teresa of Avila, John was a great spiritual influence starting in this period. He and Teresa were the founders of the Discalced Carmelites. Tyson continues, both Teresa and John advocated an experiential spiritual expression. John especially pressed for emptiness and purification of the soul by contemplation physical mortification (apophatic mysticism) with a goal toward Divine union.

A brief mention of Puritan piety (1600s) of the post-Reformation period is worthwhile. Puritan spiritual writings were often drawn from Thomas á Kempis and medieval Catholic mysticism and nonconformists according to Lovelace.[90] Lovelace also acknowledged Puritan study of Augustine, Ambrose, Gregory the Great, and the Cappadocians as a nodding to those of spiritual sympathy but only after their devotion to the Reformers and apostles. According to Lovelace,[91] Puritan spirituality pressed a piety that reached into every area of life as the Christian's daily service. The Puritans brought an awareness of God's holiness and grandeur, human impurity and desire for sanctification. All beings are symbols and expressions of God's glory and spiritual truths, in intrinsic need of extending the kingdom of God. Their rigor, although rivaling monasticism, derived from a Puritan-born biblicalism.[92]

A full examination of this period would include a thorough review of the Wesleyan movement and early African-American traditions. However, only a few mentions are able or needful for present purposes. The Wesleyans gain their name from John Wesley (1703–1791). David Trickett[93] says that although Wesley's influences were varied and complex, his reading and insights produced the belief that one must exercise discipleship both before and in communion with God and with one's neighbor as one lives an embodiment of faith in God's presence and community. In addition, to gratitude to God and benevolence to neighbors, the most select societies of Wesleyans focused on holy living, holy dying, and walking in perfect love as the purpose of their classes, bands, and penitents.[94]

Although Smith[95] proposes three areas of the black church spiritual experience, black expression through music, art, literature, and the freedom

90. Lovelace, "Puritan Spirituality," 295.
91. Ibid., 306–7.
92. Ibid., 320–21.
93. Trickett, "Spiritual Vision and Discipline," 355.
94. Ibid, 368–69.
95. Smith, "Spirituality of Afro-American Traditions," 372–73.

movement shall serve as outward expressions of inward spiritual realities. The freedom movement was, according to Smith, a "quest for transcendent community or *communitas*" in a land of bondage and disparate tribes not unlike Moses and the biblical tribes in Egypt driving toward freedom in exodus. Although, of necessity, the white Protestant experience leeched into the black church, commensurately the black experience, which is a fusion of spiritualities not unlike the development of jazz, spilled over into white, American Protestantism as much as Puritan, Calvinistic, Evangelical sources. The awareness of the 1960s has made this clear as seen in singing, dancing, walking, praying, preaching, and even laughing, of not only the American church, but American society as a whole noting a spiritual experience that is more ethnic and inclusive than solely European, rightly argues Smith.[96]

Although there are certainly other names that are associated with the black church, Martin Luther King Jr. (1929–1968) is best known and the active representative of the black church and the civil rights movement born from that experience. Tyson[97] records that King's call came from God, who took his fears and gave him peace to stand for righteousness and truth. His love and forgiveness of enemies was on display for the whole world to see. It was in love that Martin Luther King Jr. found transformation in relationship with God.[98]

Orthodox spirituality and personalities have been discussed throughout this work; however, some attention shall be given to one luminary of the period at hand before moving on to the emergent period. Although compiled by a number of Greek fathers, the revision of the love of beauty (Gk. *philokalia*) as part of the Hesychast (an eremitic tradition of prayer) revival in the eighteenth century must take pride of place among the Orthodox.[99] By his writings (twenty-five large volumes), Sherrard[100] argues, Nicodemus of the Holy Mountain (1749–1809) was responsible for Hesychast spirituality surviving into theology, liturgy, and canonical tradition.

Nicodemus also translated and published the Catholics Ignatius Loyola and Lorenzo Scupoli. His work with Macarius of Corinth (1751–1805) produced his masterwork anthology that set the Hesychast revival in modern times, establishing prayer of the heart for both laity and monks.[101] Sherrard

96. Ibid., 404–6.
97. Tyson, *Invitation to Christian Spirituality*, 426.
98. Ibid., 429–30.
99. Sherrard, "Revival of Heysychast Spirituality," 418–19.
100. Ibid., 420.
101. Ibid., 420–21.

points up the importance of Paisii Velichkovskii (1722–1794) in translating the sacramental collection, *Philokalia* into Slavonic. Its publication as *Dobrotolubiye* in Moscow in 1793 is the volume carried by the pilgrim in *The Way of a Pilgrim*. It had a deep and far reaching influence on Russian piety in the nineteenth century as testified by Dostoevsky' works by the Russian translation (1857) by Ignatius Brianchaninov (1807–1867). The rippling affects of the various translations of the *Philokalia* cannot easily be over stated.

Postmodern Spirituality

An assessment of what is presently developing in the church is only tenuous. Mursell[102] aptly noted that Christianity is in the twenty-first century (2013). It is a world changing so quickly that it is perhaps impossible to predict the future except as an obvious shift from the northern to southern hemispheres. The machines have taken hold, or as Tickle[103] says it, "Technology and the knowledge of how to use it have leveled the playing field."

If the Reformation and its reverberations are said to lead to the Great Emergence, then is the "emergence" anything more than the words attributed to Herbert Fisher in 1934.[104] That is, history has been said to have "a plot, a rhythm, a predetermined pattern," but it is no more than "one [emergence] following upon another as wave follows upon wave." So, although one may argue for Great Emergence within the church, it seems to be within the sanguine muck of human striving. Perhaps the ground of the twenty-first century was tilled by the twentieth-century actions of Pentecostal, feminist, and liberation spirituality most recently as well as all that has proceeded.

After almost twenty years into twenty-first century, or the Great Emergence, many of the cultural responses are not satisfying the distracted, over-occupied, harried, and often-frenetic lifestyles of today's disciple. The nature-abhorring vacuum within humans is too often filled with the immediate rushing in. Without offering an experiential reality living within Christianity, we have become distracted by other competing void-filling offers. As rightly noted by Cox,[105] there is a growing openness and desire for the mystical. Noted earlier, Christian experience is filled with promise of fruits, gifts, and general experience to answer the human yearning. Agreeing here with Dunn,[106] Christian theology is anchored in experience and

---

102. Mursell, *Story of Christian Spirituality*, 366–67.
103. Tickle, *Great Emergence*, 15.
104. Fukuyama, *End of History*, 5.
105. Cox, *Fire from Heaven*, 308.
106. Dunn, *Jesus and the Spirit*, 361.

cannot survive with demonstrable vibrancy apart from experience. Dialectical Materialism, earth religions, Christian denominations and sects, Bahi, Mormonism, and mental sciences are all alternatives in search of experiential truth. Cox[107] reaches far in saying the church has presently entered a time in which it is beginning to see itself and its world as less cerebral or analytical and more intuitive and immediate. It is a church with an opportunity and responsibility to model the Christian experience filled with rich daily living and intimacy with God and humans.

As any version of history can attest, upheaval has been central to human affairs. Most particularly, upheaval has been central to Christian movement. Such tumult and shifts have been the soil in which spiritual transformation flourishes. Although the authority in Christendom shifts and reforms, and although authority's present place may be unclear and under question,[108] it may produce a beneficial result. The historical resignation of Pope Benedict XVI raises questions about the Catholic Church's direction and that of its 1.2 billion followers who seem to be enamored with Pope Francis and his reforms.

The groping of uncertainty not only births new paradigms, but drives seekers into God's arms for assuring comfort and opening to new guidance and intimacy. Pope Francis, from the southern hemisphere, signals the possibility of a more spiritual, humble, and compassionate church—an imitation of the "red-letter" Jesus of Scripture. Moreover, more than a quarter of Christians "emerging" are Roman Catholic.[109] Many of the world's Catholics are looking to Pope Francis with hope for answers about the future of the church in the new millennium.

The heart's desire and seeking for intimacy with God is common to all human eras, epochs, and cycles. If life is a pilgrimage or sojourn, then humans survive all of it and its trials by an inherent sympathetic, concordance with God's Spirit as God ushers history forward. Tyson[110] speaks about spiritual diversity and how walking with the heroes of the faith, such as Polycarp, Perpetua, Martin Luther, or Martin Luther King across the ages, ushers disciples past their comfort zones to a place of spiritual growth. Tyson is correct, the paradigm shifts, and the debates that have consumed the church over the ages are the seeds of spiritual growth, and the spiritually mature overcomers produced are the examples by which we all can live and move forward.

107. Cox, *Story of Christian Spirituality*, 301.
108. Tickle, *Great Emergence*, 45.
109. Ibid., 104.
110. Tyson, *Invitation to Christian Spirituality*, 4.

Borrowing variously from Scot McKnight's article "Five Streams of the Emergent Church,"[111] there are many popular names associated with the emergent or emerging church. Postmodern epistemology and the abandonment of metanarratives have changed the field over recent years. Such as the following participants can be listed in no particular order: Mike Reddell, Mark Pierson, Jonny Baker, Ian Mobsby, Ana and Brian Draper, Sue Wallace, Tony Jones, Jason Clark, Doug Pagitt, Chris Seay, Tim Keel, Karen Ward, Ivy Beckwith, Brian McLaren, Phillis Tickle, Mark Oestreicher, Dan Kimball, Andrew Jones, Rob Bell, Jamie Smith, Kevin Vanhoozer, John Franke, and Peter Rollins. Although this is an unauthorized and partial list, names, forms, numerous books, churches, and expressions are starting to emerge. What solidified form this emergence shall finally take is yet to be seen.

Orthopraxy, however, cannot supplant orthodoxy or the church shall represent another Gospel. This might lead to a formation or transformation that does not look like that model given by Jesus Christ during his sojourn. If the missional work of the church is key to the emergent church,[112] then making disciples (Matt 28:19; 2 Cor 5:18–19) takes place of primacy for communal church activity.

POSTMODERN PROMISES

To borrow from Jean-Luc Nancy[113] regarding the deconstruction of Christianity, this book "deliberately [runs] the risk of presenting a reflection that is still under construction, trying to find its way and unable to reach any conclusion except a pragmatic and tentative one." The tension in the area of postmodern, deconstruction studies, especially as they play against Christianity is tenuous, and so what is offered here is hoped as helpful and specifically only to further the aims of our considerations. It is of worthy note to say that deconstruction of scriptural texts cannot, by itself, produce the complete event by which the God of Scripture is delivered in speech. Drawing from Jenson,[114] because filling with text or memory cannot be evaded in "union with eternity."

Biblical ritual, Jenson offers, is not assured by deriving correct theological propositions, which are "linguistic enterprises." Jenson[115] claims

111. McKnight, "Five Streams of the Emergent Church."
112. Ibid., 4.
113. Nancy, *Dis-Enclosure*, 140.
114. Jenson, "Praying Animal," 317.
115. Ibid.

deconstruction is "an alien phenomenon with Christianity." It is, according to Jenson, like some forms of meditation, a silencing, an emptying of consciousness with no necessary expectation of infilling from a known text. However, Jenson fails to recognize the deconstructive work does not look to reach into silence where there is no voice of God, or to empty without hope of clarity and a better understanding. It is this place of silence and emptiness where it is hoped that the false and distractive is peeled back for the true and singular. Against Nancy,[116] I do not accept that Christianity, by its namesake, "has ceased giving life." Any so-called deconstruction referred to herein stands squarely in the reality of the life-giving message and reality of the Scripture (John 4:10, 14; 6:27, 51; 7:38; 10:28; 17:2).

Jenson[117] asserts that silence is only a temporary, suspect devise in moving toward a meditative place with God, who is always approached by ritual, sacrament, and sacrifice, which is by nature a visible speaking. Following, deconstruction philosophy can never "make the whole event by which the biblical God is brought to speech" which is a "filling of consciousness." However, deconstruction or postmodern philosophy, in its best yielding, does not make such a claim. Rather, as it relates to PrōST, deconstruction uses promise. That is, the promise of revelation is not limited nor guaranteed by the latest speculative technique of modern, literary technique. It is the Spirit's underlying drive to truth and life on which the Christian must rely (John 6:45; 14:26; 1 Cor 2:10, 12; 1 John 2:20, 27) and by which technique finds its efficacy. If deconstruction of the law to find justice, according to Derrida,[118] is desirable, then perhaps deconstructing the Christian history (Scripture) is needed to find spiritual transformation, inclusiveness, and universalism. As an example, abolition and women's rights were defended from a kind of deconstruction of Scripture, tradition, and theology. This also is the present effort of gender rights.

As already stated, deconstruction, in any of its forms, is not defended here, but its concepts are utilized here as seen helpful to the subject. Postmodern thought proposes both disturbing and promising questions and directions. If there has been a limiting factor to spiritual experience and transformation because of the dialectics of patristic, enlightenment, and even modern interpretations, postmodernity might be construed to release standard questions, answers, and possibilities. Such movement is a shifting and has even transformed reality that opens the possibility of realities only posited for and believed to be reserved for eternity future. The

---

116. Nancy, *Dis-Enclosure*, 141.
117. Jenson, "Praying Animal," 317.
118. Vanhoozer, "Theology and the Condition of Postmodernity," 17.

demonstrated lack of expressed, spiritual transformation leads some of us to accept a delayed eschatology of waiting for the "change" (Matt 24:31; 1 Cor 15:52; 1 Thess 4:13–18) as a substitution for a cosmology inclusive of present possibilities of what I have designated PrōST (proleptic spirituality transformation). This future event still shall not happen to passive believers and requires, at best, present faithfulness that ushers the future gift of being changed (transformed [1 Cor 15:52]).

If there is any truth to the thought of Tickle,[119] that according to Karl Marx and William Friedrich Hagel good and evil are not antithetical but two parts of the same and exist as long as they are two parts in opposition, then the deconstruction takes on, among other considerations, a discernment of the same. The synthesis produces another reality; and so "life [is] . . . a becoming never a being" as is creation and the Absolute, the state according to Marx, Tickle argues. Caputo's[120] interpretation of the theopoetics of the kingdom of God draws down an even more explicit inference that can only be implied from the truth found there that the entity deconstructed is not destroyed but changed, transformed, especially in praxis, as a result of its unrestrictable proclivities. This possibility does not ignore or countermand Scripture, especially anachronistic passages (Matt 8:29, John 2:4; 7:6). Rather, these passages can be deconstructed, and understood in an unhabituated light of progressive revelation as God unfolds his original desire that humans reflect his image in unhindered expression on earth now.

Anachronisms

Although one may not be able to establish a theology solely on the following, there are a number of biblical examples that may serve to draw out anachronistic meanings, or more precisely, prolepsis, that is before time or not-yet-in-the-now examples in support of PrōST. As already noted, several scriptural passages hint at a "before time" possibility or conjecture. Moreover, in Matthew's Gospel the demons cry out to Jesus, "What have you to do with us, O Son of God? Have you come here to torment us *before the time*?" (Matt 8:29b, emphasis added). The word (Gk. *kairos*) here is referring to an appointed time. Cullmann[121] supports the idea of prolepsis in noting that, "The demoniacs themselves thus note that here, even before the time, a decision is made whose effect for the kingdom of Satan still lies in the future." Further, or a particular hour (Gk. *hóra*), in John's account of Jesus'

---

119. Tickle, *Great Emergence*, 88.
120. Caputo, *What Would Jesus Deconstruct?*, 134–35.
121. Cullmann, *Christ and Time*, 71.

response to his mother's request for wedding wine: "Woman, what does this have to do with me? *My hour has not-yet come*" (John 2:4b, emphasis added). Finally, "Jesus said to them, 'My *time* [Gk. *kairos*] has not-yet come, but your time is always here'" (John 7:6, emphasis added). The variant forms of time in these and other passages, by context, still refer to an appointment, a special time. It is less the word for or variant and more the inner meaning conveyed about special divine moments or appointments. "The day of the Lord" (Heb. *Yahweh yom*) of the Hebrew Scriptures is taken over by the New Testament writers in this context. Further, according to 1 Corinthians 15:8 Paul was untimely (Gk. *ektrōmati*) born.

If deconstruction is the "experience of the impossible,"[122] then such a deconstructed understanding of *imago Dei* is suggestive that one might experience the not-yet of transformation in the now. Stripping the Greek or Hellenistic concept of time from Christian modes leaves time and eternity as no longer simply qualitative differences. What is thought of as "eternity" in the New Testament, Cullmann[123] argues, is a continuation of time as in age (Gk. *aión*) into the future. This carries importance and weight in that the not-yet of the last (Gk., *eschatos*) is, in this construct, no longer in consideration of time as qualitative difference.

Future transformation, occupies the same quality of time-space as does the measure enjoyed today. This removes a conceptual barrier that posits the impossibility of prolepsis (PrōST). Transformation is the same, although admittedly for most it is only experienced partially and minimally. My issue or point here is that although appointments are meant to be kept, there are exceptions for extenuating circumstances by, or for, which times and hours are exempted. The argument here is that spiritual transformation, to this extent of pulling into the now the not-yet, is a reality to be enjoyed by those "born out of time." This is preparatory or preview for a complete transforming of all God's children. Paul says, "When Christ who is your life appears, then *you also will appear with him in glory*" (Col 3:4, emphasis added). And John says, "Beloved, we are God's children now, and what we will be has not yet appeared; but we know that when he appears *we shall be like him*, because we shall see him as he is" (1 John 3:2, emphasis added).[124]

These instances all refer to appointed times and hours that are specific to respective events. Yet, there are hints of the possibility of something being done out of time before its appointment. PrōST speaks to this possibility also regarding transformed living. As already alluded to above, several

---

122. Caputo, *Deconstruction in a Nutshell*, 32.

123. Cullmann, *Christ and Time*, 61–62.

124. Black, *First, Second, and Third*, 409–11; Willimon, *Who Will Be Saved?*, 84.

biblical figures were taken or resurrected out of time. Enoch walked with God and was translated (Gen 5:24); Elijah, a powerful prophet of God, was taken up into heaven by a whirlwind (2 Kgs 2:11); Jesus, the perfect man (God-man), ascended to God (Mark 16:19; Acts 1:11).[125]

This comes from spiritual readiness and divine fiat. Moreover, this particular divine καιροι of PrōST, if it belongs to someone as it did for Enoch, Noah, Elijah, Jesus, and Paul, is sometimes outside of "regular schedules" of time and better serves God's grace and kingdom. However, the exceptions to the rule in no way change the rule. That is a fallacious conjecture. But the rule is often examined and confirmed by testing. This "excepting" might better be thought of as idiosyncratic versus a strict application of law without grace. Law stands as inviolate, but grace moves and flexes freely and fulfills the intent of the original law or "rule." That God's kingdom would be manifest on earth as it is heaven (Matt 6:10), and that we would be in intimate and unhindered communion and fellowship affecting the freedom of creation, is the intent and eventual full reality of redemption and sanctification in God's heart as seen in PrōST.[126]

Application

Whatever label is affixed to contacting the divine, it seems anecdotally clear that mystics, for one, have been doing this as much as historical account and legend testify. Catherine Tomas[127] insightfully notes mysticism in the plural, arguing that mystics "are identified as being other to everydayness, other to the ordinary and other to the normal religious practice of connection to the divine" by finding various means of access to the divine through ways not necessarily prescribed by canonical charge. As Tomas, here, wrestles with Heidegger, the transformation brought by this ontological intimacy is not epistemological knowledge as truth seeking. This mystical experience is a matter of being. It is being with the Divine. In a proposal that sounds very much like Schrödinger's Cat (1935), before one encounters an entity, it is neither true nor untrue but both.

Playing off of Caputo,[128] the possibility of a singular experience or "singularity" of the not-yet in the now is an exception to the "law" of not-yet as Abraham was excepted from the curse of the law before its establish-

---

125. Bauckham, *God Crucified*, 58–61, 68; Crisp, "Divinity and Humanity," 34.

126. Berkouwer, *Studies in Dogmatics*, 112; Harrison, "God's Many-Splendored Image," 16.

127. Tomas, "Validating the Ineffable," 3.

128. Caputo, *Deconstruction in a Nutshell*, 133–35.

ment—the remnant escaping through legal cracks by faith. The not-yet calls, summons, everyone to the impossible of the not-yet now. The possibility of the not-yet now is a reality now to be experienced. This makes "the singular higher than the universal" as is the urgency for the one lost sheep over the ninety-nine.

Moltmann[129] says, "[The] truth of freedom is love." God's love brings freedom not constraint. Freedom constrains itself by love (John 14:21–24; 2 Cor 5:14). Moltmann continues that this freedom is directed toward the future in the hope of God's coming and yet to be defined potentials. "In the Spirit we transcend the present in the direction of God's future." Such a thought furthers the reality of proleptic not-yet living and draws it down in a "creative function" into the now (PrōST).

More particularly, influencing God in "direct relationship" as friends, Moltmann[130] posits, not only being God's noncontributing children but allows for free will and freedom in growing human maturity including allowance for error. God has arranged a world of progressive freedom drawn to maturity for his human creatures in relationships which moves ultimately to knowing God face to face in un-frustrated partaking in the eternal life of God himself unbounded depth, profundity, and glory.[131]

CONCLUSIONS

As stated in the introduction, the primary aim of this study has been to investigate whether we must wait for the afterlife to have purification and spiritual transformation fully or largely "worked out" (Phil 2:12–13). This chapter argued that once hindering enculturation's are cleared as phantom, foundational limitations, and misapprehensions or misunderstandings about God, that PrōST is greatly facilitated through the influence that we have with God. Such an intimate relationship, as friends with God, allows for free will and spiritual growth in relationship. Moreover, scriptural constraints and decrees, wrongly applied, were also shown as hindrances to spiritual growth. More subtly, the tensions created by postmodern, deconstruction studies, especially as they are used as interpretive methods, were shown as tenuous, and only offered to further the stated aims of this book.

Enculturation and presuppositions is key to either limiting or freeing one to pursuing intimacy with God and being changed by that potential relationship. In this chapter, some of the foundational limitations that

---

129. Moltmann, *Trinity and the Kingdom*, 216–17.
130. Ibid., 220–21.
131. Ibid., 221–22.

interrupt proleptic spiritual transformation (PrōST) were examined such as those that may generally wall-in the disciple within supposed scriptural constraints, boundaries, and directives. These constraints are not necessarily pernicious in or of themselves; they are often within historical orthodoxy of faith and practice. However, as experiential spiritualities play out, they are often varied and escape attempts to neatly package them into an obedient codification or genus. Even when falling into doctrinal lines, foundational limitations often develop in our souls against living the fullest enjoyment of what the church can be in the now especially regarding proleptic spiritual transformation (PrōST).

Because of this, the yet-to-be completed spiritual reality is presented with impediments, and suggests that such a hope may not yet be fully realizable. Nonetheless, as discussed above, admitting that there is still a future hope and fullness does not delete the present that is now available. In tension, the followers of Christ represent the kingdom although not fully so; and therefore, must live with a sense of urgency.

As presented above, some theologians, however, limit the presence of the kingdom solely to the activities of Christ. The contention of this book remains that Christ's disciples are not fully, but presently living, to an imperfect degree, the kingdom. Additionally, the environmental and biological conditions with which humans must contend to survive and evolve further helps to explain the great difficulty in trying to live the transformed life.

This chapter also examined some of the shadows of doubt or phantom pains created by false beliefs, such as materialism and specifically physicalism, which obstruct efforts to spiritual transformation. By physicalism, transformation is often thought to be beyond demonstrable scientific proof. While the sciences have been welcomed in this chapter and throughout these writings, the spiritual is not presently demonstrable and thereby ruled out from consideration by most physicalists except as pseudo-scientific conjecture.

We also examined not understanding the full extent of God's forgiveness. Unforgiveness creates a spiritual prison of self-banished solitude from God and others hindering PrōST. The forgiveness and clear conscious secured by the work of Christ's love was clarified as the approach to God. Such forgiveness is in itself transformative.

We also considered in this chapter the problem of misunderstanding God and that a subsequent pursuit of God based on such misunderstandings produces inclinations, devotions, and endeavors that are outside of divine will. Misunderstanding engenders misrepresentation of God's person and attributes that counter spiritual transformation. Partaking only in the usual sense of emptying meditation before an "ineffable eternity" leaves one with a god alien to Christianity. The foundational problem, however, is that the Christian habit of ritual prayer is not sufficient, and that such meditation is often not per Christian tenets. Practicing disciplines either way, in empty ritual or empty, unfocused prayer leaves a gap and perhaps is misdirection for the disciple.

This chapter also considered the strong objection to any approximate release from ignorance, error, tempting vagaries attributed to our existence in this age. But the truth is that no absolute perfection is possible without the continual need of increased, progressive transformation. This is a softening of the idea of moral perfectionism and sinless existence in the present life without the pernicious belief that humans must live in defeat.

Five spiritual paradigm shifts were shown above as human constructs to understand world events to be analyzed and discussed for a better understanding of human past, present, and future life. I further argued that these periods are to further us to become, through Christ, what humans already are. Moreover, the self-transcendence or exocentricity of our souls is an expression of *imago Dei* expressed in history, and the epochs of history are driven, unfolding of God's image in creation.

We also considered the promises of postmodern thought. The tension in the area of postmodern, deconstruction studies, especially as they play against Christianity I argued as tenuous, and so what was offered was hoped for help and specifically only to further the aims of this book. I noted that deconstruction of scriptural texts cannot, by itself, produce the complete event by which the God of Scripture is delivered. However, I proposed deconstruction as the experiential impossible and, yet by it, suggested that one might experience the not-yet of transformation in the now.

Finally, I argued the influence that we have with God in intimate relationship as friends in a maturity that allows for our free will even when resulting in error. God has arranged a world of progressive freedom drawn to maturity for us in relationships, which moves ultimately to knowing God face to face in un-frustrated partaking in the eternal life of God himself unbounded depth, profundity, and glory.

As a result of the arguments of the prior chapters leading up to this chapter, and its argument about the limitations of enculturation and unchallenged presupposition, the following chapter is better positioned to present the glory available to us as God has intended. Especially helpful is an understanding of the forgiveness and clear conscious secured by the work of Christ's love that frees us to unhindered relationship with God and others in expression of *imago Dei*.

6

Reflecting God's Glory

PREFATORY

THE PRIMARY AIM OF this book, as stated in the introduction, has been to understand whether individuals need wait until the afterlife to have spiritual transformation fully or largely "worked out" (Phil 2:12–13). The prior chapter advanced this aim by the argument that once hindering enculturation and misapprehensions or misunderstandings about God are understood, that PrōST (proleptic spiritual transformation) is better advanced in open, intimate relationship with God. Shown here to be especially helpful was the forgiveness and clear conscious secured by the work of Christ's love that frees the disciple to unrestrained loving relationship with God and others in expression of *imago Dei*. Lastly, I presented the tensions created by postmodern, deconstruction studies, especially as interpretive methods, as tenuous, and only offered to further the stated aims of this research in disabused interpretation of Scripture.

As a result of the arguments of the prior chapters, we are better positioned to present the potential of shared glory available to us as God intended. If, as the Westminster Shorter Catechism states, humanity's "chief end is to glorify God, and to enjoy him forever" (Ps 86:9; Isa 60:21; Rom 11:36; 1 Cor 6:20; 10:31; Rev 4:11; Ps 16:5–11; 144:15; Isa 12:2; Luke 2:10; Phil 4:4; Rev 21:3–4), then I argue, giving God glory is facilitated by living the transformed life available in the now (PrōST), which yields such things as honor, appreciation, adoration, worship, affection, praise, subjection, and reflection of God's self in glory. While we cannot share in God's intrinsic, essential glory, we can reflect God's glory back to God and to the world. "The glory of God is a human being fully alive; and to be alive consists in beholding God," as Irenaeus[1] famously said. This reflection is by expressing God's communicable attributes such as love, righteousness, peace, joy, mercy, endurance, affection, patience, kindness, virtue, steadfastness, holiness, knowledge, self control, veracity, wisdom, insight, faithfulness, benevolence, purity, truth, truthful speech, spirituality, justice, gentleness, rejoicing, godliness, patience, goodness, beauty, and the mind of Christ (cf. Matt 7:16; Rom 14:17; 1 Cor 2:16; 2 Cor 6:4–12; Gal 5:22; Eph 1:1–4, 8–9; 4:1–7, 22–24; Col 3:12–17; Phil 2:2–8; 2 Pet 1:1–11).

The foci of this chapter are to consider love and free will in the garden as a restored and elevated state for human living and expression driven by a transformed perichoretic relationship with God the Trinity. In this chapter I argue that sin has no hold, that is, that the sin problem has been dealt with by *Christus Victor* in his incarnational work. It is a work freeing us to such a relationship with God provided by transformed living in a newness of life that is enjoyed and looks like what Jesus would do if he were living one's life in the present milieu.

We also examine the paradigm of God's children matured and transformed which leads them not only into responsible viceregency but a free maturity that can only be expressed as trusted friends of God (John 15:15). This examined, transformed life lights the way for others as God in Christ exampled and intends earthly life to be lived by those in *imago Dei*.

The implications for all that is presented in chapter 6, coupled with the prior chapters, suggest the possibility of a present spiritual transformational life (PrōST). Moreover, as noted in Conclusions, the points investigated in this chapter culminate the prior chapters in the hoped outcomes of glory as it begins to manifest in the disciple's life as PrōST.

LOVE AND FREE WILL IN THE GARDEN

Faber's[2] famous hymn, "There's a wideness in God's mercy," reads in part:

> For the love of God is broader
> Than the measure of man's mind;
> And the heart of the Eternal
> Is most wonderfully kind.

---

1. Irenaeus, *Against Heresies*, 4.20.7.
2. Milligan, *Elijah*, 36.

> But we make his love too narrow
> By false limits of our own;
> And we magnify his strictness
> With a zeal he will not own.
>
> F. W. Faber (1814–1863)

Faber's hymn nicely illustrates God's grace and mercy. Although many theologies portray God to be an ogre bent on punishing humans for the Edenic failure, as discussed above, regarding *Christus Victor*, God is interested in loving recovery and elevation of his *imago Dei* to more representative levels of himself. As I argued in chapter 2, we were created with the privilege and responsibility of being God's representatives not to replace God's glory in our own exercise of power decoupled from God. Clark,[3] here again, is correct that the fall from the Eden event makes humans like God (cf. Gen 3:5, 22; 2 Sam 14:17; 1 Kgs 3:22). God saw that Adam and Eve rebelled against his wishes and took of the forbidden fruit from the tree of the knowledge of good and evil, for which God removed the moment for humans to eternally live in that state of rebellion (Gen 3:22–24). By this rebellious act, humans became mortal.[4] Deprived of the glorious immortality that would have been secured in the tree of life, we were banished from the garden and the promised life of fellowship.

Adapting a borrowed analogy from Dallas Willard[5]—a similar thought is also found in Blaise Pascal[6]—when he says, "All the unhappiness of men arises from one single fact that they cannot stay quietly in their own [room]." A child may be placed in a room or garden, in which, if she stays, she is within her parent's will, according to Willard. The child naturally believes no matter with which of the toys or items she plays it is okay, since her parents put her there to play and they must be aware of the room's (or garden's) content, although she ignores the prohibition of one item in the room. Pascal would say the problem is leaving the room. According to Willard, God leaves a great amount of essential initiative to those in Christ; in fact, it is central to God's will for our maturing that we have this freedom. In the case of the freedom of Adam and Eve, there was a forbidden tree with which they were tempted and disobediently "played" and suffered the extreme universe, affecting consequences.

This is crucial in God's allowance for humans. The "garden" is the place where God placed his prototypical first humans, and it continues as

---

3. Clark, "Legal Background," 275.
4. Feinberg, "Image of God," 245.
5. Willard, *Hearing God*, 11.
6. Pascal, *Selections*, 214.

an allegorical representation of God's placement. That is, if one remains in the place and station arranged by God, he or she is free to do all that is available there. Of course, the same prohibition still stands against the tree of the knowledge of good and evil. More to the point, we still are not allowed, in defiance of God, to decide apart from his infused, matured life, how things shall be (Rom 5:5).[7]

According to Willard,[8] a world that allows for the moral development of human beings, allows for the faults, rebellion, and evil that inevitably arise from an exercise of genuine freedom. It follows, by this conjecture, that disaffection and rebellion are largely an indication of human free will (not only sin) and consequential action in a best of all possible worlds. It is a world in which all creation waits and yearns for the salvation of humans (Rom 8:18–25). It is our free action in a world where God's greatest and deepest love for the ultimate wellbeing of his creatures is inclusive of spiritual transformation in full expression of God's image in us. This world has been created and equipped to provide for the greatest degree of our freedom and allowance for human development. Consequentially, such freedom and allowance makes necessary the possibility and the realization of great rebellion and subsequent damage to God's creation by human sin (Gen 3:17–18; Ps 107:33–34; Jer 12:4, 11; Rom 8:18–22). Malfeasant, human freedom in the garden resulted in the fall.[9]

A person in instant, intimate relationship with God is compelled or constrained by Christ's life (Rom 6:6; Gal 2:20; 2 Cor 5:14; Titus 2:11–14). That is, right and moral acts come from an intimate relationship with God and not necessarily a set, construct, or number of laws or principles. This understanding can be misconstrued as Moral Particularism. Only if in a trenchant Moral Particularism one means there is no construct of absolute moral rights and wrongs that must be equally applied in every applicable situation, then the judgment is understandable. Rather, Moral Particularism, applied here, would mean that "right" and "wrong" are especially determined in the situation or case. In a person like one in consideration in these pages, the determination of right action derives from within a person in intimate relationship with the One (God) who stands above all considerations and makes a right judgment as to appropriate and best response. This does not negate moral principles but places their highest determination into the hands of the only One who can make a determination and us as we are rightly related to the One through the exigency and yet gentle, working of

---

7. Kärkkäinen, *One with God*, 124–25; Van Huyssteen, *Alone in the World?*, 143.
8. Willard, "God and the Problem of Evil."
9. Clark, "Legal Background," 275; Feinberg, "Image of God," 245.

the Holy Spirit. It is founded in and proceeds from love (Rom 13:8, 10; Gal 5:14; 6:2; Lev 19:18; Matt 3:15; 22:39; John 13:34).[10] This love originates and derives from a selfless place of love (Gk. *agapē*) in harmony with God's heart. It is love received as a result of God's real presence, which guides one to right action (Rom 5:5).[11] Living in such a place brings a freedom that is constrained and is not antinomian (lawless).

Exceeding the Garden

God desires to restore and exceed what was lost in the garden, and his solution includes an *imago Dei* that is now inclusive of the experiential realities of the God-man Jesus Christ—the *imago Christi*. Because of Jesus' transformative work imparted by the Spirit, it is now possible for us to live a life like Jesus lived in his incarnation—short of boundless divinity. To reiterate, I have argued in this book that we may approach this same existential reality in the now in the reality of spiritual transformation into the *imago Dei* that is inclusive of the life and experiences of Jesus Christ (*imago Christi*). The image bearing, like the "man of heaven" (1 Cor 15:49), is not to be reserved only for the eternal state when all things shall be restored and even made new (Rev 21:1–5). Living such a life in the "garden" of the world in free-will expression of *imago Christi* is to live not from rules, commandments of do not handle, touch, or taste (Col 2:20–23), but to live spontaneously driven from the a mature life of a spiritually transformed person, thriving from the substance and reality of Christ (Col 2:17).[12]

Although according to Van Huyssteen,[13] the ideal relationship with God is to look to the future, not to the past, or "existential, transhistorical present," he further cites Pannennberg as judging the "exocentricity" that points us to an, as yet, unfulfilled future while creating a tension between one's self-consciousness exocentricity and an openness to others. Drawing more, the argument I have given here is that "openness to others and to the world" advances one to the superlative Other of Christ and his modeled otherness in exampled-transformation opening the way to prolepsis which brings about, to that measure, a freedom now in that reality. In fact,

---

10. Milligan, *Elijah*, 36; Moltmann, *Trinity and the Kingdom*, 216–17; Tyson, *Invitation to Christian Spirituality*, 429–30.

11. Kärkkäinen, *One with God*, 125.

12. Pannenberg, *Systematic Theology*, 2:227; Kärkkäinen, *One with God*, 130; Willard, "Spiritual Disciplines," 106.

13. Van Huyssteen, *Alone in the World?*, 139.

Pannenberg[14] claims the exocentric structure of humans shadow forward a prolepsis in humanity. It is a prolepsis of an ultimate becoming, in God's image and destiny in fulfillment, in transcendent fellowship with God in openness beyond present experience and the present world. This identity is found only in Christ in his entire fulfillment of *imago Dei*, and the present life is understood in this, Van Huyssteen continues, where humans are becoming what they already are through Christ.

If, as Van Huyssteen[15] argues, the *imago Dei* is an "original gift and a future destiny for humankind," then as Pannennberg states, per Van Huyssteen's position, future destiny is already affecting eschatological reality in us now. Freedom is given as a reflection of and enablement from God to allow us to work toward God's likeness (Phil 2:12–13), along with reason to rightly choose in this process of spiritual growth.[16] But "in the end one's choices make [one] the kind of [person] who would be at home in God's Kingdom or in the outer darkness."[17] Corresponding to Genesis 1:26, a similar substance (Gk. *homoiousios*), according to Kärkkäinen,[18] implies a divine likeness in which one has freedom in expression of God's life. Divine will and human choice are joined over time to increasingly be the same impetus—a child increasingly expressing his or her essence assisted by divine example and prompting.

Freedom in Transformation

Freedom must derive from a transformed life. To try, by super human effort, to exercise against the temptations of life and to exercise for the necessities and good of life invariable meet with failure (Rom 7), despite the early historical encouragements from the desert fathers and mothers to the contrary.[19] A changed nature, that is, a life generated, cantered, and focused in God by the Spirit, is the essential need to work out one's salvation (Phil 2:12–13). "Although God's compassion and all embracing love is not irresistible, in the end it is unconquerable and invincible."[20] This is in opposition to any permissive thoughts such as "bold sinning" often liberally attributed

---

14. Ibid., 139–40.
15. Ibid., 141.
16. Harrison, "God's Many-Splendored Image," 13–17.
17. Ibid., 16; Willard, "Spiritual Formation."
18. Kärkkäinen, *One with God*, 20–21.
19. Harrison, "God's Many-Splendored Image," 17–27.
20. Power, "Imago Dei," 140.

to the Lutheran theology in an antinomian manner. Bonheoffer[21] explains well, "Sin boldly, but believe and rejoice in Christ more boldly still" (L. *Pecca fortiter, sed fortius fide et gaude in Christo*). He says Luther's intent was that we should thoroughly admit and confess our sin and not hide from its dark realities, for Christ's costly grace is its more than capable solution. While Luther's version of justification by faith insists on "inner change," a freedom to "love and good deeds," resulting from Christ's indwelling the believer is required.[22]

Freedom is granted to those walking in their inheritance of "peace, joy, and happiness commensurate with the state of [our] own being before God and the state of the world within which [we] live."[23] God is not interested in micromanaging every step and turn of his imaged creatures. Such a proposal would be an utter waste of the beauty and glory accorded us in image bearing. Such a proposal would only produce automatons reflective of a machinist, mechanic, or engineer at best.

Agreeing here with Heschel,[24] the whole of our life and activity are implicated by the details of our life; the details or parts are given meaning by the whole. These details are openly lived out in relationship with others in and through God's creation. So then, to be free from sin and to be in the image of God in a progressive transformational state is played out by the freed being living in that reality and practice in expressing a measure of the wholeness of the reality of a divine life in God's kingdom. Divine DNA drives and draws the constituent parts of the whole person in expression of *imago Dei*. The attributes of spiritual transformation in both the now and the not-yet are driven by this Christ infused *imago Dei*. There is such real and transforming freedom in this process that a threat to God's sovereignty and glory might be mistaken. In support of such a freedom in light of God's sovereignty and prerogatives is sufficiently supported by proof texting; however, such a substantiation is beyond our scope and unnecessary for the purposes of this discussion regarding PrōST.

Karl Barth[25] spoke about this freedom as a gift from God. He claimed it as a joy in which we advance toward God's election. In this we are God's partners and God's children as "God's man." This is a freedom to live as God's child in communion and in faith, dependence, and in thanksgiving

---

21. Bonheoffer, *Ethics*, 52–53.
22. Kärkkäinen, *One with God*, 124–25.
23. Power, "Imago Dei," 139.
24. Heschel, "Holy Dimension," 119, 123.
25. Barth, *Humanity of God*, 69.

alongside of God in partnership, Barth concludes,[26] also considered friends. All free will and good-works are pleasing to God. Whether Abraham in his hospitality to God, Elijah in his enjoyment of quiet and love of God, or King David's worship in song and humility,[27] God finds us all pleasing and catalysts to spiritual growth and communion with himself.

SIN HAS NO HOLD

If Adam and Eve were born or evolved into emergent perfection and with such a sinless disposition, then it seems they would naturally possess a potential that included the possibility or disposition, even necessity, of progression toward God's intended vocation of humans toward God's full image. Webb[28] argues for progressive ability to "handle" a process of growth. This truth, on a natural and human level, is observable in cultures throughout time. However, on a spiritual and transformed level this slow process can be accelerated and even demonstrated in stepwise functions that revolutionize rather than evolve a personality, understanding, and a person's attributes. It is not solely the disciples' own development, but by fearless participation or necessary activation of one's inherent inclination given by virtue of nature of birth, argues Pannenberg,[29] as evolved to that point.

Despite the Edenic fall, as represented in the allegorical first couple, Adam and Eve, and even after the fall, Power observes,[30] in agreement with this book, that each uniquely created human being has the capacity to model and live a life after the image of God. Although there were deep damaging results from the fall, this does not include the essence of *imago Dei*. God has not left his creation without recourse, capacity, and capability. Christ has dealt with sin, giving freedom for new life in God's image (Rom 6:4, 6; 2 Cor 2:5; Gal 2:20; 5:24; Col 3:3, 10). His image in us is fully preserved and in no way damaged or diminished. Moreover, in reflecting on Gregory of Nyssa, Harrison[31] continues on to suggest that the "jar" of our capacity expands or increases in size ensuring that we shall always yearn and reach for more of God in a cycle of "eternal growth" as what we first received is exercised, increased, and expanded.

26. Ibid., 82
27. Harrison, "God's Many-Splendored Image," 20–21.
28. Webb, *Slaves, Women & Homosexuals*, 59.
29. Pannenberg, *Systematic Theology*, 2:228.
30. Power, "Imago Dei," 131.
31. Harrison, "God's Many-Splendored Image," 16–17.

As briefly considered above, and worth repeating, in part, here: biblical sin entered through Adam. However, there is no logical necessity, except ingrained "orthodox" Western theology, translational error (Rom 5:12),[32] and a primitive scientific understanding by Augustine, driving a traducianism interpretation,[33] that inherited Augustinian sin was infused into and remains in the nature of Adam's federated progeny. The great philosophical theologian, Jonathan Edwards, along with others,[34] questioned such a concept. He questioned that there was any causality between Adam and Eve's colossal blunder and their descendants inherited compunction to the same. Wyman[35] rightly points out that we cannot clearly discern the fall of the first couple as irreversible changes of human nature. Continuing, he does not say that a single couple could change the course of the entire human race, present and future, and yet themselves remain the same. An individual can act according to his or her nature, but not upon that nature without the argument supporting some form of heretical Manichaeism.[36] The proposition that the first sin changed human nature forever may have no place within the Christian consciousness, except to say that ancestors "re-present" the sin model to their descendants, which are culpable in consonant will.[37]

The concept of "original sin," if accepted as generally understood, is of great import for proleptic spiritual formation (PrōST). Stated above, I reject the conjecture of original sin as genetically inherited or ancestral sin.[38] If by this concept is meant constitutional sin, then any hope of large measures of sanctification in this life (PrōST) is futile.[39] Every human commits sin, but that is not because nature makes the requirement. Understanding this allows for the possibility of proleptic spiritual transformation, which is not delimited or nullified due to any concept of a fallen human nature. Salvation is held in spiritual transformation. Keil and Delitzsch[40] speak to this when they address the issues of Genesis 1:26 in speaking of the loss through sin as regained by Christ in expressing God's glory and essence.

---

32. Shults, *Reforming Theological Anthropology*, 192.

33. Ibid., 204–6; Meyendorff, *Byzantine Theology*, 144.

34. Pannenberg, *Systematic Theology*, 2:232–33; Shults, *Reforming Theological Anthropology*, 192, 200–201, 232–33.

35. Wyman, "Rethinking the Christian Doctrine of Sin," 206.

36. Ibid., 206–7.

37. Schleiermacher, *Christian Faith*, 298; Wyman, "Rethinking," 210–11.

38. Brunner, *Man in Revolt*, 145–47; Pannenberg, *Systematic Theology*, 2:231–33; Wiley, *Original Sin*, 206–8.

39. Finney, "Accounting for Moral Depravity," 190, 192.

40. Keil and Delitzsch, *Commentary on the Old Testament*, 39.

In part, as affects our direction here, sin has no hold because the transformation spoken of in the Bible is not a temporary state that remains as long as some numbers of spiritual practices are enjoined or some prescribed frequency of rituals are maintained. Rather, the transformation spoken of here is as irreversible as is the transformation of the caterpillar into a butterfly. Although we may enjoy a moment of joy and enlightenment in communion with God, his words, his people, or transformative circumstances, the transformation proposed here is one of permanence. It may be better referred to as permanent shift from "one degree of glory to another" (2 Cor 3:18).

NEWNESS OF LIFE: DOING AS JESUS DOES

Attempting to be "like Jesus" or following a trite, hackneyed approach of "what would Jesus do" is useless and law-based without, in some measure, being who Jesus was—is in one's life and today's milieu. Enjoying the *imago Dei* brings not only the substantive image of God the Father but also the added existential experiences of Jesus Christ here on earth, in present time-space. The kingdom is at hand (Gk., *eggizō* [Mark 1:15; Matt 3:2; 4:17]). Followers or subjects of the kingdom are to live and be in newness of life (Rom 6:4; 2 Cor 5:17; Gal 6:15; Eph 4:24; Col 3:10).

A declarational image of God, in which a likeness or similarity is shared between God and humans, argues Van Huyssteen,[41] is a sharing of communicable attributes that may then lead to a paradigmatic *imago*. Such a sharing points to a functional likeness between God and us, specifically concerning the exercise of sovereign power, referring to the human office in representing God's rule in the world. To do without or before entering this life can be seen in the example of a child attempting to be as its parent before "becoming" its parent. A child's whole being must go through radical growth and change before it can run a mile, do algebraic calculations, and generally assume the responsibilities of an adult. Spiritual transformation is about this becoming. It is the restoration of an unhindered *imago Dei* inclusive of the realities of Christ's sufferings and enrichments of this image that now contain the experiential overcoming last Adam (1 Cor 15:45).

The *imago Dei* is, at its foundation, an enjoyment of and radiating of generosity and love, which is conjoined with a shared "creative power" from God in continuing his creative work through nonviolent, "developmental and transformative," care for creation.[42] Populating and managing

---

41. Van Huyssteen, *Alone in the World?*, 156.
42. Ibid., 157–58; Middleton, *Liberating Image*, 278.

the world (Gen 1:28) in a generous and loving manner is intrinsic to this creative activity. As addressed above, this image displays God's love, mercy, and grace to all creation, making the Christian faith attractive and transformative (Matt 5:16).[43] God's gifts cause the gifted to spontaneously love God. And in response, such an image in us offers devotion and praise to God. Finally, such *imago Dei* in us is the best attraction to a dark and lost world (Matt 5:16; Luke 15:24; 2 Cor 3:3, 8–10, 18; 4:6).

Radicalized

Gordon Fee,[44] for one, speaks about the now or "already" and the "not-yet" of the eschatological realization as being in tension between what is enjoyable today and what still remains for future fulfillment. However, this tension allows for some larger measure of now than is normally proposed. Too often the not-yet part of the precept is heavily weighted in opposition to the now of Jesus' completed work. What is expected now is often left as anemic and feeble. However, the present has been judged and is passing away, while the present and future has been inaugurated in great measure (Rom 6:4; 1 Cor 7:31; 10:11; 2 Cor 5:14–17). In the same work, Fee[45] hints at a realized eschatology where he notes, "Empowered by the Spirit, we now live the life of the future in the present age, the life that characterizes God himself." Making room for some unfulfilled eschatology, he goes on to say that although we have tasted something of the life that is yet to come the full and final realization is still left for the future. Moreover, this future is so certain that "God's new people are completely radicalized as they live 'already' but 'not-yet.'" Kärkkäinen,[46] in assessing the Orthodox view of deification, asserts that its fullness is left to the future and then testifies that yet such deification must be "fulfilled ever more and more even in this present life." This is the PrōST considered here. The New Testament provides a Christology that both looks back to the creation, but more importantly "anticipates the eschatological fullness in the new creation."[47]

Van Huyssteen,[48] interacting with Pannenberg and Shults, speaks of future human destiny displayed in Christ, in whom we already share is, by the power of the Spirit of God, "already effecting the eschatological reality

---

43. Willard, "Living a Transformed Life."
44. Fee, *God's Empowering Presence*, 803–5.
45. Ibid., 804.
46. Kärkkäinen, *One with God*, 31.
47. Grenz, "Jesus as the Imago Dei," 621.
48. Van Huyssteen, *Alone in the World?*, 141.

of the new human being in them." The Gospel records are filled with the marvel of Jesus' life compared to the Christian creeds, which only speak haltingly of Christ's virgin birth, life, and suffering under Pontius Pilate. "Christ is the unexpected fulfillment of human intent, the proper word for God, and the true fulfillment of Creation in the realm of human works," Milbank[49] insightfully argues, and continues, that humans are the practical recognition of Jesus Christ "as the fulfillment of human intent by regarding our entire lives as nothing but an interpretation of Christ as presented to us in the Scriptures and in the Sacraments."

Lewis[50] addressing a question regarding humans' next evolutionary step, answers that it has already occurred in Christ as the "new man." It is a life that is to be put into humans. Lewis goes on to speak about baptism, belief, and "mysterious action." In addition to the "mysterious actions" of sacraments, I have argued for the actions of disciplines. Lewis[51] continues that this change in humanity after the image of Christ is not simply an improvement but a transformation. It is going from being creatures of God to being children of God—a step and reality beyond evolution.

Eschatologically Present

The newness of life, as Berkouwer[52] presents, is in the image of God as sanctification in the believer, and in those God's glory becomes evident to all. Jesus is God made present to the world in his followers. In the same argument, Berkouwer[53] rightly claims that transformation affects the full depths of the disciple's total existence in which Christ is visible when the disciple leads Christ's life. "The eschatological seriousness is felt in the earthly life in opposition between love and hate." Berkouwer[54] continues that the children of God are known in this way now and not hidden in obscurity (1 John 3:10). The conformation into the image of Christ, the justification, and glorification (Rom 8:29–30) are meant to begin in the now as human true destiny, Berkouwer[55] rightly claims.

---

49. Milbank, *Word Made Strange*, 13.
50. Lewis, *Mere Christianity*, 62–63.
51. Ibid., 185–86.
52. Berkouwer, *Studies in Dogmatics*, 112–13.
53. Ibid., 113–14.
54. Ibid., 116.
55. Ibid., 117.

God's kingdom is, in a real sense, already present (Matt 10:7), especially as one becomes opened and attuned to God and God's rule,[56] despite so much of what would be, and is, considered non-kingdom evidence to the contrary. The reality of a present kingdom opens the door to an experience of the numinous. In his life Jesus did many great and wondrous works. He said that whoever believes in him would do what he does and even do greater works than he (John 14:12). As Bushnell[57] submits, Christ's perfect life changes the very consciousness of humanity, and inexorably brings the kingdom life and its reign. This clearly hints at the possibility of universalism as discussed above.

Willard[58] points to Scripture in support. The path is one by which a disciple can truly, as Paul told the Ephesians, "be strong in the Lord and in the strength of his might" (Eph 6:10) and "be strengthened with power through his Spirit in your inner being" (Eph 3:16). It points to the full and abundant life (John 10:10). Willard continues it is only by receiving this abundant life that one becomes adequate to the calling. This was God's intent from the beginning. This is the expression of the newness of life (Rom 6:4; 2 Cor 5:17; Gal 6:15; Eph 4:24; Col 3:10). This is the life without grumbling or disputing. It is as blameless and innocent children of God without blemish in the midst of a crooked and twisted generation, among whom disciples shine as lights in the world, holding fast to the word of life, so that in the day of Christ we may be proud that we did not run in vain or labor in self-absorption (Phil 2:14–16).

In the thirteenth century, Aquinas[59] argued the question of what spiritual enjoyment is available now. The debate raged regarding the now and not-yet of Christ-likeness and thereby an abeyance of full transformational work in the individual until the future kingdom. Aquinas addressed a theological question that has yet to find full consensus among modern scholars, except that complete spiritual transformation is most often reserved for a future kingdom. The requirements of anything approaching a large measure of spiritual transformation are thought so great, that such scriptures as Jesus' Beatitudes are usually reserved for a future fulfillment. The deficiency of guidance and emphasis on spiritual transformation exposes a superficial notion and goal of the Christian faith. Such spiritual realities or states, in

---

56. Willard, *Divine Conspiracy*, 77.
57. Bushnell, "Protestant Views," 345.
58. Willard, "Living a Transformed Life."
59. Aquinas, *Summa Theologia*, 886–87.

their fullness, are typically limited in most theologies and popular preaching to the eternal state in God's expressed presence.[60]

In this study I have attempted to demonstrate that much of what God offers his sons and daughters is available, and, in truth, meant for now. The spiritual life, often reserved for the future *eschaton*, supposedly waiting for fulfillment in "heaven," is not only available today, but is intended for large enjoyment and expression now. Because of the frailties, failings, and apparent lack of display of transformative endeavors and demonstrations in human living, many have come to believe and expect so much less than God has offered. The horror of what society readily gives as inhumane treatment of one another and the clear failure to reflect much of God's image has caused us to despair of anything wonderful and exemplary of the kingdom having come. So we wait for a future fulfillment and vindication of Jesus' words that we shall do greater things than he did when he lived the Spirit-filled life free of sin (Rom 6:6; Gal 2:20; 5:24; Col 3:3, 10). We wait for full demonstration of power, and a life saturated with spiritual excellence thought to be beyond the reach of any except the second person of the Trinity. But Jesus came to demonstrate how life should be lived and how the image of God should be reflected in all of us.

Unified Theory and Immanentization

Although I have not discovered a unified theory or consensus among scholars regarding spiritual transformation nor do I claim one of my own, I have examined the extents, and present possible realities, as issues and questions. Nonetheless, beginning in the eighteenth century, Catholics, Orthodox, Protestants—led by Luther's practical movement and Arminius' theoretical focus—were eclipsed in spiritual matters by Wesley's movement.[61] King and O'Malley continue that Wesley's movement came to be called Methodists because of their dedication to works and holiness affected by English spiritual writers and the Moravians. They stood on an inward change of the disciple not only positional change of justification. Additionally, to the spiritual efforts of Wesley and many others named throughout this book, a potentially shared view of, in effect, becoming like God, *theōsis*, has the potential of serving as a uniting factor across camp boundaries that tease at and suggest the possibilities of a proleptic spiritual transformation (PrōST) or reality that is available to the twentieth-first-century church.[62]

---

60. Aquinas, *Summa Theologia*.
61. King, *Proceedings of the Third Ecumenical*, 257; O'Malley, "Methodists," 555.
62. Kärkkäinen, *One with God*, 119–20, 123.

Dallas Willard[63] speaks of the kingdom of God as something that is present now and for entering. Kingdom now (John 3:3, 5; Rom 14:17; Col 1:13; 4:11) is an expression of the life of Jesus, as it would be lived out through us in large enjoyment of the kingdom now. The enjoyment now of the kingdom is important to support, in some measure, the possibility of entering a proleptic spiritual transformation (PrōST). The things that are part of the kingdom in full measure are the same as those of PrōST such as joy, hope and peace and other expressions of the kingdom (Rom 14:17; 15:13; 1 Cor 13:4; Eph 5:9; Gal 5:22; Col 3:12). The gifts of the Spirit, attributes of the kingdom, and spiritual transformation are expressions of the same communicable gifts and attributes from God in expression of his image in his children.

I am not proposing an immanentization of the *eschaton*. Yes, doing as Jesus does proceeds from the kingdom. Jesus did not say that if certain people would do certain things the kingdom would arrive. No, he said it is now. This does not necessitate a physical manifestation or immanence of the kingdom as material rule. Doing kingdom things comes from the kingdom. If we have a right relationship with the kingdom, by definition the King, what proceeds from the King's rule shall be exercised. The nature of a kingdom realm, is where the sovereign's wish and will are fulfilled by the subjects of the kingdom.[64]

Jenson[65] says that "creatures" are what God speaks about, but that humans are distinguished from other creatures in that God speaks to them in addition to about them. (I am not convinced that God does not speak *to creatures beside* humans). However, this discourse between humans and God is "ineluctably embodied" in prayer, that is, communion with God. Communion changes the nature of a thing.

Jesus claims to usher in a new aeon by his arrival, obedience to God, and life (Matt 11:4–6; Luke 4:17–21; John 4:25–26). Jesus opens the entrance to this kingdom. In fact, he said that those who follow him would do greater things than he did (John 14:12). At the core in its essence, this doing proceeds from being. Grossly speaking, a person does not bodily fly without growing "wings." Such a transformation is the kind spoken of in Scripture and by Jesus himself and Paul (John 3:3; Gal 6:15). This is behind the meaning of these often quoted words regarding doing the will of God the Father,

---

63. Willard, *Divine Conspiracy*, 28.
64. Hick, "Pluralist View," 185; Willard, *Divine Conspiracy*, 408.
65. Jenson, "Praying Animal," 321.

including casting out demons and doing mighty works in the name of Jesus (Matt 7:21–23).[66]

Jesus is pointing to a reality in relationship that transforms the one who is close to him. This relationship is transformative. Beholding Jesus' beauty in an open, unveiled intimacy, is transformative (2 Cor 3:18). Such a becoming includes behaviors that are pleasing to God and "known" (Matt 7:23) by him. The transformation from such a relationship as this is proleptic.[67]

Borrowing Gadamer's[68] discussion on "copy" and applying it to the *imago Dei* of humanity, one can see that the "resemblance that lies within itself" helps to explain the God-human relationship that is of the *imago Dei*. That is, the *imago Dei* is not pointing to God as representing, but signs God as humanity's "own content." God is "represented, caught, and made present" by the degree we make present what of God is not present except as resembled by us.[69]

The famous words of Athanasius, "God became man so that man might become a god,"[70] have been a point of debate and contention since they were first uttered. Erickson,[71] not directly referring to Athanasius, says that humans shall never become gods but shall remain humans and there shall always be transcendence of God in relation to humans. More specifically, salvation is God restoring humanity to what he intended it to be, not elevating us to who or what he is.[72] However, disagreeing with Erickson, I have already argued for something more than the Edenic state.

Destined *Perichōrēsis*

We previously examined Pannenberg's words, in which he claims that humans have a common destiny in the reality and relationship of the *imago Dei*, we are destined for intimate fellowship with God now as the "inner *teleos*" of the relatedness of the *imago Dei* toward including us into God's kingdom.

---

66. O'Collins, *Westminster Dictionary*, 472; Saucy, *Case for Progressive Dispensationalism*, 106; Van Huyssteen, *Alone in the World?*, 143.

67. O'Collins, *Westminster Dictionary*, 472; Van Huyssteen, *Alone in the World?*, 143.

68. Gadamer, "Truth and Method," 413–14.

69. Ibid., 414.

70. Gross, *Divinization of the Christian*, x.

71. Erickson, *Christian Theology*.

72. Ibid., 472–74.

Perichōrēsis is the fellowship being examined here. Moltmann[73] proposes the eternal trinitarian relationship in love is the same love with which the Trinity loves within itself. This perchoretic love relationship is the basis of salvation, according to Moltmann, and corresponds to human fellowship, or "community of Christ" in *perichōrēsis* through acceptance, respect, love, and affection. Moreover, argued by Eastern Orthodoxy, divinization is the destination and the full *imago Dei* in humanity. This image, Vishnevskaya[74] says, culminates in a full perichoretic union of God and humans and is, in unhindered relational terms, a perichoretic community.

Referencing *perichōrēsis* in Moltmann[75] and Vishnevskaya,[76] rather than hazard an all-inclusive definition of *imago Dei*, a leg of this book heavily leans on Eastern Orthodox traditions that divinization is the goal and the full *imago Dei* in humans and that personality and relationships are connected and present simultaneously. Moltmann[77] claims that the Trinity exists and continues in "the common divine nature" and the Trinity "exists in relations to one another." Specifically, this image culminates in a full perichoretic union of God and human beings, and is, in unhindered relational terms, nothing less than perichoretic community.[78] Moreover, Moltmann[79] claims that humans are *imago trinitatis*, only reflecting the triune God as much as they are united with one another. In this expression of perichoretic, triune-life, is "at-oneness" of the Father, Son, Spirit in "blissful love." Moltmann[80] elsewhere says, it is not a matter of privilege or subordinate, but a communal experience of Christ. It is a Spirit, united fellowship and reality of respect, tenderness, care, and love. Moreover, Grenz[81] suggests that life in Christ is a matter of community where the divine character of Jesus Christ "truly shines forth." It is a social concept in eschatological orientation, Grenz presses, in which this new humanity is God's outworking of his intention for humanity as *imago Dei*.

In this relationship, God condescends to address and have conversation with us. The *ability* to be in conversation with God is requisite to that

---

73. Moltmann, *Trinity and the Kingdom*, 157–58.
74. Vishnevskaya, "Divinization as Perichoretic Embrace," 133–34.
75. Moltmann, *God in Creation*, 172–73, 258.
76. Vishnevskaya, "Divinization as Perichoretic Embrace," 133–34.
77. Moltmann, *Trinity and the Kingdom*, 173.
78. Vishnevskaya, "Divinization as Perichoretic Embrace," 133–34.
79. Moltmann, *God in Creation*, 216.
80. Moltmann, *Trinity and the Kingdom*, 157–58.
81. Grenz, *Social God*, 267–68.

conversation and "ineluctably embodied" in prayer.[82] Such unhindered and open conversation and even fellowship is first seen in the cool of the Edenic garden in which God walked and conversed with the prototypical humans—Adam and Eve (Gen 3:8). Karl Barth[83] completes an extended argument about God's "togetherness with man" by saying that no one is required to engage in a broad investigation "to seek out and construct who and what God truly is, and who and what man truly is, but only to read the truth about both where [truth] resides, namely, in the fullness of their togetherness, [and God's and humans] covenant which proclaims itself in Jesus Christ." In this appraisal, Barth[84] argues that the meaning and power can only be found in the context of God's history and his discourse with humans, that is to say, God's togetherness with his human creatures. Barth continues that to understand who or what God is must be sought in God's speaking and acting as the human partner although he is the completely superior partner. This communicating and fellowshipping God's deity includes his humanity as displayed in Jesus, in whom there is no separation of deity from humanity.

As briefly discussed above, Barth[85] continues by directing the reader's attention to the underlying "freedom for love" and God's ability even "capacity to bend downwards" towards humanity in Christ, which Christ is himself, which condescension through Jesus Christ is the "highest communion of God with man." Barth presses, "[God's] *deity encloses humanity in itself*" (emphasis original).[86] Barth claims that it would be a false deity of a God who is also false if God's humanity did not also directly encounter humanity. In this is the established reality that God does not exist without humans.

The Humanity of God

This fellowship is not a matter of study and knowledge of God. To know or even believe in God is surely necessary, but it is not sufficient (Jas 2:18–20). Intimate fellowship is not primarily a matter of knowledge but of abiding by God.[87] It has real affects in this life. This position stands with a Keswick

---

82. Jenson, "Praying Animal," 321.
83. Barth, *Humanity of God*, 47.
84. Ibid., 45–47.
85. Ibid., 48–49.
86. Ibid., 50.
87. Heschel, "Holy Dimension," 120.

view of sanctification and according to Boyd and Eddy,[88] against Reformed views. It is fair to note that for Confessional Lutherans, sanctification flows from faith (justification) and effects an inward moral transformation not to be completed in the present life. As referenced above unlike a single or legal-facet-Calvinistic view of justification, Confessional Lutheranism includes both regenerative and transformative elements by participating in Christ in an ontic union.[89] This transformative work is an ontological change to those justified by Christ's justifying work. Although it is an "eschatological vindication" and reality invading the present, it is an accomplishment that needs cooperation, discipline, and nurturing by the redeemed for present and progressive existential enjoyment and growth.[90]

The Wesleyans emphasized God's power to transform disciples in the present versus "a legal fiction or merely an eschatological promise." Clearly, this requires presenting oneself to God's righteousness, which leads to transformation (Rom 6:19). The new life that is given to those accepting God's solution to the sin problem and estrangement from God, self, and others receive a life that is mysterious in that it is a new birth as born by God himself in the second person of the Trinity (John 1:12; 3:3, 16, 36; 1 John 2:2). Critically important, is that this new life is "fuller" than what was experienced in the garden by those first beings enjoying God's life, presence, and fellowship. Since the incarnation, life, passion, death, resurrection, and ascension of Jesus, God has "changed," if it might be put that way. What is spoken of here is that Jesus took into the Godhead humanity as gloriously and rightfully experienced and lived in Jesus Christ.

In *The Humanity of God*, Karl Barth[91] presents it thus. God's deity cannot exclude his humanity. "It is God's freedom for love," adeptness and measure to be in both the heights and depths, to be large, great, and small for those others who are distinct from himself in offering himself in unconditional priority to them. God has the initiative, leadership, and word as his action. Moreover, Barth continues, God's deity includes humanity. Therefore, it would be falsehood if his deity did not, without hesitation, fully initiate encounters with humans. Exclusion of humans is not optional.

This reality drives one's analogy away from Gregory of Nyssa'a description of the *imago Dei* as simply a reflection of God even a glorification of God in looking upon God[92] to a more intrinsic idea of emanation or dif-

---

88. Boyd and Eddy, *Across the Spectrum*, 179.
89. Cooper, "Lutheran Response to Justification," 2–4.
90. Ibid., 3, 6.
91. Barth, *Humanity of God*, 49–50.
92. Harrison, "God's Many-Splendored Image," 38, 52.

fusion of God through the graced human being. An inanimate object may reflect something and resist or even be incapable of receiving into itself the reality and essence of the subject reflected. The mirror does not change by the sun it reflects. However, the human is changed even transformed by the God we "reflect" or manifest in life. This newness of life is that from which we live and grow (Rom 6:4; 2 Cor 5:17; Gal 6:15; Eph 4:24; Col 3:10). Furthermore, this life fills us to full capacity and simultaneously, wonderfully expands "the size of the jar."[93]

Harrison and others speak of various images to describe the imprint of God on a "soul," the reflection of God by person, and other images that seem to leave the essence of the being unchanged.[94] However, I have argued for something deeper in the person's encounter with God. Something of the "metal" of the "stamp" that is pressed into the "wax" of the person (already created in God's image) is infused into us. Something of the "sun" that is reflected by the person penetrates the whole person. The point here is that something of God is left within us and that we are forever transformed to that degree and not simply a vessel, seal, or mirror for God. We become more godlike. The dross of polluting the image of God in us is purified, and we are freed to more greatly be God's image.

Grenz[95] speaks to the intrinsic or organic reality of the *imago* in humans when he presents a short overview of the historical background of the ancient Near East in its view and development of the subject. Common and radical designations of spirit, immaterial fluid, permeate the physical substance, close unity, spiritual union, self-manifestation, and replicate copies. Grenz[96] goes on to poignantly point out that, although Jesus came to fulfill the human vocation as the *imago Dei* it is rarely mentioned. Rather, this biblical theme is overshadowed by the concern to present Jesus as the one who remedied the human sin problem.

GOD'S CHILDREN MATURED AND TRANSFORMED

Regarding Question 69, "Of the Beatitudes," Aquinas[97] claims that one possesses the end now when one hopes to possess it in the end, as children are happy because they are filled with hope. Such a beginning possession and hope draws one forward to the full possession.

93. Ibid., 16.
94. Ibid., 32.
95. Grenz, "Jesus as the Imago Dei," 621–23.
96. Ibid., 625.
97. Aquinas, *Summa Theologia*, 885–86.

Willard[98] suggests that disciples need not wait until death for eternal life, but such eternal life begins at the point of redeeming grace, wherein we are engaged in a living and interactive relationship with God. Herein, such a life naturally yields the transformation in not waiting for a future promise; the future begins now, and prolepsis is enjoined.

The freedom of God's disciples or particularly friends, versus noncontributing servants or children, in influence and shared rule, in leading to growth, is qualitative and not quantitative. It may be misleading to strictly speak of constant and progressing times and chronological dates or a point in salvific history but stratum.[99] Moltmann[100] rightly points to the only "perfect bliss in God in the kingdom of glory." In that state, God's friends shall find complete, "unhindered participation in the eternal life of the triune God himself, and in his inexhaustible fullness of glory." Nevertheless, Moltmann says God respects his friends' responsibility and liberty and seems to suggest that special times, eschatologically speaking, should not limit the expectations of these friends, but rather a full realization of PrōST in maturing progress is available now in all experiences of the freedom of God's friends.

If virtues are natural to humans,[101] then unselfish love, patience, long-suffering, wisdom, courage, compassion, justice, righteousness, courage, mercy, kindness, and many others should be expressed and observed from the unhindered and free human living in communion with God and others. This observation and proposed reality is critical to the proposal of this book. These attributes are communicable expressions of holiness from a holy God. These are thought too high and reserved for that future resurrection in which all of God's chosen ones shall live in such high liberty. It is an experience that is not burdensome or filled with Godless endeavor. The sweetness of God (Ps 2:12; 34:8; 119:103; Heb 6:5; 1 Pet 2:3) is transformative; it changes us. Moreover, the Scriptures encourage such an expression and life in the now (Lev 11:44a; Matt 5:48; Luke 6:36; John 13:34; 1 Cor 13:4, 13; Eph 4:32). In support, Willard[102] says the enjoyment of the kingdom is here and now; this is a measure of PrōST blessing.

God's gift to an individual that enables us to see God is an indication of a great measure of spiritual transformation—nothing less than a measure

---

98. Willard, "Spiritual Formation."
99. Moltmann, *Trinity and the Kingdom*, 221–22.
100. Ibid., 222.
101. Harrison, "God's Many-Splendored Image," 67.
102. Willard, "Spiritual Formation," 408.

of shared essence with God's self.[103] A measure of this transformation and shared essence is the transformed intellect, a "spiritual intellect" intimately connected with free choice.

Jesus, as the Son of God the Father, reflects in a full and real sense the glory, energy, light, and life of God. In this same manner, admittedly to a lesser degree and extent, we, human beings reflect Christ in this present life. This reflection is in increasing measure clearer and unadulterated by the vagaries of human frailties and sin. It bears repeating that "reflection" is an inadequate description of the real life and essential changes in transformation that take place with the soul and body of the growing disciple. The light may or may not affect the nature of the reflector, if it is not "porous" or receptive to the essence of the light it is reflecting. However, it seems that we do, in fact, receive and absorb God's shining. We are subjected to the light of God, that is, by its nature and properties this light is a penetrate into the human soul. The attributes of the "porous" person on this adventure are changed. Those attributes that are not Godlike are diminished and eliminated. Those communicable attributes that are shared by God with us take root and grow, transforming us from one degree of glory to the next into the very same image of God (2 Cor 3:16–18). So then, from communion and relationship with Christ, perfection and fulfillment are given and received.[104]

Cullmann[105] says, "Faith allows [us] to share at the *present time* in the saving gifts of the entire time line, even in those of the future" (emphasis added). The Holy Spirit is here spoken of as "nothing else than the anticipation of the end in the present." Perhaps Cullmann would not have consented to an application as wide and deep as the one I have proposed within theses pages. In fact, Cullmann goes on to highlight the physical acts of the Spirit's activity in healing and resurrection. However, the disciple is in a position to share in the now not only God's motivational gifts, but the fruit of the Spirit, even those most often reserved for the future, the attributes that are best a reflection and image of God. This image is often associated with and evidenced by the fruit of the Spirit as wisdom, faith, grace, power, good works, and charity (Acts 6:3, 5, 8; 11:24). Ephesians 4:24 further speaks of bearing a new life that includes a renewed mind and true righteousness and holiness.

---

103. Harrison, "God's Many-Splendored Image," 50.
104. Ibid., 118–19.
105. Cullmann, *Christ and Time*, 72, 76.

Self-Address

Maturity and transformation in humans is to include a clear "self-address" of God as human.[106] We are all intended to be unhindered and in clear focus as God's address to others, to the creation, and in speaking back to God. This is the incarnational principle at root of *imago Dei*.

This relationship reaches for a rich perichoretic union with God and humans and is clearly a perichoretic community of God and humans[107] as presented above. Moreover, according to Vlachos,[108] the Orthodox Church stands aside from the scholastic or philosophical approach to spirituality that indicates, he claims, nothing more than a confounding or loss of the focus on healing of the human condition through *theōsis*, which is salvation in completion.

In support and as otherwise noted, the Apostle Paul begins to open a view into the emergence of the liberation of the children of God into glory (Rom 8:21b). These are the firstfruits of the Spirit and are looking for bodily salvation, being conformed to the image of Christ (Rom 8:23, 29). The tension between present and future adoption remains. It is present in the sharing of present suffering and the hope of future identification with Christ in his glorification.[109] The present glorification of Christ is, to a large measure, enjoyable now in the Spirit. If salvation, including transformation, is through deification, as Clendenin[110] claims shall not be completed until the *eschaton*, or the "third birth," then the opportunity is yet beginning now. In agreement with Fee,[111] I hold with Paul and the early church, that the resurrection of Christ and the outflowing of Spirit indicated the dawning and arrival of the beginning fullness. Ludlow's[112] words further support the argument that God's salvific and restorative work are not merely a return to the beginning of a process begun in Eden but a beginning fulfillment or even a perfection of creation in the glory of Christ.

If the glory of this life is to be found essentially in a Divine DNA or some measure of God's essence shared with us, then a relation is established between God and humans. Aquinas[113] alludes to this truth when he postu-

---

106. Jenson, "Praying Animal," 320.
107. Vishnevskaya, "Divinization as Perichoretic Embrace," 133–34.
108. Vlachos, "Difference between Orthodox Spirituality."
109. Fee, *God's Empowering Presence*, 570–72.
110. Clendenin, "Partakers of Divinity," 377.
111. Fee, *God's Empowering Presence*, 573.
112. Ludlow, "Universalism," 192–93.
113. Aquinas, *Summa Theologia*, 470.

lates the *imago* as a matter of "species," and that intelligent human creatures are most in God's image by virtue of their intellects. The position I hold in this book is that human creatures are the only "species" found in God's image. If Christ is the proto-exemplar image of God and thereby radiates the glory of God, as Grenz[114] contends, and I agree, then humans should, in the fulfillment of their creation, radiate God as well in living the life exampled by Christ. Gratefully, it does not depend on humans "for [God] cannot deny himself" (2 Tim 2:13).

Looking to the full results of this relationship and the revealing of the *imago Dei* in humans, Lewis[115] sounds a warning. He says that it is an awesome prospect to live in a world of possible "gods or goddesses, dazzling, radiant." To know that the most tedious and uneventful person one might talk to will eventually be a living being which, if seen today, one would be unresistingly tempted to worship (cf. 1 John 3:2). Bushnell[116] words give support when he speaks to the awesome responsibility of desecrating and destroying a human. The glory and magnificence of such an eternity dazzles the opened eyes and causes one to tremble in awe of the power of the eternal life.

If de Chardin[117] is correct about the "Ultra-human," then the present state of human beings is still very immature, and what lies ahead is a matter of the human power "of common and unanimization that are available" to developing humans. This suggests the importance of progressive perichoretic community with God and us. Shults[118] is explicit: "The Christian dynamically receives salvation as a life in hope, as a proleptic participation (*koinōnia*) in divine glory." Van Huyssteen[119] continues that this "proleptic participation in trinitarian glory provides us with a hope-filled way of being."

In this we are to seek, honor, and thank God. It is the human disposition having been created as *imago Dei* according to Annenberg.[120] Kärkkäinen[121] informs that genuine righteousness is needed and must be sought through real obedience not the usual "legal fiction" found in a forensic theology of justification. Further, he points out the Catholic view of grace

---

114. Grenz, "Jesus as the Imago Dei," 618–19.
115. Lewis, *Mere Christianity*, 174–76.
116. Bushnell, "Protestant Views," 348.
117. De Chardin, *Future of Man*, 280–81.
118. Shults, *Reforming Theological Anthropology*, 241.
119. Van Huyssteen, *Alone in the World?*, 143.
120. Pannenberg, *Systematic Theology*, 2:227.
121. Kärkkäinen, *One with God*, 130.

in which salvation is "God's self-communication to humanity through the Spirit of God." More importantly, the very aim of justification is nothing less than *theōsis* as the very content of salvation.[122] Or as Moltmann[123] identifies it, for the eschatological hope to be entirely and fully "gathered into the eternal life of the triune God and—as the early church put it—be 'deified' (Gk. *theosis*)." St. Maximus (c. 580–662) epigrammatically defined this grace of God by his loving desire and intent to condescend to reach humanity in order to make them divine by his grace for those "who consciously travel upwards with it."[124]

Although it is an eschatological hope, the transformation begins its completion now, as pressed by Berkouwer[125] and Huyssteen,[126] while presenting some of the characteristics that reflect "the perfection of the Lord." These perfections in the "receptive life" and in the unshackled license of disciples, Berkouwer continues with Paul, can be known and read by others (2 Cor 3:2). To be sure, this is no lacuna. Moltmann[127] presents an element of the maturity in God's children. He labels human beings as *imago trinitatis* (L.). That is image of the Trinity, but only so when we are united to one another in correspondence to the Trinity.

Disruptive

Webb[128] argues for progressive ability to "handle" a process of growth. It is true and observable on a natural and human level as it is observable in cultures throughout time. However, on a spiritual and transformational level, this slow process can be accelerated and even demonstrated in step-wise functions that revolutionize rather than evolve a personality, understanding, and a person's attributes. In speaking of the incompatibility of evolution to Christianity (disagreed by me), Jenson uses the "metaphor" of the resurrection to speak of the "disruption of continuity and development."[129] Here is an opening as it might apply to spirituality in particular PrōST. Transformation is not necessarily a progressive and hindered process but a "disruptive" revolutionary activity that interrupts the "normal" state of affairs and

---

122. Ibid., 137.
123. Moltmann, *Trinity and the Kingdom*, 213.
124. Stavropoulos, *Partakers of the Divine Nature*, 35.
125. Berkouwer, *Studies in Dogmatics*, 111.
126. Van Huyssteen, *Alone in the World?*, 143.
127. Moltmann, *God in Creation*, 216.
128. Webb, *Slaves, Women & Homosexuals*, 59.
129. Jenson, "Praying Animal," 312.

progress process of "evolution." PrōST may include step-wise activity that introduces the not-yet into the now.

In the often-referenced verse, God is bold and explicit in directly averring, "You are gods, sons of the Most High, all of you" (Ps 82:6a). Not only does the psalmist reveal these words of God, but God, again, in the person of Jesus Christ, himself quotes the same declaration (John 10:34). Surely there is no stronger testimony. Peter, too, understood the reality (2 Pet 1:3–4). Becoming enlightened "partakers of the divine nature" is the foundation to faith, virtue, knowledge, self-control, steadfastness, and godliness and a host of other communicable attributes, showing that we are in the process of full deification and presently in a proleptic reality (PrōST) not exclusively reserved for the future *eschaton*.[130]

Every person is included in this image.[131] Moreover, Bushnell[132] proposes that the life of Christ is, as a perfect being, an embodiment and spirit of ideas in history, sufficient of themselves to alter the ultimate portion of humanity including our capacities for excellence.

As Keil and Delitzsch[133] present the issue, it is God's image in humans "spiritual personality" although not as self-conscious, self-determining, free agents. They argue for the shattering of God's likeness in humans by sin. Only "through Christ, the brightness of the glory of God and the expression of His essence (Heb 1:3), that our nature is transformed into the image of God again (Col 3:10; Eph 4:24)."

This "new self" is where spiritual transformation has, and is occurring from one degree of glory to another (2 Cor 3:18). Disagreeing here with Keil and Delitzsch, I contend that the image was not lost but marred in the garden and is repaired and elevated in the accomplishment of Christ. For God's disciples, the image of God in Christ is now available and inclusive of incarnation and triumphant spiritual living (PrōST).

LIGHTING THE WAY

Κατοπτριζόμενοι only occurs in 2 Corinthians 3:18 for which Berkouwer[134] interacts with F. W. Grosheide and concludes that it is a "reflection of received glory," but not a possession of the same. The glory, accordingly, is a reflection of uncovered faces in contrast to the veiled face of Moses and

---

130. Van Huyssteen, *Alone in the World?*, 143; Willard, *Divine Conspiracy*, 28.
131. Van Huyssteen, *Alone in the World?*, 120.
132. Bushnell, "Protestant Views," 344.
133. Keil and Delitzsch, *Commentary on the Old Testament*, 39.
134. Berkouwer, *Studies in Dogmatics*, 110–11.

reminds the beholder of the perfections of Christ, according to Berkouwer, and an "outpouring and manifestation" of the glory in context of transformation. The way is lightened in the manifest glory in Christian communities as visible sanctification of human epistles of Christ.[135]

As helpful as this contention may be, it does not go deep enough. As we already examined above, there is deeper encounter of humans with God. Some measure and element of the "metal" of the "stamp" that is pressed into the "wax" is infused into us. Something of the "sun" that is reflected penetrates. That is, I propose that "reflection" includes something of God that is left within the person and the person is forever transformed to that degree and not only a vessel, seal, or mirror for God. In this Berkouwer[136] seems to agree that the reflection of God's glory is a "visible expression of this decisive transformation" which is a renewed life becoming like Christ. Moreover, Berkouwer continues that although this transformation is "eschatologically oriented it is nevertheless actual in principle."

Wright[137] helps by making clear that those who accept Jesus as the resurrected Lord are given a foretaste by the Spirit of God of what the *eschaton* shall be like. Borrowing from Paul (2 Cor 5:17), Wright makes clear that this is for us who are in the Messiah and that one is claimed from the old creation for "the new creation in advance and [becomes] someone through whom it begins to happen here and now." The Spirit accompanies, rebukes, directs, grieves, and forewarns regarding the disciples' missteps by the guidance of his personal presence and honors "small steps toward true inheritance."

Inaugurated eschatology (Christ's first advent) says that spiritual transformation is both a now and not-yet actuality. The full walk in the reality of Christ is yet a future completion. This now and not-yet tension, according to Hill,[138] is a reality of the present and public Christian experience. Present Christian spiritual transformation (PrōST) is a testimony of the not-yet. Proleptic spiritual transformation (PrōST) draws down experiences of the "not-yet" now (Ezek 8:1–4; 2 Cor 12:1–6). This experience lights and points the way to others of the promised full perichoretic experience.

To be perfect, Lewis[139] says, is not idealism or a commandment for the impossible. God shall make possible and real his desire for perfection in his disciples by giving us, in essence, capability for such. God is in the process of making humans reflection of received glory (Gk. *katoptrizomenoi*).

---

135. Ibid., 112.
136. Ibid., 111–12.
137. Wright, *Simply Christian*, 126.
138. Hill, *God's Time*, 173.
139. Lewis, *Mere Christianity*, 176.

Lewis says, although it is a long and arduous process, they shall be "gods or goddesses, dazzling, radiant" reflecting towards God himself. Similar to Lewis' description and drawing in immediacy, Van Huyssteen[140] says, with Jenson,[141] that humans are self-transcendent and as close to being God's intention to the degree they reflect the not-yet in the now. This existential understanding, that is, reality, is critical to us in order to walk in a testimony of proleptic reality to some measure and not relegate to the future the majority of spiritual transformation.

If "the fundamental characteristic of the image is its immediacy, its primitive resistance to mediation,"[142] then it seems not only was Christ' direct intimacy with the Father exampled in his life and work, but that all humans were created with this purpose and ability for intimate communion with God the Father. Although Mondzain, here, is not explicitly referring to *imago Dei*, the principle is inclusive of images no matter what their derivatives.

As Christ is the light (John 3:19; 8:12; 9:5; 12:35), we are called to the same high standard (Luke 11:36; John 12:36; Eph 5:8). Not only are there direct scriptural texts to this effect, but also the *imago Dei* is inclusive of this light. This light, likened to the sun, ensures a world in which darkness and freeze do not consume the planet. Human failure to reflect God's light as *imago Dei* brought God's judgment on the earth as a result of the rebellion in Genesis 6 and limits that judgment in chapter 8. In this notion, a candidate enjoys such a *post-mortem* mercy, remediable purgation though interminable, and eventual reconciliation.[143] The hope is that God has provided reconciliation for all (universalism), which for some may be fully experienced post-mortem. There is no necessary requirement outside of polemic (and there is much) that believing confession must occur before a particular human age or even before death. As argued by Berkouwer,[144] it is not clear why the fall of human beings and God's consequent judgment is leveled against all creation. However, it seems evident that if one does not accept the creation of the earth for humanity, that the creation was at least connected to humans as it was not until we, humans, and the whole created field were completed that God pronounced it very good (Gen 1:31).

The divine light that is God, the Father, fully shines forth in Jesus, the second person of the Trinity. In this we may enjoy the same light in our

140. Van Huyssteen, *Alone in the World?*, 147.
141. Jenson, *Systematic Theology*, 64.
142. Mondzain, "Can Images Kill?," 39.
143. Talbott, "Universalism."
144. Berkouwer, *Studies in Dogmatics*, 141.

encounter with Christ as he shines forth the light as God the Father, and in this encounter of God's light shining forth through the life of Christ it is receivable, absorbable by us in the same manner and brings incorruption and "freedom from decay and from death."[145] This is important in that freedom is enjoyed and death is averted. These two are responsible for restraining transformation in the disciples' souls. To receive the cleansing and empowering light directly from God through Christ, promises the life of Christ lived out in the individual and in community in reflection of the communal existence of God. Such a life is, in part, living in the not-yet for the not-yet is held back or hindered by the corruption or "decay and death" of the now.

Rejection and Proviso

The transformation that takes place in an individual often causes one to act differently than many in our circle. The result often is rejection from those who do not understand. Shunning may follow someone who appears more nonconformist, sanctimonious, or contrary to norms. The words we speak may carry a higher standard. What we refuse to do or in fact insists on doing may seem extreme. Our life begins to reflect Christ's life more closely: Befriending the downtrodden, the "unclean," the unsavory: prostitutes, drunkards, addicts, convicts, atheists, secularists, sexual deviants, and a host of people with whom "God-fearing people" are not supposed to keep company. As with Christ, over two thousand years ago, the disciple being transformed today shall not be understood at so many levels and may be rejected for this, starting with family, friends, coworkers, and whoever is in our circle or influence.

I do not debate the various exegetical kingdom arguments found in Saucy.[146] They relate to physical and national kingdom versus ethical, moral, and spiritual kingdom realities. If the kingdom is composed of such as righteousness, love, joy, peace, patience, kindness, goodness, faithfulness, gentleness, self-control and power, then to the degree we live out these fruit and attributes, we are living the kingdom.[147] The now of the kingdom is clearly lived in this. The not-yet of the kingdom is being touched and tasted to the extent that death is overcome in the victory of Christ and we are transfigured and translated to that eternal state rarely seen, recognized or experienced.

---

145. Harrison, "God's Many-Splendored Image," 118.
146. Saucy, *Case for Progressive Dispensationalism*, 82–94.
147. Ibid., 106–7.

Moltmann[148] has a curious and supportive notion to the propositions of this work wherein he argues, "Without anticipatory awareness we should not discern something that is still in the future at all." In support, he continues that in an anticipatory awareness, we align ourselves to that which is last and final. Whether the superlatives of happiness or unhappiness or life or death, the very last item to invade our experience is the final in experience. Such light as this perceived and judged is what actually comes. Moltmann continues to argue that in planning, we link the future desired with the future considered probable. No prospect of the present as future can be matched with the actual future. I agree with Fee,[149] the power of the kingdom is now as well as not yet but a future, full inheritance. Fee is firm in that the inauguration of the kingdom was marked by the resurrection of Christ and the Spirit's pouring-out in demonstration of power. Paul held the kingdom in tension of now and not yet. Moreover, Fee[150] claims Paul lived in the presence of the not-yet with the realized now foreshadowing the not-yet kingdom and encouraged those who would hear him to live in the same reality.

This is not to merely immanentize the *eschaton* as a kind of pejorative denouncement of claiming for now what is not yet. In fact, this is the very thesis of this research: that is, the church at large is wrongly waiting for some kind of "castle in the air" transformation and perfecting and thereby misses the privilege of better enjoying and representing Christ in the now by presently, more clearly reflecting his image. Fee[151] joins Scripture in saying that the kingdom of God is not a matter of laws, practices, rules, or even words but of "righteousness, and peace, and joy . . . and power" (Rom 14:17; 1 Cor 4:20).

IMPLICATIONS

As already introduced above, Catherine[152] of Siena in her famous *Dialogue* allegorizing God as in love with a feminine, names God as one of limitless charity, eternal beauty and wisdom. Catherine claimed God's eternal goodness, mercy, and immeasurable generosity. God is eternal and one of infinite good. Yet, Catherine envisions God as a "mad lover" with an insatiable need for "her" (his creatures—human beings). God cannot live without fulfill-

---

148. Moltmann, *God in Creation*, 34–135.
149. Fee, *God's Empowering Presence*, 119–20.
150. Ibid.
151. Ibid., 118–19, 617–18.
152. Catherine of Siena, *Dialogue*, 153.

ing this need, although he is "Life itself." God has fallen in love with his creation, Catherine says, and God is "drunk" for her salvation although she flees his loving pursuit. Finally, in God's chase for her he cloths himself in flesh (incarnation) without which, he determines, he cannot be close to the desire of his heart.

In this story is shown the unrelenting, intimate desire God has for union with his *imago Dei*. A millennia before, Paul put it more theologically by reminding Titus (2:11–12, 14) that God's incarnation brought salvation for everyone, enabling renouncement of faithlessness, impiousness, unspiritual passions, and rather living in reflection of God's life (*imago Dei*) in the now. Paul reminds, as did Catherine, that God gave himself (incarnation) to possess humans, freeing them in recovery to fully express *imago Dei* in good works. Peter explicitly says that by God's "precious and very great promises" his intent is to make human creatures "partakers of the divine nature" (2 Pet 1:4), and in this they shall live the overcoming, transformed life bringing glory to God. The Apostle John and the psalmist present the seed of this growth, saying, "You are gods, sons of the Most High, all of you" (Ps 81; 82:6; John 10:34).

The prodigal returns to the father who, filled with compassion, is running to embrace and kiss his beloved, returning son (Luke 15:11–24). Perhaps not with the prodigal in mind, Lewis[153] pronounces an applicable truth that "A [person] can no more diminish God's glory by refusing to worship Him than a lunatic can put out the sun by scribbling the word, 'darkness' on the walls of his cell." The prodigal prematurely demanded from his father what was not his right to then ask, bringing communal derision on his father. But the father's love was unwavering. Paul elsewhere says, "If we are faithless, [the Father] remains faithful—for he cannot deny himself" (2 Tim 2:13). As shown above, God is faithful to the love he has for his own prodigals and, yes, the faithful as was the ungrateful elder son.

However, Lossky[154] rightly argues, that we must present ourselves in life's conditions, whether prodigal defiance or dutiful ingratitude, to cooperatively work with God to manifest such an awesome and glorious reality as union with the divine. This, of course, shall not be realized without God's active grace. Human destiny, in relationship with God, does not wait for the *eschaton*, reminds Pannenberg.[155] Herein is a reflection of the kingdom and the end of the death (1 Cor 15:24, 26) that is a hindrance to fully realized transformation by not walking in the power of God's Spirit and express-

---

153. Lewis, *Problem of Pain*, 46.
154. Lossky, *Mystical Theology*, 196.
155. Pannenberg, *Systematic Theology*, 2:227–28.

ing his reign. Rather, it is living both the now of the kingdom and a great measure of the not-yet. Disciples must be insistent revolutionaries always pressing toward the mark (Luke 16:16; John 6:27; Phil 3:14).

Ritual

Spiritual disciplines, as we examined in chapter 4, can also be found in the rubric of rituals. Thereby, rituals, in this section, are limited to spiritual practices or disciplines. Jenson[156] argues that ritual makes one "available and therefore *vulnerable* to the world beyond" (emphasis original) and to oneself, others, and God. This availability and vulnerability opens the potential for proleptic spiritual transformation (PrōST) as we are opened to the change and transformation that occurs in relationship and encounter with God. To sacrifice ourselves in the dedication and ritual of spiritual practices puts us in contact with the divine from which transformation is catalyzed. "History's sacrificers and revolutionaries are the same persons," observes Jenson.[157] These revolutionaries draw down the realities of the future transformation as displayed in the life of Jesus Christ shining forth God's glory to a dark world (Luke 11:36; John 12:36; Eph 5:8; Phil 2:14–16). Transformation is not necessarily a progressive and hindered process, but a "disruptive" revolutionary activity that interrupts the "normal" state of affairs and progressive process of "evolution." PrōST may include step-wise activity that introduces the not-yet into the now.

In these rituals, as offered herein, there is no suggestion to immanentize the *eschaton*. There is no suggestion in this study that any effort of human creatures can introduce the *kairos* of God prematurely. However, ushering in some measure of the not-yet into the now, especially as spiritual transformation is defined, seems possible. Although I make no claim or suggestion of dominion theology or kingdom-now proposals, the implications of PrōST suggest a measure of the not-yet now—a living in the not-yet, although the kingdom has not been fully manifested and the world is not yet fully transformed as God's kingdom. I am not alone in positing that "salvation/liberation," as Hick[158] argues, is not an event to wait for until the after life, but rather something that should be expected and entered into now.

---

156. Jenson, "Praying Animal," 316.
157. Ibid.
158. Hick, "Pluralist View," 185.

Transformation unto Salvation

The proposal of PrōST found in these pages suggests and perhaps necessitates a *Gestalt* that promises a reality, experience, and even an eschatological appearance in the present. Such an experience progressively introduces transformation of humans only expected in the *eschaton* of God's completed work. If this is the case, then a brief word about science here might be useful. Although I do not attempt a defense of any position on science or evolution specifically, I accept the latest advances in evolutionary science and quantum mechanics as a given throughout this book. It is worth our considering that deification, as an evolutionary process, may be a more acceptable notion than absent it from redemption, sanctification, or salvation, as Peacocke[159] posits. Although further investigation beyond the reach of this work is required, this may be a promising way to recognize scientific discovery and present the Gospel and provide further clarity for the ideas of transformation discussed herein to the uninitiated, the academics, and the world in general.

So then, as the substructure below shows in figure 2, if the kingdom is composed of such as love, righteousness, peace, joy, mercy, endurance, affection, patience, kindness, virtue, steadfastness, holiness, knowledge, self control, veracity, wisdom, insight, faithfulness, benevolence, purity, truth, truthful speech, spirituality, justice, gentleness, rejoicing, godliness, patience, goodness, beauty, and the mind of Christ (cf. Matt 7:16; Rom 14:17; 1 Cor 2:16; 2 Cor 6:4–12; Gal 5:22; Eph 1:1–4, 8–9; 4:1–7, 22–24; Col 3:12–17; Phil 2:2–8; 2 Pet 1:1–11), then to the measure that we exhibit these fruit and attributes we are living the kingdom.[160] The now of the kingdom is clearly lived to the degree that these attributes are experienced. The not-yet of the kingdom is being touched and tasted to the extent that death is overcome in the victory of Christ and we are figuratively drawn into the eternal state rarely seen, recognized, or experienced.

Regarding Galatians 5:16–21, Fee[161] cautions that although the Apostle Paul speaks about the negative behaviors that shall disqualify one from entering into the kingdom of God, that the positive should not be lost. It seems that Paul is more concerned with the good of what is expected or even required against the foil of the dark behavior he first warns. "But the fruit of the Spirit is love, joy, peace, patience, kindness, goodness, faithfulness, gentleness, self-control; against such things there is no law" (Gal 5:22–23).

---

159. Peacocke, *Theology for a Scientific Age*, 430.
160. Saucy, *Case for Progressive Dispensationalism*, 106–7.
161. Fee, *God's Empowering Presence*, 443.

"There is no law" against kingdom behavior, as displayed by the fruit of the Spirit, such as "love, joy, peace, patience, kindness, goodness, faithfulness, gentleness, self-control." Without law's application there is no death (Rom 7:5; 8:2; 1 Cor 15:56). Death broke our fellowship and communion with God and thus blocked the enjoyment of the tree of life, representing God's life flowing into humanity that would have and shall still express the spiritually transformed kingdom life (Prov 11:30a; 15:4a; Rev 2:7; 22:2, 14).

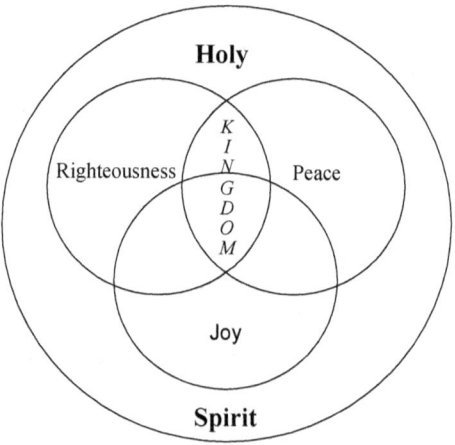

Figure 2

Aune[162] reminds that no one can look into the face of God and survive (Exod 33:17–20; John 1:18). If God being with humans (Rev 21: 3–5) is not a seeing of God's face, then it is at least a sharing in God's holiness and righteousness.[163] This is important for the complete restoration and transformation of humans. There seems to be an understanding of this need among some groups and leaders. For one the Third Lausanne Congress on World Evangelization which was attended by 4,200 evangelical leaders from 198 countries whose reach extended to perhaps hundreds of thousands of Christians, confessed that they do not live the life of obedience through Christ as taught in the Bible. They recognized, in "The Cape Town

---

162. Aune, "Disclosure of God's Eschatological Plan," 1188 (Rev 21:9—22:9).
163. Ibid.

Commitment,"[164] the best commendation of the Gospel is the transformed and holy life. "There is no biblical mission without biblical living," they affirmed.

In this kingdom relationship, there is no death or limitation except to the old life (Rom 6:6; Gal 5:24; Eph 4:22). So then to the measure Christ's disciples enjoy him as the tree of life, to that measure we live the kingdom life, that is, living within the desires of the King's rule bringing him glory. In some estimate, as demonstrated by kingdom behavior (John 13:35; 17:21; 1 John 2:3–5, 10), this is to experience not only the now kingdom of God, but the not-yet kingdom of God prior to the full manifestation in the *eschaton*. Willard[165] successfully argues that "kingdom-*now*" living is considered radical and subversive affirming that altitudinal living is *not* reserved for the afterlife millennium unless one accepts that other critical behavioral passages of walking by the Spirit in love and freedom by a new self (e.g., Rom 8:1; 1 Cor 13; Col 3; Gal 5) are also meant for the future.

Nonna Harrison[166] provides a practical vision of the *imago Dei* as less complicated or conflicted as necessarily discussed here in chapters 1 and 2. Harrison argues that *imago Dei* is universally human and that all humans, to varying degrees, share in such things as freedom of choice, a measure of closeness to God, awareness of spiritual realities, virtuous capability, dignity, care for God's creation, and an innate ability to creativity in arts and sciences. Harrison says that these common attributes draw us together to endeavor toward the "same ultimate goals" in trinitarian likeness, and that many traditions testify to this reality.

Reluctancy

There seems a reluctancy, by some theorists and practitioners, to entertain full orbed and present spiritual transformation (PrōST). Foundational to this the Israelites held, with the clear exception of Philo, a strict monotheism and overwrought belief of a transcendent God, which belief seems to have forbidden any form of deification for human beings according the report of Gross.[167] This anecdotally supports the conjecture that it is impossible to have any large measure of spiritual transformation in the present (PrōST). However, the abundant life that Christ brought (John 10:10) is not exclusive or delayed to the *eschaton*. It begins now for those who have an ear to hear

---

164. Anon, "Cape Town Commitment."
165. Willard, *Divine Conspiracy*, 105, 207.
166. Harrison, "God's Many-Splendored Image," 170.
167. Gross, *Divinization of the Christian*, 339.

(Rev 2:7). Moreover, the focus, whatever extent may be allowed, seems to be limited to parts of the soul. That is, the intellect may be offered as the focus of transformation as the best description of *imago Dei*.[168] This partitioning of the soul, leaving out such other "parts" as the emotional and conscience faculties, does not treat humans as whole persons, but rather divides and fractures us eliminating the possibility of integrated transformation and surely and consequently no possibility for present transformation. This, at best, leaves a focus on one area of the soul or another. Even if one accepts that the intellect or mind best represents God's image, to exclusively focus on this faculty is imbalanced and harmful to the idea of the whole person. However, as with this book, Christian modern spirituality pursues a holistic and integrated paradigm of persons, as supported by Schneiders,[169] including all that is spirit, soul, body, community, and socio-political commitment.

Anxiety and Free Will

Clearly, other than Jesus, no one has died in perfection. Many have an anxiety about living a worthy-of-heaven life before death and if not a present anxiety, than one of "where" or how can purification be accomplished after death so that one can enter God's presence in heaven. Many die not confessing Christ, although he is the only way to the Father (John 14:6; Acts 4:12; Heb 7:25), and so if we are still saved, then it is somehow through him, that is, if such a possibility is even allowed, as argued by me in this book. God is holy and nothing unholy can approach his presence (Rev 3:5; 21:27; 22:14). If a form of universalism or inclusivism is allowed for the non-confessing, then, as Paul say (1 Cor 1:8; Phil 1:6; 2:12), those need to have completed by God what he began in them.[170]

The deuterocanical book, 2 Maccabees 12:40–45, gives some insight into the Jewish mind of scrupulous piety and hopes for a holy Jerusalem during the time just prior to the New Testament period. Alford[171] says those of the period spoke of confidence in God who both punishes and shows mercy and dispatches his angels in guardianship. This Maccabean passage suggests the need to pray for the departed. The point at issue here is that there were needs for those who have sinned in this life and subsequently de-

---

168. Harris et al., *Theological Wordbook*, s.v. "děmuwth"; Aquinas, *Summa Theologia*, 470.

169. Schneiders, "Christian Spirituality," 1–2.

170. Hick, *Death and Eternal Life*, 71–72; Lewis, *Mere Christianity*, 176; Ludlow, "Universalism," 204–5; Plumptre, *Spirits in Prison*, 403; Talbott, "Universalism."

171. Alford, *Jewish History and Literature*, 35.

parted into death. Moreover, Matthew 12:32 makes a suggestion in the New Testament era that there is a possibility of sins being forgiven in the afterlife: "And whoever speaks a word against the Son of Man shall be forgiven, but whoever speaks against the Holy Spirit *will not be forgiven, either in this age or in the age to come*" (Matt 12:32, emphasis added).

The argument here is not for a theology of purgatory and prayers being given for the departed. Rather, there seems to be a possibility, even a need that spiritual transformation may continue after death to ready us for God's presence in fact completing what God already began in earthly time.[172] Although still being convinced, as I especially discussed, it increasingly seems to me that a form of universal salvation *may* be the message of Scripture and the heart of God. If this is the case, then it is natural to ask about human will and the possibility that some may finally decide not to be with God and thereby exclude themselves from eternal bliss in the presence of God and thereby "choose" separation from God. Fidelity requires a reminder that free will must be absolute or it is not free or culpable.

Campbell[173] argues for freedom as unbound from requisite intervention or help. Without full development here, this seems to imply the possibility of something less than universalism and rather a kind of inclusivism that posits intransigent, free-agents refusing God's work, grace, and offer in general. It seems, however, that human parents can raise children and at some point decide, for various reasons, to disown them and become estranged. God is infinitely wiser and more capable than human parents, whose DNA, like human parents, remains despite estrangement. God is never estranged from those who carry his DNA but remains loving, attractive, patient, merciful, and long-suffering. It seems that all of this and his great love shall prevail in the final analysis, and that all shall, ultimately-enlightened, choose him. This may happen sooner for some than others. For some it may happen after death. None know whether this is "hell" or "purgatory." The Scriptures are clear that God desires that no one be lost (Rom 8:31–35; Col 1:16–20). God's desire for us is so full that he went into hell to save those disobedient that had died before his arrival (1 Pet 3:19–20).

Although we considered this subject in chapter 3, Cromhout[174] does not speak about PrōST; and yet, his contentions about the afterlife are supportive of a proleptic experience of spiritual transformation. Although he leaves no room for anything other than punishment or a blessed state, for which I disagrees. If a proleptic entry or beginning experience of the

---

172. Hick, *Death and Eternal Life*, 71–72.
173. Campbell, *Self and Free-Will*, 360.
174. Cromhout, *Dead in Christ*, 85–86.

eschaton can be conjectured, even allowed, whether it is beneficial or not and simply a "post-mortem discrimination" for acts done in the body, then a proleptic spiritual transformation argument might survive. That is, even death and that existence after death are opportunities and the ground where one continues in transformation.

The probability of this argument seems almost necessary, "until we all attain to the unity of the faith and of the knowledge of the Son of God, to mature manhood, to the measure of the stature of the fullness of Christ" (Eph 4:13). It follows, all the more, since, with the exception of Jesus Christ, no one is fully perfected in the present age. Therefore, the Scriptures seem to leave room for activity after death (Matt 12:40; John 5:25; Acts 2:31; Rom 10:7; Eph 4:9; 1 Pet 3:19–20; 4:6). After the writer of Hebrews lists the dead heroes of faith, he goes on to state that they still need to be made perfect: "And all these, though commended through their faith, *did not receive what was promised*, since God had provided something better for us, that apart from us they should not be made perfect" (Heb 11:39–40, emphasis added). Although these are all the faithful before Christ's incarnation, the point is that perfecting takes place in some measure, at least with some people, *post-mortem*. Moreover, the New Testament seems to indicate a difference between the intermediate condition of the dead pre-Christian and Christian, according to Cromhout,[175] and was a better condition for Christians.

Moreover, if one accepts that the final judgment is reserved until after the general resurrection of the dead (Rev 20:13–15), then there seems to be some kind of opportunity for continued growth in the spirit in Christ until then. This opportunity is provided from the Father's heart of love to bring his children to share in his holiness (Heb 12:8–11). My argument is that some measure of God's victory and thereby glory would be diminished if someone is, in the end, lost.

Every Christian understands the privilege and importance of pleasing God: "So whether we are at home or away, we make it our aim to please him" (2 Cor 5:9). This understanding is thought of as a test and discipline while alive in our bodies before death. Yet, it is a privilege. Here, however, Paul tells the Corinthians that even if we are "away" (dead) not in the body that "we aim to please him," although, the Catholic Church does not hold out hope to those who die as unbelievers.[176] This acknowledgment or charge even says that in order to do such a thing there must be the possibility after death ("away"). The availability of the culmination of the age in the *eschaton*, in which all is put under God's "feet," is available to the departed in

---

175. Ibid., 87.
176. *Catechism of the Catholic Church*, 1030–31.

Christ, whoever we may be. In this state, we can please God and continue in perfecting before the end and the final judgment.

We may have to hold an agnostic position on this and its detailed outworking. But the implications for spiritual transformation would be greatly affected if people knew that we all shall eventually prevail in transformation. If, on the other hand, it is accepted that some or many of us shall be lost, then the focus shifts to salvific, first things. If we all are saved, then believers can focus on discipling (Matt 28:18–20) in assisting God's children to grow in his graces and to enjoy transformation. If we all are not saved, then the number one priority, if exclusiveness is not granted, becomes saving souls.

Christus Victor shows how much God loves us and is not interested in exacting a "due," but in restoring what was lost. He overcame the fall and law and their results to restore his children to intimate relationship with himself. It seems that in this restoration more than the original Edenic state is intended. Christ now brings all that was experienced and thereby included in who he is as a result of his thirty-three years on earth. His incarnation has "added" something to God and therefore what is included in "image."

Whether there is a hell or not does not erode the ground of this argument. The reality of hell must only be understood in light of whatever ultimate end is proposed for humans. Hell may be fashioned as a never-ending place for eternal, conscious punishment, a place for rehabilitation, or an invention of religious and political figures to control the masses.[177]

The real and great value of each and every human being without exception is inescapable since each of us has been created in God's image—God's own value is deposited within us.[178] We cannot exclude another once we clearly believe in the value of the other and the investment of God's very image in that same person. Moreover, we shall come to love the other as this vision takes hold. The Scriptures, theology, and philosophy viewed through this lens of value of the *humano imago Dei* shall drive an inclusive biblical interpretation in spite of various obscure and apparently non-supportive verses.

Drawing from Caputo,[179] the possibility of a singular experience or "singularity" of the not-yet now is an exception to the "law" of not-yet as Abraham was prior to Moses' law and exempt when he took Hagar. The not-yet calls, summons us to the impossible of the not-yet now. The possibility of the not-yet now is a reality now to be experienced. This makes "the

---

177. Hick, *Evil and the God of Love*, 87–89, 107–9, 341–42; Willimon, *Who Will Be Saved?*, 71.

178. Harrison, "God's Many-Splendored Image," 44, 49.

179. Caputo, *Deconstruction in a Nutshell*, 133–35.

singular higher than the universal" as is the urgency for the one lost sheep over the ninety-nine.

Even though Jenson may not have applied his thought to PrōST, he opens the possibility "in which what we have been and what we must or shall be somehow rhyme to make a coherent whole."[180] If this "rhyme" is coherent and if only a God from the future is worthy of the focus of ritual,[181] then what of the future can be "pulled-back" or "pulled-in" for present experience and enjoyment in the now of the lasting real from the not-yet? Moreover, in the Gospel of Matthew, Jesus is recorded as saying, "From the days of John the Baptist until now the kingdom of heaven has suffered violence, and the violent take it by force" (Matt 11:12). This greatly contested text can be interpreted in positive or negative terms.[182] However, as Derrida[183] has suggested, if we are so dedicated, even devoted, to what we are engaged, that we warp and distort it, then we are bringing a violence into the pursuit.

In discussing deconstruction and asking questions to overturn existing boundaries, Bowman[184] through meticulous examination of texts, engaged judgments, and deconstructed "ideological assumption." So the question, "Under what circumstances, no matter how unlikely or contrary to present orthodoxy, would the idea of proleptic spiritual transformation make sense?" should be answered in order to move toward an opening of possible acceptance of some part of living in the not-yet now. Kärkkäinen[185] agrees with Lossky, yet he does not own a full proleptic spiritual transformation (PrōST), but the "more and more in the present life" suggests the possibility of something more than is usually allowed by theologians and clergy alike.

Full redemption begins here and now from release of the necessity of fallen bodily nature. "The *testimonium Spiritus Sancti internum* [L. internal witness of the Holy Spirit] also enables the human being to give himself up to the instinct, the impulse and guidance of the Holy Spirit: the Spirit is present and at work in the feelings and in the unconscious as well."[186] In this same discussion, and more to the issue, Moltmann continues to argue that all living things, which are part of "open systems," subsist in the direction of their future. Future is the realm of open possibilities only limited by the

---

180. Jenson, "Praying Animal," 312.
181. Ibid., 312–13.
182. Hagner, *Matthew 1–13*, 306–7.
183. Bowman, "Deconstruction Is a Martial Art," 1.
184. Ibid., 18.
185. Kärkkäinen, *One with God*, 31.
186. Moltmann, *God in Creation*, 264–65.

living's past and environment. It follows that our drives, realizations, and our ways of behaving have an anticipatory character. Humans live in a particular direction consciously chosen or not. This "anticipatory structure" is inclusive of the whole physical, mental, and spiritual person inclusive of that which is subjective and objective. Clearly, PrōST is prefigured even designed into such a reality.

Revolutionaries and Gods

Harrison[187] proposes that we are made in God's image, and therefore possess the "capacities to use reason, priestly mediation, and royal power in [our] relationships with the natural world." We have obscured the magnificence of the human being, by familiarity (commonplace), difficult, and dissolute living resulting in a marred visage. Nevertheless, a deep look into the face of a person, especially the face of one who has, to some degree, been transformed by beholding God's face, Levinas[188] argues, can see what of God has been left behind as he "withdraws" from the world. I disagree that God "withdraws" from humans in anyway. Moltmann[189] argues, and I agree, from biblical tradition (Exod 34:33–35; Matt 17:2; 1 Cor 3:12; 2 Cor 3:18; 4:6; Rev 1:16), that the human face is a place that God's glory, in relationship with persons, can be recognized. A reading of the New Testament will reveal that Jesus' disciples reflected the glory of his life.

If, as Milbank[190] derives from the Apostle John, Jesus is himself the message, then humans, in reflection of Jesus, must be a reflection of that message in their doing and being. Milbank[191] explains that the "divine-human person," Jesus, is divinity overtaking and completing the purposes of human beings. Although as God, Jesus is the essence and origination of meaning, as a "human person" he is the inheritor of the constituted human meaning. Milbank concludes that Jesus is the complete metaphor representing the totality of humanity's intent. Whereas, Van Huyssteen[192] rightly states that the *imago Dei* is both an original gifting by God and a future destiny by God for humanity in the kingdom.

---

187. Harrison, "God's Many-Splendored Image," 144.
188. Levinas, "Otherwise than Being," 18.
189. Moltmann, *God in Creation*, 221.
190. Milbank, *Word Made Strange*, 135.
191. Ibid., 36.
192. Van Huyssteen, *Alone in the World?*, 141.

Willard[193] speaks of the kingdom of God as something that is present and for entering now. The enjoyment now of the kingdom is important to support, in some measure, the possibility of entering a proleptic spiritual transformation (PrōST). The things that are part of the kingdom in full measure are the same as those of PrōST, such as joy, hope and peace and other expressions of the kingdom (Rom 14:17; 15:13; 1 Cor 13:4; Eph 5:9; Gal 5:22; Col 3:12). The gifts of the Spirit, attributes of the kingdom, and spiritual transformation are expressions of the same communicable gifts and attributes from God in expression of his image in his children. Kingdom now (John 3:3, 5; Rom 14:17; Col 1:13; 4:11)[194] is an expression of the life of Jesus, as it would be lived out through his disciple in full enjoyment of the kingdom now. Doing as Jesus does proceeds from the kingdom. Jesus did not say that if certain people would do certain things the kingdom would arrive. No, he said it was now. Doing kingdom things comes from kingdom living. If we have a right relationship with the kingdom, that is the King, then we shall do the things of the kingdom. The subjects of the kingdom naturally fulfill the sovereign's wishes and will.

The new life that is given to those accepting God's solution to the sin problem and estrangement from God, self, and others receive a life that is mysterious in that it is a new birth as born by God himself in the second person of the Trinity (John 3:16; 1 John 1:1–4; 4:9–10, 19). Critically important is that this new life is "fuller" than what was experienced in the garden by those first beings enjoying God's life, presence, and fellowship. Since the incarnation, life, passion, death, resurrection, and ascension of Jesus Christ, God has "changed," if it might be put that way. What I am speaking of here is that Jesus took into the Godhead humanity as gloriously, rightfully experienced, and lived in Jesus Christ. In *The Humanity of God*, Karl Barth[195] notes that God's deity could not exclude humanity as a part of himself. It is God's freedom for love, he says, and by that love he holds the capacity to dwell in the heights and descend to the depths and to be both great and small. This kingdom capability is not only for himself but also for his creatures distinct from himself.

God addresses and has conversation with humans. The *ability* to be in conversation with God is requisite to that conversation and "ineluctable embodied" in prayer.[196] Such unhindered and open conversation and even fellowship is first seen in the cool of the Edenic garden, in which God

---

193. Willard, *Divine Conspiracy*, 28.
194. Saucy, *Case for Progressive Dispensationalism*, 106.
195. Barth, *Humanity of God*, 49–50.
196. Jenson, "Praying Animal," 321.

walked and conversed with the prototypical humans—Adam and Eve (Gen 3:8–10). Barth continues, that God's relationship to his creatures is "the unconditional priority." According to Barth, and agreed by me, God's act is his decisive word, his initiative, and his leadership. Jesus is the ultimate human in full commune with God. There is no exclusion of humanity in God in order for God to be God. God's deity now includes humanity, a humanity that encompasses humanity in total. Barth concludes in this same thought the amazing conjecture that "God does not exist without [humans]."

On a spiritual and transformational level this usually slow process of fully reflecting such a God-man in *imago Dei* can be accelerated in a stepwise function that revolutionizes rather than evolves a disciple relationship with God and the world, transforms understanding, and a person's attributes. Disciples must be insistent, tenacious revolutionaries pressing toward the mark (Luke 16:16; John 6:27; Phil 3:14) in divine fellowship. Although perhaps labeled revolutionaries, they draw down the realities of the future transformation as displayed in the life of Jesus Christ shining forth God's glory now (Luke 11:36; John 12:36; Eph 5:8; Phil 2:14–16). There is, in this, a "disruption of continuity and development."[197]

CONCLUSIONS

As stated in the introduction, this chapter continued to examine whether individuals need wait until the afterlife to have spiritual transformation fully or largely "worked out" (Phil 2:12–13). My primary aim of the present chapter was to look at God's glory in human reflection of him. Perichoretic fellowship with God, I proposed here, is central to this process. Following the conjectures of the prior chapters the present chapter was better positioned to present the glory available to humans as God has intended. As we discussed, the transformed life is a God glorifying life.

The beginning point of this chapter was to consider love and free will in the garden as a restored and elevated state for human living and expression driven by a transformed perichoretic relationship with God the Trinity. The freedom provided is only licensed by remaining in God's chosen place for us. In this "place" or way, we are compelled or constrained by Christ's life. Moreover, in this chapter I argued that sin has no hold, that is, that the sin problem has been dealt with by Christ's victorious incarnational work freeing us to such a relationship with God. The freedom provided by transformed living, is the newness of life that is enjoyed and looks like what Jesus would do if he were living our lives in the present milieu. Freed from the

197. Ibid., 312.

limiting affects of sin, each unique human being has the capacity to model and live a glory-reflecting life in the image of God.

We examined in this chapter the paradigm of God's children matured and transformed, which leads us not only into responsible viceregency, but a free maturity that can only be expressed as trusted friends of God (John 15:15). Disciples do not need to wait until death for eternal life, but such a life begins now in redeeming grace engaged in living and interactive, integrative relationship with God. Such a life yields transformation, rather than waiting for a future promise. The future in prolepsis is enjoined now.

We also examined in this chapter the transformed life as it lights the way for others as exampled by Jesus Christ and his followers. I showed how God intends earthly life to be lived by us in *imago Dei* by reflecting God's glory. The glory is a reflection by uncovered faces, unlike the veiled face of Moses, and reminds the beholder of the perfections of Christ. I also argued for an outpouring and display of glory in the context of proleptic spiritual transformation (PrōST).

The implications for all that we have considered in chapter 6, coupled with the prior chapters of this study, suggest the possibility of a present spiritual transformational life (PrōST). Paul reminds that God gave himself (incarnation) to possess humans, freeing us in recovery to fully express *imago Dei* in good works. Peter explicitly says that by God's "precious and very great promises" his intent is to make us "partakers of the divine nature" (2 Pet 1:4), and in this we shall live the overcoming, transformed life bringing glory to God. The Apostle John and the psalmist boldly present the seed of this growth, saying, "You are gods, sons of the Most High, all of you." Moreover, as noted in Conclusions, the points we investigated in this chapter culminate the prior chapters in the hoped outcomes of glory as it begins to manifest in the disciple's life as PrōST. There is no law competing with kingdom behavior, which is displayed by such as love, joy, peace, patience, kindness, goodness, faithfulness, gentleness, and self-control. Without law's application there is no death (Rom 7:5; 8:2; 1 Cor 15:56). Death broke fellowship and communion with God and thus blocked the enjoyment of the tree of life, representing God's life flowing into humanity that would have and shall still express the spiritually transformed kingdom life.

It is God's freedom for love, and by that love he holds the capacity to dwell in the heights and descend to the depths and to be both great and small. This capability is lavished on his creatures that are distinct from himself. God's relationship to his creatures is his, the unfettered priority. Jesus is the ultimate human in full communion with God. There is no exclusion of humanity in God in order for God to be God. God's deity now includes humanity, a humanity that encounters in expression humanity in total. God no longer exists without us. Such a reality is glorious.

7

Summary and Conclusions

INTEGRATION AND WHOLENESS

THE PRIMARY AIM OF this book has been to investigate whether individuals must wait until the afterlife for spiritual transformation to be fully or largely "worked out." That is, what, if any, is the possible opportunity to largely "work out [our spiritual transformation] with fear and trembling [now]" (Phil 2:12–13). In this book we investigated and answered affirmatively that God's economy (Gk. *oikonomia*) or administration grants a present enjoyment of the *imago Dei* in transformation as inclusive of the experiential life of Christ. Such a transformation, as unhindered *imago Dei*, is to be represented by us in time and in relation to God and creation. More particularly, we demonstrated that an experience of spiritual transformation usually reserved for heaven in eternity is greatly available today (PrōST: proleptic spirituality transformation), if by God's grace and mercy, we cooperate with the Spirit of God. However, I did not argue for or find a basis for present perfectionism. The integration and wholeness of the subject, as listed below by five questions, was foundational to the book throughout and is referenced in this conclusion.

The following questions were addressed, and related research objectives were pursued to gain an understanding throughout this investigation to support the stated primary aim of this study. They are presented here followed by summary responses as conclusions:

Summary and Conclusions 247

- ❖ What does God's heart, in relationship, imply toward an image-bearing human spiritually, and what, if any, are the implications on this from the Edenic fall?

- ❖ In what measure is God actively interested in recovery of his image in humanity as the remedy to the spiritual effects of the fall and in PrōST?

- ❖ How does God reveal or unveil his heart, truth, and intents toward creation and humanity in particular in the plan of spiritual recovery/PrōST?

- ❖ What are the transformative and soteriological implications of PrōST?

- ❖ What are the conclusions of this book; do they imply a unified theory regarding PrōST?

The research of this book utilized a postfoundationalism to enfold deconstructive principles and an eclectic hermeneutic to address the primary aim and these five objectives. In support of the primary aim of this book, this research affirms all of these queries and questions with the single exception of the last bullet (a unified theory) as addressed below. What follows, in answer to the primary aim and objectives, is the distilled support, in conclusion, drawn from the arguments, concepts, and research from the body of this dialogue.

The first query was addressed variously in these pages as scripturally knowable with ostensible, theologically-professed implications:

- ❖ What does God's heart, in relationship, imply toward an image-bearing human spiritually, and what, if any, are the implications on this from the Edenic fall?

The central theoretical argument has been that we were originally created in the "image and likeness" of God (Gen 1:26–27); however, the enjoyment and expression of this *imago Dei*, not its essence, has been greatly blemished, marred, and damaged by a God-defying willfulness of humanity (Gen 2:16; 3). The only real differentiation needed was that something of God's essence, here referred to as *imago Dei*, is inviolate, and some part, attribute, or expression of humanity is not exempt from harm and corruption. It is that which is in need of recovery and transformation.

I argued for the very best possible world for God's purposes into which God created and made humans with an ineffaceable drive within us as God's children and vice-regents to care for the creation, and to desire, serve, worship, and love God. To have us created in God's image as the capstone to creation is to survey the whole in satisfaction which brings a pronouncement of "very good" or "completely perfect" in reflection of God's heart. God created the very best possible world in which are found the means for our seeking and transformation. God's economy, in creating a world that is most conducive to his goals and means, is seen in the evolving and progressing world in which we inhabit. God's heart and desire are toward a world that he created the best possible—one that allows for the *summum bonum* of God's creation.

A priori, the goodness of God's creation is, in part, simply because God created it (Ps 119:68; 1 Tim 4:4). By definition, whatever God does must be particularly, essentially, and consequentially of teleologically good, if God is beneficent and in no way maleficent. It is designed, and has continued to evolve and develop, as the best soil and means to transformationally develop the heart of God in each of us in expression of God's image and in proleptic spiritual expression (PrōST), as is expressed throughout this work.

I proposed that despite human rebellion, God's desires have been accomplished through the victorious incarnation (*Christus Victor*)—a yet to be fully manifested, restoration of the enjoyment and expression of his image in us. We spoke to and contend that the ineffaceable drive within humans as *imago Dei* to find God is a reciprocated response to God, who first sought and continues to seek us. It is a correlate and concomitant seeking by us in response to God.

God's heart yearns and is in the process of restoring and deepening the rich and intimate conditions that were enjoyed in Eden, as reflected in the parable of the Prodigal (Gen 2; 3:6a; Luke 15:11–32), and as elevated in the life of Jesus Christ (Matt 5:44, *et al.*). God desires fellowship and intimacy with us enjoying and living out his image to the full, beginning in the now. Despite the Edenic fall, as represented in the archetypical first couple (i.e., initial group of prehistorical humans), Adam and Eve, and even after the fall, Power[1] observes, in final agreement with this book, that each uniquely created human person has the capacity to a life in the image of God. Although there were deep, damaging results from the fall, God did not leave his creation without recourse, capacity, and capability. Christ has dealt with sin, bringing freedom for new life (Rom 6:4, 6; 2 Cor 2:5; Gal 2:20; 5:24; Col 3:3, 10). God's image in us is fully preserved and in no way damaged or diminished.

I showed that it requires a loosing of the restraints of sin as phantom pains that also create false beliefs such as physicalism, which obstruct efforts

---

1. Power, "Imago Dei," 131.

to spiritual transformation. Based in the work of Schleifer,[2] the phenomenon of phantom-limb pain seen in amputees (a sense of pain in a severed limb) is drawn from physiological/psychological phenomenon in which brain-commands cause pain when the source of pain is no longer present. Phantom pain, here, is a spiritual, illusionary fixation. These false beliefs or phantom pains (further discussed below), I argued, keep people in the shadows of inability for relationship with God and one another.

This phenomenon is demonstrated in Teresa of Avila's shared pain of the suffering Christ.[3] She hoped to become one with Christ who, of course, is no longer suffering. The phantom pains of sin (Rom 6:11; 1 John 1:9),[4] long ago dealt with by the redemptive, regenerative, victorious work of Christ, must not be allowed to stall and interrupt the process and expression of a transformed life. Otherwise, as I have argued, the progression of the expressed life of *imago Dei* may be frustrated by the disbelief of its possibility and acceptance of the phantom pains of unrequited sin. Bushnell,[5] although not so labeling it, agrees: God must become the focus of love and replace those sinful habits once held and insisting on attention although they have lost their hold by Christ's freeing work.

The phantom pains of the prior condition of humanity, before Christ, trouble most disciples to such an extent that we cannot accept the possibility of a proleptic spiritual transformation (PrōST). However, once hindering enculturation is cleared as phantom, foundational limitations, and misapprehensions or misunderstandings about God, PrōST is greatly facilitated through the intimate influence that we have with God. Not understanding that sin has been dealt a deathblow, firmly-held beliefs of other limitations often interrupt the reality of God's heart toward those created in his image that have been freed from subjugating sin into the kingdom of his son.

As was supported in the body of this book, God seeks an intimate and vital relationship with humans and is injured by its frustration or loss of any part of that relationship (Luke 13:34; 19:41; John 11:33; 13:21). We do not lose value as God's image due to the fall or other disruptions. So then, whether according to the Hebrew or Christian Scriptures, the image of God remains intact after the Edenic fall no matter the explications, impressions, or actions to the contrary. Toward this desire of relationship, after the Edenic fall in time, God's heart immediately reached out to restore fallen humanity to a loving relationship within the Triune, perichoretic community, one

2. Schleifer, "Intangible Materialism," 152–54.
3. Ibid., 154.
4. Farley, *Naked Gospel*, 151.
5. Bushnell, "Protestant Views," 347.

another, and creation (Gen 3:8–11; Lev 26:12; Deut 23:14; 2 Cor 6:16). God desires to be in conversational, intimate relationship with us as friends who freely live in God's expressive will and glory (Exod 29:43–46; 33:11; Ps 23; Isa 41:8; John 15:14; Heb 13:5–6).[6] Therefore, as a result of the introduction of the lawlessness of sin, through consequential human freedom, God determined to intervene through incarnation to put down the rebellion that had, to some degree, veiled the *imago Dei* in us, and created estrangement from God.

God is Spirit and spiritual and has created us in the same fashion as *imago Dei*. This way of creation speaks about God's heart in seeking to fully recover and express his image in humanity. It is a perichoretic relationship as the remedy to the spiritual effects of the fall responding as proleptic spiritual transformation (PrōST). It is a response from us to God who first sought and continues to seek us. It is a correlate and resultant seeking in response to God.

Already addressed, but worth repeating here, Catherine[7] of Siena in *The Dialogue*, spoke about God's love at a devotional level, "Because you have fallen in love with what you have made!" This enamored, benevolent-desire of God is the essential reason that we desire God in concordant, harmonious response, which response, is, at its core, a reflection of God's desire for us (1 John 4:10, 19). It is a consonant-response, reflection, and echo of the very image of God, responding, reflecting, and echoing back to God and to the whole of creation (Eccl 3:11). Included in this transmission or transaction, as I have argued, is the necessary and naturally spontaneous worship generated by such an encounter with the living God.

The second query showed God's interest and his extents to fully recover, in richer measure, a manifest *imago Dei* in humans:

- ❖ In what measure is God actively interested in recovery of his image in humanity as the remedy to the spiritual effects of the fall and in PrōST?

The book's central intent was a focus on the accomplishment of God's intent and desire for the recovery and transformation of creation, with humans as his heart's special intent to be vice-regents and the catalyst to universal recovery and transformation of all creation. Moreover, the fall of humanity, as recorded in Genesis, is instructive whether one believes in an archetypical Adam and Eve, a literal first pair of disobedient humans, or

---

6. Willard, *Hearing God*, 10.
7. Catherine of Siena, *Dialogue*, 325.

SUMMARY AND CONCLUSIONS   251

an initial group of prehistorical humans (the position of this book) from which modern humans descended. As discussed earlier and considered at the beginning of this study, the biblical fall records both a becoming and a fall in that becoming. Moreover, Welker[8] claimed that this image had been expressed, damaged, and started toward recovery. While disagreeing with Welker that the image-bearing was damaged, I posit an obscuring of the expression and continuing enjoyment of image. The image-bearing and image-obscuring were in fact, incredibly, both brought on by a God-defying willfulness of humanity (Gen 3). I have throughout disagreed that the image-bearing was damaged, but argued for an obscuring of the expression and full enjoyment of the image. Nevertheless, I have agreed that such hubris by humanity greatly wounded the communion, fellowship, and intimacy between God and humans and introduced an alienation from God and others that has warped the perceptions, desires, and directions of humanity and creation. Moreover, remaining in humans and yearning for expression, is an overwhelming resonance for full expression and enjoyment of *imago Dei*, relationship to God and one another, and creation as a whole.

Gadamer,[9] in an exchange with Hagel, suggested as we interact with, even sacrifice for, the universal, we gain an intense sense of ourselves. It is in this progressive expansion of relationship to the world and creation, in whole, that the intimate heart of God is experienced and expressed putting on display the expansiveness and grandeur of *imago Dei*. Here, in such an intimate and open relationship, we find particularity and ourselves in the largeness of the whole. It is a relational *imago Dei* in caring for God's creation as vice-regents.

In agreement here, Paul reminds, as did Catherine of Siena, that God gave himself in incarnation to possess humans in a nurturing embrace, freeing us in recovery to fully express *imago Dei* by good works in creation. Peter explicitly says that by God's "precious and very great promises" his intent is to make us "partakers of the divine nature" (2 Pet 1:4), and in this we shall live the overcoming, transformed life bringing glory to God and liberating the creation in transformation (Ps 8:6; Rom 8:18–25; Col 2:13–15; Heb 2:14–15).[10] The Apostle John and the psalmist present the seed of this growth, saying, "You are gods, sons of the Most High, all of you" (Ps 81; 82:6; John 10:34). God is interested in loving full expression and elevation of his *imago Dei* to more representative levels of himself (2 Cor 3:18). We were created with the privilege and responsibility of being God's representatives

---

8. Welker, *Creation and Reality*, 75.
9. Gadamer, *Century of Philosophy*, 7, 59.
10. Grenz, "Jesus as the Imago Dei," 621.

not to replace God's glory in our exercise of power decoupled from God but to exercise viceregency as friends of God in his reflection.

Van Huyssteen[11] and Feinberg[12] claim that there is no ground to plant the seed of a lost or even distorted *imago Dei*. Despite the conjecture according to Altmann[13] that "by faith and obedience to the will of God as expressed in the Scriptures . . . [humans can] regain the lost status of *imago Dei*," I have argued that the *imago* is not lost but only obscured. Central to the point is that people are restored not the *imago Dei*. Contrary to Feinberg,[14] the image is not in need of restoration or perfecting. God's image in humans was not and cannot be lost; it is the status of all human beings, as rightly argued by Kilner.[15] Yes, conformation to God's image is the immediate and ultimate destination (Rom 8:29; 12:2), but that refers to the accidents and not the essential human, which is inviolate. In either case, whether we insist on a lost or obscured paradigm, such a recovery of *imago* or experience and enjoyment of *imago* is not dependent on the weak efforts of human beings exercising faulty attributes. It is the working of God (1 Cor 1:8; Phil 1:6; 1 Thess 3:13).

In this description is shown, the unrelenting, intimate desire God has for union with his human creatures as *imago Dei*. More than a millennia before, Paul put it more theologically by reminding Titus (2:11–12, 14) that God's incarnation brought salvation for everyone, enabling renouncement of faithlessness, impiousness, unspiritual passions, and rather in their place living in the reflection of God's life (*imago Dei*) in the now. God is ecumenical, merciful, generous, and does not refuse assistance to anyone.

According to Mahoney and Pargament,[16] and I agree, a formal conversion experience is not required or needed to proceed to human inherent, elemental, and inexpungible propensity for transformation. Potential is intrinsic to humans and follows from a relationship with God as fully recovered and experienced by Christ's incarnational work in securing the means to a transformed life for the rest of God's children. In this universal eschatological nature of the reality of God's transformative work, universal restoration shall not be frustrated or interrupted (2 Pet 2:9). Since this has not been an exhaustive study of soteriology, further investigation is needed regarding salvific constructs of universalism in the particularism of Christ,

---

11. Van Huyssteen, *Alone in the World?*, 135.
12. Feinberg, "Image of God," 245.
13. Altmann, "Homo Imago Dei," 257.
14. Feinberg, "Image of God," 246.
15. Kilner, "Humanity in God's Image," 611–12, 615.
16. Mahoney and Pargament, "Sacred Changes," 481.

especially among the works of Tillich, Balthasar, Barth, Origen, Talbott, McDonald, Schleiermacher, Hick, and others.

As I have argued in the body of this work, God has not forgotten his design that humans would express him in this life as his image (Rom 8:29; 1 Cor 15:49; 2 Cor 3:18; Eph 1:11; Col 2:13; 3:10; 2 Tim 1:9; 1 Pet 5:10). Moreover, I have argued that *imago Dei* now carries something more—the God-man. God's image in Jesus the Christ now carries the existential realities of his incarnate life toward which PrōST (Proleptic Spiritual Transformation) drives in the now (Rom 8:29; 2 Cor 4:4; Col 1:5). *Imago Dei*, or God's self-address, now carries the God-man (*imago Christi*). This study examined the conventional partitioning of the "now" and "not-yet" and proposed a new balance and paradigm in expressed PrōST toward expressed *imago Dei*.

The third query considered the revelation of God's heart toward creation and PrōST:

❖ What are the means by which God reveals or unveils his heart, truth, and intents toward creation and humanity in particular in the plan of spiritual recovery/PrōST?

As shown in the body of this work, it may appear presumptuous to speak as though one might know something about God's heart, truth, and intents. After all, God is transcendent, eternal, immortal, immutable, and invisible—the magnificent creator of the universe and the maker of heaven and earth and all their content, seen and unseen, experienced and never to be experienced. What can be experienced of God, however, is to be found in Christ. God exists in unapproachable glory "outside," "above," "below," "before," "after" space-time and yet contains space-time (Gen 1:31; Eccl 8:17; 1 John 4:12; 1 Tim 1:17; 6:16). God contains all; all is in God (Job 12:10; Dan 5:23b; Acts 17:28). God is the uncreated-creator and uncaused-cause of reality and all of its content. He sustains the entire "universe by the word of his power" (Col 1:17; Heb 1:3). As Anselm famously said, God is that being than which nothing greater can be conceived.[17] Yet, this transcendent God is revealed in Christ Jesus (John 1:18; 6:46; 8:19; 14:7–10).

My primary aim, objectives, and intents in this book were further advanced, in part, by considering the means and methods by which God reveals and unveils his heart, truth, and purposes toward creation including humanity. I argued here that God utilizes both general and special revelation with a view to present spiritual recovery (PrōST). Creation, especially humans, and various other means were also considered as methods of God's

---

17. Fairweather, *Scholastic Miscellany*, 75.

communication. The Scriptures (Ps 19:1–4; Rom 1:20) show that because of general revelation, we can be excused for not knowing what God has made accessible about himself, his heart, and his creation. I proposed special revelation particularly to be a method and means of God in revealing a reality fully dependent upon God's intent for self revelation, which is a far more specific telling of God's heart, attributes, intents, and, actions. Both general and special revelations were examined as intents and methods to aid and enable spiritual recovery or transformation in the now (PrōST).

We considered Scripture as revealing an omnipresent, omniscient God, who feels, knows, and empathizes with the needy and abused, as well as having a full response to the errant feelings and actions of the stray and willfully, defiant person. We thought about the passibility of God as God's willingness to change his "mind" and to withhold judgment if his creatures listen to his warnings and heed his direction. God, I argued, can be influenced by the will of human beings.

We examined the theory, thought, and theology of an unknowable God, a God that is transcendent, ineffable and "transcategorial, meaning [God who is] beyond the range of our human systems of concepts or mental categories,"[18] but as mainly in Christ. Notwithstanding, there is a vast list that can be numbered regarding the revelation of God's heart in Scripture and following that God is to some measure and at some level knowable. I discussed herein the evidential testimony to God's heart as found in Scripture as indeed, *a priori*, multitudinous. Nonetheless, the intent and subject of this book has been specific to spiritual transformation and the possibility of proleptic, spiritual reality as modeled in Christ. God's heart, specifically regarding this subject, graciously presents as seminal, knowable, vital, and central. My focus has been directed toward human persons.

In addition to God's heart being seen in his works, as was further investigated, the Judeo-Christian Scriptures display the heart of God and help derive his desires (Ps 19:1; 50:6; 144:6; Rom 1:19–20). I presented the anthropological personifications used in Scripture to describe God, although only partial and incomplete, to be adequate to the task of revelation for human understanding (2 Tim 3:15–17). We also examined other manners such as Scripture, and spiritual disciplines including prayer, fasting, confession, and meditation. The mysterious and the beautiful array of truth in narrative, story, and fiction, displaying suffering in the process exposing God's passibility were also examined by our focus. More pointedly, in the hands of the Yahwist, they are the "boldest anthropomorphisms" and necessary to

---

18. Hick, "Who or What Is God?"

God's, self-revelation.[19] God's heart is laid open in the histories, narratives, poetry, psalms, parables, allegories, and directives of Hebrew and Christian canon and deuterocanonical writings.

Although much is asserted regarding the revelations of God's heart in creation—experiential tales by individuals and communities—God and God's heart is at the deepest level a mystery. As testified by these storied accounts, God determined to make known to humans the "mystery of his will" in service to God's purpose (Eph 1:7–10; 3:3). This mystery (Gk. *mustérion*) indicates that God's will, in plan, was first hidden. God's self-revelation opens his heart to human knowledge, experience, and transformation. Moreover, God's self-revelation now makes possible for us to join and serve God's heart desire in fulfilling his will and plan.

John Calvin[20] spoke to this mystery with poignant counsel in that the "most perfect way" to seek God is not to attempt to satiate our curiosity by attempting to probe and investigate his essence but rather to adore and meditate on him as can be seen in his great works. It is by these works that God is close and known to his children, and by which he communes with his creatures.[21] I presented spiritual disciplines in this book as a means to this goal of adoration and meditation.

I further discussed in the body of this work God's heart for his eternal plan in response to the fall and its remedy through incarnation. More to the point of this study, God seeks to fully recover and express his image in humanity now as proleptic spiritual transformation (ProST) in perichoretic relationship with the Trinity.

We looked at some examples of God's heart to include the following: God's heart is overflowing with love for his creation and creatures (John 3:16; Rom 5:8; 8:32; Eph 2:4; 1 John 4:9–10). God is desirous of beauty (Ps 8:1; 19:1; Eccl 3:11a; Acts 14:17; 17:24; Rom 1:18–19) and of righteousness and justice (Gen 6:6–7; Ps 23:3; 89:14; 97:2). God's heart is for the disadvantaged, downtrodden, orphan, widow, poor, sick, possessed, dispossessed, all nations, children, women, men, animals, the planet, the universe, and all disadvantaged issues, situations and involved people (Matt 5:1–11; 11:5; Mark 1:40–41; 10:14; Luke 4:18; Gal 3:8). God is for his kingdom (Dan 6:26; Matt 13:44–46; John 2:17). God is for the salvation of everyone (John 3:16; 1 John 4:9; Rom 4:25; 5:8; 1 Cor 15:22; 1 Tim 2:6; 4:10; Titus 2:11). God's heart is against idolatry, covetousness, irresponsibility, and a host of

---

19. Rad, *Genesis*, 25–26.
20. Calvin, *Institutes*, I.V.9.
21. Ibid.

immoral and unrighteous actions and thoughts (Deut 4–5; 2 Kgs 15:5; Matt 23:27–29; 2 Pet 2:9).

I argued that from the beginning of the scriptural record, God displayed a heart and intent to share his essence with humanity as he created us in his image (*imago Dei*) and breathed into us his very life (Gen 2:7; John 5:21). Moreover, and to the point of this study, God's heart still yearns for a full, rich, and transformative relationship with us (Ps 34:8; Song 8:1; John 14:23; 17:21–23; Rom 12:2; 2 Cor 3:18; 6:16).

The *imago Dei* in humans is not an allusion to royal theology. A prince is not the focus of bearing this image, but us, all human beings.[22] All persons are *imago Dei*, and are included in proleptic spiritual transformation (PrōST), as per God's intent. The fulfillment of human destiny as *imago Dei* is a growing representation of PrōST's fulfillment. Such a life is modeled in Jesus Christ proleptically, regarding or representing all humanity by the man Jesus. God determined to put down human rebellion through the incarnation of Christ. Putting down this rebellion accomplishes the goal of transformation. Christ exampled God's heart (anthropomorphically speaking) regarding the intended life meant for us. As Pannenberg,[23] notes, it was a life that cannot be exceeded by any other model of intimacy between God and humans. Although we are only too often seen as in the image of the man of dust, humans shall, one day, be the full expression and bear the unencumbered image of the man of heaven in full manifest *Christosis* (1 Cor 15:47, 49).

This comes from spiritual readiness and divine fiat. Moreover, this particular divine καιροι (divine appointment) of PrōST, if it belongs to someone as it did for Enoch, Noah, Elijah, Jesus, and Paul, is sometimes outside of "regular schedules" of times and better serves God's grace and kingdom. However, the exception to the rule in no way changes the rule. Such a thought is a fallacious conjecture. But the rule is often examined and confirmed by testing. This "excepting" might better be thought of as idiosyncratic versus a strict application of law without grace. Law stands as inviolate, but grace moves and flexes freely and fulfills the intent of the original "rule." That God's kingdom would be manifest on earth as it is in heaven (Matt 6:10), and that we would be in intimate and unhindered communion and fellowship affecting the freedom of creation is the intent and eventual full reality of redemption and sanctification in God's heart as seen in PrōST.

---

22. Moltmann, *God in Creation*, 219.
23. Pannenberg, *Systematic Theology*, 2:225.

Summary and Conclusions

The fourth query examined PrōST in relation to soteriology:

❖ What are the transformative and Soteriological implications of PrōST?

Although not a polemic, a defense, or an apology for a particular soteriological construct, a brief consideration or précis of some key theological concepts, that were shown to affect the objectives and goals of this work, were considered in this book. As in Schleiermacher,[24] taking care not to do violence to individual scriptural passages by wrenching them from contextual considerations, reference was made with the larger support of contextual and dogmatic considerations. Yet the necessary limited survey and wanting of further details of these considerations, were only in support of the more specific and primary aim of this study to investigate whether individuals must wait for the afterlife to have purification and spiritual transformation fully or largely "worked out" (Phil 2:12-13).

We considered two lines of reasoning that greatly affect salvific presuppositions. The first had to do with the intent and broadness of God's heart: Who receives God's salvation and who may not, creates broad spiritual effects. The second reasoning had to do with the human heart, especially in reflection of God's heart. Soteriological constructs were not exhaustively developed, but some amount of discussion was necessarily given for the full proposal of the present work.

I presented a gloss of soteriological constructs during the course of this work. However, there were no arguments given by me for a pluralistic theology in which all religions are equal. I argued Christian Exclusivism as salvation found only in and through Christ (John 14:6; 1 John 5:12) and contested as a construct in which only a limited number of persons shall be saved in the final judgment. Giving more room, yet not sufficient, Christian Inclusivism was also considered in this book as most shall, in fact, be saved except those who remain intransigently hardened and intent to resist all of God's mercies and graces. Finally, although thorough future research is needed, Christian universalism, as I presented here, posited that Christ is the only way to God (particularism) and *hoped* that all shall be saved and redeemed through Christ perhaps after some respective or required time of purgation. A form of universal salvation it seems to me, or at least I hope, to be the message of Scripture and the heart of God. Karl Barth, along with others, was shown to hold such a universal hope.[25] Barth, as representative, was shown to hold salvation as found in none other than the particularism

---

24. Schleiermacher, *Christian Faith*, 116.
25. Greggs, *Barth, Origen*, 30-31, 41.

of Jesus Christ; that is, Christian universalism is particularism that remains in the Christian fold.[26]

Moreover, if one accepts that the final judgment is reserved until after the general resurrection of the dead (Rev 20:13–15), then there seems to be some kind of opportunity for continued growth in the spirit in Christ until then. This opportunity is provided from the Father's heart of love to bring his children to share in his holiness (Heb 12:8–11). We can argue that some measure of God's victory and thereby glory would be diminished if someone is, in the end, lost to God.

An understanding and belief about salvation and subsequent transformation opens horizons to human destiny. Considered in these pages was who is included in transformation, and to what degrees they are included. Nevertheless, despite various conflicting doctrinal assertions and popular testimonies, this book could not say with certainty, what salvific construct is correct. All possible, falsifiable understandings were set-aside as distractions and challenges to the objectives of this study regarding PrōST. Nevertheless, it is the belief and hope presented by me that Christian universal salvation founded in the particularity of Christ wins out in the eschatological end. The practical presumption of such a hope presents all people with the dignity and deference of a destined magnificent of God's choosing and availability for PrōST and who shall be made into a radiant gods or goddesses.[27] Such a conceptualization or vision provides a particular view of our selves, and all others, that it in turn drives an attitude and response that facilitates communion and open fellowship with God and others. As I argued, such fellowship makes available God's transformative activity to all persons.

Orthodoxy says humans are justified by grace; however, suffering in no way appeases God but is a means to express God and display God's unconquerable love.[28] By this, besides our own sinful and often-tragic devices, God-arranged situations, argued here by me to place persons in difficulty for transformational means. This is more palatable if everyone's eventual destination is God. However, I admit, along with Vorster's solution,[29] that some difficulties and outright tragedies cannot easily be found in the heart of a loving God. Nevertheless, it seems that God is inclined to use such difficulty and tragedy for spiritual transformation (PrōST).

---

26. Ibid., 310.
27. Lewis, *Mere Christianity*, 176.
28. Bushnell, "Protestant Views," 350.
29. Vorster, *Created in the Image of God*, 2011:47.

Summary and Conclusions 259

Although considering the world's creation and Jesus crucifixion, we cannot absolve God.[30] Nevertheless, Augustine[31] protests, no fault can be found in God regarding sin in creation simply because God is creator. His judgments are as a "great deep"; God is unsearchable (Rom 11:33).[32] However, seeing no right to judge the creator of the universe, neither Israel nor primitive Christianity dared to accuse God of evil (Isa 45:9; Jer 18:6; Rom 9:20).[33] Contrary to usual Augustinian thought, humans are indeed capable of will and directed to workout transformational ends (Phil 1:6; 2:12).[34] This capability to workout our salvation must not be allowed frustration by churning on irreconcilable struggles and misery of this life that might wrongly even cause accusations that God is maleficent or at least neglectful not resting in a resolved salvific construct.

Although there is no theological consensus, there are several reasons, which I have presented, why Christian or trinitarian universalism may be the best reflection of the Gospel. Among them, I showed Scripture to support such a view in that God's love for all of his children cannot be defeated. Additionally, Jesus Christ's salvific work cannot be defeated in the smallest degree. Existentially, there is a witness, an instinct, and deep in the soul of every human to everlasting life in a better condition at rest. As reviewed in this work, there is an early historical testimony to this view. Moreover, I presented philosophical and scientific reasons to support the continued existence of the human soul.

Lacking the full expression of a universal image hinders the manifestation of God's kingdom on earth as it is in heaven (Matt 6:10; 13:19; Rom 12:2). If one holds to an exclusive belief of salvation, it would results in fewer souls attracted to the Gospel as it is impotently lived out. The "righteousness and peace and joy in the Holy Spirit," that is of the kingdom of God (Rom 14:17), is expressed by those of us who enjoy some measure of spiritual transformation from which to spontaneously express these attributes. This too-neglected movement I showed to be at the heart of God's desire and intent for PrōST.

Plantinga,[35] the Christian analytic philosopher, shares the same hope. Although he does not quite believe universalism, he does not disbelieve it either and rather thinks universalism is something for which Chris-

---

30. Pannenberg, *Systematic Theology*, 2:166.
31. Augustine, Tractate 53.
32. Ibid.
33. Pannenberg, *Systematic Theology*, 2:163.
34. Irenaeus, *Against Heresies*, 4.37.6–7; Willard, "Spiritual Disciplines," 106.
35. Plantinga, "Can a Person Be a Soul?"

tians should at least hope. As noted, God is making his people gods and goddesses, Lewis[36] envisions, who are such beautiful creatures and who are radiant and filled with the love seen in Christ. In its effects, the degree to which this image is obscured is the measure of hindrance of the manifestation of God's kingdom on earth as it is in heaven (Matt 6:10; 13:19; Rom 12:2). The "righteousness and peace and joy in the Holy Spirit," that is of the kingdom of God (Rom 14:17), is expressed by disciples who enjoy some measure of spiritual transformation, that is, *imago Christi* (image of Christ), from which to spontaneously express these attributes of righteousness, peace and joy in God's Spirit as did Christ. This too-neglected movement is at the heart of God's desire and intent.

The fifth query was to investigate conclusions and the possibility of a unified theory of PrōST:

❖ What are the conclusions of this book; do they imply a unified theory regarding PrōST?

First, no clear unified theory was found to exist nor was one developed; although various elements begin to emerge that might suggest a "recombinant" possibility. Emerging from Christian spirituality is a rich, varied, and long history of mystics, seekers, and the uninitiated simply desirous of the divine. Although I was not able to discern a broadly accepted understanding of present Christian spiritual transformation (PrōST), this rich history of spiritual practices and seeking suggests a human intrinsic foundational desire for relationship with the divine. What spiritual conditions or attributes of God are communicably and fully available to humans, though enjoyed by some availed disciples, have not been clearly and thoroughly presented and broadly made available in Christian literature. Moreover, there does not seem to be any addressing of proleptic spirituality transformation (PrōST) in the construct as presented in this work. The "not-yet" of these communicable conditions and attributes available "now" for humanity to enjoy of God's restorative and progressive work of spiritual transformation is lacking foundational agreement.

In consideration of the spiritual efforts of many named throughout this book, a potentially shared view of, in effect, becoming like God, *theōsis*, has the potential of serving as a uniting factor across camp boundaries that tease at and suggest the possibilities of a proleptic spiritual transformation (PrōST) or a reality that is available to the twenty-first-century church,

---

36. Lewis, *Mere Christianity*, 176.

according to Kärkkäinen.[37] Moreover, more in depth investigation into soteriological and theodical constructs is needed, especially as related to Christian Universalism. Spiritual practices and the extent of *imago Dei* are also in need of further investigation. Further research into these areas may yield such a unified theory. However, it does not appear necessary for experience. A clear unified theory is left for future investigation and formulation, while PrōST, as a reality to be experienced, was founded in individual opportunity and *praxis* as we examined in these pages.

Setting aside unified theories for later research, this entire chapter is founded as a summary in conclusions. Particular concluding thoughts are given above in answer to the five queries and in the sections that follow. As asserted in the beginning of this research, the human pursuit for God has reached across time, place, and all cultures and milieus.[38] As told herein, the search for God has been a particularly intense quest that, at times, has been told and experienced in often-opposing perspectives.

Mystics and contemplatives variously claim that the Judeo-Christian God, in particular, is experienced in both presence and absence, that is, cataphatic and apophatic expression.[39] These differences are not solely academic distinctions. As was considered in this book, their paradigms presage existential outcomes. This study demonstrated that the nature of the Christian relationship with God directs or even determines any transformative affect of that relationship upon the life of the seeker, initiate, or experienced disciple.

Exchange in this work about the extent of spiritual transformation ranged from the anemic to full-orbed experiential enjoyment. This discussion defined spirituality or the lived experience of spirituality as our conscious participation in life synthesis through an experiential integration of self-transcendence toward ultimate value.[40] Unambiguously, Pargament[41] says spiritual transformation mainly points to a basic change in the place or character of the sacred as life's significance. Integration of one's life into the sacred is a change in spiritual quality, vivacity, function, character, or condition from one experiential level to another that may have collateral affects on soul, body, and creation. Moreover, such transformation alters our relationship with others and with God. This research demonstrates that we need not wait for the *eschaton* to begin spiritual transformation. In fact,

37. Kärkkäinen, *One with God*, 119–20, 123.
38. Cady, "Loosening the Category," 23–25.
39. McGinn, *Foundations of Mysticism*, xviii.
40. Schneiders, "Christian Spirituality," 1.
41. Pargament, *Spiritually Integrated Psychotherapy*, 21.

it is my conclusion that we are expected and facilitated by God to PrōST (proleptic spiritual transformation).

The intrinsic likeness to God of human beings in creation, the experiential realities that foster change and transformation, the spiritual disciplines, and the inner working of God's Spirit all make PrōST possible. This answers our primary aim: Must individuals wait until the afterlife for spiritual transformation to be fully or largely "worked out"; that is, what, if any, is the possible opportunity to largely "work out [our spiritual transformation] with fear and trembling [now]" (Phil 2:12–13). That is, no; no one must wait until the afterlife for spiritual transformation to be fully or largely "worked out." The opportunity is experientially present and available now (PrōST).

FORWARD WAYS

More particularly, God was also shown in this work as revelatory in special ways and means for more specific telling of himself, attributes, and intents communicating to particular individuals, using Scripture, literature, visions, dreams, preaching, and even earthly creatures, and nature (Gen 1:26–27; Num 12:6; 22:27–30; Matt 16:17; John 5:17, 19; Luke 19:40; 2 Tim 3:16; Heb 1:1). Through various means God continues to use revelation in his desire to draw persons into an intimate relationship with himself now (PrōST). Particularly, this study examined and suggested how God continues to communicate himself to us.

Facilitations of this communication were considered throughout this study. Specifically, beginning entrance into spiritual disciplines was examined by which we might avail ourselves to God for spiritual growth. This writing showed that God speaks into the harmonizing, sympathetic, and resonating heart of humans created in the *imago Dei*. Available means were also presented herein including disciplines such as prayer, fasting, confession, and meditation. I postulated disciplines as only a sampling for opening one to God's presence and transformative in-working to persons inclusive of spirit, soul, and body. Furthermore, disciplines are only means. They are not to be confused with goals, ends, or warrant for God's earned grace.

In these pages we also forwarded the idea that sentient human beings proceed through mind shifting and transforming through scriptural story, allegory, and parable toward a spiritual relationship issuing in God's unwarranted grace. This grace we showed to be with the "unknowable" God despite God's apparent, often enigmatic communication. I also put forth in this work the teleological intent in leading from PrōST to unobscured *imago Dei* in unhindered divine presence expressing God in creation.

We postulated in this best of all possible worlds, that theodicy, or particularly the mystery of human suffering under the eye of an omnipotent, all-beneficent God is an enigmatic means for God's transformative work no matter suffering's causes. These chapters have not attempted a thorough review of the historical and personal implications of the full subject, but suggested that suffering, whatever its causes, is used by God for ultimate purposes in creation. It is important to consider that whatever the full reasons of suffering in the world, God's heart is still inclined to the best environment for spiritual transformation of his human creatures. God is especially interested in spiritual transformation in the now (PrōST) availing present suffering.

Contending against our primary aim was and is the commonly held belief that God is ineffable and unknowable. Such a belief frustrates any hope of enjoying God in any measure of perichoretic relationship. God, however, as shown in this research, has made whatever of himself is needful for intimate communication and spiritual transformation manifest and knowable in Christ. The communal experience found in narrative and especially story, fictional or otherwise, was shown by this study as the heavenly community, a trinitarian experience in reflection of the perichoretic communal reality. Story, as found throughout the biblical narrative, is not dependent on linear historical fact as the central intent to speak of and lead one into spiritual truth and experience. God uses various literary devices to press past the ingrained mental habits of persons. Story, allegory, poetry, and parable are common devices found in Scripture by which God speaks of deeper and higher truths than are readily seen by simple propositions and historical accounts. This is dressed in the beauty and pleasure of story pointing and reaching for the teleological goals of the creator of the universe particularly our spiritual maturation beginning now.

This work also examined the transformed life as it lights the way for others as exampled by Jesus Christ and his followers. This treatise showed how God intends earthly life to be lived by those in *imago Dei* by reflecting God's glory. The glory is a reflection by uncovered faces unlike the veiled face of Moses and reminds the beholder of the perfections of Christ. I proposed in these pages an outpouring and display of glory in the context of proleptic spiritual transformation (PrōST).

Interacting with Emmanuel Levin as, Caputo[42] spoke of the face of the "other" with whom one encounters as being the trace of God that is left behind as he withdraws. The allusion is enticing and lovely; however, although God implants himself and provides a trace of himself that can be seen by

---

42. Caputo, *Deconstruction in a Nutshell*, 98.

the attentive observer in one in whom the *imago Dei* is being expressed, this study concluded that God does not withdraw himself. Perception of withdrawal is simply that—perception. God uses such imperceptible times, where presence is not discerned, for the purposes of maturing and transforming us (2 Cor 2:10).

As has been argued in this study, perhaps more of the not-yet is available now than is usually proposed. Van Hyussteen[43] claimed that the human being is transcendent and as close to being itself to the degree it reflects the not-yet in the now. "Proleptic participation in trinitarian glory [is] a hope-filled way of being."[44] This existential understanding, now reality, is critical to one walking in a proleptic reality to some measure and not relegating to the future the majority of spiritual transformation.

Salvation is held in spiritual transformation. Keil and Delitzsch[45] speak to this when they address the issues of Genesis 1:26 and speak of it as a loss through sin to be regained by Christ in expressing God's glory and essence. This "new self" is where spiritual transformation has, and is occurring from one degree of glory to another (2 Cor 3:18). Disagreeing here with Keil and Delitzsch, I hold that the image was not lost but marred in the garden and is repaired and elevated in the accomplishment of Christ. For God's disciples, the image of God in Christ is now available and inclusive of incarnation and triumphant spiritual living (PrōST).

SHIFTS AND CONCERNS

A mental, or paradigm, shift is necessary to militate the yet-to-be completed spiritual reality as it is presented with impediments that suggest such a hope may not yet be realizable. Admitting that there is still a future hope and fullness does not delete the present possibility now available. In anticipation, the disciples of Christ presently represent the kingdom although not fully so; and therefore, we must live in tension with a sense of urgency.

Not understanding the full extent of God's completed forgiveness is a hindrance to PrōST. Unforgiveness creates a spiritual prison of self-banished solitude from God and other persons hindering spiritual transformation (PrōST). The forgiveness and clear conscious secured by the work of Christ's love is the approach to God in relationship. Such forgiveness is, in itself, transformative.

---

43. Van Hyussteen, *Alone in the World?*, 147.
44. Ibid., 143.
45. Keil and Delitzsch, *Commentary on the Old Testament*, 39.

Despite the attempts to include disciples in present transformation, some theologians limit the presence of the kingdom solely to the activities of Christ. My contention has been, and remains, that Christ's disciples are not fully, but presently living, to an imperfect degree, the kingdom. The environmental and biological conditions in which we must contend to survive and evolve, further explain the tremendous difficulty in trying to live a transformed life. Most observers object strongly to any present release from ignorance, error, and tempting vagaries, attributed to our existence in this age. I made no claim of absolute perfection without the continual need of increased, progressive transformation. This was shown herein as a softening of the idea of moral perfectionism and sinless existence in the present life without the injurious belief that humans must live in defeat.

Again, since a general exclusive view of salvation holds sway in most modern Christian theology and preaching, initial salvation is the main, slavish focus of most of what occupies God's church. This contributes to the neglect of making disciples that reflect God's image. Such image shows forth God's love, mercy, and grace to creation. Furthermore, such a lack hinders the manifestation of God's kingdom on earth as it is in heaven. Admittedly, to identify and describe proleptic spiritual transformation (PrōST) is not to make spiritual transformation happen. The theory and even theology of such a proposed state or process does not equal practice. Doxy does not equate with praxy.

However the development, this proclivity to winning converts seems blind to the very words of Jesus Christ to "make disciples of all nations" (Matt 28:18–20). Grudem[46] provides a reminder that to see God "face to face" brings a *beatific* response from the beholder. There is a vital need to behold the face of the one who leads into a Christ-like transformation and response (2 Cor 3:18) not only conversion. The "righteousness and peace and joy in the Holy Spirit" (Rom 14:17), that is of the kingdom of God, is expressed by disciples who enjoy some measure of transformation and formation to spontaneously express these attributes of righteousness, peace and joy in the Holy Spirit. This movement is at the heart of God's desire and intent.

This study investigated and utilized postmodern thought and theology, Open Theism, philosophy, science, psychology, story, and consequences and implications among the consequent direction dictated by the research. This study also considered means to spiritual transformation and examined the markers of transformation and how they are the "down payment" and taste of the eternal steady-state reality in God's presence.

---

46. Grudem, *Systematic Theology*, 190.

My intent was to speak to the establishment of the inclusive nature of God's transformative work, and that it cannot be frustrated or interrupted. I further examined whether God's transformative work excludes, disallows, or leaves behind any persons. We found God's transformative work to include those that have too often been judged as outside the veil of Christian orthodoxy and orthopraxy. Included are the non-confessing, the homosexual, the heretic, the agnostic and atheist, the profligates, and the others outside the pale of acceptable Christian belief and practice included or excluded.

This demonstrated contention of inclusion weighed on the present analysis as a consideration of the extent of spiritual transformation and its reach. Further, we limited our review of soteriology to the extent, strength, and efficacy of God's salvific work only as it relates to and effects spiritual transformation. Principally, our argument has been if all were lost because of the one man, Adam, and all are saved through the one man, Jesus, then everyone must receive eventual spiritual transformation (Rom 5:12–21). Therefore, that which does not transpire in this life must then continue after death (2 Macc 12:46; Matt 5:26; 12:32; Phil 1:6; Rev 21:27). Further work is required to establish the extent of God's salvific accomplishment and by that who is included in PrōST.

More so, since justification in salvation has been accomplished, we answered the after-life question as reference to sanctification or transformation, which cannot be partitioned from justification.[47] This sanctification or transformation is included in a full and unhindered image of God. So while the Roman Catholic view of purgatory is that a saved person who has not been perfected must be purged to ready himself or herself for heaven and God's holy presence,[48] the Orthodox view is that *post-mortem* tests may determine individual eternity. What I propose is that any supposed or possible purgatory, limbo, or after-life purification is to complete the work God has begun and not a matter of punishment, salvation, eternal perishing, or recompense.

But one must not wait or wager for the afterlife to have this worked out. The marvelous opportunity is available now. This is the proleptic experience available to all today if one but cooperates with the Spirit of God by his grace and mercy. It is a reality in tension. That is, individuals are fully dependent on God and yet need to "work" as if God was only cheering on the accomplishment. God's ability is made perfect in the disciples' inability. This proposal was argued as not being anachronistic, out of time and place,

---

47. Walls, "Purgatory for Everyone."
48. Catechism of the Catholic Church, CCC 1030.

and not obtainable in this age or dispensation but a present reality to be enjoyed.

THE END AS BEGINNING

The beginning point is intimate love with humans and God and human free will in the garden. The end or conclusion is this beginning point restored in an elevated state for human fellowship and expression driven by a transformed life reflective of the experiential life of Christ in perichoretic relationship with the Trinity. Freedom provided is only licensed by remaining in God's chosen place. In this "place" or way, we are compelled or constrained by Christ's life. More firmly, sin has no hold, that is, the sin problem of the fall in the beginning has been extinguished by Christ's victorious incarnational work freeing us to an intimate relationship with God as friends. Transformed living provides a beginning freedom or the newness of life that is enjoyed in Jesus now (PrōST). It is the life Jesus Christ would live in the embrace of the Father, if he were living our life in the present milieu. Unbound from the limiting affects of sin, each of us, as *imago Dei*, have the capacity to model and live a glory-reflecting life in the image of the Godman. It is the beginning of what was lost in the garden realized at a higher level in the experientiality of Christ's life.

It is God's reciprocated freedom in love for us that began in the garden. In the end it is the same freedom, however, with a larger capacity to dwell in the heights and descend to the depths and to be both great and small with God. This capability is lavished on persons who are distinct from him. God's free, intimate relationship with humans is his unfettered priority. Jesus is and models the ultimate human in full communion with God. There is no exclusion of humanity in God in order for God to be God. God's deity now includes humanity, a humanity that encounters experientially in the humanity of Jesus Christ in total. God no longer exists without us. Such a reality is glorious now and carries us into the end.

As Fee[49] presents the kingdom of God, it is not a matter of laws, practices, rules, or even words, but of "righteousness, and peace, and joy . . . and power" (Rom 14:17; 1 Cor 4:20). In further support of this, Fee[50] continues with his interpretation of Paul as holding the kingdom in a tension of "now" and "not-yet." He claims Paul lived in the not-yet and realized the now as a foreshadowing of the kingdom as not-yet and tried to convince any who would listen to experience the same.

---

49. Fee, *God's Empowering Presence*, 118–19, 617–18.
50. Ibid., 119–20.

This book portrayed a reflection of the kingdom or the end of death in prolepsis (1 Cor 15: 24, 26). Living by the kingdom life removes the hindrance to fully realized transformation by walking in the power of God's Spirit and expressing God's reign. It is living both the now of the kingdom and a great measure of the not-yet. What is here termed proleptic is nothing less than what God, in Christ, has illustrated in such places as the Sermon on the Mount. It seems for the future and is most often not expected until the eternal state of believers. And so, while I, like many others, hold that something more does wait in the eternal state, the kingdom life is largely accessible now (PrōST). The attributes attached to the kingdom life are available now and should be growing and developing in each Christ-follower in the present life. It is an injustice to God and Christ's accomplishments to put off, until the future eternal-state, what was naturally intended by God for present enjoyment. God, by his ways and means, persuades and prevails now for those walking in that reality. He shall complete what he has begun, even when he must say regarding all that we know, "You have heard it said, but I say to you . . ." (Matt 5).

Moreover, the prodigal returns to the father who had been waiting filled with restrained compassion, now broken out, running to embrace and kiss his beloved, returning child (Luke 15:11–24). Wandering and squandered living changed the prodigal. He came to know the blessing of being with his father even in the lowest state or position. Perhaps not with the prodigal in mind, Lewis[51] pronounces an applicable truth that "a [person] can no more diminish God's glory by refusing to worship Him than a lunatic can put out the sun by scribbling the word, 'darkness' on the walls of his cell." The prodigal prematurely demanded from his father what was not his right to yet ask to live in darkness, denying his place and bringing communal derision on his father and his rightful position. But the father's love was unwavering. Paul elsewhere says, "If we are faithless, [the Father] remains faithful—for he cannot deny himself" (2 Tim 2:13). As shown above, God is faithful to the love he has for his own prodigals and, yes, the faithful as was the ungrateful elder son. He is drawing all of his sons and daughters to his heart in transformation. For those that can receive it, the transformation is proleptic (PrōST).

Finally, Lossky[52] rightly argues, that persons must present themselves in life's conditions, whether disciplined disciple, prodigal defiance, or dutiful ingratitude, to cooperatively work with God to manifest such an awesome and glorious reality as union with the divine in the present (PrōST).

---

51. Lewis, *Problem of Pain*, 46.
52. Lossky, *Mystical Theology*, 196.

This, of course, requires God's active mercy and grace. Human destiny, in relationship with God, does not wait for the *eschaton*, reminds Pannenberg.[53] Herein is a reflection of the kingdom and the end of the death (1 Cor 15: 24, 26). It is a removal of the hindrance to fully realized transformation by walking in the power of God's Spirit and expressing his reign. It is living both the now of the kingdom and a great measure of the not-yet (PrōST). We must be insistent revolutionaries always pressing toward the mark (Luke 16:16; John 6:27; Phil 3:14) of the primary aim.

We have variously demonstrated through interdisciplinary investigation that we need not wait until the afterlife for spiritual transformation to be largely "worked out"; that is, there is great opportunity to largely "work out [our spiritual transformation] with fear and trembling [now]" (Phil 2:12–13). An experience of spiritual transformation usually reserved for heaven in eternity is greatly available today (PrōST: proleptic spirituality transformation), if by God's grace and mercy, we cooperate with the Spirit of God.

---

53. Pannenberg, *Systematic Theology*, 2:227–28.

Bibliography

Al- Bitar, S. M. "A Critical Analysis of Thomas Aquinas's Doctrine of the Image of God." *Damascus University Journal* 19 (2003) 17–33.
Alcorn, R. "Reflections on *The Shack*." Eternal Perspectives Ministries. September 26, 2012. http://www.epm.org/resources/2012/Sep/26/reflections-shack.
Alford, B. H. *Jewish History and Literature under the Maccabees and Herod*. London: Longmans, Green, 1913.
Altmann, A. "Homo Imago Dei in Jewish and Christian Theology." *Journal of Religion* 48 (1968) 235–59.
Anderson, B. W. *Understanding the Old Testament*. 5th ed. With S. Bishop and J. H. Newman. Upper Saddle River, NJ: Pearson Education, 2007.
Anon. *Theologia Germanica*. Edited by Peiffer. Translated by S. Winkworth. http://www.ccel.org/ccel/anonymous/theologia.i.html.
Aquinas, T. *Summa Theologia*. 5 vols. Translated by Fathers of the English Dominican Province. Westminster, MD: Christian Classics, 1981.
Aristotle. *Categories and De Interpretatione*. Translated by L. J. Ackrill. Clarendon Aristotle Series. New York: Oxford University Press, 1975.
Athanasius. *De Incarnatione Verbi Dei: Athanasius on the Incarnation*. Translated by Penelope Lawson. http://www.ccel.org/ccel/athanasius/incarnation.iii.html.
Augustine. *Augustine: Earlier Writings*. Translated by J. H. S. Burleigh. Library of Christian Classics. Philadelphia: Westminster, 1953.
———. *City of God*. Translated by M. Dods. New York: Modern Library, 1993.
———. *City of God and Christian Doctrine*. Translated by M. Dods. In vol. 2 of *Nicene and Post-Nicene Fathers*, ser. 1. Grand Rapids: Christian Classics Ethereal Library. http://www.ccel.org/ccel/schaff/npnf102.pdf.
———. *On Christian Doctrine*. Translated by J. Shaw. In vol. 14 of *Nicene and Post-Nicene Fathers*, ser. 1. Buffalo, NY: Christian Literature Publishing, 1887. Revised and edited for New Advent by K. Knight. http://www.newadvent.org/fathers/12020.htm.
———. *Sermon LXVII*. In vol. 6 of *Nicene and Post-Nicene Fathers*, ser. 1. Grand Rapids: Christian Classics Ethereal Library. http://www.ccel.org/ccel/schaff/npnf106.vii.lxix.html.
———. *Tractate 53 (John 12:37–43)*. Translated by J. Gibb. In vol. 7 of *Nicene and Post-Nicene Fathers*, ser. 1. Buffalo: Christian Literature. Revised and edited for New Advent by K. Knight. http://www.newadvent.org/fathers/1701053.htm.

Aulén, G. *Christus Victor: An Historical Study of the Three Main Types of the Idea of Atonement.* Translated by A. G. Herbert. Eugene, OR: Wipf & Stock, 2003.

Aune, D. E. "The Disclosure of God's Eschatological Plan (4:1—22:9)." Chapter 3 of *Revelation 17–22.* Word Biblical Commentary 52c. Nashville: Nelson Reference & Electronic, 1998.

Azkoul, M. "What Are the Differences between Orthodoxy and Roman Catholicism?" *Orthodox Christian Witness* 27.48, 28.6, 28.8 (1994). http://www.ocf.org/OrthodoxPage/reading/ortho_cath.html.

Badiu, A. *Being and Event.* Translated by O. Feltham. New York: Continuum, 2010.

Balserak, J. *Divinity Compromised: A Study of Divine Accommodation in the Thought of Calvin.* Studies in Early Religious Reforms. Dordrecht, Netherlands: Springer, 2006.

Balthasar, H. U. von. *Dare We Hope "That All Men Be Saved"? With a Short Discourse on Hell.* Translated by D. Kipp and L. Krauth. San Francisco: Ignatius, 1988.

Banks, R. *Redeeming the Routines: Bringing Theology to Life.* Grand Rapids: Baker Academic, 2001.

Barclay, W. *William Barclay: A Spiritual Autobiography.* Grand Rapids: Eerdmans, 1977.

Barna. "Americans Describe Sources of Spiritual Fulfilment and Frustration." Barna Group. November 29, 2004. https://www.barna.org/component/content/article/5-barna-update/45-barna-update-sp-657/199-americans-describe-sources-of-spiritual-fulfillment-and-frustration.

———. "A Faith Revolution Is Redefining 'Church' according to New Study." Barna Group. November 30, 1999. https://www.barna.org/component/content/article/5-barna-update/45-barna-update-sp-657/170-a-faith-revolution-is-redefining-qchurchq-according-to-new-study#.Vng2u8ArKAw.

———. "Self-Described Christians Dominate America but Wrestle with Four Aspects of Spiritual Depth." Barna Group. September 13, 2011. https://www.barna.org/barna-update/faith-spirituality/524-self-described-christians-dominate-america-but-wrestle-with-four-aspects-of-spiritual-depth#.Vng3IsArKAx.

———. "Six Megathemes Emerge from Barna Group Research in 2010." Barna Group. December 13, 2010. https://www.barna.org/barna-update/culture/462-six-megathemes-emerge-from-2010#.Vng3ZMArKAw.

Barnes, G. "Why Don't They Listen? John Stott on the Most Pernicious Obstacles to Effective World Evangelism." *Christianity Today*, September 1, 2003. http://www.christianitytoday.com/ct/2003/september/2.50.html.

Barrett, C. K. *The Gospel according to St. John: An Introduction with Commentary and Notes on the Greek Text.* 2nd ed. Philadelphia: Westminster, 1978.

Barrett, D. B., et al. *World Christian Encyclopedia: A Comparative Survey of Churches and Religions in the Modern World.* 2 vols. New York: Oxford University Press, 2001.

Bartlett, D. L. "The First Letter of Peter." In *The New International Commentary on the New Testament*, vol. 12. Grand Rapids: Eerdmans, 1998.

Barth, K. *Church Dogmatics: III. 2.: The Doctrine of Creation.* New York: T. & T. Clark International: A Continuum Imprint, 2004.

———. *The Humanity of God.* Translated by J. N. Thomas and T. Wieser. Louisville: Westminster John Knox, 1960.

Barton, R. H. *Invitation to Solitude and Silence: Experiencing God's Transforming Presence.* Downers Grove: InterVarsity, 2004.

Bauckham, R. *God Crucified: Monotheism and Christology in the New Testament*. Carlisle, UK: Paternoster, 1998.

———. *MacBears of Bearloch*. Bauckham's website. 2005. http://richardbauckham.co.uk/index.php?page=the-macbears-of-bearloch.

———. "'Only the Suffering God Can Help': Divine Passibility in Modern Theology." *Themelios* 9.3 (1984) 6–12. http://www.theologicalstudies.org.uk/article_god_bauckham.html#27.

———. *2 Peter*. Word Biblical Commentary 50. Nashville: Nelson Reference & Electronic, 1983.

———. "Universalism: A Historical Survey." *Themelios* 4.2 (1978) 47–54. http://www.theologicalstudies.org.uk/article_universalism_bauckham.html.

Beegle, D. M. "Anthropomorphism." In *Evangelical Dictionary of Theology*. Edited by W. A. Elwell. Grand Rapids: Baker, 1992.

Bell, R. H. *Love Wins: A Book about Heaven, Hell, and the Fate of Every Person Who Ever Lived*. New York: HarperOne, 2011.

Berkouwer, G. C. *Man: The Image of God*. Studies in Dogmatics. Grand Rapids: Eerdmans, 1984.

Berndt, F. "Did Martin Luther Lean towards Universal Salvation?" http://www.tentmaker.org/articles/martin_luther_universalist.html.

Black, C. C. "The First, Second, and Third Letters of John." In *The New Interpreter's Bible*, vol. 12. Nashville: Abingdon, 1998.

Blackwell, C. B. "Christosis: Pauline Soteriology in Light of Deification in Irenaeus and Cyril of Alexandria." PhD thesis, Durham University, 2010. http://etheses.dur.ac.uk/219.

Boettner, L. *The Reformed Doctrine of Predestination*. Phillipsburg, NJ: Presbyterian and Reformed, 1932.

Bonhoeffer, D. *The Cost of Discipleship*. Translated by R. H. Fuller. New York: Touchstone, 1995.

———. *Ethics*. Edited by E. Bethge. Translated by N. H. Smith. New York: Touchstone, 1995.

Borg, M. "Religious Pluralism: Seeing Religions Again with Marcus Borg." Lecture given March 2002, Wesley Foundation at UCSD. Youtube video, uploaded January 31, 2008. http://www.youtube.com/watch?NR=1&feature=endscreen&v=jHIv-c-Rpzw.

Bowman, P. "Deconstruction Is a Martial Art." In *Enduring Resistance: Cultural Theory after Derrida* [La résistance persérvère: La théorie de la culture (d')aprés Derrida], edited by S. Houppermans et al., 37–56. New York: Rodopi, 2010.

Boyd, G. "Christus Victor View." Chapter 1 of *The Nature of the Atonement: Four Views*. Edited by J. Beilby and P. R. Eddy. Downers Grove: InterVarsity, 2006.

———. "The 'Christus Victor' View of Atonement." Christus Victor Ministries, 2008. http://reknew.org/2008/01/the-christus-victor-view-of-the-atonement.

Boyd, G., and P. R. Eddy. *Across the Spectrum: Understanding Issues in Evangelical Theology*. Grand Rapids: Baker Academic, 2009.

Bozack, M. J. "Conjugate Properties and the Hypostatic Union." *Science in Christian Faith: Journal for the American Scientific Affiliation* 39 (1987) 105–7. http://www.asa3.org/ASA/PSCF/1987/PSCF6-87Bozack.html.

Bratt, J. "Wolfhart Pannenberg: Imago Dei as Gift and Destiny." Unpublished paper, Princeton Theological Seminary, 2005.

Bruce, F. F. *The Epistles to the Colossians, to Philemon, and to the Ephesians.* New International Commentary on the New Testament. Grand Rapids: Eerdmans, 1991.

———. *The Epistle to the Hebrews.* New International Commentary on the New Testament. Grand Rapids: Eerdmans, 1985.

Brunner, E. *Man in Revolt: A Christian Anthropology.* Cambridge, UK: Lutterworth, 2002.

Burridge, R. A. "Jesus and the Origins of Christian Spirituality." Introduction to *The Story of Christian Spirituality: Two Thousand Years, from East to West*, edited by G. Mursell. Minneapolis: Fortress, 2001.

Bushnell, H. "The Protestant Views of the Atonement." Chapter 32 of *Man's Need and God's Gift*, edited by M. J. Erickson. Readings in Christian Theology 2. Grand Rapids: Baker, 1992.

Cady, L. E. "Loosening the Category That Binds: Modern 'Religion' and the Promise of Cultural Studies." Chapter 2 of *Converging on Culture: Theologians in Dialogue with Cultural Analysis and Criticism*, edited by Delwin Brown et al. New York: Oxford University Press, 2001.

Cairns, E. E. *Christianity through the Centuries: A History of the Christian Church.* Grand Rapids: Academie, 1981.

Calvin, J. *Commentaries on the First Book of Moses Called Genesis.* Translated from Latin by John King. Vol. 1. Christian Classics Ethereal Library. http://www.ccel.org/ccel/calvin/calcom01.txt.

———. *Commentary on Psalms.* 5 vols. Translated by J. Anderson. Grand Rapids: Christian Classics Ethereal Library, 1999. http://www.ccel.org/ccel/calvin/calcom08.titlepage.html.

———. *Institutes of the Christian Religion.* 2 vols. Edited by J. T. Mitchell. Library of Christian Classics. Louisville: Westminster John Knox, 2006.

Campbell, C. A. *The Self and Free-Will: Philosophical Paradox and Discovery.* 2nd ed. A. J. Minton and T. Shipka. New York: McGraw-Hill, 1982.

Campbell, J. *The Masks of God.* Vol. 1, *Primitive Mythology.* New York: Penguin, 1991.

Campbell, T. "Asceticism." In *The Catholic Encyclopaedia.* Vol. 1. New York: Robert Appleton. http://www.newadvent.org/cathen/01767c.htm.

Canlis, J. *Calvin's Ladder: A Spiritual Theology of Ascent and Ascension.* Grand Rapids: Eerdmans, 2010.

The Cape Town Commitment. 2010. http://www.lausanne.org/en/documents/ctcommitment.html.

Caputo, J. D., ed. *Deconstruction in a Nutshell: A Conversation with Jacques Derrida.* Perspectives in Continental Philosophy 1. New York: Fordham University Press, 1997.

———. *What Would Jesus Deconstruct? The Good News of Postmodernism for the Church.* Grand Rapids: Baker Academic, 2007.

Carson, D. A. *The Gospel of John.* New International Commentary on the New Testament. Grand Rapids: Eerdmans, 1995.

———. *Matthew, Mark, Luke.* Expositor's Bible Commentary 8. Grand Rapids: Zondervan, 1984.

Carter. C. *Science and the Near-Death Experience: How Consciousness Survives Death.* Rochester, VA: Inner Traditions, 2010.

Catechism of the Catholic Church. 1993. http://www.vatican.va/archive/ENG0015/__P2N.HTM.
Catherine of Siena. *The Dialogue*. Classics of Western Spirituality. Mahwah, NJ: Paulist, 1980.
Chafer, L. P. *Systematic Theology*. 8 vols. Grand Rapids: Kregel, 1993.
Chan, S. *Spiritual Theology: A Systematic Study of the Christian Life*. Downers Grove: InterVarsity, 1998.
Chesterton, G. K. *The Everlasting Man*. San Francisco: Ignatius, 2008.
———. *The Incredulity of Father Brown*. Cornwall, UK: House of Stratus, 2008.
Christensen, M. J., and J. A. Wittung. *Partakers of the Divine Nature: The History and Development of Deification in the Christian Traditions*. Grand Rapids: Baker Academic, 2008.
Clark, G. H. "The Image of God in Man." *JETS* 12 (1969) 215–22. http://www.etsjets.org/JETS/12-4.
Clark, W. M. "A Legal Background to the Yahwist's Use of 'Good and Evil' and Genesis 2–3." *Journal of Biblical Literature* 88 (1969) 266–78.
Clendenin, D. B. "Partakers of Divinity: The Orthodox Doctrine of Theosis." *JETS* 37 (1994) 365–79. http://www.etsjets.org/files/JETS-PDFs/37/37-3/JETS_37-3_365-379_Clendenin.pdf.
Clines, D. J. A. "The Image of God in Man." *Tyndale Bulletin* 19 (1968) 53–103. http:/www.tyndalehouse.com/tynbul/library/TynBull_1968_19_03_Clines_ImageOfGodInMan.pdf.
Collins, C. J. *The God of Miracles: An Exegetical Examination of God's Action in the World*. Wheaton, IL: Crossway, 2000.
Cox, H. *Fire from Heaven: The Rise of Pentecostal Spirituality and the Reshaping of Religion in the Twenty-First Century*. Cambridge, MA: De Capo, 1995.
Collins, R. "The Incarnational Theory of Atonement." http://home.messiah.edu/~rcollins/AT7.HTM.
Cooper, J. "A Lutheran Response to Justification: Five Views." *Logia: A Journal of Lutheran Theology*, July 31, 2012. http://www.logia.org/logia-online/216?rq=Lutheran%20Response%20to%20Justification.
Craig, W. L. *No Other Name: A Middle Knowledge Perspective on the Exclusivity of Salvation through Christ*. Faith and Philosophy 6 (1989) 172–88.
Crisp, O. D. *Divinity and Humanity: The Incarnation Reconsidered*. Current Issues in Theology 5. New York: Cambridge University Press, 2007.
———. "On Barth's Denial of Universalism." *Theomelios* 29 (2003) 18–29. http://s3.amazonaws.com/tgc-documents/journal-issues/29.1_Crisp.pdf.
Cromhout, M. *The Dead in Christ: Recovering Paul's Understanding of the After-Life*. HTS Teologiese Studies / Theological Studies 60 (2004) 83–101. http://www.hts.org.za/index.php/HTS/article/view/520.
Cullmann, O. *Christ and Time: The Primitive Christian Conception of Time and History*. London: SCM, 1957.
D'Aquili, E. G., and A. B. Newberg. *Mystical Mind: Probing the Biology of Religious Experience*. Minneapolis: Fortress, 1999.
———. "The Neuropsychological Basis of Religions, or Why God Won't Go Away." *Zygon* 33 (1998) 187–201. http://bigfatgenius.com/3340/Aquili%20Newberg%20-%20Why%20God%20Wont%20Go%20Away.pdf.

D'Costa, G. *Christian Uniqueness Reconsidered: Myth of Pluralistic Theology of Religions.* Faith Meets Faith Series in Interreligious Dialogue 2. Maryknoll: Orbis, 1990.

De Caussade, J.-P. *The Sacrament of the Present Moment.* Translated by K. Muggeridge. New York: HarperSanFrancisco, 1982.

De Chardin, P. T. *The Divine Milieu.* New York: Harper Perennial Modern Classics, 2001.

———. *The Future of Man.* New York: Image/Doubleday, 2004.

Decock, P. "Origen of Alexandria: The Study of the Scriptures as Transformation of Readers into Images of the God of Love." *HTS Teologiese Studies / Theological Studies* 67 (2011). http://www.hts.org.za/index.php/HTS/article/viewFile/871/1527.

De Duve, C., and N. Patterson. *Genetics of Original Sin: The Impact of Natural Selection on the Future of Humanity.* New Haven: Yale University Press, 2011.

Derrida, J. "Structure, Sign, and Play in the Discourse of Human Sciences." In *A Postmodern Reader*, edited by J. P. Natoli and Hutcheon, 223–42. Albany: State University of New York Press, 1993.

———. "To Forgive: The Unforgivable and the Imprescriptible." Part 1 of *Questioning God*, edited by J. D. Caputo et al. Bloomington: Indiana University Press, 2001.

Downey, M. *The Upper Room Dictionary of Christian Spiritual Formation.* Edited by K. Beasly-Topliffe. Nashville: Upper Room, 2003.

Dunn, J. D. G. "The First and Second Letters to Timothy and the Letter to Titus." In *The New Interpreter's Bible*, vol. 11. Nashville: Abingdon, 2000.

———. *Jesus and the Spirit: A Study of the Religious and Charismatic Experience of Jesus and the First Christians as Reflected in the New Testament.* Grand Rapids: Eerdmans, 1997.

———. "The Justice of God: A Renewed Perspective on Justification by Faith." Henton Davies Lecture, Regent's Park College, Oxford, 1991. *JTS* 43 (1992) 1–22.

Dyrness, W. A., and V.-M. Kärkkäinen, eds. *Global Dictionary of Theology: A Resource for the Worldwide Church.* Downers Grove: InterVarsity, 2008.

Earp, B. D. "Do I Have More Free Will Than You Do? An Unexpected Asymmetry in Intuitions about Personal Freedom." *New School Psychology Bulletin* 9 (2011) 21–27. http://www.academia.edu/1288624/Do_I_have_more_free_will_than_you_do_An_unexpected_asymmetry_in_intuitions_about_personal_freedom.

Edwards, D. L., and J. R. W. Stott. *Evangelical Essentials: A Liberal-Evangelical Dialogue.* Downers Grove: InterVarsity, 1988.

Eichrodt, W. *Theology of the Old Testament.* Vol 2. Translated by J. A. Baker. Old Testament Library. Philadelphia: Westminster, 1967.

Einstein, A. *The Expanded Quotable Einstein.* 2nd ed. Edited by A. Calaprice. Princeton: Princeton University Press, 2000.

Eller, D. B. "Universalism." In *New 20th-Century Encyclopedia of Religious Knowledge*, edited by J. D. Douglas. 2nd ed. Grand Rapids: Baker, 1991.

Endean, P. "Spirituality and Theology." In *The New Westminster Dictionary of Christian Spirituality*, edited by P. Sheldrake. Louisville: Westminster John Knox, 2005.

Erickson. M. J. *Christian Theology.* 3rd ed. Grand Rapids: Baker, 2013.

Fairweather, E. R., ed., trans. *A Scholastic Miscellany: Anselm to Ockham.* Library of Christian Classics, Ichthus ed. Philadelphia: Westminster, 1956.

Farley, A. *The Naked Gospel: The Truth You May Never Hear in Church.* Grand Rapids: Zondervan, 2009.

Fee, G. D. *God's Empowering Presence: The Holy Spirit in the Letters of Paul.* Peabody: Hendrickson, 1994.

———. *Pauline Christology: An Exegetical-Theological Study.* Peabody: Hendrickson, 2007.

Feinberg, C. L. "The Image of God." *Bibliotheca Sacra* 12 (1972) 235–46. https://faculty.gordon.edu/hu/bi/ted_hildebrandt/otesources/01-genesis/text/articles-books/feinberg-image-bs.pdf.

Finlan, S., and V. Kharlamov, eds. *Theosis.* Vol. 2, *Deification in Christian Theology.* Princeton Theological Monographs 156. Eugene, OR: Pickwick, 2006.

Finney, C. G. "Accounting for Moral Depravity." Chapter 15 of *Man's Need and God's Gift*, edited by M. J. Erickson. Readings in Christian Theology 2. Grand Rapids: Baker, 1976.

Foster, R. J. *Celebration of Discipline: The Path to Spiritual Growth.* Rev. ed. New York: HaperCollins, 1988.

———. *Prayer: Finding the Heart's True Home.* San Francisco: HaperCollins, 1992.

———. *Streams of Living Water: Celebrating the Great Traditions of Christian Faith.* San Francisco: HaperCollins, 1998.

Foster, R. J., and E. Griffin. *Spiritual Classics: Selected Readings for Individuals and Groups on the Twelve Spiritual Disciplines.* San Francisco: HaperCollins, 2000.

Fukuyama, F. *The End of History and the Last Man.* New York: Free Press, 1992.

Gadamer, H.-G. *A Century of Philosophy: A Conversation with Riccardo Dottori.* New York: Continuum International, 2006.

———. *Philosophical Hermeneutics.* 30th anniversary ed. Berkley: University of California Press, 1976.

———. *Truth and Method.* New York: Continuum International, 2006.

Galli, M. "Heaven, Hell, and Rob Bell: Putting the Pastor in Context." *Christianity Today*, March 2, 2011. http://www.christianitytoday.com/ct/2011/marchwebonly/rob-bell-universalism.html?paging=off.

Gamble, Richard C. "Calvin as Theologian and Exegete: Is There Anything New?" *Calvin Theological Journal* 23 (1988) 178–94.

Geivett, R. D., and W. G. Phillips. "Response to John Hick." In chapter 1 of Okholm and Phillips, *Four Views on Salvation in a Pluralistic World.*

Geivett, R. D., and C. Pinnock. "The Beautiful Campus of the Southern Baptist Theological Seminary." *SBJT* 2 (1998) 26–38. http://www.sbts.edu/media/publications/sbjt/sbjt_1998summer3.pdf.

Gerrish, B. A. "'To the Unknown God': Luther and Calvin on the Hiddenness of God." *Journal of Religion* 53 (1973) 263–92. http://www.jstor.org/stable/1202133.

Goldstein, V. S. "The Human Situation: A Feminine View." *Journal of Religion* 40 (1960) 100–112. http://www.jstor.org/stable/1200194.

Gomes, A. W. "Evangelicals and the Annihilation of Hell, Part One." *Christian Research Institute Journal*, Spring 1991, 1–14. http://www.iclnet.org/pub/resources/text/cri/cri-jrnl/web/crj0085a.html.

Gomes, P. J. *The Scandalous Gospel of Jesus: What's So Good about the Good News?* New York: HarperCollins, 2007.

Gorsuch, R. L. *Integrating Psychology and Spirituality?* Pasadena: Fuller Seminary Press, 2007.

Gottstein, A. G. "The Body as Image of God in Rabbinic Literature." *Harvard Theological Review* 87 (1994) 171–95.

Govett, R. *Calvinism by Calvin: Being the Substance of Discourses Delivered by Calvin and the Other Ministers of Geneva on the Doctrines of Grace.* Miami Springs, FL: Conley & Schoettle, 1984.

Greathouse, W. M. "Sanctification and the Christus Victor Motif in Wesleyan Theology." *Wesleyan Theological Journal* 38 (2003) 217–29. http://wesley.nnu.edu/fileadmin/imported_site/wesleyjournal/2003-wtj-38-2.pdf.

Green, J. B. "Kaleidoscopic View." Chapter 4 of *The Nature of the Atonement: Four Views*, edited by J. Beilby and P. R. Eddy. Downers Grove: IVP Academic, 2006.

Greggs, T. *Barth, Origen, and Universal Salvation.* New York: Oxford University Press, 2009.

Gregory of Nyssa. "On the Soul and the Resurrection." Translated by H. Leclercq. *The Catholic Encyclopedia.* NY, New York: Robert Appleton. New Advent. http://www.newadvent.org/cathen/07016a.htm.

———. *The Lord's Prayer, the Beatitudes.* Ancient Christian Writers: The Works of the Fathers in Translation 18. Mahwah, NJ: Paulist, 1954.

Grenz, S. "Jesus as the Imago Dei: Image-of-God Christology and the Non-Linear Linearity of Theology." *JETS* 47 (2004) 617–28.

———. *Social God and the Relational Self: A Trinitarian Theology of the Imago Dei.* Louisville: Westminster John Knox, 2001.

Greyson, B. "Implications of Near-Death Experiences for a Postmaterialist Psychology of Religion and Spirituality." *Psychology of Religion and Spirituality* 2 (2010) 37–45. http://www.medicine.virginia.edu/clinical/departments/psychiatry/sections/cspp/dops/greyson-publications/postmaterialist-PRS.pdf.

Griffen, D. R. *God, Power and Evil: A Process Theodicy.* Louisville: Westminster John Knox, 2004.

Gross, J. *The Divinization of the Christian according to the Greek Fathers.* Anaheim: A & C, 2002.

Grudem, W. *Systematic Theology: An Introduction to Biblical Doctrine.* Grand Rapids: Zondervan, 1994.

Guyon, Madame [Jeanne-Marie Bouvier de la Motte-Guyon]. *Experiencing the Depths of Jesus Christ.* Sargent, GA: Christian, 1975.

Habermas, G. R., and J. P. Moreland. *Immortality: The Other Side of Death.* Nashville: Nelson, 1992.

Hackett, S. E. *The Reconstruction of the Christian Revelation Claim: A Philosophical and Critical Apologetic.* Grand Rapids: Baker, 1984.

Hagner, D. A. *Matthew 1–13.* Word Biblical Commentary 33. Nashville: Nelson Reference & Electronic, 1993.

Harris, R. L., et al. *Theological Wordbook of the Old Testament.* 2 vols. Chicago: Moody Bible Institute, 1980.

Harrod, J. B. "Two Million Years Ago: The Origin of Art and Symbol." *Continuum* 2 (1992) 4–29. http://www.originsnet.org/old.pdf.

Harrison, N. V. *God's Many-Splendored Image: Theological Anthropology for Christian Formation.* Grand Rapids: Baker Academic, 2010.

Haub, C. "How Many People Have Ever Lived on Earth?" *Population Reference Bureau.* October 2011. http://www.prb.org/Articles/2002/HowManyPeopleHaveEverLivedonEarth.aspx.

Hefner, P. "Imago Dei: The Possibility and Necessity of the Human Person." Chapter 5 of *The Human Person in Science and Theology*, edited by N. H. Gregersen et al. Issues in Science and Theology. Edinburgh: T. & T. Clark, 2000.
Herzfeld, N. "Imago Dei." In *The New Westminster Dictionary of Christian Spirituality*, edited by P. Sheldrake. Louisville: Westminster John Knox, 2005.
Heschel, A. J. "The Holy Dimension." *Journal of Religion* 23 (1943) 117–24.
Hick, J. H. "D Z Phillips on God and Evil." John Hick: The Official Website. 2009. http://www.johnhick.org.uk/jsite/index.php/articles-by-john-hick/17-d-z-phillips-on-god-and-evil.
―――. *Death and Eternal Life*. Louisville: Westminster John Knox, 1976.
―――. *Dialogues in the Philosophy of Religion*. New York: Palgrave Macmillan, 2001.
―――. *God and the Universe of Faiths*. 2nd ed. Chatham, NY: Oneworld, 1994.
―――. *God Has Many Names*. Philadelphia: Westminster, 1982.
―――. *An Interpretation of Religion*. New Haven: Yale University Press.
―――. "A Pluralist View." Chapter 1 of Okholm and Phillips, *Four Views on Salvation in a Pluralistic World*.
―――. "Reincarnation and the Meaning of Life." Talk given to the Open End, Birmingham, December 2002. John Hick: The Official Website. http://www.johnhick.org.uk/article7.html.
―――. "Response to Alister E. McGrath." In Okholm and Phillips, *Four Views on Salvation in a Pluralistic World*, 181–86.
―――. "The Soul-Building Argument." Chapter 2 of *Philosophy: Paradox and Discovery*, edited by T. Shipka and A. Minton. 5th ed. New York: McGraw-Hill, 2003.
―――. "Who or What Is God?" John Hick: The Official Website. 2001. http://www.johnhick.org.uk/article1.html.
―――. *Evil and the God of Love*. New York: Palgrave Macmillian, 2010.
Hick, J. H., and P. F. Knitter, eds., *The Myth of Christian Uniqueness: Toward a Pluralistic Theology of Religions*. Eugene, OR: Wipf & Stock, 2005.
Hill, C. C. *In God's Time: The Bible and the Future*. Grand Rapids: Eerdmans, 2002.
Hodge, C. *The Bible and the Future*. Grand Rapids: Eerdmans, 1994.
―――. *Systematic Theology*. Vol. 1. New York: Scribner, Armstrong, 1873.
Hoekema, A. A. *Created in God's Image*. Grand Rapids: Eerdmans, 1986.
Hoeksema, H. C. A. "Scriptural Presentation of God's Hatred." *Protestant Reformed Theological Journal* 1 (1967) 7–33.
Hooker, M. D. "The Letter to the Philippians." In *The New Interpreter's Bible*, vol. 11. Nashville: Abingdon, 2000.
Houston, J. *The Heart's Desire: A Guide to Personal Fulfilment*. Oxford: Lion, 1992.
Hryniewicz, W. *The Challenge of Our Hope: Christian Faith in Dialogue*. Polish Philosophical Studies 7. Washington, DC: Council for Research in Values and Philosophy, 2007.
Irenaeus. *Against Heresies*. Christian Classics Ethereal Library. http://www.columbia.edu/cu/augustine/arch/irenaeus.
Jankélévitch, V. *Forgiveness*. Translated by A. Kelly. Chicago: University of Chicago Press, 2005.
Jenson, R. W. "The Praying Animal." *Zygon* 18 (1983) 311–25.
―――. *Systematic Theology*. Vol. 2, *The Works of God*. New York: Oxford University Press, 1999.

John of the Cross. *Dark Night of the Soul*. Translated and edited by E. A. Peers. New York: Image/Doubleday, 2005.
Jukes, A. *The Second Death and the Restitution of All Things: With Some Preliminary Remarks on the Nature and Inspiration of Holy Scripture*. London: Longmans, Green, 1881.
Kant, I. *Lectures on Philosophical Theology*. Ithaca: Cornell University Press, 1986.
Kärkkäinen, V.-M. "The Human Prototype." *Christianity Today*, January 2012, 28–31.
———. *One with God: Salvation as Deification and Justification*. Collegeville: Liturgical, 2004.
———. *Pneumatology: The Holy Spirit in Ecumenical International, and Contextual Perspective*. Grand Rapids: Baker Academic, 2002.
Keil, C. F., and F. Delitzsch. *Commentary on the Old Testament*. Vol. 1, *The Pentateuch*. Peabody: Hendrickson, 2006.
Kierkegaard, S. A. *Parables of Kierkegaard*. Princeton: Princeton University Press, 1989.
Kilner, J. F. "Humanity in God's Image: Is the Image Really Damaged?" *Journal of Evangelical Theology Society* 53 (2010) 601–17.
King, M. J. *Proceedings of the Third Ecumenical Methodist Conference Held in City Road*. Edited by H. Crawford et al. Whitefish, MT: Kessinger, 1901.
King, M. L. "Loving Your Enemies." Chapter 5 of *Invitation to Christian Spirituality: An Ecumenical Anthology*, edited by J. R. Tyson. New York: Oxford University Press, 1999.
Kinnaman, D., and G. Lyons. *Unchristian: What a New Generation Really Thinks about Christianity . . . And Why It Matters*. Grand Rapids: Baker, 2007.
Küng, H. *The Beginning of All Things: Science and Religion*. Grand Rapids: Eerdmans, 2008.
———. *On Being a Christian*. New York: Image, 1984.
Ladd, G. E. *The Presence of the Future: The Eschatology of Biblical Realism*. Grand Rapids: Eerdmans, 1974.
Laing, J. D. "Middle Knowledge." *Internet Encyclopedia of Philosophy: A Peer Reviewed Academic Resource*. http://www.iep.utm.edu/middlekn.
Lam, J. "The Biblical Creation in Its Ancient Near Eastern Context." *BioLogos*, April 21, 2010. http://biologos.org/uploads/projects/lam_scholarly_essay.pdf.
Leroi-Gourhan, A., and A. Michelson. "The Religion of the Caves: Magic or Metaphysics?" *October* (MIT Press Journals) 37 (1986) 6–17.
Leibniz, G. W. *Theodicy: Essays on the Goodness of God, the Freedom of Man, and the Origin of Evil*. La Salle, IL: Open Court, 1998.
Levinas, E. *Otherwise than Being*. Translated by A. Lingis. Martinus Nijhoff Philosophy Texts 3. Dordrecht, Netherlands: Kluwer Academic, 1991.
Lewis, C. S. *God in the Dock: Essays on Theology and Ethics*. Edited by W. Hooper. Grand Rapids: Eerdmans, 1970.
———. *The Great Divorce*. New York: Macmillan, 1946.
———. *Mere Christianity*. New York: Touchstone, 1996.
———. *The Problem of Pain*. New York: HarperCollins, 1966.
———. *The Screwtape Letters*. San Francisco: HarperCollins, 2001.
Lioy, D. *Evolutionary Creation in Biblical and Theological Perspective*. Studies in Biblical Literature 148. New York: Lang, 2011.
———. *Jesus as Torah in John 1–12*. Eugene, OR: Wipf and Stock, 2007.

———. "Two Contrasting Views on the Historical Authenticity of the Adam Character in the Genesis Creation Narratives." Review article. *Conspectus* (South African Theological Seminary) 14 (2012). http://www.sats.edu.za/userfiles/Dan%20Lioy.pdf.

Lohse, B. *Martin Luther's Theology: Its Historical and Systematic Development*. Translated and edited by R. A. Harrisville. Minneapolis: Fortress, 1999.

Longenecker, R. N. "Acts." In *The Expositor's Bible Commentary with the New International Version*, vol. 9. Grand Rapids: Zondeervan, 1981.

———. *Galations*. Word Biblical Commentary 41. Nashville: Nelson Reference & Electronic, 1990.

Lossky, V. *In the Image and Likeness of God*. Crestwood, NY: St. Vladimir's Seminary Press, 1974.

———. *The Mystical Theology of the Eastern Church*. Crestwood, NY: St. Vladimir's Seminary Press, 1976.

———. *Orthodox Theology: An Introduction*. Translated by I. Kesarcodi-Watson. Crestwood, NY: St Vladimir's Seminary Press, 1978.

Louth, A. *The Origins of the Christian Mystical Tradition: From Plato to Denys*. 2nd ed. Oxford: Oxford University Press, 2007.

Lovelace, R. C. "Puritan Spirituality: The Search for a Rightly Reformed Church." Chapter 10 of *Christian Spirituality: Post-Reformation and Modern*, edited by L. Dupre and D. E. Saliers. World Spirituality 18. New York: Crossroad, 1989.

Ludlow, M. "Universalism in the History of Christianity." Chapter 5 of Parry and Partridge, *Universal Salvation? The Current Debate*.

Ludwig, K. "Why the Difference between Quantum and Classical Physics Is Irrelevant to the Mind/Body Problem." *Psyche* 2 (1995). http://www.theassc.org/files/assc/2350.pdf.

Luther, M. *Bondage of the Will*. Originally published 1525. Translated by H. Cole 1823. http://ebookbrowse.com/gdoc.php?id=322690222&url=42cb76a465ac0735285eebe5f2e75624.

———. *Heidelberg Disputation*. 1518. The Book of Concord: The Confessions of the Lutheran Church. http://bookofconcord.org/95theses.php.

Mahoney, A., and K. I. Pargament. "Sacred Changes: Spiritual Conversion and Transformation." *Journal of Clinical Psychology* 60 (2004) 481–92.

MacDonald, G. *Creation in Christ: Unspoken Sermons*. Vancouver, BC: Regent College Publishing, 2004.

———. *Unspoken Sermons, Third Series*. London: Longmans, Green, 1889.

Mackintosh, H. R. *Immortality and the Future: The Christian Doctrine of Eternal Life*. New York: Hodder & Stoughton, 1915.

Mann, C. C. "Every Now and Then the Dawn of Civilization Is Reenacted on a Remote Hilltop in Southern Turkey." *National Geographic*, June 2011, 34–59.

Mantzaridis, G. I. *The Deification of Man: Saint Gregory Palamas and the Orthodox Tradition*. Translated by L. Sherrard. Crestwood, NY: St. Vladimir's Seminary Press, 1984.

Marshall, C. D. *Beyond Retribution: A New Testament Vision for Justice, Crime, and Punishment*. Grand Rapids: Eerdmans, 2001.

Masi, R. "The Credo of Paul VI: Theology of Original Sin and the Scientific Theory of Evolution." *L'Osservatore Romano*, weekly edition in English, April 17, 1969. http://www.ewtn.com/library/Theology/SINEVOL.HTM.

Maximovitch, J. "Life after Death: A Description of the First 40 Days after Death." Website of St. Nicholas Russian Orthodox Church (McKinney, TX). http://www.orthodox.net/articles/life-after-death-john-maximovitch.html#n4.

McGinn, B., ed. *The Essential Writings of Christian Mysticism*. New York: Modern Library, 2006.

———. *The Flowering of Mysticism: Men and Women in the New Mysticism—1200–1350*. Presence of God: A History of Western Christian Mysticism 3. New York: Crossroad, 1998.

———. *The Foundations of Mysticism: Origins of the Fifth Century*. Presence of God: A History of Western Christian Mysticism 1. New York: Crossroad, 2005.

———. *The Growth of Mysticism: From Gregory the Great to the Twelfth Century*. Presence of God: A History of Western Christian Mysticism 2. London: SCM, 1994.

McGinn, B., and J. Meyendorff, eds. *Christian Spirituality: Origins to the Twelfth Century*. World Spirituality 16. New York: Crossroad, 1985.

McGrath, A. E. *The Intellectual Origins of the European Reformation*. Malden, MA: Blackwell, 2004.

———. *Luther's Theology of the Cross*. Cambridge, MA: Blackwell, 1993.

———. "A Particularist View: A Post-Enlightenment Approach." Chapter 3 of Okholm and Phillips, *Four Views on Salvation in a Pluralistic World*.

McGuckin, J. A. "The Eastern Christian Tradition, 4th to 18th Centuries." Chapter 4 of *The Story of Christian Spirituality: Two Thousand Years, from East to West*, edited by G. Mursel. Minneapolis: Fortress, 2001.

McKnight, S. "Five Streams of the Emerging Church." *Christianity Today*, January 19, 2007, 1–6. http://www.christianitytoday.com/ct/2007/february/11.35.html?order=&start=1.

Mesle, R. C. "The Problem of Genuine Evil: A Critiques of John Hick's Theodicy." *Journal of Religion* 66 (1986) 412–30.

Metaxas, E. *Bonheoffer: Pastor, Martyr, Prophet, Spy*. Nashville: Nelson, 2010.

Meyendorff, J. *Byzantine Theology: Historical Trends and Doctrinal Themes*. New York: Fordham University Press, 1979.

———. "Liturgy and Spirituality." Chapter 14 of McGinn and Meyendorff, *Christian Spirituality: Origins to the Twelfth Century*.

Middleton, J. R. *The Liberating Image: The Imago Dei in Genesis 1*. Grand Rapids: Brazos, 2005.

Milbank, J. *Theology and Social Theory: Beyond Secular Reason*. Malden, MA: Blackwell, 2006.

———. *The Word Made Strange: Theology, Language, Culture*. Malden, MA: Blackwell, 1998.

Milligan, W. *Elijah: His Life and Times*. New York, 1880s.

Moltmann, J. *God in Creation: A New Theology of Creation and the Spirit of God*. Gifford Lectures, 1984–1985. Minneapolis: Fortress, 1993.

———. *The Trinity and the Kingdom: The Doctrine of God*. Minneapolis: Fortress, 1993.

Mommaers, P. *Riddle of Christian Mystical Experience: The Role of the Humanity of Jesus*. Louvain Theological & Pastoral Monographs 29. Louvain: Peeters, 2003.

Mondzain, M.-J. "Can Images Kill?" Translated by S. Shafto. *Critical Inquiry* 36 (2009) 20–51.

Moore, E. "Origen of Alexandria (185–254 CE)." *Internet Encyclopedia of Philosophy: A Peer Reviewed Academic Resource.* http://www.iep.utm.edu/origen-of-alexandria/#SH5a.

Moreland, J. P. *Kingdom Triangle: Recover the Christian Mind, Renovate the Soul, Restore the Spirit's Power.* Grand Rapids: Zondervan, 2007.

Mosser, C. "The Greatest Possible Blessing: Calvin and Deification." *SJT* 55 (2002) 36–57. http://www.academia.edu/185246/_The_Greatest_Possible_Blessing_Calvin_and_Deification.

Mounce, W. D. *Pastoral Epistles.* Word Biblical Commentary 46. Nashville: Nelson, 2000.

Mouw, R. J. "More Thoughts about 'Generous Orthodoxy.'" Mouw's Musings, Fuller Theological Seminary. March 29, 2011. http://cms.fuller.edu/rjmouw/root/Home/Blogs/03-_More_Thoughts_about_%E2%80%9CGenerous_Orthodoxy%E2%80%9D.

Murray, A. *The Inner Life.* Springdale, PA: Whitaker House, 1984.

———. *The Spirit of Christ.* Minneapolis: Bethany Fellowship, 1979.

Mursell, G., ed. *The Story of Christian Spirituality: Two Thousand Years, from East to West.* Minneapolis: Fortress, 2001.

Myers, D. B. "Exclusivism, Eternal Damnation, and the Problem of Evil: A Critique of Craig's Molinist Soteriological Theodicy." *Religious Studies* 39 (2003) 407–19.

Nancy, J.-L. *Dis-Enclosure: The Deconstruction of Christianity.* Translated by B. Bergo et al. Perspectives in Continental Philosophy. New York: Fordam University Press, 2008.

Nash, R. H. "Is Belief in Jesus Necessary? The Answer to Religious Inclusivism." Part 2 of 3. *Christian Research Journal* 27 (2004). http://www.equip.org/PDF/JAJ772.pdf.

National Academy of Sciences. *Teaching about Evolution and the Nature of Science.* Washington, DC: National Academies, 1998.

Neuhaus, R. J. *Death on a Friday Afternoon: Meditations on the Last Words of Jesus from the Cross.* New York: Basic, 2001.

———. "Will All Be Saved?" *First Things*, August 2001. http://www.firstthings.com/article/2009/02/will-all-be-saved-30.

Newberg, A. B. *Principles of Neurotheology*, London: Ashgate, 2010.

Newberg, A. B., and E. D'Aquili. "Wired for the Ultimate Reality: The Neuropsychology of Religious Experience." *Science & Spirit Magazine,* 1999. http://www.pbs.org/wgbh/questionofgod/voices/newberg.html.

Newsom, C. A. "The Book of Job as Polyphonic Text." In *The Book of Job: A Contest of Moral Imaginations.* Oxford: Oxford University Press, 2003. http://home.nwciowa.edu/wacome/newsom.html.

Niebuhr, R. *The Nature and Destiny of Man: A Christian Interpretation.* 2 vols. Louisville: Westminster John Knox, 1996.

Nicholas of Cusa. *On the Peace of Earth: De Pace Fidei* (1453). Translated by H. L. Bond. http://www.appstate.edu/~bondhl/bondpeac.htm.

Nietzsche, F. *Twilight of Idols and The Anti-Christ; or, How to Philosophize with a Hammer.* Translated by W. Kaufmaan and R. J. Hollingdale. London: Penguin, 2003.

Oakley, F. "The Absolute and Ordained Power of God in Sixteenth and Seventeenth-Century Theology." *Journal of the History of Ideas* 59 (1998) 437–61.

Okholm, D. L., and C. H. Pinnock, eds. *Four Views on Salvation in a Pluralistic World*. Grand Rapids: Zondervan, 1996.

O'Malley, J. S. "Methodists." In *New 20th-Century Encyclopedia of Religious Knowledge*, edited by J. D. Douglas. 2nd ed. Grand Rapids: Baker, 1991.

Origen. *De Principiis I and II* (1885). Translated by Frederick Crombie. Ante-Nicene Fathers 4. Buffalo, NY: Christian Literature. http://www.newadvent.org/fathers/0412.htm.

Ouspensky, L. "Icon and Art." Chapter 15 of McGinn and Meyendorff, *Christian Spirituality: Origins to the Twelfth Century*.

Packer, J. I. "Hell's Final Enigma." *Christianity Today*, April 2002. http://www.christianitytoday.com/ct/2002/april22/27.84.html.

———. "Justification." In *Evangelical Dictionary of Theology*, edited by W. Elwell. Grand Rapids: Baker, 1992.

Palmer, R. E. "Postmodern Hermeneutics and the Act of Reading." *Notre Dame English Journal* 15 (1983) 55–84.

Pannenberg, W. *Systematic Theology*. Vols. 1–3. Grand Rapids: Eerdmans, 1994–2009.

———. *What Is Man? Contemporary Anthropology in Theological Perspective*. Minneapolis: Fortress, 1970.

Pargament, K. I. "The Meaning of Spiritual Transformation." In *Spiritual Transformation and Healing: Anthropological, Theological*, edited by J. Koss-Chioino and P. J. Hefner, 10–24. Lanham, MD: AltaMira, 2006.

———. *Spiritually Integrated Psychotherapy: Understanding and Addressing the Sacred*. New York: Guilford, 2007.

Parry, R. A., and C. H. Partridge, eds. *Universal Salvation? The Current Debate*. Grand Rapids: Eerdmans, 2003.

Pascal, B. *Pascal Selections*. Edited by R. H. Popkin. New York: Macmillan, 1989.

Peacocke, A. R. *Evolution: The Disguised Friend of Faith?* West Conshohocken, PA: Templeton, 2004.

———. *Theology for a Scientific Age: Being and Becoming—Natural, Divine, and Human*. Minneapolis: Fortress, 1993.

Peters, T. *Sin: Radical Evil in Soul and Society*. Grand Rapids: Eerdmans, 1994.

Peterson, E. H. *The Jesus Way: A Conversation on the Ways that Jesus Is the Way*. Grand Rapids: Eerdmans, 2007.

———. *A Long Obedience in the Same Direction: Discipleship in an Instant Society*. Downers Grove: InterVarsity, 2000.

Pinnock, C. H. "The Destruction of the Finally Impenitent." McMaster Divinity College Hamilton, Ontario, Canada. 1990. http://www.onthewing.org/user/Esc_Annihilationism%20-%20Pinnock.pdf.

———. "An Inclusivist View." Chapter 2 of Okholm and Phillips, *Four Views on Salvation in a Pluralistic World*.

———. "Response to John Hick." In Okholm and Phillips, *Four Views on Salvation in a Pluralistic World*, 60–64.

———. *A Wideness in God's Mercy: The Finality of Jesus Christ in a World of Religions*. Theology and the Sciences. Grand Rapids: Zondervan, 1992.

Plantinga, A. C. "Is Belief in God Properly Basic?" *Noûs* 15 (1981) 41–51.

———. *God, Freedom, and Evil*. Grand Rapids: Eerdmans, 1974.

———. "Can a Person Be a Soul?" Interview. http://www.closertotruth.com/series/can-person-be-soul#video-2840.

Plested, M. *Orthodox Readings of Aquinas. Changing Paradigms in a Historical and Systematic Theology.* Oxford: Oxford University Press, 2012.

Plumptre, E. H. *The Spirits in Prison and Other Studies on the Life after Death.* London: Isbister, 1884. http://books.google.com/ebooks/reader?id=LcUrAAAAYAAJ&printsec=frontcover&output=reader&pg=GBS.PR3.

Power, W. L. "Imago Dei: Imitatio Dei." *International Journal for Philosophy of Religion* 442 (1997) 131–41.

Pseudo-Dionysius. *Dionysius the Areopagite: On the Divine Names and the Mystical Theology.* Translayed by C. C. Rolt. London: Christian Classics Ethereal Library, 2010.

Punt, N. *A Theology of Inclusivism.* Allendale, MI: Northland, 2008.

Rad, G. von. *Genesis: A Commentary.* Translated by J. H. Marks. Old Testament Library. Philadelpia: Westminister, 1973.

———. *Old Testament Theology.* Vol. 1, *The Theology of Israel's Historical Traditions.* Translated by D. M. G. Stalker. Old Testament Library. Louisville: Westminster John Knox, 2001.

Raitt, J., ed. *Christian Spirituality: High Middle Ages and Reformation.* In collaboration with B. Mcginn and J. Meyendorff. World Spirituality 17. New York: Crossroad, 1988.

Ranft, P. *How the Doctrine of the Incarnation Shaped Western Culture.* Plymouth, UK: Lexington, 2013.

Rathbone, R. *Post-Rapture Radio.* San Francisco: Jossey-Bass, 2005.

Rauser, R. *Finding God in The Shack.* Colorado Springs: Paternoster, 2009.

Reid, W. S. "Calvinism." In *Evangelical Dictionary of Theology*, edited by W. A. Elwell. Grand Rapids: Baker, 1992.

Richardson, A., and J. Bowden, eds. *The Westminster Dictionary of Christian Theology.* Philadelphia: Westminster John Knox, 1983.

Richardson, H. N. "God's Search for Man in Biblical Thought." *Journal of Bible and Religion* 23 (1955) 9–16.

Ridderbos, H. N. *Coming of the Kingdom.* Phillipsburg, NJ: P & R, 1962.

Rollins, P. *How Not to Speak to God.* Brewster, MA: Paraclete, 2009.

Russell, N. *The Doctrine of Deification in the Greek Patristic Tradition.* Oxford: Oxford University Press, 2006.

Ruusbroed, J. *The Spiritual Espousals: Christ Guides Us to Seeing.* Spiritual Classics: Selected Readings for Groups on the Twelve Spiritual Disciplines. New York: HarperCollins, 2000.

Sanders, J. E. *The God Who Risks: A Theology of Divine Providence.* 2nd ed. Downers Grove: InterVarsity, 2007.

Sapolsky, R. "The Uniqueness of Humans." 2009 Class Day Lecture, Stanford University. June 13, 2009. Video. http://news.stanford.edu/news/2009/june17/videos/557.html.

Saucy, R. L. *The Case for Progressive Dispensationalism.* Grand Rapids: Zondervan, 1993.

Seim, T. K., and J. Økland, eds. *Metamorphoses Resurrection, Body and Transformative Practices in Early Christianity.* Berlin: de Gruyter, 2009.

Schaff, P. *History of the Christian Church.* Vol. 1, *Apostolic Christianity A.D. 1–100.* Grand Rapids: Eedmans, 1978.

Schleiermacher, F. D. E. *The Christian Faith.* New York: T. & T. Clark, 1999.

Schleifer, R. *Intangible Materialism: The Body, Scientific Knowledge, and the Power of Language*. Minneapolis: University of Minnesota Press, 2009.

Schneiders, S. M. "Christian Spirituality: Definitions, Methods and Types." In *The New Westminster Dictionary of Christian Spirituality*, edited by P. Sheldrake. Louisville: Westminster John Knox, 2005.

———. "Religious Life: The Dialectic between Marginality and Transformation." *Spirituality Today* 40 (winter 1988 supplement) 59–79. Conference Proceedings from For the Trumpet Shall Sound: Protest, Prayer, and Prophecy, Aquinas Center of Theology, Emory University, Atlanta, October 26–30, 1988. http://www.spiritualitytoday.org/spir2day/884056schneiders.html.

Schwartz, S. B. *All Can Be Saved: Religious Tolerance and Salvation in the Iberian Atlantic World*. New Haven: Yale University Press, 2008.

Shahan, T. "Second Council of Constantinople." In *The Catholic Encyclopedia*. New York: Appleton. http://www.newadvent.org/cathen/04308b.htm.

Sherrard, P. "The Revival of Heysychast Spirituality." Chapter 13 of *Christian Spirituality: Post-Reformation and Modern*, edited by L. Dupre and D. E. Saliers. World Spirituality 18. New York: Crossroad, 1989.

Shults, F. L. *Reforming Theological Anthropology: After the Philosophical Turn to Relationality*. Grand Rapids: Eerdmans, 2003.

Simoni, H. "Divine Passibility and the Problem of Radical Particularity: Does God Feel Your Pain?" *Religious Studies* 33 (1997) 327–47.

Smith, T. H. "The Spirituality of Afro-American Traditions." Chapter 12 of *Christian Spirituality: Post-Reformation and Modern*, edited by L. Dupre and D. E. Saliers. World Spirituality 18. New York: Crossroad, 1989.

Spencer, J. "The Destruction of Hell: Annihilationism Examined." *Christian Apologetics* (Southern Evangelical Seminary) 1 (1998). http://www.gospelanswers1.com/HellandAnnihilationismSP.pdf.

Spurgeon, C. H. "The Hope of Future Bliss" (1855). Sermon. http://www.spurgeon.org/sermons/0025.htm.

Stapp, H. P. "Why Classical Mechanics Cannot Naturally Accommodate Consciousness but Quantum Mechanics Can." *Psyche* 2 (1995). http://www.theassc.org/files/assc/2345.pdf.

Stavropoulos, A. C. *Partakers of the Divine Nature*. Translated by S. Harakas. Minneapolis: Light & Life, 1976.

Steeves, P. D. "The Othodox Tradition." In *Evangelical Dictionary of Theology*, edited by W. A. Elwell. Grand Rapids: Baker, 1992.

Steinberg, J. R. "Leibniz, Creation and the Best of All Possible Worlds." *International Journal for Philosophy of Religion* 62 (2007) 123–33.

Strong, J. *Strong's Exhaustive Concordance*. Nashville: Crusade Bible, 1978.

Stronstad, R. *The Charismatic Theology of St. Luke*. Peabody: Hendrickson, 1984.

Talbott, T. "Christ Victorious." Chapter 2 of Parry and Partridge, *Universal Salvation?*

———. "The Essential Role of Free Will in Universal Reconciliation." Evangelical Universalist.com. Posted February 3, 2009. http://www.evangelicaluniversalist.com/forum/viewtopic.php?f=50&t=205.

———. *The Inescapable Love of God*. Boca Raton, FL: Universal, 1999.

———. "A Pauline Interpretation of Divine Judgment." Chapter 3 of Parry and Partridge, *Universal Salvation? The Current Debate*.

———. "Towards a Better Understanding of Universalism." Chapter 1 of Parry and Partridge, *Universal Salvation? The Current Debate*.

———. "Universalism and the Supposed Oddity of Our Earthly Life: Reply to Michael Murray." *Faith and Philosophy* 18 (2001) 102–9. http://www.willamette.edu/~ttalbott/murray4.pdf.

Tennant, F. R. "Evolutionary Theory of the Empirical Origin of Sin." Chapter 9 of *Man's Need and God's Gift*, edited by M. J. Erickson. Readings in Christian Theology 2. Grand Rapids: Baker, 1976.

Thurman, H., and R. Eyre. "An Interview with Howard Thurman and Ronald Eyre." *Theology Today* 38 (1981) 208–13.

Tickle, P. *The Great Emergence: How Christianity Is Changing and Why*. Grand Rapids: Baker, 2008.

Tomas, C. "Validating the Ineffable through a Reinterpretation of Truth: Mystical Experience as a Form of Heidegger's Ἀλήθεια (Aletheia)." Conference presentation. http://www.academia.edu/2972366.

Trickett, D. "Spiritual Vision and Discipline in the Early Wesleyan Movement." Chapter 11 of *Christian Spirituality: Post-Reformation and Modern*, edited by L. Dupre and D. E. Saliers. World Spirituality 18. New York: Crossroad, 1989.

Turner, D. *Faith, Reason and the Existence of God*. Cambridge: Cambridge University Press, 2004.

Tyson, J. R., ed. *Invitation to Christian Spirituality: An Ecumenical Anthology*. New York: Oxford University Press, 1999.

US Bureau of Labor Statistics. American Time Use Survey Summary. Economic News Release. Wednesday, June 24, 2015. http://www.bls.gov/news.release/atus.nro.htm.

Van Huyssteen, J. W. *Alone in the World? Human Uniqueness in Science and Technology*. Grand Rapids: Eerdmans, 2006.

Vanhoozer, K. J. "Theology and the Condition of Postmodernity: A Report on Knowledge (of God)." Chapter 1 of *The Cambridge Companion to Postmodern Theology*, edited by K. J. Vanhoozer. Cambridge: Cambridge University Press, 2003.

Venema, D. "Mitochondrial Eve, Y-Chromosome Adam, and Reasons to Believe." *BioLogos*, October 28, 2011. http://biologos.org/blog/understanding-evolution-mitochondrial-eve-y-chromosome-adam.

Vilshnevskaya, E. "Divinization as Perichoretic Embrace in Maximus the Confessor." In *Partakers of the Divine Nature: The History and Development of Deification in the Christian Traditions*, edited by M. J. Christensen and J. A. Wittung, 115–31. Grand Rapids: Baker Academic, 2007.

Vlachos, H. "The Difference between Orthodox Spirituality and Other Traditions." Orthodox Christian Information Center. http://orthodoxinfo.com/inquirers/hierotheos_difference.aspx. Originally from chapter 2 of *Orthodox Spirituality: A Brief Introduction*, translated by E. Mavromichali. Levadia, Greece: Birth of the Theotokos Monastery, 1994.

Vorster, N. "Calvin's Modification of Augustine's Doctrine of Original Sin." In *Restoration through Redemption: John Calvin Revisited*, edited by H. Van Den Belt. Leiden: Nijhoff, 2013.

———. *Created in the Image of God: Understanding God's Relationship with Humanity*. Princeton Theological Monograph. Eugene, OR: Pickwick, 2011.

———. "Transformation in South Africa and the Kingdom of God." *HTS Teologiese Studies / Theological Studies* 62 (2006) 731–53. http://www.hts.org.za/index.php/HTS/article/view/357.
Walvoord, J. F. "Realized Eschatology." *Bibliotheca Sacra* 127 (1970) 313–23. http://www.galaxie.com/article/bsac127-508-04.
Wall, R. W. "The Acts of the Apostles." In *The New Interpreter's Bible*, vol. 10. Nashville: Abingdon, 2002.
Wallis, J. L. Purgatory for Everyone. *First Things*. August/September. 2001. Available: http://www.firstthings.com/article/2007/01/purgatory-for-everyone-49, 2002.
Watson. D. F. "The Second Letter of Peter." In *The New Interpreter's Bible*, vol. 12. Nashville: Abingdon, 1998.
Ware, T. *The Orthodox Church*. New ed. New York: Penguin, 1997.
Webb, W. J. *Slaves, Women & Homosexuals: Exploring the Hermeneutics of Cultural Analysis*. Downers Grove: InterVarsity, 2001.
Welker, M. *Creation and Reality*. Minneapolis: Fortress, 1999.
Wesley, J. *The Works of the Reverend John Wesley, A. M.* Vol. 6. Translated by J. Emory. London: Collard, 1831.
Whitney, D. S. *Spiritual Disciplines for the Christian Life*. Colorado Springs: NavPress, 1991.
Wilke, J. D. "Churchgoers Believe in Sharing Faith, Most Never Do." *LifeWay Research*. 2012. http://www.lifeway.com/article/research-survey-sharing-christ-2012.
Wilkins, M. J. *Following the Master: Discipleship in the Steps of Jesus*. Grand Rapids: Zondervan, 1992.
Willard, D. "The Absurdity of 'Thinking in Language.'" Paper presented 1972 meeting of American Philosophical Association. *Southwestern Journal of Philosophy* 4 (1973) 125–32. http://www.dwillard.org/articles/artview.asp?artID=11.
———. *The Divine Conspiracy: Rediscovering Our Hidden Life in God*. New York: HarperCollins, 1997.
———. "God and the Problem of Evil." 2011. http://www.dwillard.org/articles/artview.asp?artID=30.
———. *Hearing God: Developing a Conversational Relationship with God*. Downers Grove: InterVarsity, 1999.
———. "Living a Transformed Life Adequate to Our Calling." 2005. http://www.dwillard.org/articles/artview.asp?artID=119.
———. *The Spirit of the Disciplines: Understanding How God Changes Lives*. New York: HarperCollins, 1988.
———. "Spiritual Disciplines, Spiritual Formation, and the Restoration of the Soul." *Journal of Psychology and Theology* 26 (1998) 101–9. http://www.dwillard.org/articles/artview.asp?artID=57.
———. "Spiritual Formation as a Natural Part of Salvation." Presented at 2009 Wheaton Theological Conference. http://www.dwillard.org/articles/artview.asp?artID=135.
———. "The Unhinging of the American Mind—Derrida as Pretext." In *European Philosophy and the American Academy*, edited by B. Smith, 3–20. LaSalle, IL: Hegeler Institute, 1994. http://www.dwillard.org/articles/artview.asp?artID=69.
Williams, A. N. *The Ground of Union: Deification in Aquinas and Palamas*. Oxford: Oxford University Press, 1999.
Willimon, W. H. *Who Will Be Saved?* Nashville: Abingdon, 2008.

Wiley, T. *Original Sin: Origins, Developments, Contemporary Meanings*. Mahwah, NJ: Paulist, 2002.
Wittgenstein, L. *Remarks on Colour*. Edited by G. E. Anscombe et al. 30th anniversary ed. Berkeley: University of California Press, 2007.
Wooldridge, D. "Christian Spiritual Transformation: God's Calling and Provision and the Human Response; A Schema for Spiritual Life." MDiv thesis, Columbia Evangelical Seminary, Longview, WA, 2008.
Wright, D. F. "Calvin's Accommodating God." In *Calvinus Sincerioris Religionis Vindex* [Calvin as protector of the purer religion], edited by W. H. Neuser and B.G. Armstrong, 19. Kirksville, MO: Sixteenth Century Journal Publishers, 1997.
Wright, N. T. *Simply Christian: Why Christianity Makes Sense*. New York: HarperCollins, 2006.
———. "Towards a Biblical View of Universalism." *Themelios* 4 (1978) 54–58. http://s3.amazonaws.com/tgc-documents/journal-issues/4.2_Wright.pdf.
Wyman, W. E., Jr. "Rethinking the Christian Doctrine of Sin: Friedrich Schleirmacher and Hick's 'Irenaean Type.'" *Journal of Religion* 74 (1994) 199–217. http://www.jstor.org/stable/1205 5276.
Young, W. P. *The Shack*. Los Angeles: Windblown, 2007.
Žižek, S., and J. Milbank. *The Monstrosity of Christ: Paradox or Dialectic?* Edited by C. Davis. Cambridge: MIT Press, 2009.
Zizioulas, J. D. "The Early Christian Community." Chapter 2 of McGinn and Meyendorff, *Christian Spirituality: Origins to the Twelfth Century*.

www.ingramcontent.com/pod-product-compliance
Lightning Source LLC
Chambersburg PA
CBHW071238230426
43668CB00011B/1490